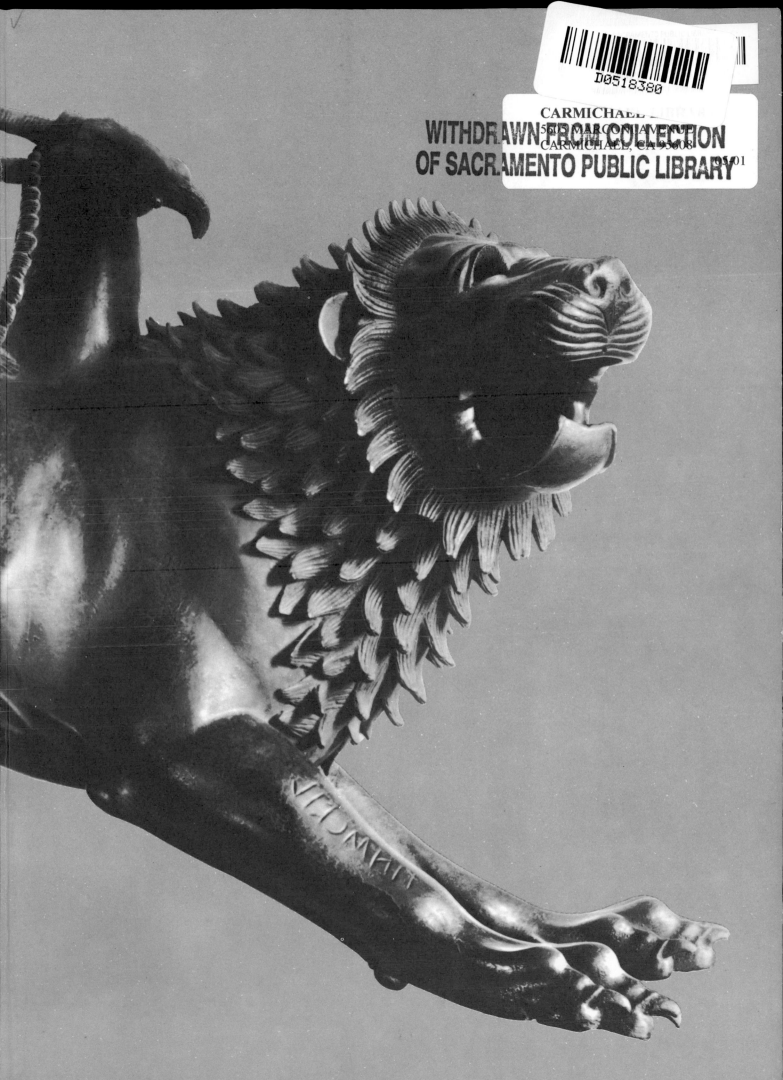

New Larousse Encyclopedia of Mythology

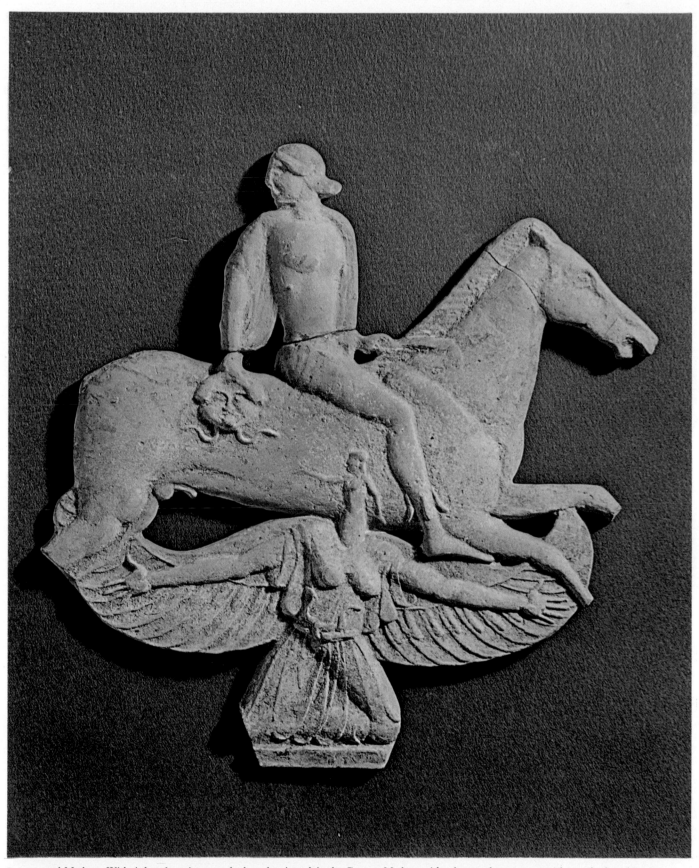

Perseus and Medusa. With Athene's assistance, the hero has just slain the Gorgon Medusa with a bronze *harpe*, or curved sword, given him by
by Hermes and now, seated on the back of Pegasus who has just sprung from her bleeding neck and holding her still-dripping decapitated head
in his right hand, he turns to watch her two sisters who are pursuing him in fury. Beneath him kneels the headless body of the Gorgon
with her arms and golden wings outstretched. From her neck emerges Chrysaor, the father of the monster Geryon. Perseus later
presented Medusa's head to Athene who placed it on her shield. Relief from Melos. British Museum.

New Larousse Encyclopedia of Mythology

Introduction by
Robert Graves

Prometheus Press

Other titles in this series:
Larousse Encyclopedia of Animal Life
Larousse Encyclopedia of Astronomy
Larousse Encyclopedia of Prehistoric and Ancient Art
Larousse Encyclopedia of Byzantine and Medieval Art
Larousse Encyclopedia of Renaissance and Baroque Art
Larousse Encyclopedia of Modern Art
Larousse Encyclopedia of the Earth
Larousse Encyclopedia of Ancient and Medieval History
Larousse Encyclopedia of Modern History
Larousse Encyclopedia of World Geography
Larousse Encyclopedia of Music
Larousse Encyclopedia of Archaeology
Larousse World Mythology
Larousse Science of Life

First published in 1959

New edition 1968
Seventh Impression 1973

New Larousse Encyclopedia of Mythology
Translated by Richard Aldington and Delano Ames
and revised by a panel of editorial advisers from the
Larousse Mythologie Générale edited by Felix Guirand
and first published in France by
Augé, Gillon, Hollier-Larousse, Moreau et Cie,
the Librairie Larousse, Paris

Printed in Hong Kong by Toppan for
THE HAMLYN PUBLISHING GROUP LIMITED
LONDON · NEW YORK · SYDNEY · TORONTO
Hamlyn House, The Centre, Feltham, Middlesex, England

© 1959 Paul Hamlyn
ISBN 0 600 02351 6

INTRODUCTION

By Robert Graves

Mythology is the study of whatever religious or heroic legends are so foreign to a student's experience that he cannot believe them to be true. Hence the English adjective 'mythical', meaning 'incredible'; and hence the omission from standard European mythologies, such as this, of all Biblical narratives even when closely paralleled by myths from Persia, Babylonia, Egypt and Greece; and of all hagiological legends. Otherwise, the New Larousse Encyclopedia of Mythology offers a comprehensive and compact *Who's Who* or *Who Was Who* of the better known gods, goddesses, heroes, monsters, demons, angels and saints from all over the world, including certain Moslem ones. It does not discuss philosophic theory or religious experience, and treats each cult with the same impersonal courtesy.

Myth has two main functions. The first is to answer the sort of awkward questions that children ask, such as: 'Who made the world? How will it end? Who was the first man? Where do souls go after death?' The answers, necessarily graphic and positive, confer enormous power on the various deities credited with the creation and care of souls – and incidentally on their priesthoods.

The second function of myth is to justify an existing social system and account for traditional rites and customs. The Erechtheid clan of Athens, who used a snake as an amulet, preserved myths of their descent from King Erichthonius, a man-serpent, son of the Smith-god Hephaestus and foster-son of the Goddess Athene. The Ioxids of Caria explained their veneration for rushes and wild asparagus by a story of their ancestress Perigune, whom Theseus the Erech-

theid courted in a thicket of these plants; thus incidentally claiming cousinship with the Attic royal house. The real reason may have been that wild asparagus stalks and rushes were woven into sacred baskets, and therefore taboo.

Myths of origin and eventual extinction vary according to the climate. In the cold North, the first human beings were said to have sprung from the licking of frozen stones by a divine cow named Audumla; and the Northern afterworld was a bare, misty, featureless plain where ghosts wandered hungry and shivering. According to a myth from the kinder climate of Greece, a Titan named Prometheus, kneading mud on a flowery riverbank, made human statuettes which Athene – who was once the Libyan Moon-goddess Neith – brought to life, and Greek ghosts went to a sunless, flowerless underground cavern. These afterworlds were destined for serfs or commoners; deserving nobles could count on warm, celestial mead-halls in the North, and Elysian Fields in Greece.

Primitive peoples remodel old myths to conform with changes produced by revolutions, or invasions and, as a rule, politely disguise their violence: thus a treacherous usurper will figure as a lost heir to the throne who killed a destructive dragon or other monster and, after marrying the king's daughter, duly succeeded him. Even myths of origin get altered or discarded. Prometheus' creation of men from clay superseded the hatching of all nature from a world-egg laid by the ancient Mediterranean Dove-goddess Eurynome – a myth common also in Polynesia, where the Goddess is called Tangaroa.

A typical case-history of how myths develop as culture spreads: – Among the Akan of Ghana, the original social system was a number of queendoms, each containing three or more clans and ruled by a Queen-mother with her council of elder women; descent being reckoned in the female line, and each clan having its own animal deity. The Akan believed that the world was born from the all-powerful Moon-goddess Ngame, who gave human beings souls, as soon as born, by shooting lunar rays into them. At some time or other, perhaps in the early Middle Ages, patriarchal nomads from the Sudan forced the Akans to accept a male Creator, a Sky-god named Odomankoma; but failed to destroy Ngame's dispensation. A compromise myth was agreed upon: Odomankoma created the world with hammer and chisel from inert matter, after which Ngame brought it to life. These Sudanese invaders also worshipped the seven planetary powers ruling the week – a system originating in Babylonia. (It had spread to Northern Europe, by-passing Greece and Rome; which is why the names of pagan deities – Tuisto, Woden, Thor and Frigg – are still attached to Tuesday, Wednesday, Thursday and Friday.) This extra cult provided the Akan with seven new deities, and the compromise myth made both them and the clan-gods bisexual. Towards the end of the fourteenth century A.D., a social revolution deposed Odomankoma in favour of a Universal Sun-god, and altered the myth accordingly. While Odomankoma ruled, a queendom was still a queendom, the king acting merely as a consort and male representative of the sovereign Queen-mother, and being styled 'Son of the Moon': a yearly dying, yearly resurrected, fertility godling. But the gradual welding of small queendoms into city-states, and of city-states into a rich and populous nation, encouraged the High King – the king of the dominant city-state – to borrow a foreign custom. He styled himself 'Son of the Sun', as well as 'Son of the Moon', and claimed limitless authority. The Sun which, according to the myth, had hitherto been re-born every morning from Ngame, was now worshipped as an eternal god altogether independent of the Moon's life-giving function. New myths appeared when the Akan accepted the patriarchal principle, which Sun-worship brought in; they began tracing succession through the father, and mothers ceased to be the spiritual heads of households.

This case-history throws light on the complex Egyptian corpus of myth. Egypt, it seems, developed from small matriarchal Moon-queendoms to Pharaonic patriarchal Sun-monarchy. Grotesque animal deities of leading clans in the Delta became city-gods, and the cities were federated under the sovereignty of a High King (once a 'Son of the Moon'), who claimed to be the Son of Ra the Sun-god. Opposition by independent-minded city-rulers to the Pharaoh's autocratic sway appears in the undated myth of how Ra grew so old and feeble that he could not even control his spittle; the Moon-goddess Isis plotted against him and Ra retaliated by casting his baleful eye on mankind – they perished in their thousands. Ra nevertheless decided to quit the ungrateful land of Egypt; whereupon Hathor, a loyal Cow-goddess, flew him up to the vault of Heaven. The myth doubtless records a compromise that consigned the High King's absolutist pretensions, supported by his wife, to the vague realm of philosophic theory. He kept the throne, but once more became, for all practical purposes, an incarnation of Osiris, consort of the Moon-goddess Isis – a yearly dying, yearly resurrected fertility godling.

Indian myth is highly complex, and swings from gross physical abandon to rigorous asceticism and fantastic visions of the spirit world. Yet it has much in common with European myth, since Aryan invasions in the second millennium B.C. changed the religious system of both continents. The invaders were nomad herdsmen, and the peoples on whom they imposed themselves as a military aristocracy were peasants. Hesiod, an early Greek poet, preserves a myth of pre-Aryan 'Silver Age' heroes: 'divinely created eaters of bread, utterly subject to their mothers however long they lived, who never sacrificed to the gods, but at least did not make war against one another.' Hesiod put the case well: in primitive agricultural communities, recourse to war is rare, and goddess-worship the rule. Herdsmen, on the contrary, tend to make fighting a profession and, perhaps because bulls dominate their herds, as rams do flocks, worship a male Sky-god, typified by a bull or a ram. He sends down rain for the pastures, and they take omens from the entrails of the victims sacrificed to him.

When an invading Aryan chieftain, a tribal rain-maker, married the Moon-priestess and Queen of a conquered people, a new myth inevitably celebrated the marriage of the Sky-god and the Moon. But since the Moon-goddess was everywhere worshipped as a triad, in honour of the Moon's three phases – waxing, full, and waning – the god split up into a complementary triad. This accounts for three-bodied Geryon, the first king of Spain; three-headed Cernunnos, the Gallic god; the Irish triad, Brian, Iuchar, and Iucharba, who married the three queenly owners of Ireland; and the invading Greek brothers Zeus, Poseidon, and Hades who, despite great opposition, married the pre-Greek Moon-goddess in her three aspects, respectively as Queen of Heaven, Queen of the Sea, and Queen of the Underworld.

The Queen-mother's decline in religious power, and the goddesses' continual struggle to preserve their royal prerogatives, appears in the Homeric myth of how Zeus ill-treated and bullied Hera, and how she continually plotted against him. Zeus remained a Thunder-god, because Greek national sentiment forbad his becoming a Sun-god in Oriental style. But his Irish counterpart, a thunder-god named The Dagda, grew senile at last and surrendered the throne to his son Bodb the Red, a war-god – in Ireland, the magic of rain-making was not so important as in Greece.

One constant rule of mythology is that whatever happens among the gods above reflects events on earth. Thus a father-god named 'The Ancient One of the Jade' (Yu-ti) ruled the pre-revolutionary Chinese Heaven: like Prometheus, he had created human beings from clay. His wife was the Queen-mother, and their court an exact replica of the old Imperial Court at Pekin, with precisely the same functionaries: ministers, soldiers, and a numerous family of the god's sisters, daughters and nephews. The two annual sacrifices paid by the Emperor to the August One of the Jade – at the winter solstice when the days first lengthen and at the spring equinox when they become longer than the nights – show him to have once been a solar god. And the theological value given to the number 72, suggests that the cult started as a compromise between Moon-goddess worship and Sun-god worship: 72 means three-times-three, the Moon's mystical number, multiplied by two-times-two-times-two, the Sun's mystical number, and occurs in solar-lunar divine unions throughout Europe, Asia and Africa. Chinese conservatism, by the way, kept these gods dressed in ancient court-dress, making no concessions to the new fashions which the invading dynasty from Manchuria had introduced.

In West Africa, whenever the Queen-mother, or King, appointed a new functionary at Court, the same thing happened in Heaven, by royal decree. Presumably this was also the case in China; and if we apply the principle to Greek myth, it seems reasonably certain that the account of Tirynthian Heracles' marriage to Hera's daughter Hebe, and his appointment as Celestial Porter to Zeus, commemorates the appointment of a Tirynthian prince as vizier at the court of the Mycenaean High King, after marriage to a daughter of his Queen, the High Priestess of Argos. Probably the appointment of Ganymede, son of an early Trojan king, as cup-bearer to Zeus, had much the same significance: Zeus, in this context, would be more likely the Hittite king resident at Hattusas.

Myth, then, is a dramatic shorthand record of such matters as invasions, migrations, dynastic changes, admission of foreign cults, and social reforms. When bread was first introduced into Greece – where only beans, poppy-seeds, acorns and asphodel-roots had hitherto been known – the myth of Demeter and Triptolemus sanctified its use; the same event in Wales produced a myth of 'The Old White One', a Sow-goddess who went around the country with gifts of grain, bees, and her own young; for agriculture, pig-breeding and bee-keeping were taught to the aborigines by the same wave of neolithic invaders. Other myths sanctified the invention of wine.

A proper study of myth demands a great store of abstruse geographical, historical and anthropological knowledge; also familiarity with the properties of plants and trees, and the habits of wild birds and beasts. Thus a Central American stone-sculpture, a Toad-god sitting beneath a mushroom, means little to mythologists who have not considered the world-wide association of toads with toxic mushrooms or heard of a Mexican Mushroom-god, patron of an oracular cult; for the toxic agent is a drug, similar to that secreted in the sweat-glands of frightened toads, which provides magnificent hallucinations of a heavenly kingdom.

Myths are fascinating and easily misread. Readers may smile at the picture of Queen Maya and her pre-natal dream of the Buddha descending upon her disguised as a charming white baby elephant – he looks as though he would crush her to pulp – when 'at once all nature rejoiced, trees burst into bloom, and musical instruments played of their own accord'. In

English-speaking countries, 'white elephant' denotes something not only useless and unwanted, but expensive to maintain; and the picture could be misread there as indicating the Queen's grave embarrassment at the prospect of bearing a child. In India, however, the elephant symbolises royalty – the supreme God Indra rides one – and white elephants (which are not albinos, but animals suffering from a vitiliginous skin-disease) are sacred to the Sun, as white horses were for the ancient Greeks, and white oxen for the British druids. The elephant, moreover, symbolises intelligence, and Indian writers traditionally acknowledge the Elephant-god Ganesa as their patron; he is supposed to have dictated the *Mahabharata*.

Again, in English, a scallop-shell is associated either with cookery or with medieval pilgrims returning from a visit to the Holy Sepulchre; but Aphrodite the Greek Love-goddess employed a scallop-shell for her voyages across the sea, because its two parts were so tightly hinged together as to provide a symbol of passionate sexual love – the hinge of the scallop being a principal ingredient in ancient love-philtres. The lotus flower sacred to Buddha and Osiris has five petals, which symbolise the four limbs and the head; the five senses; the five digits; and, like the pyramid, the four points of the compass and the zenith. Other esoteric meanings abound: for myths are seldom simple, and never irresponsible.

CONTENTS

ix

COLOUR PLATES

PREHISTORIC MYTHOLOGY

THE RELIGION OF THE FIRST MEN

Mythology, which will be examined in the following chapters by specific regions and epochs, implies a belief in supernatural forces, that is to say in beings who are both different from and superior to living men in that they exercise, either directly or through the intermediary of natural phenomena, a benign or harmful influence. It is the function of ritual practices or ceremonies to encourage the former influence and prevent or neutralise the latter.

As an introduction to the study of the varied forms and the often poetic embellishments which these beliefs assumed among different peoples throughout the ages, it is appropriate to inquire into their origins: when in the life of mankind did such beliefs first appear?

Supernatural beings, the objects of these beliefs, can be divided into two categories which, though in principle distinct, overlap in a number of cases. On the one hand there are the dead, ancestors or *manes*, who have been known to their contemporaries in the form and condition of normal men. On the other hand there are the divinities, strictly speaking, who never existed as ordinary mortals.

Our information about the religious beliefs of peoples known to history can be derived from written documents; about primitive peoples who still exist we have the oral reports of travellers and ethnologists. But for prehistoric ages both of these sources of information are entirely lacking, and we never find ourselves in the actual presence of prehistoric religious beliefs. The only materials we possess are either physical traces of what appear to be vestiges of ritual practices or else pictorial representations of such practices from which can be inferred – with the aid of ethnological parallels – a belief in the existence of the supernatural beings to whom they were addressed. One cannot, therefore, insist too strongly on the hypothetical character of conclusions based on such material.

We shall confine ourselves to the study of those people we call Palaeolithic because of their industry in chipped, not polished, stone, and who lived during the Pleistocene geological epoch. We shall retrace our way cautiously through the course of time and, ignoring facts which are too ambiguous, try to discover what may reasonably be conjectured about their religious beliefs.

Mythology in the strict sense of the word. It is not impossible that the Magdalenians – the least ancient of Palaeolithic peoples – had a mythology in the strict sense of the word: that is to say, that they attributed to certain supernatural beings not only a specific form but specific acts. This at least is an acceptable interpretation of wall-drawings discovered in the cavern of the Trois-Frères in the Ariège department of southern France. There are three of them, and two at least seem to form an intentional group. Objectively the one on the right depicts a personage whose upright posture, legs and rump belong to a man. He has a horse's tail, a bison's head and the front legs of an animal, with one hoof distinctly cloven. He is perhaps dancing, and is certainly playing some kind of bowed musical instrument. He is preceded by an animal which turns its

Part of the Relief Frieze of Le Roc, Charente (according to Dr. Henri Martin). Effigies of female animals connected with fertility magic.

Engraved shaft from the Mège Shelter at Teyjat, Dordogne
(according to H. Breuil). Men disguised as chamois. Hunting magic.

head towards him. To be sure, the human figure may be a magician
in disguise who is charming the animal in front of him; but it would
seem difficult to disguise the arms of an actual man with imitation
hooved forelegs. Moreover, neither of the two animals who precede
him is altogether real. The one nearest to him, a female whose sex is
carefully accentuated, has the hind-quarters of the deer tribe and
the forequarters of a bison. The forelegs of the reindeer in front
terminate in the hooves of anything but a reindeer. We may thus
suppose that this group of figures, of which not one entirely corresponds to reality, was intended to represent a mythological scene –
a sort of Palaeolithic Orpheus charming equally mythical animals
by means of his music and dancing.

The Magicians. But this interpretation of the Trois-Frères group
is by no means the only one possible. Actually, the combination in
the same animal of characteristics belonging to different species is
found again elsewhere, not only in other drawings from the same
cave. In the Trois-Frères cavern there are two bears, one with a
wolf's head, the other with a bison's tail. A Solutrean bas-relief at
Roc in the Charente shows a swine with a bull's back.

Such figures, as we shall see, are connected with the magic of
hunting and fertility and represent not mythological but real animals
who are partially deformed in order to avert the hostility which
might be aroused in them were their exact resemblance drawn.
In addition, personages who combine human and animal characteristics occur elsewhere in Magdalenian art, both in wall-paintings
and household possessions. Some of them also seem to be dancing
and – according to ethnological parallels – may quite probably
represent magicians in disguise. Such are, to cite only the least
debatable specimens, another figure carved and painted on a wall
of the same Trois-Frères cave – a man with a bearded head, bull's
ears, stag's antlers and a horse's tail – and the three personages with
chamois heads carved on a staff found in the Mège shelter at Teyjat
in the Dordogne. Though all these figures may equally be interpreted
as either divinities or magicians, it would seem that the figure cut
on one side of a limestone pebble from La Madeleine, in which
human features are represented under a covering mask, must be
that of a magician. On the other face of the same stone there is a
feminine figure whose animal head is not so certainly a mask. If we
assume that she also is a magician we reach the interesting conclusion
that at least in the Lower Magdalenian period magic functions were
not an exclusively masculine prerogative.

Egyptian terracotta figurine. Fashioned from Nile
mud, these female figures were probably fertility goddesses
or served as simple representations in magic rites.
Prehistoric period.

Whether any of the figures mentioned above actually represented
a hybrid deity or not, it is easy to see how the use of magic disguise
contributed to the belief in such deities. The power of the magician
was attributed to his disguise. It played the role of establishing a
mystic communion, a fusion of essence, between him and the animals
on which he proposed to act. Magic power and the magician's
appearance were naturally associated. His aspect, simultaneously
animal and human, naturally led to the conception of gods under
the same hybrid form. The god possessed similar powers, and the
magician, at least in the exercise of his functions, was in some way
the god's incarnation. In any case, whether these figures represented
divinities or magicians, they bear witness to the existence of religious
beliefs. There can be no doubt that during the Magdalenian period
many caverns, either wholly or at least in their lower depths, were
sanctuaries.

Wall Engraving in the Trois-Frères, Ariège (according to H. Begouen and H. Breuil). Mythical scene or representation of some form of hunting magic.

Hunting Magic. Food in Palaeolithic times depended primarily on hunting, and the essential role of magic was to assure its success. Mimetic magic with animal disguises must have contributed. But Magdalenian man certainly had recourse to sympathetic or homoeopathic magic, which relies on the theory that an operation performed on an image of a real being will produce the same effect on the being itself. Many of the drawings and clay figures of the cave of Montespan in the Haute-Garonne seem to have been made in order to be slashed or pierced with holes with the object of wounding real animals. Particularly remarkable is a statue of a bear cub, modelled in the round and placed on a stand, which seems to have been destined for this purpose. The statue never had a head. There is a cavity in the neck which seems to have been produced by a wooden peg supporting some object – and the skull of a bear cub was found on the ground between the statue's two front paws. This suggests that the headless statue, which is riddled with more than thirty holes, was completed by the head of an actual animal. There are other indications that it was perhaps covered with an animal's hide which also played a part in the magic ceremony.

Also sculptured in the round at Isturitz in the Basses-Pyrénées is a feline creature, perforated in a manner which does not seem to suggest that the holes were made in order to hang up the figure. They must therefore represent wounds; and there are also arrows or harpoons scratched on the figure's thighs and spine. Another sculpture in the same grotto was even more obviously intended for sympathetic magic. This is a bison in sandstone. On its flank there is a deep vertical incision, at the side of which an arrow is cut. It is even possible that the original fracturing of the head and feet was the result of intentional mutilation which completed the magic ceremony.

From these examples, in which the magic operation consists of actually wounding the animal's image, ancient man passed gradually to merely portraying the wounds or even simply evoking them by drawing the weapons which were supposed to inflict them. This can be seen, among many other examples, in a wall-drawing of a bear at Trois-Frères. Its body is depicted as having been stoned. It bristles with arrows, and from the muzzle flow copious streams of blood.

In these figures, and in others which seem to represent animals being hunted not with weapons but with snares, it is almost certain that the portrayal of a wished-for event was intended to bring about the event itself.

Two drawings on limestone of animals pierced with arrows, a rhinoceros and a stag, found at La Colombière in the Ain, must antedate the Magdalenian and correspond chronologically to the Solutrean period in a region to which this civilisation did not penetrate.

Fertility Magic. Since hunting of necessity required the existence of game it is natural that Palaeolithic man, in order that game should be plentiful, also practised fertility magic. In this case sympathetic magic could not, as with hunting magic, consist of performing in animal images the operations which would produce the desired result on the animals themselves. Fertility could only be caused artificially in effigy. We can therefore consider the representation of certain animal couples, and certain females, as examples of fertility magic. Such animal couples are the clay-modelled bisons of Tuc d'Audoubert, the reindeer sculptured in ivory of Bruniquel

and the bull following a cow at Teyjat. To these may be added a wall-drawing of bison at Altamira. A female fertility figure is the drawing on a flagstone at La Madeleine of a doe accompanied by her fawn. All these specimens are of the Magdalenian period. But the older Solutrean frieze at Roc presents several bas-reliefs of female forms: the sow with cow's back already mentioned and some mares, one of which seems to be accompanied by the rough outline of a male.

It is possible, though disputable, that certain figures of wounded men – for example a drawing in the shelter at Saltadora – were intended to bewitch an enemy, and thus correspond to a war magic similar to hunting magic. We consider it even more doubtful that representations of amorous scenes between human beings or the figurines of women with exaggerated bellies were intended to cause fertility among women. There is the Magdalenian 'Woman with a Reindeer' of Laugerie-Basse and the luxuriant females who are particularly abundant in, though not exclusive to, the Aurignacian period. But their role, we believe, was purely erotic. There is, however, a curious drawing on a blade of bone at Isturitz in which a woman, followed by a man, bears on her thigh a harpoon similar to those which in the picture on the opposite side of the blade have wounded a bison. This we are tempted to interpret as a love charm.

To sum up, there seem to be no indications of hunting magic or fertility magic during Aurignacian times. They only appear with the Solutrean and continue into the Magdalenian period, reaching their apogee in its first phase.

Pre-Mousterian Offerings. Different religious practices are encountered in pre-Mousterian central Europe, a period which goes back to the last ice age. The most characteristic remains come from Drachenloch, above Vättis in the valley of the Tamina (canton of Saint-Gall, Switzerland), which is the highest known Palaeolithic cavern, over 7,500 feet above sea level. In two of the chambers there are low stone walls nearly three feet high, which were certainly made by the hand of man. They run along the cave wall, leaving between it and them a space about fifteen inches wide. This space is filled with the bones of cave bears. These bones are chiefly skulls and are usually accompanied by the two first cervical vertebrae. There are also leg bones belonging, with rare exceptions, to different individual bears. At the entrance and in the forepart of one of these chambers similar bone-heaps were accumulated in half a dozen rectangular stone chests, covered by large slabs which form lids. In the far end of the same chamber three skulls were gathered together in an empty space between fallen blocks. Another skull had been carefully placed beneath a huge stone which was wedged in a manner to protect it

Negative hand print in red ochre. A very early example of man expressing man, leading later to more complicated examples and to sympathetic magic. Grotte de Gargas (Hautes-Pyrénées).

Designs resembling symbolic suns which from their frequency
in the later engraving period would appear to point to the existence
of sun worship in this area. Cave in the Matopo Hills, Rhodesia.

Male bison about to mount a female. Representations of animals
coupling are believed to have been made as part of fertility rites.
Clay figures of the Magdalenian period. Le Tuc d'Audoubert (Ariège).

Wall Engraving from the Trois-Frères (according to H. Begouen
and H. Breuil). Bear stoned and pierced with arrows, vomiting
blood. Sympathetic magic.

against the pressure of the earth. It was encircled by a sort of stone
crown adapted to the shape of the head.

All these collections of bears' remains were certainly deliberate.
Since the skulls were generally attached to the first two vertebrae,
they were not deposited there fleshless, but in a state to be eaten.
Moreover, the brain, like the legs with their meat and marrowbones,
represented the most succulent part of the animal. They were thus in
all probability offerings to some supernatural power. It is, of course,
arbitrary to see in this power a Supreme Being like our own God,
and more likely these choice morsels were offered to conciliate the
spirits of the game, to give them thanks for the success of a past
hunting expedition and to solicit the continuance of their favour
in the future. In any case we have here what may be the oldest known
example of practices addressed to supernatural powers.

THE CULT OF THE DEAD

The dead, too, were considered to be supernatural powers.
Corpses were the object of practices which give evidence not only
of deference but also, in the broad sense of the word, of a cult. The
skeletons which have been found in artificially dug trenches or
surrounded and covered by durable materials, like stones or bone
fragments, were incontestably buried with funerary intention.

Many of them, moreover, were buried with funerary furnishings
such as the jewels and ornaments which have been found on or near
them. Doubtless these were objects which they had owned during
their lifetimes. But even if they had not been presented with these
ornaments on burial, at least the survivors had not, in spite of their
considerable value, taken them away as they could have done. The
fact that they belonged to the dead rendered them in some way
taboo. And then other objects found with the bodies could only
have been placed there by the survivors, and constitute genuine
funerary furnishings, destined for the use of the dead man in after-
life: utensils, works of art, food.

In many cases red ochre (clay coloured with haematite or iron
peroxide) was sprinkled over the corpse's grave and has left traces
of its colour on the skeleton and surrounding objects. Because of its
colour certain primitive peoples of to-day, in particular the Austra-
lian aborigines, liken red ochre to blood (even we call it haematite)
and for this reason consider it a symbol of life and strength. It is
reasonable to suppose that the ochre spread over the tombs and
bodies of Palaeolithic man was intended, like the deposits of food,
to strengthen the dead one during his journey to the after-world
and his sojourn in his new abode.

Among numerous examples of these various funeral practices
we shall call attention only to those that are particularly characteristic, and establish at which periods such practices were in force.

The Magdalenian skeleton of Hoteaux in the Ain, covered with
red ochre, was found in a small trench. Behind the head a large stone
had been placed. Beside it were chipped flint instruments and a
chieftain's staff in reindeer horn on which was engraved a stag. The
skeleton of Sordes in the Landes had several slabs placed on its
skull and had been covered with red ochre. Beside it were found
about forty bears' and three lions' canine teeth, almost all carefully
pierced. Some twenty of them were carved with seals, fish and
arrows. In view of their position they must have constituted a
necklace and a belt. The perforated shellfish which formed the
adornment of 'the crushed man' of Laugerie-Basse belonged to
two species which are native to the Mediterranean. Having come
from such a distance they must have been especially valuable.

Under the right hand of the skeleton of Solutré there were
numerous flints chipped in the shape of laurel leaves and also a
pierced scallop shell. Found with it were two crude statuettes of
reindeer in stone.

The skeleton of Klause in Bavaria was enclosed between boulders
fallen from the ceiling. They had been arranged to make a place for
the body. It was completely surrounded by a mass of red powder.
Above and beneath the head was a great heap of fragments of
mammoths' tusks.

For the Aurignacian period a number of consonant facts have
been established in the caverns of Grimaldi, near Menton. In the
grotto 'des Enfants' the two negroid skeletons lie in a trench about
thirty inches deep. The head of the old woman was found in a tightly
closed chest formed by two lateral blocks of stone, covered over by

Funeral scene. The large reclining figure in the upper half is a masked and bandaged body, probably of a chief or someone of rank, wearing an antelope mask and ready for burial. The figure below with raised knees is possibly a wife mourning him, but she could also be prepared for burial with him – in effect to follow him into the next world. The curved lines in the lower part may represent a river, a frequent symbol among primitive peoples for the barrier to be crossed before reaching the next world. Numerous other figures are shown, and offerings of food. Rock painting believed to be about 5,000 years old at 'Diana's Vow' Farm near Rusape, Rhodesia.

Thutmoses III pours a libation to the god Amon-Ra. The pharaoh stands before the seated god pouring a double libation with his right hand and holding burning incense in his left. The god is portrayed seated on a throne wearing his head-dress of a crown surmounted by two tall plumes and holding a sceptre and the *ankh,* or symbol of life. Originally a god of Thebes, Amon was raised by the conquests of Thutmoses III to the position of supreme god of the known world. Tomb of Thutmoses III from Deir el-Bahri. Eighteenth dynasty, 1580 to 1350 B.C.

a horizontal slab. The young man was wearing a sort of crown made of four rows of pierced nassas. The same shellfish provided the two bracelets on the old woman's left arm. This tomb contained red powder in the rubble, around the head and on parts of the young man's skeleton. The two children, to whom the cave owes its name, were wearing a kind of apron made of thousands of perforated nassas. In the same cave a female skeleton was covered over with animal bones, the jawbones of a wild boar and some chips of flint. Under its head there was a white stone bearing traces of red colouring. It was literally lying in a bed of trochus shells. Not being pierced, these shells could not have been for adornment, but had been put near the body for food.

At La Barma Grande the three bodies stretched side by side were placed in an obviously man-made trench and had a bed of red earth. They wore adornments composed of shells, teeth, fish vertebrae and artificial pendants in bone and ivory. Particularly remarkable is the young man's necklace, which was held in its original position by a coating of clay and, in the symmetry and rhythm of its arrangement, bears witness to a sense of artistry. These skeletons were accompanied by very beautiful flint instruments, and the woman's head reposed on the femur of an ox.

The corpse of Paviland in Wales was powdered with iron oxide which stained the earth and burial objects, and in some places formed a coating on the bones. Although probably male, it has for this reason been christened 'The Red Lady'. Beside it was found the entire head of a mammoth complete with tusks. Near the thighs were found two handfuls of small shells drenched in red, and near the chest some fifty fragments of round ivory rings.

At Predmosti in Moravia twenty human skeletons were gathered under a veritable lid of stones. A child's skeleton wore a necklace of fourteen pendants. Beside the skeleton of Brno there were more than six hundred fragments of fossilised shells, strung together to form conical tubes. Some were still inserted in each other and together they must have made a kind of breastplate for the body. Near it were also found large perforated stone disks, small disks decorated with incisions, three solid disks made of mammoth's or rhinoceros's ribs, some rhinoceros ribs, and finally an ivory statuette of a human being. The skeleton and some of the objects in the tomb were partially stained red.

The skeleton of La Chapelle-aux-Saints belongs to the Mousterian period. It lay in a trench a little less than five feet long, about three feet wide and a foot deep. The head lay against a corner of the trench, propped by stones and covered over with broad slabs of bone. At La Ferrassie the two children at least were laid in artificial trenches. The man's skeleton was covered by rubble and protected by chips of bone. The skeleton of Moustier had its skull placed on a sort of pillow formed by a heap of flint fragments carefully adapted to the shape of the head. The nose seems to have been especially protected by two chips of flint. The bodies of both La Chapelle-aux-Saints and Moustier were provided with funerary furnishings, instruments and joints of game.

The use of red ochre has not been observed in the Mousterian period, but burial rites are as apparent then as in later Magdalenian times. What, then, was their intention? Since they were performed for people whose earthly life was finished they imply a belief that the dead continue after death to lead some kind of existence. This posthumous life appears to have been conceived as similar to life on earth, with the same needs and the same means of satisfying them. This explains the ornaments left with the dead, the implements, the food (quarters of venison and piles of shellfish) and the red ochre.

In thus providing for the posthumous needs of the dead, the survivors seem, however, to have acted less from disinterested affection than from self-interest. Their care seems to have been to encourage the deceased's favourable disposition towards themselves, to soften his possible hostility or to put him physically in a position where he could do no harm. Generally speaking, primitive people believe that death, like sickness, is the result of a magic operation. Deaths to which we assign natural causes are attributed by them to an evil spell, the author of which, whether unconscious or malevolent, they attempt to discover by various means.

This being so, it can be understood that the dead were thought to harbour vengeance against their presumed murderers and, in consequence of the idea of collective responsibility, against all those who survived them. At the very least they would entertain sentiments

Carved stone stele discovered near Avignon.
The face probably represents a deity and the stele itself would have been erected at a cult centre. Neolithic period.

Rock drawing of a woman giving birth, almost certainly an example of sympathetic magic.
The signs near the drawing are believed to be an early form of pictograph. Sha'ib Samma in the Yemen.

Spear thrower in carved bone. The spear shaft fitted into the hole to provide additional leverage. The figure of the horse suggests that wild horses were hunted for food. Palaeolithic period.

Engraved Bone from Isturitz (according to R. de Saint-Périer). On one side bison with arrows (hunting magic); on the other side, man following a woman with an arrow in her thigh (possibly love charm.)

of envy towards those who still enjoyed the earthly life of which they themselves had been deprived. It seems, then, that the basic attitude towards the dead was one of fear, and that burial rites were originally measures of protection against the deceased. Thus Palaeolithic trenches and tombs may have been intended less to shelter the dead than to imprison them. The statuette of Brno, very probably masculine and buried with a masculine corpse, could have played the role of a 'double', meant to keep the dead one in his tomb and prevent him from 'returning' to torment the living. This would account for the statuette's being made with neither legs nor right arm.

Particularly remarkable is the trussed-up position in which many of these bodies were found. A typical example from the Magdalenian period is the old man of Chancelade in the Dordogne, covered with red ochre, with arms and legs folded and the vertical column bent to such a degree that the skeleton only occupies a space little more than two feet long and sixteen inches wide. In the grotto 'des Enfants', which is Aurignacian, the negroid young man's legs were completely drawn up to his thighs. The old woman's thighs were raised as far as possible so that her knees reached the level of her shoulders. The legs were sharply folded under the thighs and the feet nearly touched the pelvis. The forearms were bent upwards so that the left hand was just beneath the shoulder-blade. In the Mousterian period the woman of La Ferrassie had her legs doubled up; the bent right forearm rested along the thigh, the hand on a knee. This arm and the legs formed a letter 'N', the knee reaching a distance of only six inches from the shoulder. The legs of the skeleton of La Chapelle-aux-Saints were folded and raised so that the kneecaps were more or less on a level with the chest.

This contracted condition which has been observed in so many skeletons from the Mousterian until the Magdalenian period could, of course, only have been imposed on the body by those who buried it. In addition, it means that the body must have been tied up at the moment of death: for rigor mortis would later have prevented its being forced into such a position. It seems, then, that among Palaeolithic as among other primitive peoples who share similar burial customs, the doubled-up posture of the body was only a result of the trussing-up and binding – this being the essential operation, intended to prevent the dead from coming back to torment the living. This also explains the diversity of positions in which Palaeolithic bodies are found: provided that they were securely bound and could not leave their graves, the actual position of the body was of secondary importance and could be left to individual initiative.

Although fear of the dead seems to have been the dominant sentiment it does not follow that in some cases at least there was not also a belief that the dead could be helpful and beneficent, especially when funeral rites devised to assure their maximum well-being in the after-life had been performed. This seems to account for certain practices which differed from burial in the strict sense, in that they tended not to set the dead apart from the living but, on the contrary, to preserve their remains and keep them, as it were, to hand. Such, notably, was the practice of stripping the flesh from the body before burial. This was done by various means, especially by natural putrefaction in a provisional grave. The object was to conserve the skeleton or its bones, which were sometimes worn by the survivors as amulets. The practice seems to have existed from Palaeolithic times. A Lower Magdalenian example is found in the grotto of Le Placard in the Charente. An entire skull of a woman, complete with lower jawbone, was placed on a rock and surrounded by a hundred and seventy shells of different sorts, some pierced, some not. Skulls in the same cave, belonging to Lower Magdalenian and Upper Solutrean periods, show clear traces of deliberate flesh-stripping and have undoubtedly been cut and altered. In the Aurignacian cave of Le Cavillon at Grimaldi three such bones were found: the broken radius of a child and two bones from a man's foot, coloured a vivid red. Scattered nearby was a set of pierced and unpierced shells. A tomb at Predmosti contained only a few bone-remains which had been scraped; the head was missing but must once have been there, for two teeth still remained. A Mousterian skeleton, found in a trench at La Ferrassie, had its skull, deprived of face and jawbone, placed nearly four feet away from the body. At Le Pech de l'Aze the skull of a five or six years old child was surrounded by deliberately broken animal bones, by teeth and by a quantity of implements. Finally, we must take into

Stone age men armed with bows and arrows preparing for battle or the hunt. In the world of primitive magic success in either was sought by formal representations such as these. From a cave painting at Teruel.

Pottery figure discovered in Lake Maracaibo, Venezuela. Of unknown date, it probably represents a primitive mother goddess. The sun sign on the base would seem to anticipate the later sun cultures.

Two female figures with goats, probably engaged in some kind of ritual. Rock painting from Tanzoumaitak, Tassili N'Ajjer.

Ivory Statuette from the Cave of Les Rideaux at Lespugne, Hte. Garonne (according to R. de Saint-Périer). Connected with fertility magic.

account many finds of isolated human bones from all periods, generally skulls or jawbones.

Sinanthropus. The deposits of Fu-Ku-Tien near Peking permit us to go back to the earliest Pleistocene times. They have yielded – together with abundant vestiges of fire, and work in bone and stone – the remains of a dozen human beings, halfway between Pithecanthropus man of Java and Neanderthal man of Mousterian Europe. For the moment these remains are confined to skull and lower jaw, without traces of cervical vertebrae, while the animals on which these men fed are represented by bones from all parts of the body. There can thus be no question of cannibalism or of the heads being cut from corpses immediately after death. To all appearances these skulls must have been preserved after the bodies had been stripped of flesh.

Hence from the remotest times when, on the evidence of the skull which is all we have of his body, man was still closely related to the ape, it would seem that there are proofs of his industry and that, at least in the form of a cult of the dead, he revealed traces of religion.

EGYPTIAN MYTHOLOGY

Isis, the sorrowing wife and eternal mother. Protectress of the dead, the goddess stands mourning with upraised arms at the foot of a sarcophagus. She bears a throne upon her head, the ideogram of her name. Below is the *djed* symbol of stability, which also represents her husband Osiris. Stone relief.

Horus, in the form of a falcon with a human arm, delivers six thousand captives to King Narmer, who is brandishing his mace over the defeated chief. First Dynasty, about 3200. Cairo.

INTRODUCTION

No one who strolls through the Egyptian galleries of a museum can fail to be struck by the multitude of divinities who attract attention on all sides. Colossal statues in sandstone, granite and basalt, minute statuettes in glazed composition, bronze, even in gold, portray gods and goddesses frozen in hierarchical attitudes, seated or standing. Sometimes these male or female figures have heads with human features. More often they are surmounted by the muzzle of an animal or the beak of a bird. The same divinities, receiving adoration and offerings or performing ritual gestures for the benefit of their worshippers, can be seen again on the bas-reliefs of massive sarcophagi or sculptured on funerary stelae and stone blocks stripped from temple walls. They recur on mummy cases and in the pictures which illuminate the papyri of the Book of the Dead.

In view of such a multiplicity of divine images it may seem strange to suggest that the religion of Ancient Egypt is very imperfectly known to us. Such, however, is the case; though we know the names of all these gods and goddesses and the temples in which they were worshipped, we understand little of their nature and seldom know even the legends concerning them.

It is true that the innumerable religious texts which have survived

often allude to mythological occurrences. The full stories themselves, however, are almost never set down; for they were known to every early Egyptian and handed down from generation to generation by word of mouth alone.

Only the myth of Osiris – one of the greatest gods in the Egyptian pantheon – has been transmitted in detail to us by Plutarch. Plutarch, though Greek and writing of times already long past, was evidently well informed; for in ancient texts we find frequent references to the events he relates, notably in those texts which the old kings of the sixth dynasty had engraved inside their pyramids – twenty-five centuries before him.

It seems that the earliest representations of Egyptian deities appeared about the middle of the fourth millennium, long before the first hieroglyphs. In those days the inhabitants of the Nile valley lived in tribes. Each tribe had its own god, who was incarnated in the form either of an animal, of a bird or of a simple fetish. There is a fragment of a palette for grinding malachite in the Louvre on which we see men of one of these early tribes setting forth to hunt. They are bearded, unlike the clean-shaven men of later historical epochs, and they wear only a belted loin-cloth. At the back of the belt is attached the bushy tail of an animal. At their head marches their chief. In one hand he brandishes a club. In the other he grasps the staff of a standard or totem pole which bears a kind of perch for a falcon. On other objects of the same class the hawk is replaced by an ibis, a jackal, a scorpion, or perhaps by a thunderbolt, a bucranium, or two crossed arrows on a shield. These are the gods of the tribe who led their followers into battle and, when necessary, fought for them. Often, indeed, one of the divine animal's paws is a human hand which grasps a weapon to slaughter the enemy or an implement to attack his fortress.

These animal deities, however, gradually gave way to gods in human form, and at the end of his anthropomorphic evolution nothing of the primitive animal is left except the head surmounting the body of a man or woman. Sometimes the head, too, has become human and all that remains are vestigial ears or horns.

From the second dynasty on, the divine types seem to have become definitely fixed and to remain unchanged until the end of paganism. Like the hunters of the ancient tribes seen on the palette in the Louvre, the gods of the historical epoch are shown dressed in short loin-cloths ornamented by animals' tails. The goddesses, like great ladies, wear a narrow robe, held at the shoulders by shoulder-straps and falling nearly to their ankles.

Gods and goddesses alike often retain the head of the animal from which they were derived. They wear heavy wigs, thanks to which the transition between the snout of an animal or the beak of a bird and their human bodies takes place so smoothly that our aesthetic sense is scarcely violated and these hybrid beings seem almost real.

At other times the head is human, and in this case the shaven chin of the god is adorned by an artificial plaited beard, which recalls the bearded faces of the first Egyptians.

These divinities are distinguished and immediately identified by their different head-dresses and by various attributes inherited from the original fetish or from the primitive animal which surmounts their heads. Sometimes too their names are written in hieroglyphic signs. Like the ancient tribal chieftains, the gods carry sceptres with one end forked and the other decorated by, say, the head of a greyhound. Goddesses bear in their hand a simple stalk of papyrus.

By the time that the animals and fetishes of the prehistoric epoch had become divinities in human form the nomad warriors whom they once led into battle had long since settled down to till the soil. Their gods were installed in the towns they built, and were thus transformed from tribal into local deities. Every town, village and district had its god who bore the title: 'Lord of the City'. There he resided and yielded priority of rank to no one. Conceived in the image of a man, but of a man infinitely strong and powerful, he possessed a vital fluid – the 'sa' – which he could renew at will by having another god, better provided, lay hands on him. But he could not defend himself for ever against old age, and sometimes he even died. He delighted in revealing himself to men, and he would become incarnate in the temple statue, in a fetish, or in a chosen animal which the initiated could recognise by certain signs.

At first the god lived alone, jealous of his authority. But the Egyptian could not conceive of life without a family and soon he married off his god or goddess and gave him or her a son, thus forming a divine triad or trinity in which the father, moreover, was not always the chief, contenting himself on occasion with the role of prince consort, while the principal deity of the locality remained the goddess. This occurred at Dendera, where the sovereign was the goddess Hathor.

The god resided in the temple, which was his palace, with his family and sometimes with other gods whom he permitted to surround him. Only Pharaoh, the king, whom he called his 'son' had the right to appear in his presence. But as the king naturally could not officiate everywhere at once he delegated high priests to each sanctuary to perform in his place the ceremonies of the cult, while numerous priests and priestesses composed the domestic staff of the god and administered his sometimes immense domains. On certain dates the 'Lord of the City' brought joy to his people by deigning to show himself to them in all his glory. Abandoning the deep shadows of the naos (the inner sanctuary of the temple) where only Pharaoh's representative had the privilege of worshipping him daily, he would emerge majestically and be borne through the streets in his golden barque on the shoulders of his priests.

In addition to such local gods, some of whom imposed their authority over several provinces at a time and even throughout the entire land, the Egyptians worshipped, though generally without cult, the great divinities of nature: the Sky, the Earth, the Sun, the Moon and the mighty river which, in the words of Herodotus, created Egypt – the Nile.

In the Egyptian language the word 'sky' is feminine. Thus the Egyptians made the sky a goddess, Nut or Hathor, whom they represented either as a cow standing with her four feet planted on earth, or as a woman whose long, curved body touches the earth only with the tips of her toes and fingers. It was the starry belly of the goddess which men saw shining in the night above them. Sometimes also they imagined the sky as the head of a divine falcon whose eyes, which he opened and closed alternately, were the sun and the moon.

The earth, on the contrary, is masculine. Thus it was a man lying prone, from whose back sprouted all the world's vegetation. They called him Geb, the earth-god.

The sun had many names and gave rise to extremely varied interpretations. In his aspect of solar disk the sun was called Aten. Depending upon whether he rose, or climbed to the zenith, or set, he was given the names Khepri, Ra or Atum. He was also called Horus and it was under this name, joined with that of Ra, that he later reigned over all Egypt as Ra-Harakhte. It was claimed that he was reborn every morning of the celestial cow like a sucking calf, or like a little child of the sky-goddess. He was also said to be a falcon with speckled wings flying through space, or the right eye only of the great divine bird. Another conception of him was that of an egg laid daily by the celestial goose, or more frequently a gigantic scarab rolling before him the incandescent globe of the sun as, on earth, the sacred scarab rolls the ball of dung in which it has deposited its eggs.

The moon, too, was called by different names: Aah, Thoth, Khons. Sometimes he was the son of Nut, the sky-goddess. Sometimes he was a dog-headed ape, or an ibis; at others, the left eye of the great celestial hawk whose right eye was the sun.

Not content with explaining the phenomena of the external world, the priests of the principal sanctuaries busied themselves in constructing cosmological systems to demonstrate how the gods had successively appeared and how all that exists had been created. We have a fair knowledge of four of these systems which were taught in the four great religious centres of Hermopolis, Heliopolis, Memphis and Busiris. In each of these sanctuaries the priests attributed the work of creation to the great local god.

In his own temple Thoth, Ra, Ptah and Osiris was each proclaimed to have created the world, but each in his own way. Sometimes it was taught that the gods had issued from the mouth of the Demiurge and that all had been created by his voice. Sometimes it was alleged that they were born when the creator spat or performed an even cruder act. Again it was said that men had been engendered by his sweat or by a flood of tears gushing from his eyes. Another explanation was that men, together with the entire animal world, had emerged from the sun-dried mud of the Nile. It was also taught that the Demiurge had modelled them from the earth and fashioned them on a potter's wheel.

Like all people in antiquity the Egyptians explained everything by the intervention of a god, and for them there was nothing which was not capable of containing supernatural power. Consequently the number of gods worshipped in the Nile valley was considerable, and a list found in the tomb of Thuthmosis III enumerates no fewer than seven hundred and forty. Of most of them we know only the names and it would serve no useful purpose to mention them here.

We shall limit ourselves in this study to those deities who enjoyed a genuine cult or who occupied a real place in Egyptian mythology, beginning with the study of the gods and goddesses associated with the Ennead (or company of gods) of Heliopolis; that is to say, with the cosmological system taught by the priests of Heliopolis. We shall then review the great protective divinities of the Pharaohs and the kingdom, enumerating them in chronological order when in the course of the royal dynasties they appear particularly important.

Afterwards we shall come to river gods and desert gods not included in the above categories; then to the various divinities who concerned themselves with men's birth or death; and finally to deified humans among whom will be found the living Pharaoh who was himself a veritable god.

We shall conclude with a study of the sacred animals which,

Geb, the earth god, tries to reach his wife and twin sister, the goddess Nut, after being separated from her on the orders of Ra. With her body arched over the world, which she touches only with her toes and finger-tips, she forms the vault of the sky. Papyrus of Tameniu, twenty-first dynasty, 1102 to 952 B.C.

towards the end of paganism, were without doubt the most popular divinities in Egypt. We append a list of quadrupeds, birds and even insects from whom the gods and goddesses borrowed either the features or the attributes.

THE ENNEAD OF HELIOPOLIS AND THE FAMILY OF OSIRIS

Nun (or **Nu**) is Chaos, the primordial ocean in which before the creation lay the germs of all things and all beings. The texts call him the 'father of the gods', but he remains a purely intellectual concept and had neither temples nor worshippers. He is sometimes found represented as a personage plunged up to his waist in water, holding up his arms to support the gods who have issued from him.

Atum (or **Tum**), whose name seems to come from a root which signified 'not to be' and 'to be complete', was originally a local god of Heliopolis where his sacred animal was the bull Merwer (Greek Mnevis). From very early times his priests identified him with Ra, the great sun god. They taught that inside Nun, before the creation, there had lived a 'spirit, still formless, who bore within him the sum of all existence'. He was called Atum, and he manifested himself one day under the name of Atum-Ra and drew from himself gods, men and all living things.

Later, Atum was personified as the setting sun and the sun before its rising. His cult spread rather widely through Egypt, conjointly with that of Ra.

Atum was ordinarily considered to be the ancestor of the human race. He is always represented with a man's head, wearing the double crown of the Pharaohs – the 'pschent'. Originally unmarried, Atum was supposed to have fathered the first divine couple without the aid of a wife. Only later was he given a spouse, indeed two – since at Memphis he was united sometimes with Iusaas and sometimes with Nebhet Hotep, who bore him the twin gods Shu and Tefnut.

Ra (or **Re** or **Phra**), which probably signifies 'creator', is the name of the sun, sovereign lord of the sky. He had his principal sanctuary at Heliopolis. The priests of this city affirmed that it was here Ra first manifested himself in the stone object in the form of an obelisk called benben, piously preserved in the temple named for this reason Het Benben – the 'palace of the obelisk'.

Formerly, according to the priests of Heliopolis, the sun-god reposed, under the name of Atum, in the bosom of Nun, the primordial ocean. There, in order that his lustre should run no risk of being extinguished, he took care to keep his eyes shut. He enclosed himself in the bud of a lotus until the day when, weary of his own impersonality, he rose by an effort of will from the abyss and appeared in glittering splendour under the name of Ra. He then bore Shu and Tefnut who, in their turn, gave birth to Geb and Nut, from whom issued Osiris and Isis, Set and Nephthys. These are the eight great gods who with their chief Ra – or more exactly Ra Atum, since Ra and Atum were identified with each other – form the divine company or Ennead of Heliopolis.

Ra drew from himself and without recourse to woman the first divine couple. It is not until much later that he was given as his spouse Rat – which is only his own name feminised – or Iusaas, Eus-os, Uert-Hekeu, 'the great of magic'. As for men and all other living creatures, it was said that they came from Ra's tears – perhaps a play on words as 'tears' and 'men' sound the same in Egyptian.

At the same time Ra had created a 'first' universe, different from the present world, which he governed from the 'Prince's Palace' in Heliopolis where he normally resided. The Books of the Pyramids minutely describe for us his royal existence and how, after his morning bath and breakfast, he would get into his boat and, in the company of his scribe, Weneg, inspect the twelve provinces of his kingdom, spending an hour in each.

As long as Ra remained young and vigorous he reigned peacefully over gods and men; but the years brought with them their ravages and the texts depict him as an old man with trembling mouth from which saliva ceaselessly dribbles. We shall see later how Isis took advantage of the god's senility, made him reveal his secret name and thus acquired sovereign power.

Even men perceived Ra's decrepitude and plotted against him. These projects finally reached Ra's ears. Justly enraged, he summoned his council and, having consulted the gods one by one on the measures which should be taken, he decided to hurl his divine Eye against his rebellious subjects. Farther on we shall tell how the divine Eye (taking the form of the goddess Hathor) rushed upon the guilty and massacred them without pity until Ra, appeased, managed to put an end to the bloodshed; for his goodness would not permit him to allow the entire human race to be exterminated.

The ingratitude of men had, however, inspired in him a distaste for the world and a desire to withdraw himself beyond reach. So on the orders of Nun, the goddess Nut changed herself into a cow and took Ra on her back. She raised him high into the vault of heaven and at the same time, as we shall later relate, the present world was created.

From the moment that the sun-god left earth for heaven his life was immutably regulated. During the twelve daylight hours he rode in his boat from east to west across his kingdom. He took great care to avoid the attack of his eternal enemy Apep, the great serpent who lived in the depths of the celestial Nile and sometimes – for instance during total eclipses – succeeded in swallowing the solar barque. But Apep was always at last vanquished by Ra's defenders and cast back into the abyss.

During the twelve hours of darkness the perils which Ra faced were even greater. But again they were overcome and at night he passed from cavern to cavern, receiving the acclamations of the inhabitants of the underworld who waited with impatience for the light he bore and after his departure fell back into the agony of darkness.

Ra, it was also taught, was born each morning in the guise of a child who grew until midday and afterwards fell into decline, to die that night an old man.

We see him represented in many fashions: as a royal child resting on the lotus from which he sprang at his birth; as a man, seated or walking, whose head is surmounted by the solar disk around which is wreathed the Uraeus, the terrible sacred asp who spits flame and destroys the god's enemies; as a man with a ram's head, Efu Ra, in whom the dead sun is embodied during his nocturnal transit.

Often also we find a personage with the head of a falcon, surmounted by a disk with the Uraeus. This is Ra-Harakhte, the great solar god of Heliopolis, sovereign lord of Egypt. The forms and names of Ra are innumerable and the Litanies of the Sun, engraved at the entrance of the royal tombs, list no fewer than seventy-five.

Universally recognised as the creator and ruler of the world, Ra, with whom all the other gods were finally identified, became from the time of the Old Kingdom the divinity particularly revered

The creation of the universe. Shu, the god of the atmosphere, holds aloft the body of Nut, the sky goddess, whom he has just separated from her husband Geb. The latter lies at his feet resting on one elbow with his knees raised and forming with the angles of his body the hilly surface of the earth. Painted coffin of Butehamon.

Harmakhis, the Great Sphinx of Gizeh, with the pyramid of Cheops in the background. A personification of the rising sun, the sphinx was carved out of the solid rock on the orders of King Khephren nearly five thousand years ago and consists of a lion's body surmounted by a portrait of the king. Fourth dynasty, 2900 to 2750 B.C.

The two gods of the Nile binding the ties of lotus and papyrus to symbolise the union of Upper and Lower Egypt – the symbolic gesture of *sam-taui*. The god on the left represents Upper Egypt and wears a crown of lotus plants, that on the right, Lower Egypt, with a crown of papyrus. Bas-relief from a pedestal beneath the colossal statues of Rameses II in front of the great temple at Abu Simbel. Nineteenth dynasty, 1375 to 1202 B.C.

A statue of Osiris showing him swathed in mummy wrappings, wearing the *atef* crown and *uraeus*. His arms are free and he carries the crook and flail, supreme symbols of power. To those who passed the final ordeal of judgment he gave the blessing of eternal happiness.

by the Pharaohs, who called themselves 'sons of Ra'. One story tells us how the sun-god came to Reddedet, the high priest's wife, in the guise of her husband and how from this union were born the three first kings of the fifth dynasty. Each time that a Pharaoh was conceived Ra was said to return to earth to espouse the queen.

Of the celebrated sanctuary of Heliopolis, where the god was worshipped in the form of a gigantic obelisk – a petrified sun's ray – and where he used to take the form of the bull Merwer, or, at times, the bird Bennu, there remain to-day only shapeless ruins and an obelisk, the oldest in Egypt, erected during the twelfth dynasty by the king, Senusert I.

Khepri (or **Khepera**) signifies at the same time 'scarab' and 'he who becomes'. For the Heliopolitans he represented the rising sun which, like the scarab, emerges from its own substance and is reborn of itself. Khepri was the god of the transformations which life, for ever renewing itself, manifests. He is represented as a scarab-faced man or as a man whose head is surmounted by this insect. Sometimes he appears simply as a scarab.

Shu, who with Tefnut his twin sister comprised the first couple of the Ennead, was created by Ra without recourse to woman. His name derives from a verb which means 'to raise' and can be translated as 'he who holds up'. He is the Atlas of Egyptian mythology and supports the sky. It was told of him how, on the orders of Ra, he slipped between the two children, Geb the earth-god and Nut, goddess of the sky, who had until then been closely united. He threw them violently apart and elevated Nut high into the air, where he maintained her with his upraised arms.

Shu is also the god of air: emptiness deified. But like the other great divinities of nature he enjoyed no especial cult.

He is always represented in human form. On his head he nor-mally wears, as a distinctive sign, an ostrich feather which is an ideogram of his name.

Shu succeeded Ra as king on earth. But like his father he experienced the vicissitudes of power; for the children of Apep plotted against him and attacked him in his palace of At Nub. He vanquished them, but disease riddled him so that even his faithful followers revolted. Weary of reigning, Shu abdicated in favour of his son Geb and took refuge in the skies after a terrifying tempest which lasted nine days.

Tefnut seems to have been a theological conception rather than a real person. At Heliopolis she was said to be Shu's twin sister and wife, but she appears to have been paired in earlier times with a certain god Tefen of whom we know nothing but the name.

Goddess of the dew and the rain, it seems, she also had a solar character. She was worshipped in the form of a lioness or of a woman with the head of a lioness, and the Greeks sometimes identified her with Artemis. She is depicted in the texts as a pale copy of Shu, whom she helps to support the sky and with whom each morning she receives the new-born sun as it breaks free from the eastern mountains.

Anhur (the Greek rendering is *Onouris*) seems to signify 'he who leads what has gone away' but has also been translated as 'sky-bearer'. God of Sebennytus and This, it is believed that he symbolised the creative power of the sun. He was very soon identified with Shu and invoked under the name Anhur-Shu. He is assumed to be a warlike personification of Ra, and was identified by the Greeks as Ares, the god of battle.

He is represented with the traits of a warrior wearing a head-dress adorned with four tall straight plumes. He is covered by a long embroidered robe and often brandishes a lance. Sometimes

Symbolic Tableau representing the course of the Sun. Two jackal-headed gods and two falcon-headed gods worship the god Khepri, whose human head is surmounted by a scarab. Above, four dog-headed apes greet the birth of the sun. To the left four lesser divinities, with serpent and scarab heads, triumphantly bear Ra-Harakhte across his kingdom. New Kingdom, 1580 to 1090. Papyrus in the Bibliothèque Nationale.

The god Atum. Often identified with the great sun god Ra under the name of Atum-Ra, he came to personify both the setting sun and the sun before its rising. The god wears the double crown of the pharaohs, the *pschent*. Bas-relief on a stone stele from Karnak, *c.* 1400 B.C.

he holds the cord by which he leads the sun. Legend recounts how an Eye of Ra which had fled from Egypt was brought back from Nubia by Anhur, and how this divine Eye became enraged upon seeing that another Eye had taken its place. Ra then set it on his forehead where it became the Uraeus which protected the god against his enemies.

Anhur was very popular under the New Empire and was called 'the Saviour' and 'the Good Warrior'. He was fervently invoked against enemies and against noxious animals, whom he hunted without respite from his chariot. His popularity was of long duration; Herodotus speaks of the great festivals he saw celebrated at Papremis and of the innumerable cudgel blows which priests and the faithful enthusiastically exchanged in honour of their god.

As a wife Anhur was given Mehit, who seems to be a mere double of Tefnut, the sister-wife of Shu. She was worshipped at This, and is pictured as a lion-headed goddess.

Geb (or **Seb, Keb**) constituted with Nut the second pair in the Ennead. Plutarch identifies him with Cronus. In reality he was the earth-god, the physical foundation of the world; but in classical times he scarcely had anything resembling a cult.

We have already seen how Geb had been separated by Shu from Nut, his sister-spouse. Since that time he had remained inconsolable and his lamentations could be heard night and day.

Geb is often represented lying under the feet of Shu, against whom he had vainly struggled to defend his wife. Raised on one elbow, with one knee bent, he thus symbolises the mountains and the undulations of the earth's crust. His body is sometimes covered with verdure.

Geb is nearly always depicted as a man without especial attributes, but on occasion his head is surmounted by a goose, which is an ideogram of his name. Certain legends, moreover, describe him as a gander – the 'Great Cackler' – whose female has laid the egg of the sun. Others make him a vigorous bull who has fertilised the celestial cow.

Most frequently, however, Geb was reputed to be the father – and Nut the mother – of the Osirian gods, and for this reason was known as the 'father of the gods'.

He was the third divine Pharaoh and succeeded Shu to the throne. His reign also was disturbed. One text tells us how Geb caused the golden box in which Ra's Uraeus was kept to be opened in his presence. Ra had deposited the box, together with his cane and a lock of his hair, in a fortress on the eastern frontier of his empire

Khepri, the scarab-god. Before him he rolls the ball of the sun, pushing it into the Other World in the evening and over the horizon in the morning as the scarab beetle pushes before itself a ball of dung. For the Egyptians he represented the rising sun and symbolised the renewal of life and the idea of eternal existence.

as a potent and dangerous talisman. When opened, the breath of the divine asp within killed all of Geb's companions then and there, and gravely burned Geb himself. Only the lock of Ra's hair, applied to the wound, could heal Geb. So great, indeed, was the virtue of this divine lock of hair that years later when it was plunged for purification into the lake of At Nub it immediately turned into a crocodile. When he was restored to health Geb administered his kingdom wisely and drew up a careful report on the condition of every province and town in Egypt.

Then he handed over his sovereignty to his eldest son, Osiris, and ascended to the heavens where at times he took the place of Thoth as Ra's herald and arbiter of the gods.

Nut, whom the Greeks sometimes identified with Rhea, was goddess of the sky, but it is debatable if in historical times she was the object of a genuine cult. She was Geb's twin sister and, it was said, married him secretly and against the will of Ra. Angered, Ra had the couple brutally separated by Shu and afterwards decreed that Nut could

Anhur. The god advances with his right arm raised to brandish his lance (now missing) wearing a long robe and his four-plumed head-dress. In his left hand he probably held the reins of his chariot. Known as 'the Saviour' and 'the Good Warrior', Anhur was invoked against enemies and noxious animals. Bronze statuette of the twenty-sixth dynasty, 672 to 525 B.C.

not bear a child in any given month of any year. Thoth, Plutarch tells us, happily had pity on her. Playing draughts with the Moon, he won in the course of several games a seventy-second part of the Moon's light with which he composed five new days. As these five intercalated days did not belong to the official Egyptian calendar of three hundred and sixty days, Nut was thus able to give birth successively to five children: Osiris, Haroeris (Horus), Set, Isis and Nephthys.

The sky-goddess is often represented as a woman with elongated body, touching the earth with toes and fingertips, while her star-spangled belly is held aloft by Shu and forms the arch of the heavens. She also sometimes appears as a cow; for this is the form she assumed when, on the orders of Nun, she bore Ra on her back to the sky after Ra, as already related, decided to abandon his rebellious subjects. The dutiful cow rose obediently to her feet, rose higher and higher until she became dizzy and it was necessary to appoint a god to each of her four legs – which became the four pillars of the sky – in order to steady them. Shu, meanwhile, supported her belly, which became the firmament and to which Ra attached the stars and the constellations to light our earth. Though she was often qualified by the title 'Daughter of Ra', Nut was also the mother of the sun, which, as we have already had occasion to see, was reborn in various fashions each morning from her womb.

When she is pictured as a woman Nut often wears a rounded vase on her head, this being an ideogram of her name. She is protectress of the dead and we frequently see her holding the deceased close in her arms. On the inner lid of sarcophagi her starry body stretches above the mummy, watching maternally over him.

Osiris, which is the Greek rendering of the Egyptian Ousir, was identified by the Greeks with several of their own gods, but principally with Dionysus and Hades. At first Osiris was a nature god and embodied the spirit of vegetation which dies with the harvest to be reborn when the grain sprouts. Afterwards he was worshipped throughout Egypt as god of the dead, and in this capacity reached first rank in the Egyptian pantheon.

Hieroglyphic texts contain numerous allusions to the life and deeds of Osiris during his sojourn on earth; but it is above all thanks to Plutarch that we know his legend so well.

The first son of Geb and Nut, he was born in Thebes in Upper Egypt. At his birth a loud, mysterious voice proclaimed the coming of the 'Universal Lord', which gave rise to shouts of gladness, soon followed by tears and lamentations when it was learned what misfortunes awaited him. Ra rejoiced at the news of his birth in spite of the curse he had pronounced against Nut; and, having Osiris brought into his presence, he recognised his great-grandson as heir to his throne.

Osiris was handsome of countenance, dark-skinned and taller than all other men. When Geb, his father, retired to the heavens, Osiris succeeded him as king of Egypt and took Isis, his sister, as queen. The first care of the new sovereign was to abolish cannibalism and to teach his still half-savage subjects the art of fashioning agricultural implements. He taught them how to produce grain and grapes for man's nourishment in the form of bread, wine and beer. The cult of the gods did not yet exist. Osiris instituted it. He built the first temples and sculptured the first divine images. He laid down the rules governing religious practice and even invented the two kinds of flute which should accompany ceremonial song.

After this he built towns and gave his people just laws, thus meriting the name Onnophris – 'the Good One' – by which, as the fourth divine Pharaoh, he was known.

Not satisfied with having civilised Egypt, he wished to spread the benefits of his rule throughout the whole world. He left the regency to Isis and set forth on the conquest of Asia, accompanied by Thoth, his grand vizier, and his lieutenants Anubis and Upuaut. Osiris was the enemy of all violence and it was by gentleness alone that he subjected country after country, winning and disarming their inhabitants by songs and the playing of various musical instruments. He returned to Egypt only after he had travelled the whole earth and spread civilisation everywhere.

On his return Osiris found his kingdom in perfect order; for Isis had governed wisely in his absence. But it was not long before he became the victim of a plot organised by his brother Set, who was jealous of his power. Farther on we shall relate in detail (see *Isis* and *Set*) how on the 17th Athyr, in the twenty-eighth year of his

Ra-Harakhte and Ament, goddess of the West. The god is falcon-headed and wears the solar disk encircled by a serpent on his head while the goddess wears her emblem, the hawk.
Originally the goddess of a Libyan province to the west of Egypt, Ament became the goddess of the underworld when 'west' came to signify the land of the dead. Fresco from the tomb of Nefertari. Nineteenth dynasty, 1375 to 1202 B.C.

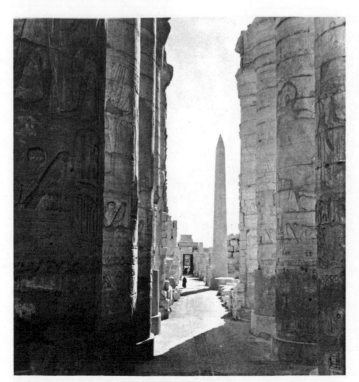

Colossal carved columns in the temple of Amon at Karnak in Thebes. Probably the largest religious building of all time, the temple was nearly a quarter of a mile long and the work of extension, rebuilding and decoration went on for a period of nearly two thousand years. A hundred men could stand on each of the capitals of the columns in the nave of its great hall.

reign, Osiris 'the Good One' fell under the blows of the conspirators and how his faithful wife found his body and bore it back to Egypt. For the moment it suffices to say that Isis, thanks to her powers of sorcery and the aid of Thoth, Anubis, and Horus, succeeded in restoring her husband's dead body to life. Osiris soon answered Set's accusations and vindicated himself before the tribunal of gods, presided over by Geb.

Resurrected and from thenceforward secure from the threat of death, Osiris could have regained his throne and continued to reign over the living. But he preferred to depart from this earth and retire to the 'Elysian Fields' where he warmly welcomed the souls of the just and reigned over the dead.

Such is the legend of Osiris. What we can guess of his actual origin suggests that he was a fetish of a conquering clan which first installed its god at Busiris in Lower Egypt. There he took the place of the preceding Lord of the City, Andjeti, whose form he borrowed. Perhaps he borrowed his name also, since later in Abydos in Upper Egypt he became identified with Khenti Amenti, the wolf-god, and became the great god of the dead, sometimes known as Osiris Khenti Amenti, 'Lord of the Westerners' – that is, the dead, who dwell in the west where the sun sets.

Here we can only indicate briefly the many cosmic interpretations which the myth of Osiris has been given.

As a vegetation spirit that dies and is ceaselessly reborn, Osiris represents the corn, the vine and trees. He is also the Nile which rises and falls each year; the light of the sun which vanishes in the shadows every evening to reappear more brilliantly at dawn. The struggle between the two brothers is the war between the desert and the fertile earth, between the drying wind and vegetation, aridity and fecundity, darkness and light.

It was as god of the dead that Osiris enjoyed his greatest popularity; for he gave his devotees the hope of an eternally happy life in another world ruled over by a just and good king.

He was worshipped throughout Egypt in company with Isis, his wife, and with Horus, his posthumous son, who formed with him a trinity. But he was particularly venerated at Abydos where priests showed his tomb to the innumerable pilgrims who visited it. Happy were the favoured ones who were buried in the shadows of the august sanctuary or who at least had a stela erected nearby in their name to assure the benevolence of Osiris in after-life!

Osiris is represented sometimes standing, sometimes seated on his throne, as a man tightly swathed in white mummy wrappings. His greenish face is surmounted by the high white mitre flanked by two ostrich feathers which is called 'Atef', the crown of Upper Egypt. Around his neck he wears a kind of cravat. His two hands, freed from the winding sheet, are folded across his breast and hold the whip and the sceptre in the form of a crook, emblems of supreme power.

The names and appellations of Osiris were countless. There are about a hundred in the litanies of the Book of the Dead.

Like many other gods he delighted in incarnations. He appeared not only in the form of various animals – the bull Onuphis, the sacred ram of Mendes, the bird Bennu – but also in the 'Djed', a simple fetish which seems to have been his primitive form in the days when he led his prehistoric followers into battle. The 'Djed' was originally the trunk of a fir or some other conifer; but in classical times it was a kind of pillar with four capitals, which certain texts alleged to be the god's vertebral column, preserved in the famous sanctuary of Busiris.

Space is lacking to describe the festivals which marked critical dates in the Osiris legend. They were publicly celebrated, and in the course of the Mysteries then presented priests and priestesses would mime the passion and resurrection of the god.

Isis (a Greek rendering of **Aset, Eset**) was identified by the Greeks with Demeter, Hera, Selene and even – because of a late confusion between Isis and Hathor – with Aphrodite. In later days the popularity of Isis became such that she finally absorbed the qualities of all the other goddesses; but originally she seems to have been a modest divinity of the Delta, the protective deity of Perehbet, north of Busiris, where she always retained a renowned temple.

Very soon she was given as wife to Osiris, the god of the neighbouring town. She bore him a son, Horus, who formed the third member of the trinity. Her popularity grew rapidly with that of her husband and son. This is her legend as Plutarch tells it to us:

The first daughter of Geb and Nut was born in the swamps of the

Tuthmoses III. wearing the *pschent*.
The Pharaohs were fond of depicting the gods in their own likenesses and during the reign of Tuthmoses III they would have resembled this portrait of the great Pharaoh which originally formed part of a statue. Red granite. *c.* 1550 B.C. From Karnak.

Delta on the fourth intercalary day. Osiris, her eldest brother, chose her as his consort and she mounted to the throne with him. She helped him in his great work of civilising Egypt by teaching women to grind corn, spin flax and weave cloth. She also taught men the art of curing disease and, by instituting marriage, accustomed them to domestic life.

When her husband departed on his pacific conquest of the world she remained in Egypt as regent. She governed wisely while awaiting his return.

She was overwhelmed with grief at the news that Osiris had been assassinated by their brother, the violent Set. She cut off her hair, tore her robes and at once set forth in search of the coffer in which the good Osiris had been enclosed and which the conspirators had cast into the Nile.

This coffer had been carried out to sea by the waters of the Nile and borne across the waves to the Phoenician coast where it came to rest at the base of a tamarisk tree. The tree grew with such astonishing rapidity that the chest was entirely enclosed within its trunk.

Now Malcandre, the king of Byblos, gave orders that the tamarisk should be cut down in order to serve as a prop for the roof of his palace. When this was done the marvellous tree gave off so exquisite a scent that its reputation reached the ears of Isis, who immediately understood its significance. Without delay she went to Phoenicia. There the queen, Astarte, confided to her the care of her newly born son. Isis adopted the baby and would have conferred immortality upon it had its mother not broken the charm by her cries of terror upon seeing the goddess bathe the baby in purificatory flames. In order to reassure her, Isis revealed her true name and the reason for her presence. Then, having been presented with the trunk of the miraculous tree, she drew forth the coffer of her husband, bathed it in tears, and bore it back in haste to Egypt where, to deceive Set, she hid it in the swamps of Buto. Set, however, regained possession of his brother's body by chance and in order to annihilate it for ever cut it into fourteen pieces which he scattered far and wide.

Isis, undiscouraged, searched for the precious fragments and found them all except the phallus which had been greedily devoured by a Nile crab, the Oxyrhynchid, forever accursed for this crime.

The goddess reconstituted the body of Osiris, cunningly joining the fragments together. She then performed, for the first time in

Seker, Taueret and Hathor – scene from the Papyrus of Ani. On the right, the goddess Hathor, in the form of a cow, emerges from the Libyan mountain to protect the tomb of Ani. Before her stands the hippopotamus goddess, Taueret, while on the left Seker, the hawk-headed god of the dead of the Memphis necropolis, stands guard. Painting on papyrus. Nineteenth dynasty, 1375 to 1202 B.C.

Efu Ra. The dead sun, portrayed as a man with a ram's head surmounted by the solar disk, is drawn in the Evening Boat through the Realm of Night. Around his cabin the serpent Mehen throws its coils to protect him from the terrible serpent Apep who sought to destroy him every night. Sketch and bas-relief on the wall of a tomb in the Valley of the Kings, Thebes.

history, the rites of embalmment which restored the murdered god to eternal life. In this she was assisted by her sister Nephthys, her nephew Anubis, Osiris' grand vizier Thoth and by Horus, the posthumous son whom she had conceived by union with her husband's corpse, miraculously re-animated by her charms.

Afterwards she retired to the swamps of Buto to escape the wrath of Set and to bring up her son Horus until the day when he should be of an age to avenge his father. Thanks to her magic powers Horus was able to overcome every danger which threatened him.

Isis, indeed, was a potent magician and even the gods were not immune from her sorcery. It was told how, when she was still only a simple woman in the service of Ra, she persuaded the great god to confide to her his secret name. She had taken advantage of the fact that the sun-god was now an old man with shaking head and dribbling mouth. With earth moistened with his divine spittle she fashioned a venomous snake which bit Ra cruelly. Ra was incapable of curing himself of a wound whose origin he did not understand, and had recourse to the spells of Isis. But Isis refused to conjure away the poison until Ra, overcome with pain and hiding himself from the other gods, consented to reveal his true name, which he caused to pass directly from his own bosom into that of Isis.

Isis, in the Osirian myth, represents the rich plains of Egypt, made fruitful by the annual inundation of the Nile which is Osiris, who is separated from her by Set, the arid desert.

Her cult continued to grow in importance until it ultimately absorbed that of nearly all other goddesses. It even crossed the frontiers of Egypt; seamen and merchants in the Graeco-Roman era carried her worship as far as the banks of the Rhine – Isis, star of the sea, and patron divinity of travellers.

In the Nile valley she kept her worshippers until well into Christian times. It was not until the middle of the sixth century, in the reign of Justinian, that the temple of Philae – her chief sanctuary in the extreme south of the country – was closed to her cult and turned into a church.

Great festivals were celebrated in spring and autumn in honour of Isis. The splendours of the processions which then took place have been described to us by Apuleius, who was an initiate in the mysteries of Isis. Thanks to him we can raise a corner of the veil which conceals the secret ceremonies of initiation.

Isis is normally represented as a woman who bears on her head a throne, the ideogram of her name. Occasionally, but later, her head-dress is a disk, set between cow's horns, occasionally flanked with two feathers. Finally we sometimes find her represented with a cow's head set on a human body. These horns and the cow's head merely prove that Isis was by then identified with Hathor; but Plutarch, though he says he does not believe it, gives us another explanation. Isis, he tells us, wished to intervene on behalf of Set who, though her husband's murderer, was also her own brother. She tried to cheat her son Horus of his just vengeance; but Horus turned in rage against his mother and cut off her head. Thoth then transformed it by enchantment and gave her the head of a cow.

This cow is, on the other hand, the animal sacred to Isis who also possessed, as fetishes, the magic knot 'Tat', called 'The Knot of Isis', and the Sistrum, the emblem of Hathor.

Sculpture and painting often represent her beside Osiris, whom she helps or protects – as she does the dead – with her winged arms. She may be seen mourning at the foot of sarcophagi or watching over canopic jars. She also frequently appears in the role of mother, suckling the infant Horus or joining him in his struggles with Set.

Set (Seth, Sutekh), whom the Greeks called Typhon, was the name of Osiris' evil brother who finally became the incarnation of the spirit of evil, in eternal opposition to the spirit of good.

The son of Geb and Nut, he was, Plutarch tells us, prematurely born on the third intercalary day. He tore himself violently from his mother's womb. He was rough and wild, his skin was white and his hair was red – an abomination to the Egyptians, who compared it to the pelt of an ass.

Set was jealous of Osiris, his elder brother, and secretly aspired to the throne. In order to seize it he availed himself of the great festivals which were celebrated at Memphis on the occasion of Osiris' victorious return to his kingdom. Having first assured

The facade of the great temple at Abu Simbel in Egyptian Nubia. Flanking the entrance are four colossal seated statues over sixty feet high of the Pharaoh Rameses III wearing the double crown of Upper and Lower Egypt while above it stands the falcon-headed figure of the sun god. Smaller figures represent wife, princes and gods. Nineteenth dynasty, 1375 to 1202 B.C.

himself of the presence of seventy-two accomplices he invited his brother to a banquet during the course of which he gave orders that a marvellously fashioned coffer should be brought in. This chest, he explained jokingly, would belong to whomsoever fitted it exactly. Osiris, falling in with the pleasantry, lay down in the coffer without suspicion. The conspirators at once rushed forward, closed the lid and nailed it solidly down. They threw it into the Nile, whence it was carried to the sea and across to Byblos. We have already seen how Isis brought it back to Egypt and how Set, hunting by moonlight in the swamps of the Delta, found it again by chance, and how, when he had recognised his brother's corpse, he cut it up into fourteen pieces which he scattered far and wide. This time the usurper felt that the possession of the realm was assured, and it worried him little that his wife Nephthys had left him. Nephthys, indeed, had joined the party of Osiris as most of the other gods had done, escaping from the cruelties of the tyrant by taking refuge in the bodies of various animals. Meanwhile Horus, son of Isis, was growing to maturity in the shelter of the Delta swamps, and we shall see how he avenged the murder of Osiris, his father, and reclaimed his heritage from Set.

As we have already said, Set, in Osirian myth, figures as the eternal adversary, a personification of the arid desert, of drought and darkness in opposition to the fertile earth, life-bringing water and light. All that is creation and blessing comes from Osiris; all that is destruction and perversity arises from Set.

In primitive times, however, the evil character of Set was not so accentuated. The old pyramid texts make him not the brother of Osiris, but the brother of Horus the Elder, and speak of terrible struggles between them which were terminated by the judgment of the gods, who proclaimed Horus the victor and banished Set to the desert.

It was only later, when the Osirian myth had grown and when the two Horuses had become confused, that Set was made the uncle of Horus and the eternal enemy of Osiris.

Originally Set seems to have been the Lord of Upper Egypt who was overthrown by the worshippers of the falcon god. The legendary struggles between the brother gods may thus reflect historical events.

The bas-reliefs of the Old and the Middle Kingdoms show Set and Horus together leading prisoners to the king, or else together at the base of the royal throne binding the plants of Upper and Lower Egypt around the emblem which expresses the idea of union – thus making the symbolic gesture of 'sam-taui', the union of the two countries.

Under the domination of the Hyksos, the new rulers identified Set with their own great warrior god Sutekh and had a temple built for him in Avaris, their capital. Under the New Empire Rameses II, whose father was named Seti, the 'Setian', did not hesitate to proclaim himself the 'Beloved of Set'. The worshippers of Osiris, however, were indignant that a cult should be devoted to the murderer of the 'Good One', and Seti caused the cursed image to be effaced from the engraved tablets on the walls of his tomb and proclaimed himself no longer the 'Setian' but the 'Osirian'.

It is only towards the middle of the tenth century, under the kings of the twenty-second dynasty, that the assassin of Osiris really began to undergo the punishment for his crime. His statues were broken and on the bas-reliefs his features were smashed with hammers. Anyone who wrote his name was forced to erase it. Finally he was driven from the Egyptian pantheon and made a god of the unclean. Set, the ancient Lord of Upper Egypt, ended up by becoming a kind of devil, enemy of all the gods.

Asses, antelopes and other desert animals were supposed to belong to Set, and also the hippopotamus, the boar, the crocodile and the scorpion, in whose bodies the god of evil and his partisans had sought refuge from the blows of the conquering Horus. Legend says that Set, in the guise of a black pig, had once wounded Horus in the eye. In this form each month he attacked and devoured the moon where, some said, the soul of Osiris had taken refuge.

Set is represented as having the features of a fantastic beast with a thin, curved snout, straight, square-cut ears and a stiff forked tail. This creature cannot with certainty be identified and is commonly called the 'Typhonian animal'. Sometimes Set is depicted as a man with the head of this strange quadruped.

The temple of Rameses III at Karnak. The pharaoh wears the double crown of Upper and Lower Egypt, the *pschent*. The statues in the inner court, though much damaged by time, show clearly the familiar Osiris posture with their arms folded across their breasts, holding the flail and the sceptre in the shape of a crook, the emblems of supreme power. Twentieth dynasty, 1202 to 1102 B.C.

The goddess Isis embraces Prince Amun-kher-khopsh. The protectress of the dead, the goddess wears a disk set between cow's horns on her headdress, having become identified with Hathor, the cow-goddess, by this date. The prince, who was the son of the Pharaoh Rameses III, wears the blue *khepresh*, or war helmet. Behind him stands the ibis-headed god Thoth holding a read pen in his upraised right hand and with a writing palette in his left to record the prince's deeds. Painting from the tomb of Prince Amun-kher-khopsh, Twentieth dynasty, 1202 to 1102 B.C.

Nephthys is the Greek rendering of Nebthet and is called by Plutarch Aphrodite and Nike.

She is pictured as a woman wearing on her head the two hieroglyphs with which her name, which signifies 'Mistress of the Palace', was written: i.e., a basket (*neb*) placed on the sign for a palace (*het*). In origin a goddess of the dead, Nephthys in the Osirian legend becomes the second daughter of Geb and Nut. Set, her second brother, took her for his wife, but she remained barren. She wanted a child by her eldest brother Osiris and with this object she made him drunk and drew him into her arms without his being aware of it. The fruit of this adultery was Anubis.

Nephthys, according to this legend, seems to represent the desert's edge, ordinarily arid but sometimes fruitful when the Nile floods are especially high. When Set committed fratricide his wife abandoned him in horror and, joining the party of Osiris' defenders, she helped her sister Isis to embalm the corpse of the murdered god, alternating with her in the funereal lamentations. A papyrus still preserves for us the text of these lamentations.

Just as Nephthys and Isis had protected the mummy of their brother so the 'twins', as they are often called, also watched over the bodies of the dead who, by virtue of funeral rites, had become 'Osirises'. On coffin-lids and the walls of sarcophagi we often see them represented, standing or kneeling, stretching forth their long, winged arms in a gesture of protection.

Horus is the Latin rendering of the Greek Horos and the Egyptian Hor. He was a solar god constantly identified with Apollo and represented by a falcon or a falconheaded god.

Under the name Hor – which in Egyptian sounds like a word meaning 'sky' – the Egyptians referred to the falcon which they saw soaring high above their heads, and many thought of the sky as a divine falcon whose two eyes were the sun and the moon. The worshippers of this bird must have been numerous and powerful; for it was carried as a totem on prehistoric standards and from the earliest times was considered the pre-eminent divine being. The hieroglyph which represents the idea of 'god' was a falcon on its perch.

Wherever the followers of the falcon settled, Horus was worshipped, but in the course of time and in the different sanctuaries which were dedicated to him his role and attributes varied. Thus we find in the Egyptian pantheon some twenty Horuses, among whom it is important to distinguish Horus the Elder, 'Haroeris', and other falcons of a solar character such as Hor Behdetite, Horus of Edfu, from Horus, son of Isis, of the Osirian legend – i.e., 'Harsiesis', the infant avenger of his father.

Haroeris is the Greek rendering of Har Wer, which signifies Horus the Great, Horus the Elder.

He was worshipped at Latopolis under the name Horkhenti Irti, 'Horus who rules the two eyes', and at Pharboethos under the name Hor Merti, 'Horus of the two eyes'. He is the god of the sky itself and his two eyes are the sun and the moon, whose birth, according to Herodotus, was celebrated on the last day of Epiphi, when these two astral bodies are in conjunction.

In the pyramid texts Haroeris is the son of Ra and brother of Set, and the eternal struggle between darkness and light is symbolised by the endless battles in which Set tears out the eyes of Horus while Horus emasculates his implacable enemy. We shall presently see how the tribunal of the gods gave judgment in favour of Horus, who from the end of the second dynasty was considered to be the divine ancestor of the Pharaohs in whose records he is given the title Hor Nubti: 'Horus the Vanquisher of Set'.

Behdety, 'He of Behdet' (or Hor Behdetite) is another name of the great celestial Horus. He was worshipped at Behdet, a district of ancient Edfu. The Greeks called it Apollinopolis Magna and recognised Apollo as Lord of the sanctuary.

Behdety is usually represented in the form of a winged solar disk; his followers liked to sculpture his image above temple gates. He often appears in battle scenes hovering above the Pharaoh like a great falcon with outspread wings which clutches in its claws the mystic fly-whisk and the ring, symbolic of eternity.

The bas-reliefs in the temple at Edfu portray him as a falcon-headed god leading into battle against Set the armies of Ra-Harakhte, the great god of whom we have already spoken

Horus. The falcon-headed solar god of Memphis makes a purificatory gesture towards a Pharaoh – possibly Amenhotep II. His gesture, formerly completed by the god Set, in company with whom he performed the coronation and purification of the Pharaoh, would at this period have been completed by the god Thoth. Statue of the nineteenth dynasty, 1587 to 1375 B.C.

Haroeris. The great sky-god Horus the Elder or Horus the Great is portrayed with the head of a man instead of that of a falcon probably by confusion with the younger Horus, the son of Isis and Osiris. and wears the double crown upon his head. Statue in bronze.

Snake-goddess. This tomb painting from the Valley of the Kings probably represents Mertseger, the snake goddess of the Theban necropolis, who protected the desert tombs. Another goddess also portrayed as a winged cobra was Buto, the protector of the Pharaoh. New Kingdom period, 1738 to 1102 B.C. Thebes.

(see *Ra*) who embodied in a single deity the union of Ra and a special form of Horus worshipped at Heliopolis.

Harakhtes is the Greek rendering of Harakhte and means 'Horus of the Horizon'. He represents the sun on its daily course between the eastern and western horizon. Early confused with Ra, he successively usurped all of Ra's roles until Ra, in his turn, assumed all of Horus' epithets and became pre-eminent throughout Egypt under the name Ra-Harakhte.

Harmakhis is the Greek rendering of Hor-m-akhet which means 'Horus who is on the Horizon'. The name has often been wrongly employed in the form of Ra Harmakhis for Ra-Harakhte. It is the proper name of the huge sphinx sixty feet high and more than a hundred and eighty feet long sculptured nearly five thousand years ago in the image of King Khephren in a rock near the pyramid which it guards. He is a personification of the rising sun and a

symbol (for the comfort of Khephren) of resurrection.

Raised on the edge of the desert, even its colossal size did not in ancient days protect it against the invading sands. A stela tells us how it appeared in a dream to the future Thuthmosis IV. Thuthmosis was at the time a simple royal prince and not heir to the throne. While hunting he fell asleep in the shadow of the sphinx and dreamed that it spoke to him, ordering him to remove the covering sand and promising in return to heap favours upon him. 'Oh my son Thuthmosis,' it cried, 'it is I, thy father, Harmakhis-Khepri-Atum. The throne will be thine . . . so that thou shalt do what my heart desires . . .'

Harsiesis is the Greek rendering of Hor-sa-iset, i.e. 'Horus, the son of Isis'. We have already seen how Isis was reputed to have conceived Horus without husband or lover and how the popularity of mother and son continued to increase, together with that of Osiris himself. This popularity became such that Harsiesis – originally a minor falcon-god from the neighbourhood of Buto who was called Horus the Younger in order to distinguish him from the great sky-god Horus the Elder – ended up by eclipsing all the other Horuses whose roles and attributes he successively took over.

The Osirian legend recounts the posthumous birth of the child which Isis obtained from Osiris by magical means, re-animating the corpse of the murdered god. It relates how she gave premature birth to Horus on the floating island of Chemmis, not far from Buto. In early youth he was frequently called 'the infant Horus' – Harpakhrad – or Harpokrates.

Harpokrates is represented as a baby, nude or adorned only with jewellery. His head is shaved, except for the sidelock of youth which falls over his temple. Often he is seated on his mother's lap while she offers him her breast. He sucks his thumb like a baby, a gesture which was misinterpreted by the Greeks, who took it for a symbol of discretion, and won the young god fame as the divinity of silence.

For fear of the machinations of Set, Horus was brought up in seclusion. He was extremely weak at birth and escaped from the numerous dangers which menaced him only by his mother's power of sorcery. He was bitten by savage beasts, stung by scorpions, burnt, attacked by pains in the entrails. The memory of these sufferings is preserved for us in the magic formulas which were employed by sorcerers to cure patients similarly afflicted.

The child Horus grew, and Osiris appeared frequently to him and instructed him in the use of arms so that he should soon be able to make war on Set, reclaim his inheritance and avenge his father. This glorious action earned for Horus the epithet Harendotes, which is the Greek for Har-end-yotef, 'Horus, protector of his father'.

The campaigns of the young god against the murderer of Osiris are sculptured on the walls of the temple at Edfu whose great god Behdety was, in this later epoch, identified with Horus, while Set was confused with Apep, the eternal enemy of the sun. In a long series of bas-reliefs we see him, under the name Hartomes, 'Horus the Lancer', piercing his adversaries with his lance while his followers cut Set's followers – who vainly attempt to seek refuge in the bodies of crocodiles, hippopotami, antelopes and so on – into pieces.

The war dragged on, and in order to terminate it a tribunal of the gods summoned the two adversaries before it. Set pleaded that his nephew was a bastard, only the alleged son of Osiris; but Horus victoriously established the legitimacy of his birth. The gods, after condemning the usurper, restored Horus' heritage and declared him ruler of the two Egypts, by which he then earned the two further titles: Harsomtus or Heru Sam Taui ('Horus who unites the two countries') and Har-pa-neb-taui ('Horus, Lord of the two lands').

He now everywhere re-established the authority of Osiris and the solar cycle. He erected temples in which he was represented in the various forms he had assumed during the wars against his irreconcilable enemies, the followers of Set. He then reigned peacefully over Egypt, of which he always remained the national god, ancestor of the Pharaohs, who each took the title of 'the Living Horus'.

With his father Osiris and his mother Isis, Horus was worshipped throughout Egypt. He figures in the triads or trinities of numerous sanctuaries, either as chief, as prince consort, or as divine infant. Thus at Edfu and at Ombos he is the great god with Hathor as his companion; while Hathor is the uncontested mistress at Dendera, and Horus, in his role of the sovereign's husband, only a privileged guest.

Until the beginning of the New Kingdom, temple figures represent Horus acting in consort with Set to crown and purify the king. They show the king into the sanctuary or perform the symbolic gesture of 'sam-taui'. But later Thoth everywhere replaces Set. Elsewhere we see Horus fighting Set and his partisans, mourning Osiris and performing for him the burial duties. Finally in the next world Horus ushers the deceased into the presence of 'the Good One' and often presides over the weighing of his soul.

Hathor (Athyr) is the name of the great Egyptian deity whom the Greeks identified with Aphrodite.

A sky-goddess, she was originally described as the daughter of Ra and the wife of Horus. She was, however, sometimes called the mother of Horus; for her name can also signify 'the dwelling of Horus' and it was explained that within her the sun-god resided, being enclosed each evening in her breast, to be born again each morning.

Hathor and the Pharaoh Seti I. The goddess, wearing an embroidered robe and a horned head-dress with the solar disk and the *uraeus* embraces the Pharaoh and presents him with the 'Menat' collar, thus transmitting to him her protective fluid.
Painted bas-relief. Nineteenth dynasty, 1350 to 1202.

The texts also say that she was the great celestial cow who created the world and all that it contains, including the sun.

She is in consequence represented as a cow – her sacred animal – or as a cow-headed goddess. Still more often she is given a human head adorned either with horns or simply cow's ears and heavy tresses framing her face.

Hathor also had a fetish in which she liked to embody herself: the sistrum, a musical instrument which drove away evil spirits. It was in a spirit of piety that the architect of Dendera conceived the columns of Hathor's temple as so many colossal sistrums.

Hathor was the protectress of women and was supposed to preside at their toilet. She enjoyed immense popularity as the goddess of joy and love. She was proclaimed mistress of merriment and sovereign of the dance, mistress of music and sovereign of song, of leaping and jumping and the weaving of garlands. Her temple was

Selket. One of the four goddesses who protected the dead, Selket, wearing her sacred animal, the scorpion, on her head, spreads her winged arms around the sarcophagus of the young Pharaoh Tut-ankh-Amon. The other three goddesses were similarly carved in high relief at each of the other corners of the sarcophagus. Yellow quartzite. Eighteenth dynasty, 1587 to 1375 B.C.

Sebek, the crocodile god. In this bas-relief on the small south-western outer wall of the court of the temple of Kom Ombo where his triad was worshipped, Sebek is portrayed as a seated man with a crocodile's head though he could also be represented as the animal itself. At one time a patron of the Pharaohs, he was later reviled in some areas as an enemy of Osiris.

Sekhmet, the terrible lioness-headed goddess of war and battle. The goddess of vengeance, who at one time attempted to exterminate the human race and who punished the damned in the Underworld, she was also a fire goddess and symbolised the devouring fire of the sun. Head of a statue in the third court of the temple of Mont at Karnak. Eighteenth dynasty, c. 1400 B.C.

Anubis, 'Lord of the Land' (i.e. the cemetery). The jackal-headed god advances wearing the double crown of Upper and Lower Egypt. Originally the fourth son of Ra, he was later admitted into the family of Osiris, and from being the god of death of the Pharaoh only, became the god of death for all. Bronze statuette.

the 'home of intoxication and a place of enjoyment'.

Hathor nourished the living with her milk. We see her giving her breast to the king whom she holds in her arms or on her knees and, again, in the form of a cow, suckling the Pharaoh.

Although she was well disposed towards those who were alive she cherished the dead even more tenderly. Under the name 'Queen of the West' she was the protectress of the Theban necropolis. Vignettes in the Book of the Dead show the good cow half-emerged from the Libyan Mountain – the westernmost limit of human habitation – to welcome the dead on their arrival in the other world. Those who understood how to beseech her aid by means of the prescribed formulas she would carry in safety on her back to the after world.

She was also called 'the Lady of the Sycamore', for she would sometimes hide in the foliage of this tree on the edge of the desert and appear to the dead with the bread and water of welcome. It was she, they believed, who held the long ladder by which the deserving could climb to heaven. More and more the goddess specialised in her role of funerary deity until in the last epoch a dead person was no longer called 'an Osiris' but 'a Hathor'.

Her principal sanctuary was at Dendera where she was worshipped in company with her husband, Horus of Edfu, who here ceded first place to her, and with their son Ihi (Ahi), 'the Sistrum Player', who is represented as an infant jingling the sistrum at her side. Great festivals were celebrated in this temple, above all on New Year's Day, which was the anniversary of her birth. Before dawn the priestesses would bring Hathor's image out on to the terrace to expose it to the rays of the rising sun. The rejoicing which followed was a pretext for a veritable carnival, and the day ended in song and intoxication.

Hathor was also worshipped at Edfu with Horus, Lord of the temple, and their son Harsomtus, as well as at Ombos, where she took part in both trinities at the same time.

Even beyond Egypt, on the coast of Somaliland, she was called 'Mistress of the land of Punt', from which perhaps she had come in very ancient times. In the Sinai peninsula she was known as 'Mistress of the land of Mefket'; and in Phoenicia, where part of the Osirian legend had early taken root, as 'the Lady of Byblos'.

Anubis, the Greek rendering of Anpu, was identified with Hermes, Conductor of Souls. It was Anubis who opened for the dead the roads of the other world. He is represented as a black jackal with a bushy tail, or as a blackish-skinned man with the head of a jackal or the head of a dog, an animal sacred to Anubis. For this reason the Greeks called the chief city of his cult Cynopolis.

From the earliest dynasties Anubis presided over embalmments. Funeral prayers, in which he was always to occupy a preponderant position, were in those days almost exclusively addressed to him.

In the pyramid texts Anubis is the 'fourth son of Ra' and his daughter is Kebehut, the goddess of freshness. But later he was admitted into the family of Osiris and it was said that Nephthys, left childless by her husband Set, bore him adulterously to Osiris.

Abandoned by his mother at birth, he was, it is related, found by his aunt, Isis. Isis, feeling no rancour at the thoughtless infidelity of her husband, undertook to bring up the baby. When he had grown to man's estate Anubis accompanied Osiris on his conquest of the world, and when 'the Good One' was murdered he helped Isis and Nephthys to bury him.

It was on this occasion that Anubis invented funeral rites and bound up the mummy of Osiris to preserve him from contact with the air and subsequent corruption. He was known, therefore, as 'Lord of the Mummy Wrappings'. From then on he presided over funerals and it is in this role that we often see him, first proceeding with the mummy's embalming and later receiving it at the door of the tomb. Anubis also makes sure that offerings brought by the deceased's heirs actually reach him.

Afterwards we see Anubis take the dead by the hand and, in his capacity of Osiris' usher, introduce him into the presence of the sovereign judges before whom he then weighs the soul of the dead.

This role of god of the dead won Anubis a universal cult and his admission into the circle of Osiris kept his worship alive until the latest epoch when, because of his identification with Hermes, Conductor of Souls, he was given the name Hermanubis. In the great procession in honour of Isis which Apuleius describes, it is the dog-headed god, bearing in his hands the caduceus and the palms, who marches at the head of the divine images.

Upuaut (or **Ophois Wepwawet**) is a wolf-headed or jackal-headed god who should not be confused with Anubis. Upuaut signifies 'he who opens the way'. In prehistoric representations we see the wolf-god, borne high upon his standard, guiding the warriors of his tribe into enemy territory. Similarly, during his principal

Anubis preparing a mummy. The
god bends forward to adjust the
mask of the bandaged mummy
which lies on a lion-headed couch.
Anubis was believed to have
invented funeral rites and the
art of embalming when he
bound up the body of Osiris to
preserve it from corruption.
Painting from the first tomb of
Sennedjem at Deir el Medinah in
the necropolis of Thebes.
Twentieth dynasty, 1202
to 1102 B.C.

Head of Thoth. Represented generally as an ibis or an ibis-headed man, Thoth was worshipped at Hermopolis as the divine ibis who created the world. The god of learning, the inventor of hieroglyphs and the scribe of the gods, he was also portrayed as a dog-headed baboon, probably as the result of a fusion in early times with another deity. Bronze.

Thoth as a baboon. The god is seated and wears a crescent moon upon his head. Worshipped as a lunar deity throughout Egypt, he was believed to take the place of Ra in the sky while the latter made his journey through the Underworld during the hours of night, and was responsible for regulating the months and seasons.

procession, Upuaut, carried on his shield, leads the cortège at the festivals of Osiris. Sometimes he is also shown piloting the sun's boat during its nocturnal voyage and, if necessary, towing it along the edge of the southern and northern sky.

A former warrior-god, he was also worshipped as god of the dead; and notably at Abydos, before Osiris deposed him, he was worshipped as Lord of the Necropolis under the name Khenti Amenti 'he who rules the West'.

Upuaut was feudal god of Siut, the Greek Lycopolis, and a later addition to the Osirian legend. He was an ally of Osiris and, with Anubis, one of his chief officers during the conquest of the world. As such, they both sometimes appear in later times dressed as soldiers.

Thoth is the form which the name Djehuti or Zehuti had taken in Graeco-Roman times. He was identified by the Greeks with Hermes, Messenger of the Gods, and was worshipped throughout Egypt as a moon-god, patron of science and literature, wisdom and inventions, the spokesman of the gods and their keeper of the records.

Djehuti seems merely to mean 'he of Djehut', the name of the old province in Lower Egypt whose capital, Hermopolis Parva, must have been the cradle of Thoth's cult before he had established his principal sanctuary at Hermopolis Magna in Upper Egypt.

Thoth is ordinarily represented with the head of an ibis, often surmounted by a crescent moon, or simply as an ibis. He liked to appear as a bird of this sort, but also at times as a dog-headed ape, which makes us suspect that the god of historical ages may have been derived from a fusion, in very remote times, of two lunar divinities, one figured as a bird, the other as an ape.

According to the theologians of Hermopolis, Thoth was the true universal Demiurge, the divine ibis who had hatched the world-egg at Hermopolis Magna. They taught that he had accomplished the work of creation by the sound of his voice alone. When he first awoke in the primordial 'Nun' he opened his lips, and from the sound that issued forth four gods materialised and then four goddesses. For this reason the future Hermopolis was called Khnum, 'City of the Eight'. Without real personality these eight gods perpetuated the creation of the world by the word; and the texts tell us that they sang hymns morning and evening to assure the continuity of the sun's course.

In the Books of the Pyramids, Thoth is sometimes the oldest son of Ra, sometimes the child of Geb and Nut, the brother of Isis, Set and Nephthys. Normally, however, he does not belong to the Osirian family and is only the vizier of Osiris and his kingdom's sacred scribe.

He remained faithful to his murdered master and contributed powerfully to his resurrection, thanks to the trueness of his voice which increased the force of his magic incantations, and to the thoroughness of the way in which he purified the dismembered body of Osiris. Afterwards he helped Isis to defend the child Horus against the perils which beset him. We are told how on the orders of the gods he drove out the poison from the child's body when he had been stung by a scorpion. Later we see him intervene in the merciless struggle between Horus and Set, curing the former's tumour and the latter's emasculation by spitting on their wounds. Finally, when the two irreconcilable enemies were summoned to appear before the tribunal of the gods sitting in Hermopolis, Thoth earned the title 'He who judges the two companions'. He decided between the two adversaries and condemned Set to return his nephew's heritage.

As he had been the vizier of Osiris, so afterwards was he that of Horus. When Horus resigned earthly power Thoth succeeded him to the throne. During three thousand two hundred and twenty-six years Thoth remained the very model of a peaceful ruler.

Endowed with complete knowledge and wisdom, it was Thoth who invented all the arts and sciences: arithmetic, surveying, geometry, astronomy, soothsaying, magic, medicine, surgery, music with wind instruments and strings, drawing and, above all, writing, without which humanity would have run the risk of forgetting his doctrines and of losing the benefit of his discoveries.

As inventor of hieroglyphs, he was named 'Lord of Holy Words'. As first of the magicians he was often called 'The Elder'. His disciples boasted that they had access to the crypt where he had locked up his books of magic, and they undertook to decipher and learn 'these formulas which commanded all the forces of nature and subdued the very gods themselves'. It is to this infinite power which his followers attributed to him that he owes the name Thoth – three times very, very great – which the Greeks translated as Hermes Trismegistus.

After his long reign on earth Thoth ascended to the skies where he undertook various employments.

First of all he was the moon-god, or at least the god in charge of guarding the moon; for this astral body had its own individuality and name: Aah-te-Huti. We have already recounted the legend (see *Nut*) which tells how Thoth played draughts with the moon and won a seventy-second part of its light from which he created the five intercalary days. Elsewhere we are told that the moon is the left eye of Horus, watched over by either an ibis or a dog-headed ape. On the other hand a passage in the Book of the Dead tells us that Ra ordered Thoth to take his own place in the sky whilst he himself 'lighted the blessed in the underworld'. The moon then appeared and in its boat began its nocturnal voyages, each month exposed to the attack of monsters who slowly devoured it but who, happily, were constrained by the moon's faithful champions to disgorge it.

In his quality of lunar divinity Thoth measured the time, which he divided into months (to the first of which he gave his own name) and into years, which in turn were divided into three seasons.

He was the divine regulative force and charged with all calculations and annotations. At Edfu we see him before the temple trinity presenting the register in which is recorded all that concerns the geographical division of the country, its dimensions and resources. At Deir el Bahri we see him proceeding scrupulously with an inventory of treasures brought to the gods of Egypt by a naval expedition on its return from the land of Punt.

Nekhebet, the goddess, in the form of a vulture with outstretched wings, hovers protectively over the Pharaoh Mem-kau-Heru, of the Fifth Dynasty. Louvre.

Thoth was the keeper of the divine archives and at the same time the patron of history. He carefully noted the succession of the sovereigns and, on the leaves of the sacred tree at Heliopolis, wrote the name of the future Pharaoh whom the queen had just conceived after union with the Lord of the Heavens. On a long palm shoot he also inscribed the happy years of reign which Ra had accorded to the king.

He was the herald of the gods and also often served as their clerk and scribe. 'Ra has spoken, Thoth has written', we read. And during the awful judgment of the dead before Osiris we see Thoth, who has weighed the heart and found it not wanting, proclaim in a loud voice the verdict 'not guilty' which he has just registered on his tablets.

He was invested with the confidence of the gods and chosen by them as arbiter. We have already seen him awarding judgment to Horus and condemning Set. Also, at least from the time of the New Empire, he everywhere replaces Set in coronation scenes, in scenes in which libations are offered to the king, and in the symbolic ceremony of 'sam-taui'.

The texts often couple him with Maat, the goddess of Truth and Justice; but in no temple do we find them together. On the other hand two spouses of his were known, Seshat and Nehmauit, 'she who uproots evil'. In Heliopolis they form with him two triads with, in the first instance, Hornub as divine son, and in the second Nefer Hor.

Plutarch tells us that the chief festival of the ibis-headed god was celebrated on the nineteenth of the month of Thoth, a few days after the full moon at the beginning of the year. His friends were then approached with the words, 'Sweet is the Truth', and they were presented with many gifts of sweetmeats, honey, figs and other dainties.

Seshat (or **Sesheta**) was Thoth's principal spouse. In reality she is, in her quality of goddess of writing and history, merely his double. At first she was portrayed with the features of a woman wearing on her head a star inscribed in a reversed crescent, surmounted by two long straight plumes, an ideogram of her name which signifies 'the secretary'. Later, due probably to a misunderstanding on the part of sculptors, the crescent was replaced by two long, turned-down horns, from which the goddess derived the title Safekh-Aubi, i.e. 'she who wears (or, perhaps, raises) the two horns'.

She was a stellar divinity who served to measure time; to her – as to Thoth – was ascribed the invention of letters. She was called 'mistress of the house of books'.

She was also called 'mistress of the house of architects' and was represented as the foundress of temples, helping the king to determine the axis of a new sanctuary by the aid of the stars, and marking out the four angles of the edifice with stakes.

As goddess of history and record-keeper for the gods, we see her, alone or in the company of her husband, writing the names of the sovereigns on the leaves of the sacred tree at Heliopolis, or registering on a long palm-leaf the years of reign accorded to the Pharaoh and, on this occasion, drafting the minutes of jubilee celebrations.

As mistress of the scribes she writes on a tablet the balance due to the king from captured enemy booty. When the great sovereign of the eighteenth dynasty, Queen Hatshepsut, sends an expedition to the land of Punt it is Seshat who, on the expedition's return to Thebes, makes the inventory of the treasures brought back. 'Thoth made a note of the quantity', we are told, 'and Seshat verified the figures.'

PROTECTIVE DIVINITIES OF THE PHARAOHS AND THE KINGDOM

In the course of this study we have already met several gods who enjoyed the especial favour of the kings who considered them to be their divine ancestors. Such were Set, formerly Lord of Upper Egypt, but later expelled from the Egyptian pantheon; Horus, of whom every Pharaoh boasted that he was the living incarnation; and Ra, whose son each Pharaoh from the fifth dynasty onwards, proclaimed himself to be. We shall now review, in the chronological order in which their dynastic importance appears most marked, certain other divinities.

Nekhebet, who was identified by the Greeks as Eileithyia, protectress of childbirth, was from the earliest times the protective goddess of Upper Egypt. The centre of her cult was at El Kab, the former Nekheb, which the Greeks called Eileithyiaspolis, capital of the oldest kingdom in the South.

In war and offertory scenes she often appears hovering over the Pharaoh's head in the form of a vulture, holding in her claws the fly-whisk and the seal.

She is also sometimes portrayed as a divinity with the bald head of a vulture, or as a woman wearing the white crown of Upper Egypt either on her head or on a headdress shaped like a vulture.

As a mother goddess Nekhebet suckled the royal children; often we see her suckling the Pharaoh himself.

Buto, a transcription of Per Uadjit, 'the dwelling of Uadjit', was the name which the Greeks gave to the Delta town and also to the goddess who was worshipped there. She was the ancient protectress of Lower Egypt.

The Osirian legend recounts that Buto, sovereign of the Delta, allied herself with Isis and helped protect her infant child. She gathered up the baby Horus from the floating island of Chemmis, for which reason she was afterwards identified with Latona, the mother of Apollo.

Buto was a snake-goddess, frequently represented in the form of a cobra, sometimes winged and sometimes crowned. She also often has the features of a woman wearing, either directly on her head or on a head-dress in the form of a vulture, the red crown of the North, of which she was the official protectress as Nekhebet was of the white crown of the South.

The vulture-goddess and the cobra-goddess, known conjointly as Nebti – 'the two mistresses' – appear side by side on royal documents. Sometimes they embellish the Pharaoh's forehead in order to protect him against his enemies, though normally only the Uraeus appears.

Mont (Menthu) was the Theban god of war whom the Greeks, because of his solar character, identified with Apollo. He appears at the beginning of the Middle Kingdom when he was particularly venerated by the kings of the eleventh dynasty, many of whom took the name Menthu-hetep, 'Mont is satisfied'.

He is usually represented as a personage whose falcon head is surmounted by the solar disk and two tall straight plumes. At a later period he also appears as a man with a bull's head embellished with the same attributes. The bull was actually the animal sacred to him. The bull in which he preferred to become incarnate was the celebrated Buchis which was piously tended at Hermonthis, the sun's residence in Upper Egypt. Hermonthis was the former capital of this region and Mont, the sun-god, was for many long centuries its lord and master before he was demoted to second rank by his former vassal, Amon of Thebes, who became king of the gods.

Having ousted Mont, Amon, whose wife was barren, wished to adopt him as divine son in the Theban Triad; but the former sovereign of the entire region could not long be happy in such a subordinate position. Mont therefore chose to dwell apart at Hermonthis, of which he remained the uncontested master, and at Medamud, in the suburbs of Thebes, where numerous votaries came to worship him in company with his wife Rat-taui.

A solar god of warlike character, Mont was represented as the god of war under the New Kingdom. He brandished the *khepesh,* which was a kind of very curved scimitar, and cut off the heads of the Pharaoh's enemies. We see him offering the Pharaoh his invincible weapon and leading his vanquished enemies in chains. Temple bas-reliefs also often show Mont, as sun-god of the South, with Atum, sun-god of the North, escorting the king into the sanctuary.

Amon (Amun, Ammon) is the name of the great Egyptian deity who was often given the title 'king of the gods'. For this reason the Greeks identified him with Zeus. He was almost unknown in the time of the Old Kingdom. His name – which seems to be derived from a root meaning 'hidden' – only appears four times in the Heliopolitan texts of the pyramids. Perhaps he originally belonged to the cosmological system of Hermopolis which we have already discussed, and was one of those 'eight gods' who emerged from the mouth of Thoth. Thebes, which afterwards was to erect such gigantic temples in his honour, was at that time only a village in the fourth nome (or province) of Upper Egypt, the capital of which was Hermonthis, city of Mont, who was then Lord of all that region.

It was with the first king of the twelfth dynasty, whose name, Amenemhat, signifies 'Amon leads', that Thebes and its god began to take on an importance which was to become considerable under the great conquerors of the eighteenth dynasty – called Thuthmosis and Amenhotep and proudly proclaiming themselves to be 'sons of Amon'.

Amon by this time had dispossessed Mont and become the great divinity of the whole country of which Thebes – which was called Nut Amon, the 'city of Amon', or simply Nut, 'the city' – was henceforth the capital.

Amon normally appears with bronzed human features wearing as a head-dress a kind of crown which supports two straight tall parallel plumes. Sometimes he is seated majestically on a throne. Sometimes he stands with a whip raised above his head, in the ithyphallic pose of the god Min.

He is also at times represented with the head of a ram with curled horns, and at Karnak an animal of this sort was religiously tended, a living incarnation of the god. They also kept a goose which was Amon's other sacred animal.

The phallic Amon represented the forces of generation and reproduction. He was often called 'his mother's husband' and was supposed to initiate and then maintain the continuity of creative life. He was the god of fertility, and we see the king, in his presence, sowing grain and cutting the first sheaf.

He was the patron of the most powerful Pharaohs; he acknowledged them as his sons and gave them victory over their enemies. It was, then, quite natural that the god of Thebes should become pre-eminently the national god. The faithful proclaimed him 'king of the gods' under the name Amon-Ra; for when the theologians had obligingly identified him with Ra, the old sun-god, Amon assumed Ra's position as universal Demiurge and chief of the great Ennead. Pictured in the royal tombs we see Amon-Ra enthroned in the sun's boat and, during the twelve hours of night, illuminating the underworld.

Ra, however, had never abdicated his ancient authority, and under the name of Ra-Harakhte he always enjoyed his own distinct cult. Indeed, under the reign of Amenhotep III, there was a reaction in Ra's favour, no doubt encouraged by the priests of Heliopolis who were jealous of Amon's immense fortune and the omnipotence which this parvenu among the gods claimed. The texts and bas-reliefs on the walls of the temple of Luxor glorify the divine birth of Amenhotep as a result of Amon's love for the queen-mother, wife of Thuthmosis IV. But on the death of Amenhotep the cult of Ra-Harakhte gained new importance. Under the already venerable name 'Aten of the Day' – i.e. 'The solar disk whence issues the light of day', his visible form and true name – Ra-Harakhte, it would seem, engaged in a struggle against his rival Amon which was so successful that Amon was momentarily humbled. In the fourth year of his reign Amenhotep's son and successor proclaimed a great religious reform and decreed that only the religion of Aten was official.

Full of zeal for his new god, the reforming Pharaoh began by changing his name Amenhotep ('Amon is satisfied') to Akhenaton ('The glory of Aten'). He hastened to abandon Thebes for a new capital city, Akhetaten – the present-day Tell-el-Amarna – which he had built in Middle Egypt to the glory of the solar disk.

There were no statues of Aten. Bas-reliefs and paintings always represent him in the form of a great red disk from which fan out long rays tipped with hands which have seized offerings laid on altars, or which present to the king, the queen and their daughters the hieroglyphs of life and strength. The Pharaoh was his only priest, and his cult was celebrated in a temple resembling the ancient solar temples of the Old Kingdom and called, like the celebrated sanctuary of Ra at Heliopolis, Het Benben, 'the Palace of the Obelisk'. There, at the extremity of a vast courtyard, rose the obelisk of the sun. The ceremony consisted of an oblation of fruits and cakes and the recitation of hymns of great beauty, which were composed by the king himself, in honour of his god. In them the sun was glorified, as in olden days, as creator of mankind and benefactor of the world, but without those allusions to early mythological legends of which the ancient hymns to Ra had been full. The hymns could thus be sung and understood not only by the inhabitants of the Nile

Pillars decorated with stylised lotus and papyrus plants in the temple of Amon at Karnak, one of two great sanctuaries dedicated to the sovereign god of Thebes. Amon was worshipped here in company with Mut, his wife, and their son Khons.

Amon. The god is portrayed in human form wearing his characteristic plumed head-dress and seated on a throne. Between his knees he holds a headless figure of Tut-ankh-Amon whom he places under his protection. Having suffered a temporary eclipse under Akhenaton, the god had been restored to his position of supremacy by the young Pharaoh, probably under pressure from the priests. Statue from Thebes. Eighteenth dynasty, 1587 to 1375 B.C.

Amon. The king of the gods is represented seated on his throne and with the head of a ram. Originally represented as a goose or a ram when still a local deity of Thebes, he retains here, in addition to the ram's head, two goose feathers which he wears upon his head. His curved horns were adopted by Alexander the Great after he was recognized as the Son of Amon in 332 B.C. Statuette of the twenty-sixth dynasty, 672 to 525 B.C.

Akhenaton and Nefertiti, followed by one of their daughters, present offerings to their god Aten, who is represented by a solar disk the rays of which terminate in hands. Stela of the Eighteenth Dynasty, 1580 to 1350. Cairo.

Gods of the Underworld. Two zoomorphic gods, one bullheaded, the other ram-headed, holding knives and a bough, stand guard over the third gate of the Underworld. Detail from the second shrine of Tut-ankh-Amon. Relief incised into gold foil on a thin layer of gesso. Eighteenth dynasty, 1587 to 1375 B.C.

Valley but also by foreigners. All men, they proclaimed, were equally the children of Aten. In this modified attempt at monotheism we may suspect plans for an Empire-wide religion, especially if it is remembered that at this time Egyptian domination extended as far as Asia, where the Syrians worshipped Adonis and the Jews worshipped Adonai.

As long as the king lived there was no official god in Egypt but Aten. The other gods were proscribed and bitter war declared against them, especially against Amon and his trinity. Their temples were despoiled and their riches given to the solar disk. Their statues were broken and the bas-reliefs on which they appeared were mutilated, while Amon's name was harried from the most inaccessible places. It was chiselled off and removed from all the royal tablets, even from those of Amenhotep III, the Pharaoh's own father.

The new religion, it is true, was ephemeral, and on the death of the reformer, or very shortly afterwards, his own son denied his father's name and restored the cult of Amon. He changed his heretical name Tut-ankh-Aten ('Living image of Aten') into the orthodox Tut-ankh-Amon ('Living image of Amon'). Wherever it was found, the old name was replaced by the new. But there were oversights, and on the magnificent throne of the young Pharaoh, recently removed from his celebrated tomb, we can still read the two names almost side by side – a silent witness to the prince's heresy and to its abjuration.

Restored to all his former splendour by Horemheb and the kings of the nineteenth dynasty who heaped his temples with gifts, Amon, from thenceforth definitely incorporated with Ra, saw his fortune grow to such a point that it reached three-quarters of that of all the other gods combined. An inventory of his wealth made under Rameses III tells us that he possessed, among other riches, 81,322 slaves and 421,362 head of cattle. His high priests, the first prophets of Amon, were chosen from among the most powerful lords. They soon became hereditary and, after playing the role of royal comptrollers to the weak sovereigns of the twentieth dynasty, finally seized the crown itself. Herihor, the priest, succeeded the last of the Rameses to the throne. During the troubles that ensued Thebes ceased to be the royal seat and political capital of Egypt. It remained from then on the exclusive property of Amon and became a kind of theocratic state where the god wielded power, either directly through his oracles or by the mediation, no longer as in the past of his chief prophet, but of his earthly spouse. This was normally the king's daughter, 'the god's wife', 'the god's adorer'. She was paid the highest honour, ruled the town and administered the immense domains of the god, her husband.

Sovereign of Thebes, Amon extended his power beyond the frontiers of Egypt into Ethiopia where, through his oracles at Napata and Meroe, he himself chose the kings. He deposed them and ordered their death, thus exercising a tyrannical domination which only ended in the third century B.C. when Ergamenes threw off the priests' yoke and had them put to death.

Amon's power over the desert tribes of Libya was equally great and until the latest epoch pilgrims crowded in great numbers to that venerable oasis-temple of Amon – or of Jupiter Ammon – where the celebrated oracle had, in 332 B.C., saluted Alexander the Great and called him 'Son of Amon'.

Amon's most magnificent sanctuaries were, however, at Thebes on the right bank of the Nile, at Luxor and at Karnak, whose ruins to-day still fill us with admiration, and where he was worshipped in company with Mut, his wife, and their son Khons. On the bas-reliefs which cover the walls and columns we see the king of the gods on his throne, where he receives the perpetual adoration of the Pharaoh, whom at times he embraces and whom he infuses with the magic fluid 'sa'. Elsewhere he gives the breath of life to him and grants him long years of reign. He hands him the *khepesh* of battle and, trampling the vanquished underfoot, delivers over enemy towns. Finally Amon is shown holding on his knees the queen with whom he will unite in order to produce the next Pharaoh, his son.

Mut, being Amon-Ra's wife, was identified by the Greeks with Hera. She is a vague and ill-defined deity whose name signified 'Mother'. She is represented as a woman wearing a head-dress in the form of a vulture, an ideogram of her name. Again she wears a heavy wig surmounted by the *pschent* – the double crown to which, as wife of the king of the gods, she had a right.

She grew in stature along with her spouse and when he, under the name Amon-Ra, had become the great god of the heavens she also became a solar deity. She was sometimes identified with Bast, whose cat-form she assumed; and with Sekhmet, from whom she borrowed the head of a lioness.

A text tells us that as a sky-goddess she remained – in the form of a cow – behind Amon when he emerged from the waves and broke from the egg at Hermopolis. 'He mounted on her back, seized her horns, and dismounted where it pleased him so to do.'

When she had long been childless Mut first adopted Mont, then Khons. It is with Khons as child that she entered the celebrated Theban triad of which Amon was the chief.

Khons (Khensu), whose name means 'the Navigator' or 'He who crosses the sky in a boat', seems originally to have been a moon-god, little known beyond the region of Thebes. It is a puzzle why the Greeks sometimes identified him with Hercules.

Khons is ordinarily represented in the form of a personage swathed like Ptah, whose composite sceptre he holds before him. His head is completely shaven except for one temple which is adorned by the heavy tress of a royal child. He wears a skullcap surmounted by a disk in a crescent moon. At first rather obscure, Khons rose to the ranks of the great gods when he was adopted by Amon and Mut and replaced Mont as their son in the Theban triad. It is only under the New Kingdom, however, that he seems to have begun to enjoy great popularity as an exorcist and healer. The possessed and the sick from all over Egypt and even from abroad had recourse to him. In the case of those from abroad Khons delegated his powers to a statue in which he incarnated a double of himself, commanding it to go forth and cure his suppliants. Thus we see the great Khons Neferhotep of Karnak, whose aid the Syrian prince of Bakhtan had implored on behalf of his daughter, delegate a second Khons in Syria who was named 'He who executes the designs and who expels the rebels'. Space is lacking to recount in detail how the divine substitute accomplished his mission and drove from the princess's body the demon which had tormented her; how at the end of three years and nine months he appeared in a dream to her father in the form of a golden falcon who flew swiftly towards Egypt; and how the grateful prince then hastened to take back the divine statue with the greatest ceremony together with costly gifts which were deposited in the temple of Karnak at the feet of the great Khons Neferhotep.

Khons was much venerated at Thebes and also worshipped at Ombos where he formed the third person in the triad of Sebek under the name Khons Hor, who was represented as a man with a falcon's head surmounted with a disk in a crescent moon.

In conclusion it may be remarked that one of the months of the year was named Pakhons, which means 'the month of Khons'.

Sebek (in Greek, Suchos) is the name of a crocodile divinity who figured among the patrons of the kings of the thirteenth dynasty, many of whom were called Sebekhotep, 'Sebek is satisfied'.

The god was represented either as a man with the head of a crocodile or simply as a crocodile. In a lake attached to his chief sanctuary an actual crocodile was kept. It was called Petesuchos, 'He who belongs to Suchos' (or to Sebek), and it was said that the god was incarnate therein.

We know little of the origins of Sebek. A pyramid text calls him the son of Neith. But, as Maspero has pointed out, it is easy to conceive that the presence nearby of a swamp or a rock-encumbered rapid could have suggested to the inhabitants of the Fayyum of Ombos that the crocodile was the supreme god who must be appeased by sacrifice and prayers. To his worshippers no doubt Sebek was none other than the Demiurge who, on the day of creation, issued from the dark waters where until then he had reposed, in order to arrange the world – as the crocodile emerges from the river to deposit her eggs on the bank. Possibly because the name Sebek sounds in Egyptian a little like Geb he was sometimes given Geb's titles.

Sebek was especially venerated in the Fayyum. The whole province was under his protection and his principal sanctuary was in the former Shedet, the Crocodilopolis of the Greeks. We shall have occasion to speak further of this when we study the animals sacred to the Egyptians.

Sebek was the object of a cult in Upper Egypt also. One can still see to-day at Kom Ombo – the former Ombos – ruins of the temple where Sebek's triad was worshipped, as was a second triad of which Horus was the chief. Perhaps here Sebek really replaced the former Lord, Set the Ombite, whom the pious worshippers of Horus would not tolerate. What is certain is that Sebek often shared Set's evil reputation. He was reproached with having aided the murderer of Osiris when Set, to escape punishment for his crime, took refuge in the body of a crocodile. That was why these animals, worshipped in certain provinces, were hunted down and destroyed in others.

Khons. A later addition to the Theban triad in which he replaced Mont as the son of Amon and Mut, Khons, a local moon god, wears the crescent moon upon his head and is represented as a youthful mummy wearing the tress of the royal children on his right temple and carrying the crook and flail and a sceptre. Bronze statuette of the twenty-sixth dynasty, 672 to 525 B.C.

A vulture, the sacred animal of Mut, the wife of Amon in the Theban triad and the adoptive mother first of Mont and later of Khons. The goddess was often represented wearing a head-dress in the form of a vulture which was an ideogram of her name. One of many animals held to be sacred by the Egyptians.

Ptah of Memphis, in his aspect of protector of artisans and artists, was identified by the Greeks with Hephaestus. He is normally represented as a mummified figure, often raised on a pedestal inside the *naos* of a temple, his skull enclosed in a tight head-band and his body swathed in mummy-wrappings. Only his hands are free and hold a composite sceptre uniting the emblems of life, of stability and of omnipotence.

He was worshipped from the earliest times at Memphis where, south of the ancient 'White Wall' of Menes, he possessed the celebrated temple of Ptah-Beyond-the-Walls. Ptah must always have been of first importance as sovereign god of the old capital of the North, the city where the Pharaohs were crowned. But little is known of his role before the advent of the nineteenth dynasty, whose great kings, Seti I and Rameses II, held him in particular devotion, while one sovereign of the same dynasty even bore the name Siptah, which signified 'Son of Ptah'.

It was, however, after the extinction of the last of the Rameses, when the political role of the Delta had become predominant,

that the god of Memphis attained his full glory. Of all the gods of Egypt he was then third in importance and wealth, yielding only to Amon and Ra; and not even to them in the estimation of his own priest, who proudly proclaimed him to be the Universal Demiurge who had with his own hands fashioned the world.

Ptah was the patron of artisans and artists and the inventor of the arts. He was at the same time designer, smelter of metal and builder. His high priest at Memphis bore a title analogous to the 'Master Builder' of our medieval cathedrals. It was he who during the construction of a temple directed architects and masons.

To-day there remain only shapeless ruins of the celebrated temple of Memphis where priests showed Herodotus the ex-votos commemorating the great miracles performed by Ptah. Among others was the occasion on which he had saved Pelusium from Sennacherib's attacking Assyrians by raising an army of rats, who forced the assailants to retreat by gnawing their bowstrings, quivers, and the leather thongs of their shields.

In this temple Ptah was worshipped in company with his consort

Ptah. The sovereign god of Memphis, the old capital of the north, Ptah was proclaimed the creator of the world by his priests and was the object of the particular devotion of a number of the Pharaohs. He was normally represented as a mummified figure holding a composite sceptre uniting the emblems of life, stability and omnipotence. Bronze statue.

Sekhmet. 'The Beloved of Ptah' is represented as a woman with the head of a lioness seated on a throne. Originally a divinity of Latopolis to the north of Memphis, she joined the Memphis triad as the wife of Ptah to whom she bore a son, Nefertum, later replaced by the deified human, Imhotep. Black granite statue of the eighteenth dynasty from Karnak c. 1500 B.C.

Sekhmet and their son Nefertum, who was later succeeded by Imhotep, a human hero deified. Near the sanctuary was piously tended the celebrated bull Apis, a living incarnation of the god. We shall speak of Apis in the final section of this study.

Although Ptah was apt to be called 'fair of face' he is sometimes depicted as a deformed dwarf with twisted legs, hands on hips and a huge head, shaved except for the childish lock. Thus represented, Ptah plays the role of protector against noxious animals and against all kinds of evils. He was early identified with the very ancient and obscure earth-god Tenen and also with Seker, of whom we shall write briefly below. He was frequently invoked under the names Ptah Tenen, Ptah Seker and even Ptah Seker Osiris.

Seker (the Greek rendering is Sucharis) was doubtless a vegetation god before he became the god of the dead in the Memphis necropolis. There, in the form of a greenish hawk-headed mummy, he was worshipped in a sanctuary called Ro Stau ('the doors of the corridors') which communicated directly with the underworld. He was early identified with Osiris and brought to Osiris all his own local worshippers. It was under the name Seker Osiris that the god of the dead was usually worshipped in Memphis. In the end the great funerary divinity became Ptah Seker Osiris.

Sekhmet (rendered in Greek as Sakhmis) is the name of the terrible goddess of war and battle who is usually represented as a lioness or a woman with the head of a lioness.

Her name, which means 'the Powerful', is simply a title of Hathor which was given to Hathor on the occasion when in the form of a lioness she hurled herself on the men who had rebelled against Ra. As we have already seen she attacked them with such fury that the sun-god, fearing the extermination of the human race, begged her to arrest the carnage. 'By thy life', she answered him, 'when I slay men my heart rejoices', and she refused to spare her victims. For this reason she was later given the name Sekhmet and represented in the form of a savage lioness. In order to save what remained of the human race Ra had recourse to a stratagem. He spread across the bloody battlefield seven thousand jugs containing a magic potion composed of beer and pomegranate juice. Sekhmet, who was thirsty, mistook this red liquid for human blood and drank it so avidly that she became too drunk to continue the slaughter. The human race was saved; but to appease the goddess, Ra decreed that 'on that day there should be brewed in her honour as many jugs of the philtre as there were priestesses of the sun'. This was henceforth done annually on the feast day of Hathor. The great massacre had taken place on the twelfth day of the first month of winter; thus the calendar of lucky and unlucky days carefully notes: 'Hostile, hostile, hostile is the 12th Tybi. Avoid seeing a mouse on this day; for it is the day when Ra gave the order to Sekhmet.'

The goddess was called 'the beloved of Ptah'; for, though originally a divinity of Latopolis, she joined the Memphis Triad as Ptah's wife, bearing him a son, Nefertum.

Attached to her cult were bone-setters who, with her intercession, cured fractures.

Nefertum, which the Greeks rendered as Iphtimis, is the name of the original divine son of the Memphis Triad. The Greeks identified him with Prometheus, perhaps because his father was said to be Ptah Hephaestus, the discoverer of fire.

He is habitually represented as a man armed with the curved sabre called the *khepesh*. His head is surmounted by an open lotus flower from which springs a horned stalk, and he often appears standing on a crouched lion. Sometimes he has the head of this lion, which he doubtless owes to his mother, the lion-goddess Sekhmet.

His name, which signifies 'Atum the Younger', clearly indicates that he was at first an incarnation of Atum of Heliopolis, a rejuvenated Atum who at dawn sprang from the divine lotus, asylum of the sun during the night. A native of Lower Egypt, he was considered as the son of Ptah, and his mother became that god's spouse. He therefore occupied – before Imhotep – the third place in the oldest Memphis Triad.

Bast (Bastet) was identified by the Greeks with Artemis, probably by confusion with the lioness-headed goddess Tefnut. She was local goddess of Bubastis, capital of the eighteenth nome or pro-

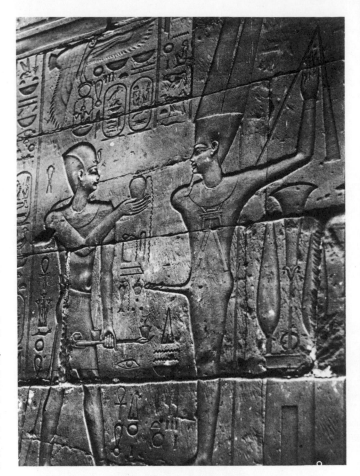

Min receiving a libation. The ithyphallic fertility god stands with his flail raised behind his head and wearing a plumed head-dress which was probably borrowed from Amon.
The Pharaoh pours him a libation with his right hand and holds burning incense in his left. The local god of Coptos, Min was chiefly worshipped in the classical period as the protector of travellers. Bas-relief, Luxor.

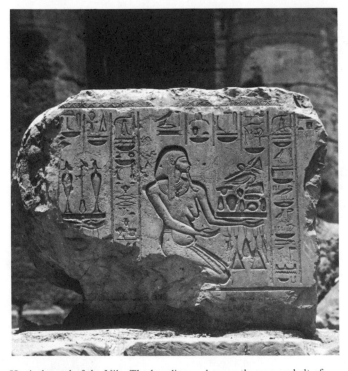

Hapi, the god of the Nile. The kneeling god wears the narrow belt of the Nile fishermen and boatmen and holds in his hands the riches provided by the fertilising waters. Invoked to procure the flooding of the river, Hapi was not connected with any theological system.
Bas-relief in the temple of Medinet Habu.
Twentieth dynasty, 1202 to 1102 B.C.

vince of Lower Egypt. Bubastis is a transcription of Per Bast, i.e. 'The House of Bast'. She became the great national divinity when, about 950 B.C., with Sheshonk and the Libyan Pharaohs of the twenty-second dynasty, Bubastis became the capital of the kingdom.

Though in origin a lioness-goddess, personifying the fertilising warmth of the sun, her sacred animal later became the cat, and she is represented as a cat-headed woman holding in her right hand either a sistrum or an aegis, composed of a semi-circular breastplate surmounted with the head of a lioness. In her left hand she carries a basket.

She was related to the sun-god whom some called her father and others her brother-spouse; and she became – like Sekhmet, with whom she is frequently confused in spite of their very dissimilar characters – the wife of Ptah of Memphis and with him formed a a triad in which Nefertum was the third person.

Although, as patron of the kings of Bubastis, Bast had already become one of the great divinities of Egypt, it was in the fourth century B.C. that she achieved her greatest popularity. She existed also in secondary forms as Pekhet, the cat or lion-headed goddess of Speos Artemidos, to the east of Beni Hasan.

Like Hathor she was a goddess of pleasure and loved music and the dance. She would beat time with the sistrum, often decorated with the figure of a cat, which she grasped in her hand. In her benevolence she also protected men against contagious disease and evil spirits.

Great and joyful festivals were periodically celebrated in her temple at Bubastis. Herodotus tells us that it was one of the most elegant in Egypt and recounts how the devout came in hundreds of thousands from all over the country for the huge annual fair. The journey took place by barges to the sound of flutes and castanets. Buffoonery and jokes were bandied between the pilgrims and the women on the banks of the river who watched the barges as they passed, and everything was a pretext for pleasantry and masquerade. On the appointed day a splendid procession wound through the town and festivities followed during which, it seems, more wine was drunk than during all the rest of the year.

To please the cat-goddess her devotees consecrated statues of this animal in great numbers, and in the shadow of her sanctuaries it was a pious custom to bury the carefully mummified bodies of cats who during their lifetime had been venerated as animals sacred to Bast. (See *Sacred Animals*.)

Neith (Neit), whom the Greeks identified with their Pallas Athene, is the name of a Delta divinity. She was protectress of Sais, which became capital of Egypt towards the middle of the seventh century B.C. when Psammetichus I, founder of the twenty-sixth dynasty, mounted the throne, thus assuring the wealth and importance of his local goddess.

She was, in fact, an extremely ancient divinity; for her fetish – two crossed arrows on an animal skin – was carried on the standard of a prehistoric clan, and two queens of the first dynasty derived their names from hers.

Her epithet Tehenut, 'the Libyan', suggests that she probably originated in the west. She always remained important in Sais after having been, in very early times perhaps, considered to be the national divinity of Lower Egypt whose red crown she habitually wears. The crown was called 'Net', which sounds like her own name.

In the beginning she was worshipped in the form of a fetish composed of two crossed arrows on a shield or the mottled skin of an animal. Later she was represented with the features of a woman wearing the crown of the North and holding in her hand a bow and arrows. Still later her attribute became a weaver's shuttle, an ideogram of her name, which she sometimes wears on her head as a distinguishing emblem.

Neith, indeed, appears in a double role: as a warrior-goddess and as a woman skilled in the domestic arts. This is why she was identified with Athene, who also played this double role.

When, with the advent of the Sais dynasty, her preponderance was established, she played a part in many cosmogonic myths. She was made a sky-goddess like Nut and Hathor, and she was proclaimed to be mother of the gods in general and of Ra in particular 'whom she bore before childbirth existed'.

She was the great weaver who wove the world with her shuttle as a woman weaves cloth. Under the name Mehueret she was the Celestial Cow who gave birth to the sky when nothing existed.

She was introduced into the Osirian cult and confounded with Isis; she became protectress of the dead and we sometimes see her offering them the bread and water on their arrival in the other world.

Just as Isis and Nephthys are frequently found together in pictures and texts, so Neith often appears with Selket, either as guardian of the mummy and viscera of the dead, or as protectress of marriage.

To-day nothing remains of her celebrated temple at Sais where, Plutarch tells us, could be read the following inscription: 'I am all that has been, that is, and that will be. No mortal has yet been able to lift the veil which covers me.'

To this sanctuary was annexed a school of medicine, 'The House of Life', directed by the priests. Later, under the Persians, Darius' Egyptian doctor boasted that he had re-organised this medical school under royal protection.

DIVINITIES OF RIVER AND DESERT

Khnum (Khnemu), which was rendered in Greek as Khnoumis, was a god of the region of the Cataracts. He is portrayed as a ram-headed man with long wavy horns, unlike the curved horns of the ram-headed Amon.

He was a god of fecundity and creation and was originally worshipped under the form of a ram or a he-goat. Like all gods of this sort he doubtless, according to Maspero, symbolised the Nile which comes from the heavens to fertilise the earth and make it fruitful. His chief sanctuary was near the Cataracts, not far from the spot where the earliest Egyptians placed the source of their great river, on that Isle of Elephantine of which Khnum was proclaimed sovereign lord.

From his temple, where he received offerings in company with his two wives, Sati and Anukis – who were, as far as we know, childless – Khnum watched over the sources of the Nile.

Khnum means 'the Moulder' and it was taught that he had formerly fashioned the world-egg on his potter's wheel. At Philae, moreover, he was called 'the Potter who shaped men and modelled the gods'. We see him moulding the limbs of Osiris; for it was he, they said, who 'shaped all flesh – the procreator who engendered gods and men'.

In this quality he presided over the formation of children in their mothers' wombs. Temple bas-reliefs show him fashioning the body of the young Pharaoh on his sculptor's turntable. At Armant this young Pharaoh is none other than the son of Julius Caesar and Cleopatra, here identified with the divine child Harsomtos.

The celebrity of Khnum soon crossed the nearby frontier and penetrated Nubia, whose god Doudoun was also a ram, or a ram-headed god. This facilitated the identification of the two gods and attracted new and numerous worshippers to the Isle of Elephantine.

Harsaphes, the Greek rendering of Hershef ('He who is on his lake'), was the name of another ram-headed god identified by the Greeks with Hercules. His principal sanctuary was at Heracleopolis Magna in the Fayyum. Probably a Nile god, like all ram-headed gods according to Maspero, Harsaphes was from the earliest times the object of great veneration; for already under the first dynasty we see King Ousaphais consecrating a *naos* to him.

Sati (Satet) was one of Khnum's two wives and as such a guardian goddess of the Cataracts. According to Maspero her name signifies 'She who runs like an arrow'. She is the Archer who lets fly the river's current with the force and rapidity of an arrow. She is represented as a woman wearing the white crown of the South, flanked by two long horns. Like Neith she often holds arrows and a bow in her hands. She was worshipped in the extreme south of Egypt, where her favourite abode was on the island of Seheil. She gave her name to the first *nome* of Upper Egypt which was called Ta Setet, the 'Land of Sati'. Its capital was Abu, 'City of the Elephant', the Elephantine of the Greeks, where Sati took her place in the temple of Khnum in company with Anuket.

Anuket (Anquet), the Greek for which was Anukis, was Khnum's second wife. She is represented as a woman wearing a tall plumed crown. Her name seems to mean 'the Clasper' – she who clasps the river bank and presses the Nile between the rocks of Philae and Syene. She was worshipped at Elephantine with Khnum and Sati as a regional goddess of the Cataracts. She liked to reside on the island of Seheil, which was consecrated to her.

Min, whom the Greeks identified with Pan, was a very ancient god whose totem, a thunderbolt apparently, appeared at the top of old prehistoric standards. Wearing a crown surmounted by two tall straight plumes which seem to have been borrowed from Amon, Min is always represented standing with a flail raised in his right hand behind his head and always with phallus erect.

This latter trait seems to indicate that Min was originally considered by his priests to be the creator of the world. He is often identified with Horus; and we may wonder if his name was not in earlier days simply a special name for the sun-god.

Be this as it may, Min was in the classical epoch chiefly worshipped as god of the roads and protector of travellers in the desert. The principal centre of his cult was Coptos, 'the town of caravaneers', a point of departure for commercial expeditions. Their leaders, before risking themselves in the deserts, never failed to invoke the great local god Min, god of the Eastern desert and 'Lord of Foreign Lands'.

He was worshipped also as a god of fertility and vegetation and protector of crops. On temple walls we see scenes from the ceremonies which were celebrated in his honour as harvest-god during the king's enthronement. We see the Pharaoh offering him the first sheaf which he has just cut and we see the homage which is rendered to the white bull, sacred to Min.

As well as in Coptos he was worshipped in Akhmin, the former Chemmis, known as Panopolis to the Greeks, who identified Min with Pan. There in his honour gymnastic games were celebrated, and it is perhaps for this reason that the Greek historian Herodotus praised the inhabitants of Panopolis for being the only Egyptians who liked Greek customs.

Hapi was the name of the deified Nile. He is given the figure of a man, vigorous but fat, with breasts developed like those of a woman, though less firm and hanging heavily on his chest. He is dressed like the boatmen and fishermen, with a narrow belt which sustains his massive belly. On his head he wears a crown made of aquatic plants – of lotus if he is the Nile of Upper Egypt, of papyrus if he represents the river in Lower Egypt.

Hapi, in fact, played the two parts of Southern Nile and Northern Nile. There were two corresponding goddesses who personified the river banks and they are sometimes seen standing with outstretched arms, as though begging for the water which will render them fertile.

The Egyptians thought of the Nile as flowing from Nun, the primordial ocean which waters the visible as well as the invisible world. It was also said that Hapi resided near the First Cataract, on the Isle of Bigeh, in a cavern where he poured water to heaven and earth from his urns. Towards the middle of June the Nile would rise and the devotees of Osiris affirmed that the inundation – on the height of which depended the year's prosperity – was caused by Isis weeping for her husband, treacherously slain by his wicked brother Set. The suitable height of the inundation was, in Graeco-Roman times, fixed at sixteen cubits – as the sixteen infants which decorate the famous statue of the Nile in the Vatican indicate. In order that the river should attain this height the Egyptians in June would make offerings to Hapi, imploring him with fervour and singing hymns, often of great poetic quality.

Apart from this, Hapi scarcely played a part in religion as such, and he was not connected with any theological system.

In temples he occupied a secondary role, and appears as a servant offering his river products to the great gods. On the foundations of buildings we often find long processions of alternate gods and goddesses who resemble Hapi and are known as 'Niles'. They represent the sub-divisions of the two Egypts bringing, in tribute to the Lord of the sanctuary, the products of all the provinces.

DIVINITIES OF BIRTH AND DEATH

Taueret (Apet, Opet) 'the Great' was a popular goddess of childbirth and symbolised maternity and suckling.

She is represented as a female hippopotamus with pendant mammae, standing upright on her back legs and holding the hieroglyphic sign of protection, 'sa', a plait of rolled papyrus. She was especially worshipped in Thebes where, under the New Kingdom, she enjoyed great popularity among people of the middle class, who often gave her name to their children and decorated their houses with her images.

As well as her role of protectress Taueret sometimes fulfilled that of an avenging deity: then she would appear as a goddess with the body of a hippopotamus but the head of a lioness who brandished a dagger in a menacing manner.

Heket was a frog-goddess or a frog-headed goddess who, it seems, symbolised the embryonic state when the dead grain decomposed and began to germinate.

A primitive goddess, it was taught at Abydos that she came with Shu from the mouth of Ra himself and that she and Shu were the ancestors of the gods. She was, they also said, one of the midwives who assisted every morning at the birth of the sun. In this aspect she figures, like Nekhebet and others whom we shall mention, among the patrons of childbirth.

Meskhent is sometimes represented as a woman wearing on her head two long palm shoots, curved at their extremities. She was a goddess of childbirth and personified the two bricks on which, at the moment of delivery, Egyptian mothers crouched. Sometimes we see Meskhent in the form of one of these bricks, terminated by a human head.

She appeared beside the expectant mother at the precise moment the baby was born; and she was said to go from house to house bringing relief to women in labour. Often, too, she played the role of fairy godmother and pronounced sentence on the newly born and predicted its future.

The old story in which the birth of the three first kings of the fifth dynasty is described permits us to determine the roles which these various divinities played during childbirth. When, we read, Reddedet approached the term of her confinement, Ra, the true father of the child she bore in her womb, ordered Isis, Nephthys, Heket and Meskhent to go to her bedside. The four goddesses, disguised as dancers and accompanied by Khnum who carried their luggage, set forth. When the moment had come Isis placed herself in front of Reddedet, Nephthys, behind her, while Heket helped her. Isis received the child. The goddesses then washed it and placed it on a bed of bricks. Finally Meskhent approached the newborn baby and said: 'It is a king who will rule over all the land.' Khnum then put health and strength into its body.

The Hathors were kinds of fairy godmothers who sometimes appeared at the birth of the young Egyptian to prophesy his destiny, much as we have seen Meskhent do. There were seven or even nine of them and we see them, in the form of young women, at the confinement of Ahmes at Deir el Bahri, of Mutemuia at Luxor and of Cleopatra at Armant. Their predictions were sometimes favourable, sometimes not; but no one escaped the fate they foretold.

Shaï was 'Destiny', and was sometimes made a goddess: Shaït. He was born at the same moment as the individual, grew up with him and shadowed him until his death. Shaï's decrees were inescapable. After death, when the soul was weighed in the presence of Osiris, Shaï could be seen in the form of a god without special attributes attending the trial in order – Maspero says – 'to render exact account before the infernal jury of the deceased's virtues and crimes, or in order to prepare him for the conditions of a new life'.

Renenet was the goddess who presided over the baby's suckling. She nourished him herself and also gave him his name – and, in consequence, his personality and fortune. At his death we see her with Shaï when his soul is weighed and judged. She is variously represented: as a woman without attributes, as a snake-headed woman, as a woman with the head of a lioness, or as a uraeus, dressed and with two long plumes on her head. As a nursing goddess she symbolised nourishment in general and sometimes appears as a harvest goddess with the title, 'Lady of the Double Granary'. She gives her name to the month of Pharmuti, 'the month of Renenet', which was, in later epochs, the eighth month of the Egyptian calendar.

Renpet was the goddess of the year, the goddess of springtide and of youth. As a deity of time's duration she was called 'Mistress

The Hippopotamus goddess Taueret, supported by two plaits of rolled papyrus which form the hieroglyphic sign 'sa'.
Statuette of the twenty-sixth Dynasty, 663 to 525. Cairo.

Bes. A foreign god who was introduced into Egypt, Bes is represented as a hideous bearded dwarf dressed in a leopard skin and wearing an ostrich-feather head-dress. One of the most popular gods in Egypt, he was both a protector and the guardian of sheep. Statue of the twenty-sixth dynasty.

of Eternity'. She is represented as wearing above her head a long palm-shoot, curved at the end – an ideogram of her name.

Bes often appeared at birth, but chiefly he was a marriage-god and presided over the toilet of women.

Bes was a popular god who perhaps originated in the land of Punt of which he was sometimes called the Lord. He appears in the form of a robust dwarf of bestial aspect. His head is big, his eyes huge, his cheeks prominent. His chin is hairy and an enormous tongue hangs from his wide-open mouth. For head-dress he has a bunch of ostrich feathers; he wears a leopard skin whose tail falls behind him and is visible between his bandy legs. In bas-reliefs and paintings he is frequently represented full-face, contrary to the old Egyptian usage of drawing only in profile. He is normally immobile, hands on hips; though occasionally he skips cheerfully but clumsily and plays the harp or tambourine or, again, brandishes a broad dagger with a terrible and menacing air.

At once jovial and belligerent, fond of dancing and fighting, Bes was the buffoon of the gods. They delighted in his grotesque figure and contortions, just as the Memphite Pharaohs of the Old Kingdom enjoyed the antics of their pygmies.

At first Bes was relegated to the lowest rank among the host of genii venerated by the common people, but his popularity grew; and under the New Kingdom the middle classes liked to place his statue in their houses and name their children after him.

From this epoch we often see Bes represented in the *mammisi* of temples – that is to say, in the birth houses where divine accouchements took place. He thus presided over childbearing and at Deir el Bahri he appears with Taueret and other tutelary genii beside the queen's bed as a protector of expectant mothers.

He also presided over the toilet and adornment of women, who were fond of having his image carved on the handles of their mirrors,

rouge boxes and scent bottles. Bed-heads are also frequently found ornamented with various representations of Bes; for he was the guardian of sleep who chased away evil spirits and sent the sleeper sweet dreams.

He was moreover an excellent protector not only against evil spirits but against dangerous beasts: lions, snakes, scorpions, crocodiles. Against their bite or sting the whole family could be preserved by taking care to place in the house a little stela or pillar, covered with magic formulas, on which was sculpted Bes' menacing mask above a figure of the infant Horus, standing on two crocodiles.

At the end of paganism Bes was even supposed to be the protector of the dead, and for this reason became as popular as Osiris.

After the triumph of Christianity Bes did not immediately vanish from the memory of man; for we are told of a wicked demon named Bes whom the holy Moses had to exorcise because he was terrorising the neighbourhood. To this day, it would seem, the monumental southern gate of Karnak serves as a dwelling-place for a knock-kneed dwarf whose gross head is embellished with a formidable beard. Woe to the stranger who, coming across him in the dusk of evening, laughs at his grotesque figure! For the monster will leap at his throat and strangle him. He is the Bes of Ancient Egypt who, after long centuries, is not yet resigned to abandoning altogether the scenes which once witnessed his greatness.

Selket (Selquet) is the name of the old scorpion-goddess who was depicted as a woman wearing on her head a scorpion, the animal sacred to her. She was also at times a scorpion with a woman's head.

According to certain texts she was a daughter of Ra. She often played the role of guardian of conjugal union. At Deir el Bahri she appears with Neith supporting the hieroglyph of the sky, above which Amon is united with the queen-mother. The two goddesses protect the couple from all annoyance.

Meskhent, the goddess of childbirth. The goddess wears her palm-shoot head-dress and an elaborate wig and carries the crook and flail. The personification of the two bricks on which Egyptian women crouched to give birth, she brought relief to women in labour and foretold the future of the child.
Relief carving on stone.

Selket played an especial part in the ceremony of embalming. She protected the entrails and, as we shall later explain, guarded the canopic vase which contained the intestines.

As we have already noticed, Selket is often found in company with Neith, as Isis is with Nephthys. Like the other three goddesses, Selket protected the dead, and like them we see her extending winged arms across the inner walls of sarcophagi.

The four sons of Horus, who were members of the Third Ennead, were supposed to have been born to Isis; but it was also said that Sebek, on Ra's orders, caught them in a net and took them from the water in a lotus flower. It is on a lotus flower that they stand before the throne of Osiris during the judgment of the dead.

They were appointed by their father, Horus, to guard the four cardinal points. He also charged them to watch over the heart and entrails of Osiris and to preserve Osiris from hunger and thirst.

From then on they became the official protectors of viscera. Since the time of the Old Kingdom it had been usual to remove the viscera from the corpse, to separate them and preserve them in cases or jugs called – wrongly – 'canopic' jars. Each of these was confided to the care not only of one of the four genii but also of a goddess.

Thus the human-headed Imsety watched with Isis over the vase containing the liver. The dog-headed Hapi guarded the lungs with Nephthys. The jackal-headed Duamutef with Neith protected the stomach. And the hawk-headed Qebhsnuf with Selket had charge of the intestines.

The Four Sons of Horus. From left to right, the jackal-headed Duamutef, the human-headed Imsety, the hawk-headed Qebhsnuf and the dog-headed Hapi. As protectors of the viscera their heads appeared on the lids of the so-called 'canopic' jars, Duamutef guarding the stomach, Imsety the liver, Qebhsnuf the intestines and Hapi the lungs.

Ament, whose name is a simple epithet meaning 'the Westerner', is represented as a goddess wearing an ostrich feather on her head or sometimes an ostrich plume and a hawk.

This feather, the normal ornament of Libyans, who wore it fixed in their hair, was also the sign for the word 'Western' and was naturally suitable to Ament, who was originally the goddess of the Libyan province to the west of Lower Egypt.

Later 'the West' came to mean the Land of the Dead, and the goddess of the West became the goddess of the dwelling-place of the dead.

At the gates of the World, at the entrance of the desert, one often sees the dead being welcomed by a goddess who half-emerges from the foliage of the tree she has chosen to live in to offer him bread and water. If he drinks and eats he becomes the 'friend of the gods' and follows after them, and can never return. The deity who thus welcomes the dead is often Ament, though she may frequently be Nut, Hathor, Neith or Maat, who take their turn in replacing the goddess of the West.

Mertseger (Merseger), whose name signifies 'the Friend of Silence' or 'the Beloved of Him who makes Silence' (i.e. Osiris), was the name of a snake-goddess of the Theban necropolis. More accurately she pertained to one part of the funerary mountain at Thebes – the peak, shaped like a pyramid, which dominated the mountain chain and earned Mertseger the epithet Ta-dehnet, 'the peak'.

She is represented as a human-headed snake or even as a snake with three heads: namely, a human head surmounted by a disk flanked by two feathers between two others: a snake's head similarly embellished and a vulture's head. Although Mertseger was benevolent she could also punish. We have the confession of Neferabu, a modest employee at the necropolis, who admitted having sinned and been justly stricken with illness. Afterwards he proclaims that he has been cured by 'the Peak of the West', having first repented and ardently besought her forgiveness.

The Judges of the Dead and the Weighing of the Soul. When, thanks to the talismans placed on his mummy and especially to the passwords written on the indispensable Book of the Dead with which he was furnished, the deceased had safely crossed the terrifying stretch of country between the land of the living and the kingdom of the dead, he was immediately ushered into the presence of his sovereign judge, either by Anubis or by Horus. After he had kissed the threshold he penetrated into the 'Hall of Double Justice'. This was an immense room at the end of which sat Osiris under a *naos,* guarded by a frieze of coiled uraeus: Osiris, 'the Good One', redeemer and judge who awaited his 'son who came from earth'. In the centre was erected a vast scale beside which stood Maat, goddess of truth and justice, ready to weigh the heart of the deceased. Meanwhile Amemait, 'the Devourer' – a hybrid monster, part lion, part hippopotamus, part crocodile – crouched nearby, waiting to devour the hearts of the guilty. All around the hall, to the right and to the left of Osiris, sat forty-two personages. Dressed in their winding-sheets, each held a sharp-edged sword in his hand. Some had human heads, others the heads of animals. They were the forty-two judges, each corresponding to a province of Egypt; and each was charged with the duty of examining some special aspect of the deceased's conscience.

The deceased himself began the proceedings and without hesitation recited what has been called 'the negative confession'. He addressed each of his judges in turn and called him by name to prove that he knew him and had nothing to fear. For, he affirmed, he had committed no sin and was truly pure.

Then followed the weighing of his soul, or psychostasia. In one of the pans of the balance Anubis or Horus placed Maat herself, or else her ideogram, the feather, symbol of truth. In the other he placed the heart of the deceased. Thoth then verified the weight, wrote the result on his tablets and announced it to Osiris. If the two pans of the balance were in perfect equilibrium Osiris rendered favourable judgment. 'Let the deceased depart victorious. Let him go wherever he wishes to mingle freely with the gods and the spirits of the dead.'

The deceased, thus justified, would lead from then on a life of eternal happiness in the kingdom of Osiris. It is true that it would be his duty to cultivate the god's domains and keep dykes and canals in good repair. But magic permitted him to avoid all dis-

Nephthys. One of the four tutelary goddesses who protected the dead, Nephthys wears her ideogram on her head – a basket surmounting the sign for a palace. With Hapi she was responsible for the lungs of the corpse and here she guards the canopic shrine containing the viscera of Tut-ankh-Amon. Carved wood overlaid with gold upon gesso. Eighteenth dynasty, 1587 to 1375 B.C.

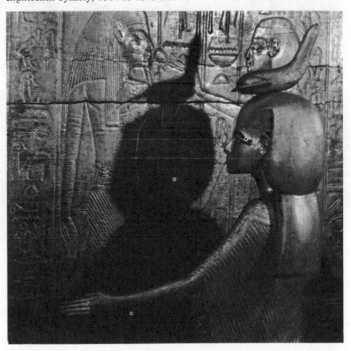

Selket guarding the canopic shrine of Tut-ankh-Amon. The scorpion goddess wears the *khaet* head-dress surmounted by her ideogram and extends her arms in a gesture of protection. The fourth of the tutelary goddesses, she was responsible for the intestines of the dead person in company with Qebhsnuf. Carved wood overlaid with gold upon gesso. Eighteenth dynasty, 1587 to 1375 B.C.

agreeable labour. For at burial he would have been furnished with *Shabtis (Ushabtis)* or 'Answerers' – those little statuettes in stone or glazed composition which have been found in tombs by the hundreds and which, when the dead man was called upon to perform some task, would hasten to take his place and do the job for him.

Maat is depicted as a woman standing or sitting on her heels. On her head she wears the ostrich feather which is an ideogram of her name – truth or justice. She was the goddess of law, truth and justice. The texts describe her as the cherished daughter and

Judgment scene from the Book of the Dead. The dead man, dressed in white, is led into the judgment hall by Anubis who then weighs his heart while the monster Amemait and the ibis-headed Thoth look on. Horus then conducts him into the presence of Osiris who is seated on a throne set upon water from which springs a lotus bearing the Four Sons of Horus. Behind him stand Isis and Nephthys. Above, the dead man is shown addressing the forty-two personages. Painting on papyrus, c. 1450. B.C.

The goddess Isis. The wife of Osiris and the chief of the four goddesses who protected the dead, Isis kneels with her winged arms outstretched in a gesture of protection, wearing her ideogram on her head. With her wings she was believed to have transmitted the breath of life to the dead Osiris. Wall painting from the tomb of Seti I. Nineteenth dynasty, 1375 to 1202 B.C. Thebes.

confidante of Ra, and also the wife of Thoth, the judge of the gods who was also called 'the Master of Maat'.

She formed part of the retinue of Osiris, and the chamber in which the god held his tribunal was named the 'Hall of Double Justice', for Maat was often doubled into two absolutely identical goddesses who stood one in each extremity of the vast hall. As we have just seen, Maat also took her place in one pan of the balance opposite the heart of the dead in order to test its truthfulness.

In reality Maat was a pure abstraction, deified. The gods, it was taught, loved to nourish themselves on truth and justice. Thus, in the ritual of the cult, it was the offering of Maat which genuinely pleased them; and in the temples we see the king, at the culminating point of divine office, presenting to the god of the sanctuary a tiny image of Maat – an offering which was more agreeable to him than all the others he had received, no matter how rich they were.

Neheh (Heh), 'Eternity', is another deified abstraction. The god of eternity is represented as a man squatting on the ground in the Egyptian manner and wearing on his head a reed, curved at the end. We often see him thus, carved on furniture and other homely objects, holding in his hands the sign for millions of years and various emblems of happiness and longevity.

MEN DEIFIED AND THE PHARAOH GOD

Imhotep, in Greek Imuthes, signifies 'He who comes in peace'. Imhotep was by far the most celebrated among those ancient sages who were admired by their contemporaries during their lifetime and after their death finally worshipped as equals of the gods.

Imhotep lived at the court of the ancient King Zoser of the third

Maat. The goddess of truth and justice, Maat wears an ostrich feather on her head-dress, the ideogram of her name.
The goddess played an important part in the judgment of the dead, either herself or her feather being placed in the scales opposite the heart of the dead person in order to test its truthfulness. Painted relief from the tomb of Nefertari. Nineteenth dynasty, 1375 to 1202 B.C.

Amenhotep, son of Hapu, the architect and vizier of Amenhotep III, the father of Akhenaton. Like Imhotep before him, Amenhotep was revered as a sage during his lifetime and was finally deified. He is portrayed as a scribe seated cross-legged with a papyrus unrolled on his knees. Life-size statue in black granite. Eighteenth dynasty, 1587 to 1375 B.C. Karnak.

dynasty. He was Zoser's greatest architect and Zoser was the constructor of the oldest of the pyramids. During his reign, as recent discoveries have revealed, the stone column seems to have been employed for the first time in the history of architecture.

By the time of the New Kingdom Imhotep was already very famous. He was reputed to have written the 'Book of Temple Foundations', and under the Pharaohs of Sais his popularity increased from year to year. Some time later, during the Persian domination, it was claimed that Imhotep was born not of human parents but of Ptah himself. He was introduced into the Triad of Memphis with the title 'Son of Ptah', thus displacing Nefertum.

He is represented with shaven head like a priest, without the divine beard, crown or sceptre and dressed simply as a man. He is generally seated or crouching, and seems to be attentively reading from a roll of papyrus laid across his knees.

He was patron of scribes and the protector of all who, like himself, were occupied with the sciences and occult arts. He became the patron of doctors. Then – for ordinary people who celebrated his miraculous cures – he became the god or, more accurately, the demi-god of medicine. He was thus identified by the Greeks with Asclepius. Towards the end of paganism Imhotep seems even to have relegated his father Ptah to second rank, and to have become the most venerated god in Memphis.

Amenhotep, son of Hapu, whom the Greeks called Amenophis, was a minister of Amenhotep III and lived in Thebes in the fifteenth century B.C.

'A sage and an initiate of the holy book,' we are told, 'Amenhotep had contemplated the beauties of Thoth.' No man of his time better understood the mysterious science of the rites. He was remembered by the Thebans for the superb edifices he had had built. Among these, one of the most imposing was the funeral temple of the king, his master, of which to-day there remain only the two statues that embellished the façade. They are gigantic statues and one of them was renowned throughout antiquity under the name of the Colossus of Memnon. Throughout the centuries the renown of Amenhotep continued to grow. In the Saite epoch he was considered to be a man 'who, because of his wisdom, had participated in the divine

nature'. Magic books were attributed to him and miraculous stories told about him.

In the temple of Karnak there were statues of Amenhotep, son of Hapu, to which divine honours were paid; but he never became a real god like Imhotep, son of Ptah. He was, however, venerated in company with the great divinities in the little Ptolemaic temple of Deir el Medineh.

The old sage is generally portrayed as a scribe, crouching and holding on his knees a roll of papyrus.

Pharaoh must also be named among the gods of Egypt; for the king's divinity formed part of the earliest dogmas. To his subjects, moreover, he was the Sun-god, reigning on earth. He wore the Sun-god's uraeus which spat forth flame and annihilated his enemies. All the terms which were used in speaking of him, of his palace and of his acts could apply equally to the sun. It was taught that he actually perpetuated the solar line; for, whenever there was a change of king, the god Ra married the queen, who then bore a son who, in his turn, mounted the throne of the living.

In temples, and particularly those of Nubia, many ancient kings and the living king himself were often worshipped in company with the great gods. Thus we sometimes see pictures of the reigning Pharaoh worshipping his own image.

Among the countless sacred animals which, especially in later times, were worshipped in the Nile Valley we shall here give details of only the most celebrated, those who were worshipped under their own names in the temples.

THE SACRED ANIMALS

Apis is a Greek rendering of Hapi. As the 'Bull Apis' he is to-day the best known of the sacred animals. Very popular and honoured throughout Egypt, he was tended and worshipped at Memphis, where he was called 'the Renewal of Ptah's life'. He was Ptah's sacred animal and believed to be his reincarnation. Ptah in the form of a celestial fire, it was taught, inseminated a virgin heifer

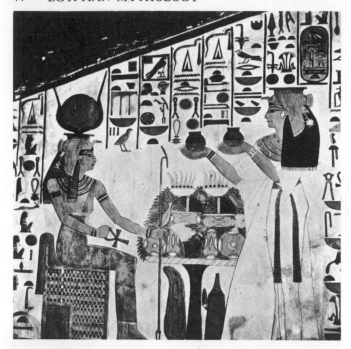

The goddess Hathor receiving an offering.
The goddess is represented seated on a throne wearing a horned head-dress and holding a sceptre and the *ankh*. Before her stands Queen Nefertari, the wife of Rameses II, who presents her with two vases.
The protectress of women, Hathor, as 'Queen of the West', was also protectress of the Theban necropolis. Wall-painting from the tomb of Queen Nefertari. Nineteenth dynasty, 1375 to 1202 B.C.

Akhenaton, the heretical Pharaoh. Head from an Osirian pillar-statue portraying the king at the beginning of his reign from the temple of Ra-Harakhte to the east of Karnak. It was the Aten.
or solar disk of the Rising Sun that Akhenaton was soon to adopt as the sole god of his new religion. Eighteenth dynasty, 1587 to 1375 B.C.

and from her was himself born again in the form of a black bull which the priests could recognise by certain mystic marks. On his forehead there had to be a white triangle, on his back the figure of a vulture with outstretched wings, on his right flank a crescent moon, on his tongue the image of a scarab and, finally, the hairs of his tail must be double.

As long as he lived Apis was daintily fed in the temple which the kings had had built for him in Memphis opposite the temple of Ptah. Every day at a fixed hour he was let loose in the courtyard attached to his temple, and the spectacle of his frolics attracted crowds of the devout. It also drew the merely curious; for a visit to the sacred animals was a great attraction for the tourists who were so numerous in Egypt during the Graeco-Roman era.

Each of his movements was interpreted as foretelling the future; and when Germanicus died it was remembered that the bull, shortly before this, had refused to eat the delicacies which Germanicus had offered him.

Normally Apis was allowed to die of old age. Ammianus Marcellinus, however, tells us that if he lived beyond a certain age he was drowned in a fountain. During the Persian tyranny the sacred bull was twice assassinated, by Cambyses and by Ochus. Space is lacking to describe how the Egyptians mourned the death of Apis, and their transports of joy at the announcement that his successor had been found. We should also have liked to describe the vast subterranean chambers discovered in 1850 at Saqqarah where the mummified bodies of the sacred bulls were, after splendid funeral services, buried in immense monolithic sarcophagi of sandstone or pink granite.

Above these underground galleries arose a great temple of which to-day nothing remains. In Latin it was called the Serapeum. Here the funeral cult of the dead bull was celebrated. He had become, like all the dead, an 'Osiris' and was worshipped under the name Osiris Apis. This in Greek was Osorapis, which caused him quickly to be confused with the foreign god Serapis, who was worshipped according to a purely Greek ritual in the great Serapeum at Alexandria. A god of the underworld, Serapis was confused at Memphis with Osorapis and was worshipped with Osorapis in his funerary temple. Due to this confusion the temple was thenceforth called Serapeum.

Other Sacred Bulls. To be brief we shall only enumerate the three other important bulls of Egypt.

Mneuis is the Greek rendering of Merwer, the Bull of Meroe also called Menuis. He was the bull sacred to Ra Atum at Heliopolis. It seems that he was of a light colour, although Plutarch speaks of his black hide.

Buchis, the Greek for Bukhe, was the bull sacred to Menthu at Hermonthis. According to Macrobius, the hair of his hide, which changed colour every hour, grew in the opposite direction from that of an ordinary animal. The great vaults where the mummies of Buchis were buried were discovered near Armant by Robert Mond, who in 1927 had already found the tombs of the cows which bore these sacred bulls.

Onuphis, the Greek rendering of Aa Nefer, 'the very good', was the bull in which the soul of Osiris was said to be incarnated, as Ra Atum re-appeared in Mneuis and Mont was re-embodied in Buchis.

Petesuchos is the Greek rendering of an Egyptian word meaning 'he who belongs to Suchos' (or Sebek). He was the sacred crocodile in which was incarnated the soul of Sebek, the great god of the Fayyum who had his chief sanctuary in Crocodilopolis, the capital of the province, which was called Arsinoe from the time of the second Ptolemy.

At Crocodilopolis, in a lake dug out near the great temple, Petesuchos was venerated. He was an old crocodile who wore golden rings in his ears. His devotees riveted bracelets to his forelegs. Other crocodiles, also sacred, composed his family and were fed nearby.

In the Graeco-Roman era the crocodiles of Arsinoe were a great attraction for tourists. Strabo tells us how in the reign of Augustus he paid a visit to Petesuchos. 'He is fed,' Strabo writes, 'with the bread, meat and wine which strangers always bring when they come to see him. Our friend and host, who was one of the notabilities of the place and who took us everywhere, came to the lake with us, having saved from our luncheon a cake, a piece of the roast and a small flagon of honey. We met the crocodile on the shore of the lake. Priests approached him and while one of them held open his jaws another put in the cake and the meat and poured in the honey-wine. After that the animal dived into the lake and swam towards the opposite shore. Another visitor arrived, also bringing his offering. The priests ran round the lake with the food he had brought and fed it to the crocodile in the same manner.'

For many centuries no one has worshipped Petesuchos, but in

Bast. The cat-headed goddess of Bubastis wears a long embroidered robe and in her left hand holds the 'aegis of Bast' – a semi-circular breastplate surmounted by the head of a lion. Originally a lioness-goddess, she was frequently confused with Sekhmet and as a goddess of pleasure became one of the most popular Egyptian deities. Bronze statuette.

Horus. The great sky-god is portrayed as a falcon in this statue in the court of the temple of Edfu in Upper Egypt – one of the great temples dedicated especially to his worship. Closely connected with the Pharaoh, he wears the double crown of Upper and Lower Egypt. The falcon was considered the pre-eminent divine being from the earliest times and was the ideogram of 'god'. Twenty-sixth dynasty, 672 to 525 B.C.

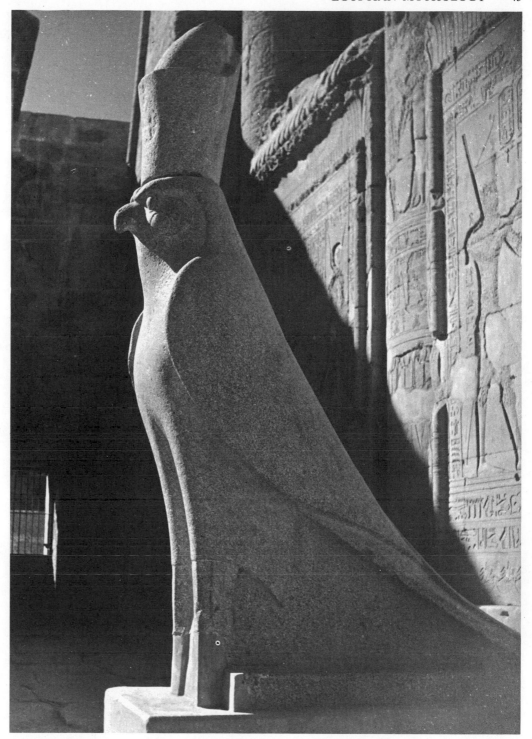

the centre of Africa those who dwell on the southern shores of Lake Victoria-Nyanza today still venerate Lutembi, an old crocodile who for generations has come to the shore each morning and evening at the call of the fishermen to receive from their hands the fish they offer him.

Like Petesuchos of old, the crocodile Lutembi has become a profitable source of revenue for his votaries. For, since many people come to see him out of curiosity, the natives demand a fee for calling him to the shore and make the visitor pay well for the fish they give him.

Sacred Rams were also very popular in Egypt. Chief among them was Ba Neb Djedet, 'the soul of the lord of Djedet', a name which in popular speech was contracted into Banaded and in Greek rendered as Mendes. In him was incarnated the soul of Osiris, and the story which Herodotus brought back about the ram – which he wrongly calls 'the He-goat of Mendes' – confirms the veneration in which this sacred animal was held. Thoth himself, said his priests, had formerly decreed that the kings should come with offerings

to the 'living ram'. Otherwise infinite misfortune would spread among men. When Banaded died there was general mourning; on the other hand immense rejoicing greeted the announcement that a new ram had been discovered, and great festivals were held in order to celebrate the enthronement of this king of Egyptian animals.

The Bird Bennu must also be mentioned among the sacred animals; for, though he was purely legendary, the ancients did not doubt his reality. Worshipped at Heliopolis as the soul of Osiris, he was also connected with the cult of Ra and was perhaps even a secondary form of Ra. He is identified, though not with certainty, with the Phoenix who, according to Herodotus' Heliopolitan guides, resembled the eagle in shape and size, while Bennu was more like a lapwing or a heron. The Phoenix, it was said, appeared in Egypt only once every five hundred years. When the Phoenix was born in the depths of Arabia he flew swiftly to the temple of Heliopolis with the body of his father which, coated with myrrh, he there piously buried.

Alabaster head of a cow sacred to Hathor. The great celestial cow who created the world and all it contains, Hathor was represented as a cow or as a cow-headed woman or, more often, simply wearing cow's horns upon her head. Special reverence was paid to the sacred cows at the temple of Deir el Bahri where the goddess had a chapel. Eighteenth dynasty, 1587 to 1375 B.C.

CONCLUSION

Much more remains to be said on the subject of the sacred animals. In most sanctuaries the god or goddess of the locality was supposed to be incarnate in the animal kept: a cat in the temple of Bast, a falcon or an ibis in the temple of Horus or Thoth. In addition, popular superstition in later times so grew that every individual of the species of animal in whose body the provincial god was incarnate was regarded as sacred by the inhabitants of that province. It was forbidden to eat them, and to kill one was a heinous crime. Since, however, different nomes venerated different animals it could happen that a certain species which was the object of a cult in one province was mercilessly hunted in the neighbouring province. This sometimes gave rise to fratricidal wars such as that which, in the first century of the Christian era, broke out between the Cynopolitans and the Oxyrhynchites. The latter had killed and eaten dogs to avenge themselves on the former for having eaten an oxyrhynchid, a kind of spider crab. Plutarch writes:

'In our days, the Cynopolitans having eaten a crab, the Oxyrhynchites took dogs and sacrificed them and ate their flesh like that of immolated victims. Thus arose a bloody war between the two peoples which the Romans put an end to after severely punishing both.'

Certain animals – cats, hawks, ibis – were venerated all over Egypt and to kill them was punishable by death. 'When one of these animals is concerned,' writes Diodorus, 'he who kills one, be it accidentally or maliciously, is put to death. The populace flings itself on him and cruelly maltreats him, usually before he can be tried and judged. Superstition towards these sacred animals is deeply rooted in the Egyptian's soul, and devotion to their cult is passionate. In the days when Ptolemy Auletes was not yet allied to the Romans and the people of Egypt still hastened to welcome all visitors from Italy and, for fear of the consequences, carefully avoided any occasion for complaint or rupture, a Roman killed a cat. The populace crowded to the house of the Roman who had committed this "murder"; and neither the efforts of magistrates sent by the king to protect him nor the universal fear inspired by the might of Rome could avail to save the man's life, though what he had done was admitted to be accidental. This is not an incident which I report from hearsay, but something I saw myself during my sojourn in Egypt.'

Cats, indeed, were so venerated that when a building caught fire the Egyptians, Herodotus tells us, would neglect the fire in order to rescue these animals whose death to them seemed more painful than any other loss they might sustain. When one of the sacred animals died it was considered an act of great merit to provide for its funeral; and in certain cases, such as the bull Apis, the king himself made it his duty to take charge of the obsequies.

Pity for dead animals reached an almost unbelievable degree. To give an idea of this it may be mentioned that crocodile cemeteries have been discovered where the reptiles were carefully mummified and buried with their newly born and even with their eggs.

The goddess Hathor protecting the Pharaoh Psammetichus.
The goddess is represented as a cow, her sacred animal,
with the solar disk and the uraeus between her horns.
A protector and nourisher of the living, Hathor came
increasingly to be regarded as the protector of the dead.
Copy of a statue of the twenty-sixth dynasty, 572 to 525 B.C.

Petesuchos, the sacred crocodile. 'He who belongs to Suchos (or Sebek)'. Petesuchos was venerated in a lake dug out near Sebek's great temple at Crocodilopolis, it being believed that the god's soul was incarnate in him. Worshipped in some provinces, crocodiles were hunted down in others. Bas-relief in the tomb of Seti Meremptah in the Valley of the Kings. Nineteenth dynasty, 1375 to 1202 B.C. Thebes.

Animals, birds, fish, reptiles of all kinds that were venerated by the ancient inhabitants of the Nile valley were interred by the hundreds of thousands. An example of the abundance of these corpses can be found at Beni Hasan, where the cats' cemetery has been commercially exploited for the extraction of artificial fertiliser.

Herodotus did not exaggerate when he wrote that the Egyptians were the most religious of men.

A LIST OF ANIMALS WHOSE HEADS APPEAR ON EGYPTIAN DIVINITIES

The following is a table, in alphabetical order, of those animals whose heads were borne by certain gods. Only the gods mentioned in this study are listed. We have omitted the countless genii and lesser divinities who on tomb decorations and in illustrations of funerary papyri were also represented with animal heads.

Bull:	Osorapis. See also Apis, Mont.
Cat:	Bast. (Sometimes, perhaps, Mut.)
Cow:	Hathor, Isis when identified with Hathor. See also Nut.
Crocodile:	Sebek.
Dog-faced ape:	Hapi, Thoth at times.
Donkey:	Set (in later times).
Falcon:	Ra-Harakhte, Horus, Mont, Khons Hor, Qebhsnuf.
Frog:	Heket.
Hippopotamus:	Taueret.
Ibis:	Thoth.
Jackal:	Anubis, Duamutef.
Lion:	Nefertum, sometimes.
Lioness:	Sekhmet, Tefnut (sometimes Mut and Renenet).
Ram with curved horns:	Amon.
Ram with wavy horns:	Khnum, Hershef or Harsaphes.
Scarab:	Khepri.
Scorpion:	Selket.
Serpent:	Buto. See also Mertseger and Renenet.
Uraeus:	See Serpent.
Vulture:	Nekhebet.
Wolf:	Upuaut, Khenti Amenti.
Indeterminate animal called the Typhonian Animal:	Set.

ASSYRO-BABYLONIAN MYTHOLOGY

Large copper panel from the temple of Ninkhursag at Tell-el Obeid, near Ur, showing the divine, lion-headed eagle, Imdugud, with two stags. The personification of the benevolent rainstorm after drought, his outstretched wings were believed to shroud the heavens with clouds. Originally erected over the doorway of the temple, this relief shows the balanced arrangement of figures which was one of the great creations of Sumerian art. *c.* third millennium B.C.

INTRODUCTION

From the beginning of the third millennium B.C., a flourishing civilisation existed on the lower banks of the Tigris and the Euphrates, due to two neighbouring peoples: the Akkadians and the Sumerians. The land of Sumer was situated around the upper end of the Persian Gulf, which in those days probably extended much further inland than it does to-day, although this belief has recently been challenged. The towns of Eridu to the south and Nippur to the north marked its extreme limits: other towns were Lagash, Umma, Erech, Larsa and Ur. The Sumerians had probably come from central Asia or the Siberian steppes. The land of Akkad, which lay immediately to the north of Sumer, was peopled by Semites who had probably come from northern Syria. The site of the city, Agade, from which it took its name, has not yet been identified. Its other principal towns were – from south to north – Borsippa, Babylon, Kish, Kutha and Sippar.

The question of which of these two peoples was the older has been disputed, as has the part attributable to each in the development of civilisation. As to the respective contributions of the two races to religion which is all that concerns us here, it is probably most accurate to regard Assyro-Babylonian religion as not primarily a Semitic religion but as one resulting from the semitisation of an originally Sumerian or, to employ a more general term, Asian basis.

However that may be, there was indubitably a reciprocal penetration between the religions of Sumer and Akkad. Each city doubtless venerated its own divinities, but each also welcomed those of neighbouring cities. Conquerors, moreover, would impose their own gods on regions subdued. In time, these new gods would become identified with the indigenous gods and, if not actually assimilated, form affiliations and relationships with them. It is this intermixture of the Akkadian and Sumerian pantheons, completed by the contributions of later epochs, which constitutes Assyro-Babylonian mythology.

THE CREATION

The myth of the Creation is given to us in a series of seven tablets which in the main come, like most of the other religious texts which we shall make use of, from the library of Ashurbanipal in Nineveh. Tablets date from the seventh century B.C., whilst there are some pieces from Ashur going back to 1000 B.C. The work as we have it must be based on much older original texts.

Water is the primordial element. From the fusion of sweet water (Apsu) and salt water (Tiamat) arose all beings, beginning with the gods.

The *Apsu,* which is here personified, was a kind of abyss filled with water which encircled the earth. The earth itself was a round plateau. This plateau was bounded by mountains on which rested the vault of heaven, and it floated on the waters of the Apsu. From the Apsu came the springs which broke through the surface of the earth. The Apsu may be compared to the River Oceanus of the Greeks, which Homer also called the father of all things.

Tiamat was a personification of the sea and represented the feminine element which gave birth to the world. In the continuation of the story she represents the blind forces of primitive chaos against which the intelligent and organising gods struggle.

Lakhmu and *Lakhamu* were the first two to be born. They are rather vague gods, and seem to be a pair of monstrous serpents. They gave birth to *Anshar*, the male principle, and to *Kishar*, the female principle, who represented respectively, so some think, the celestial and the terrestrial worlds. In the same way the Greek

Scene of worship. A devotee waters the sacred plant before a seated divinity, doubtless the god Shamash. Archaic stela. Louvre.

Figure of a bison. Possibly a votive offering, the tuft under its chin and the long, shaggy hair on its head and body are elaborately chased. Sumerian work. *c.* 2500 B.C. From Van (Eastern Turkey).

Sacred tree with two worshippers. Above the tree hovers the winged disk, emblem of Asshur. Assyrian cylinder. Louvre.

gods were born of the union of Uranus, the sky, and Gaea, the earth. But while in Greek mythology Gaea played an important role Kishar does not appear again in the story.

In the *Epic of the Creation* it will be noticed that the principal role is played by *Marduk*; it is he who triumphs over Tiamat and organises the universe. This is explained by the Babylonian origin of the poem, for Marduk was, as we shall later see, the great god of Babylon.

Now this is how the people of Sumer and Akkad explained the origin of the world.

In the beginning when 'the sky above had not been named and the earth below was nameless' there existed only Apsu, the primordial ocean, and Tiamat, the tumultuous sea. From their mingled waters came forth first *Mummu* (the tumult of the waves) then a pair of monstrous serpents, *Lakhmu* and *Lakhamu*, who in their turn gave birth to *Anshar*, the celestial world, and to *Kishar*, the terrestrial world. To Anshar and Kishar were born the great gods: Anu, the powerful; Ea, of vast intellect; and the other divinities. These latter were the *Igigi* who peopled the sky, and the *Anunnake* who were scattered over the earth and through the underworld.

Soon the new gods with their turbulence disturbed the repose of old Apsu who complained to Tiamat: 'During the day I have no rest and at night I cannot sleep.' The two ancestors argued about

Two worshippers. From their clasped hands and the libation vases which they hold they are believed to be substitute worshippers for two high-ranking personnages. Veined gypsum with additional paint and inlay. First half of the third millennium B.C.

A priest, or possibly a hero, approaching an altar. In his outstretched hands he holds a lotus plant. Ivory panel from Fort Shalasar, Assyria.

Adad, the Babylonian god of tempests. He could be both beneficent and terrifying – while he was feared in the fury of the storm he was also worshipped as the bringer of the life-giving rain. On this stele from Arslan-Tash he is seen riding on a bull, his emblem, and carrying thunderbolts in his hands. *c.* Eighth century, B.C.

Small seated statue of Gudea, the *patesi*, or governor, of the Sumerian city-state of Lagash. Like most rulers of his time, Gudea was also a priest. Here he is portrayed in the presence of his god wearing a turban-like head-dress and with his hands clasped before him in prayer. The original Sumerian beliefs contributed much to the myths and religion of Assyria and Babylonia. Alabaster. End of the third millennium B.C.

Votive figure of Gudea of Lagash. The *patesi* stands bare-headed wearing a simple robe which leaves his right shoulder bare and with his hands again clasped in the ritual attitude of prayer. As the result of a dream Gudea built a temple to Ningirsu at Lagash and this statue may well have come from this. Black basalt. End of the third millennium B.C.

Life-size bronze head of an Akkadian priest or king from Nineveh. The functions of priest and king were often combined during this period so that this head could well represent a man who was both. The hair, beard and eyebrows are elaborately worked while the eyes were probably made of precious stones. *c.* 2200 B.C.

The liberation of the sun god. In the centre Shamash, the sun god, rises from the Mountain of the East before a winged goddess wearing the *kaunakes*. A god with a bow and arrow stands on the left while on the right a water or river god ascends the mountain before a two-faced god. Impression from a Sumerian cylinder seal. *c.* 2250 B.C.

the annihilation of their descendants. 'Why should we destroy all that we have made?' asked Tiamat. 'Even though their way is troublesome!' But Ea, who perceived all things, learnt of Apsu's design and by his magic incantations was able to seize Apsu and Mummu. Tiamat, enraged, gathered around her a certain number of the gods and gave birth to enormous serpents 'with sharp teeth, merciless in slaughter', to terrible dragons with glittering scales, to tempest-monsters, savage dogs, to scorpion-men, furious hurricanes, fish-men and rams. To command this troop she chose *Kingu*, to whom she gave sovereignty over all the gods, pinning on his breast the tablets of fate.

Meanwhile Ea, who knew of Tiamat's plans, went to his father Anshar. 'Tiamat, our mother,' he said, 'has conceived a hatred against us. She is gathering an army together, she storms with fury.' Listening to his son, Anshar was moved. He 'struck his thigh, he bit his lip, his stomach knew no more rest'. At first he sent Anu against Tiamat, but Anu lacked the heart to confront the goddess. Ea was no more courageous. Then Ea summoned Bêl-Marduk, 'the son who makes his heart swell', and bade him to do battle with Tiamat, promising him the victory. Marduk accepted, but first insisted that the assembled gods should confer on him supreme

authority. Anshar consented and at once sent his messenger Gaga to Lakhmu and Lakhamu, as well as to the other Igigi. All hastened to the Upshukina and, having kissed each other, sat down to a banquet. After they had eaten bread and drunk wine they prepared a princely dwelling for Marduk, the king. They acknowledged his rule over all the world and accorded him the sceptre, the throne and the *palu,* giving him the unrivalled weapon which repelled all enemies, 'Go', they said to him, 'and slay Tiamat. May the winds carry her blood to secret places!'

Thus invested Marduk took in his right hand a bow, fixed the string, hung a quiver at his side, set lightning before him and made a net in which to entangle Tiamat. He loosed the winds which he posted beside him; then, taking his chief weapon, the hurricane, he mounted his chariot – a terrifying tempest – which was drawn by four swift and violent steeds, fearful in battle. Thus 'arrayed in terror' he went forth to challenge Tiamat to battle.

They rose up, Tiamat and Marduk the Wise, among the gods. The *Epic of the Creation* (Tablet IV, vs. 93-104. Dhorme's translation), tells us:

They marched to war, they drew near to give battle.
The Lord spread out his net and caught her in it.
The evil wind which followed him, he loosed it in her face.
She opened her mouth, Tiamat, to swallow him.
He drove in the evil wind so that she could not close her lips.
The terrible winds filled her belly. Her heart was seized,
She held her mouth wide open.
He let fly an arrow, it pierced her belly.

Worshipper between two divinities: the god with the axe,
the goddess with the crown. Perhaps Marduk and Ishtar.
Above, the emblem of Asshur. Assyrian cylinder. Bibliothèque Nationale.

The god with two heads leads to Anu (?) the tempest-bird Zu.
Assyrian cylinder. Louvre.

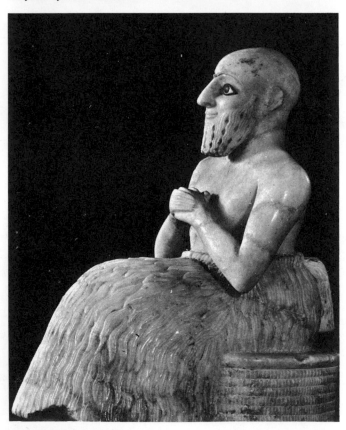

Ebih-il worshipping the goddess Ishtar. One of the most popular deities
in the pantheon, the goddess had numerous devotees.
This seated statue portrays one of them – the steward Ebih-il –
who is shown with his hands clasped before him in prayer,
ritually clad in an elaborate skirt. It was dedicated by him to the goddess
and comes from her temple at Mari in Sumeria. Alabaster. c. 2500 B.C.

Her inner parts he clove, he split her heart.
He rendered her powerless and destroyed her life.
He felled her body and stood upright on it.

The death of Tiamat spread confusion among her followers.
Her auxiliaries fled in disorder to save their lives, but Marduk
caught them in his net and took them all prisoner. With Kingu
he threw them in chains into the infernal regions. Then, returning
to Tiamat, he split her skull and cut the arteries of her blood. And,
as he contemplated the monstrous corpse, he 'conceived works of
art'. He clove the body 'like a fish into its two parts'. From one
half he fashioned the vault of the heavens, from the other the solid
earth. That done, he organised the world. He constructed a dwelling-
place for the great gods in the sky and installed the stars which
were their image; he fixed the length of the year and regulated the
course of the heavenly bodies.

Thus the earth was formed. Then 'in order that the gods should
live in a world to rejoice their hearts' Marduk created humanity.
According to the *Epic of the Creation* Marduk moulded the body
of the first man using the blood of Kingu. A neo-Babylonian text
from Eridu says that he was aided in his work by the goddess Aruru
who 'produced with him the seed of mankind'. Finally there appeared the great rivers, vegetation and animals, wild and domestic.
The work of creation had been achieved.

THE WORLD OF THE GODS

The essential privilege of the gods was immortality. But they
had the same needs and passions as mortals.

They were subject to fear. During the deluge the gods were dis-
quieted to see the waters rise. They climbed to the sky of Anu and
there:

The gods crouched like dogs; on the wall they cowered.

The gods were also greedy. When they forgathered they never
failed to feast and drink themselves into a state of boisterous intoxication. The *Epic of the Creation* says:

They grow drunk with drinking, their bodies are joyful,
They shout aloud, their hearts exult.

They were equally fond of sacrifices. When Uta Napishtim was saved
from the Deluge and, in gratitude, placed offerings on the summit
of the mountain, 'the gods smelled the good odour, the gods
swarmed like flies above him who offered them sacrifice'.

Like men the gods had wives and families. They were celestial
sovereigns and, like kings of earth, had their courts, servants and
soldiers. They inhabited palaces situated either in regions above
the sky, on the great Mountain of the East, or in the subterranean
depths of the underworld. Although each had his own sphere of
influence they would sometimes gather together to debate common
problems. They would then assemble in a hall called the Upshukina.
In particular they would congregate there at the beginning of each
year, on the feast of Zagmuk, in order to determine men's destiny.
The gods thus formed a thoroughly organised and hierarchical
society.

The divine hierarchy was not immediately established and was
often modified. The great primordial principle of fertility and
fecundity, at first worshipped by the Sumerians, was quickly dispersed into a crowd of divinities who had no precise connection
with each other. Later, under the influence of national pride, the
gods acquired rank, the dignity of which corresponded to the importance in the country as a whole of the city in which they were
particularly venerated. Finally the official theologians of Babylon
fixed the hierarchy of the gods more or less definitely, dividing them
into triads. The two principal triads were those of the great gods
Anu, Enlil and Ea, and of the astral gods Sin, Shamash and Ishtar.

THE GREAT GODS

When the victory of Marduk over Tiamat had re-established peace
and order in the world of the gods each divinity received his own
particular sphere of influence. The universe was divided into three
regions each of which became the domain of a god. Anu's share

was the sky. The earth was given to Enlil. Ea became the ruler of the waters. Together they constituted the triad of the Great Gods.

Anu. Anu was the son of Anshar and Kishar. His name signified 'sky' and he reigned over the heavens. There he resided in the uppermost region which was called the 'sky of Anu'. He was god in the highest sense, the supreme god. All the other deities honoured him as their 'father', that is to say, their chief. They came to him for refuge when danger threatened them, during the Deluge for example. It was to him they came when they had complaints to lodge. Thus the goddess Ishtar, harshly repelled by the hero Gilgamesh, goes to find Anu, her father. 'Oh my father,' she said to him, 'Gilgamesh has cursed me,' and she requested him to make 'a celestial bull' to send against Gilgamesh. In the same way Anu summoned all cases of importance before his tribunal. When Adapa broke the wings of the South Wind Anu ordered him to appear before him. He combined power and justice, all the marks of sovereignty. Before the raised throne on which he sat were placed the insignia of royalty: 'the sceptre, the diadem, the crown and the staff of command.' On monuments Anu was represented by a tiara placed on a throne. He had, moreover, an army at his command: the stars which he had created to destroy the wicked were called 'the soldiers of Anu'.

Anu never left the heavenly regions, never came down to earth. When he abandoned his majestic immobility it was to walk in that portion of the sky which was exclusively reserved for him, the name of which was 'Anu's Way'.

In spite of his uncontested supremacy he was not, however, exempt from weaknesses. We have seen, that, for example, when he was sent to do battle against Tiamat he was unable to face the monster and left the glory of victory to Marduk.

Aided by his companion, the goddess Antu, he presided from above over the fates of the universe and hardly occupied himself with human affairs. Thus, although he never ceased to be universally venerated, other gods finally supplanted him and took over certain of his prerogatives. But the great god's prestige remained such that the power of these usurper gods was never firmly established until they, too, assumed the name Anu.

Enlil (Bel). Enlil was much more involved in the events which took place on earth. In the land of Sumer, and particularly at Nippur, Enlil, Lord of the Air, had been worshipped from early times. Enlil was the god of the hurricane and his weapon was the amaru, that is, the deluge. Like the Greek Zeus he symbolised the forces of nature and again like Zeus he was soon considered to be the master of men's fates.

When the people of Babylon took over the gods of Sumer, far from overlooking Enlil they made him the second element in their supreme triad. They virtually assimilated Enlil to their god Marduk, to whom they applied the name Bel, which means 'Lord'. Bel then became Lord of the World and his rule extended throughout the earth. He was called 'King of the Land' or 'Lord of all Regions'.

Enlil, like Anu, had a reserved promenade in the heavens – 'Enlil's Way' – but he normally resided on the Great Mountain of the East.

Like Anu, Enlil (Bel) held the insignia of royalty which he dispensed to the person of his choice. Earthly kings, then, were only the representatives or vicars of Enlil (or Bel). In order to raise them above other men it was enough that the god should pronounce their name, for the word of Bel was all-powerful.

The word of Enlil is a breath of wind, the eye sees it not.
His word is a deluge which advances and has no rival.
His word above the slumbering skies makes the earth to
    slumber.
His word when it comes in humility destroys the country.
His word when it comes in majesty overwhelms houses and
    brings weeping to the land.
At his word the heavens on high are stilled.

For men, then, Enlil is the dispenser of good and evil. It was he who in an angry mood sent down the deluge to annihilate the human race.

In the most ancient period Enlil was associated with the goddess Ninkhursag, 'Lady of the Great Mountain', though to the systematising theologians his consort was Ninlil. When Bel took over

Benevolent winged genie from one of the gates of the palace of Sargon II at Khorsabad. Dressed in a long fringed robe and the horned head-dress of divinity, he holds a lustral vase and pine-cone sprinkler with which to purify those entering the palace after they have passed the guardian bulls at the entrance. His function may also have been to drive away evil spirits and demons.
Relief carving of the eighth century B.C.

Lion-headed Babylonian monster. This creature probably represents one of the seven evil genii who were believed to have been born in the Mountain of the West and lived in holes in the ground or among ruins, spreading discord and disease among men and decimating their flocks. Genii, both good and evil, were believed to play a major role in men's daily lives by the Babylonians. Terra-cotta. Seventh to sixth centuries B.C.

Ur-Nammu deified as the god Sin. On the right, the great king of Ur is shown seated on a throne extending his hand in greeting to Khashkhamer, the governor of Ishkun Sin, who is led into his presence by two goddesses wearing conical horned head-dresses with their hands raised in intercession. In the centre is a crescent moon.
Impression from a Sumerian cylinder seal. 2500 B.C.

the attributes of Enlil, his consort could correspondingly be called Belit, that is to say, 'The Lady'. Although she sometimes bore the title 'Mother of the Gods', Ninkhursag or Belit enjoyed no supremacy over the Babylonian Olympus. On the contrary, with her sacred milk she nourished those whom Bel had chosen to be kings among men. Thus, thanks to her, earthly sovereigns could boast of divine origin.

Ea. The name of this divinity, which means 'House of the Water', is alone sufficient to indicate his character and the nature of his sphere of influence. It would, however, be a mistake to identify him with the Poseidon of the Greeks. Ea was not a marine deity. His proper domain was the Apsu – in other words that stretch of fresh water which surrounded the earth and on which at the same time the earth floated. The springs which gushed from the earth, the great rivers which watered the Chaldean plain came from the Apsu. We have seen how, during the creation, the fertilising waters of the Apsu encountered the salty and tumultuous waves of the sea. In the same way the Greeks distinguished between the River Oceanus and the 'sterile sea'. While the waters of the Apsu spread abundance and happiness over the earth they were also the source of all knowledge and wisdom.

In the land of Sumer, Ea bore the name of *Enki*, 'Lord of the Earth'. As god of the Apsu he was also god of supreme wisdom. He presided over magic incantations and the gods themselves willingly consulted him. Sometimes he was also called 'Lord of the sacred Eye', *Ninigiku,* that is to say 'he whom nothing escapes'. When necessary his vigilant wisdom corrected the errors of the gods themselves. When Bel decided to drown the race of man by flood it was Ea who warned Uta-Napishtim and prevented the destruction of mankind.

God of knowledge, Ea, jointly with Shamash, spoke oracularly and he was invoked in incantations. But he also presided over men's work. Carpenters, stone-cutters, goldsmiths venerated him as their patron. It is even possible, on one interpretation of a very damaged text, that Ea was sometimes regarded as the creator of man, whom he had fashioned with clay.

The earthly residence of Ea was the holy city of Eridu which, situated in the extreme south of the land of Sumer on the Persian Gulf, had been the first city to be raised from the waters. Here Ea had his dwelling, the *Ezuab,* or the 'House of the Apsu'. Nearby rose a wondrous tree, a black *Kishkanu,* the foliage of which shone like a lapis-lazuli and cast a thick shade like that of a forest.

Ea is represented as a goat with a fish's tail. He is also seen in human form with waves springing from his shoulders or from a vase held in his hands.

Ea's companion, whose physiognomy is rather vague, bears the name of Ninki, 'Lady of the Earth', or else Damkina, or again Damgalnunna, 'The Great Spouse of the Lord'.

Such was the triad of the great gods, and such it remained until the day when Babylon became mistress of all the land of Sumer and Akkad. Then, naturally, she placed her own national god, Marduk, at the head of the pantheon.

Marduk. Marduk was the oldest son of Ea. He came from the Apsu and originally personified the fertilising action of the waters; it

was he who made plants grow and grain ripen. He thus had above all the character of an agricultural deity, as his attribute the *marru,* which is simply a spade, testifies. His fortunes grew with the greatness of Babylon, the city of his choice, and finally he occupied the first place among the gods. He had, moreover, attained this position by right of conquest. It will be remembered how, after the failure of Anu and Ea – the *Epic of the Creation* does not mention Bel in this connection – Marduk dared to face the monstrous Tiamat. And it will also be remembered how before he joined battle he insisted that the assembly of the gods should invest him with supreme authority and the privilege of determining fates. All this was accorded to him. After his victory the gods showed their gratitude by awarding him fifty titles, each of which corresponded to a divine attribute. In this way the fullness of divinity was united in Marduk. He was not only 'he who created grain and plants and made green things to grow' but also:

The light of the father who begot him,
He who renews the gods,
The Lord of pure incantation, making the dead to live,
He who knows the hearts of the gods,
Guardian of justice and law,
The creator of all things,
Among lords, the first,
The Lord of Kings,
The shepherd of the gods.

Bel conferred upon him his own title of 'Lord of the Land' and Ea, overjoyed at his son's victory, cried:

Let him, like me, be called Ea;
The commands that I command let him pronounce them!

Thus Marduk absorbed all the other gods and took over all their various functions and prerogatives. It was he who organised the universe, assigned dwelling-places to the gods, and fixed the course of the heavenly bodies. It was he who created man from the blood of Kingu; he was the 'Lord of Life', the great healer and took the place of his father, Ea, in magic incantations. From Enlil he obtained the governorship of the four quarters of the earth. Henceforward he was the supreme commander of the Anunnaki and each year he himself determined men's fates in the Duku, i.e. 'the pure abode', during the feast of *zagmuk*. Even Anu, the supreme god, felt the effects of Marduk's growing glory. Marduk took from him the *Anutu* – that is, his own dignity – and his word became 'like the word of Anu'.

It was the privilege of the supreme gods to ordain the destiny of men. The possession of the Tablets of Fate was the token of omnipotence. Now, one day, the storm-bird Zu stole the famous tablets. Anu offered the divine kingship to the one who recovered them. When approached, Adad and Shara each in turn declined. Though the text then becomes fragmentary, another composition makes it probable that it was Marduk who succeeded in overcoming the thief Zu and recovering the stolen tablets.

Marduk proved his indomitable courage on another occasion. Evil genii were provoked by the god Sin, whose watchfulness pursued nocturnal malefactors. They wove a plot against him and with the complicity of Shamash, Ishtar and Adad they succeeded in eclipsing his light. As in the days of Tiamat, Anu and Ea were seized with terror. But Marduk gave battle to the rebels, put them to flight and gave back Sin his brilliance. The poet was right when he said:

When he is angered no god can resist his wrath,
Before the sharp blade of his sword the gods flee.
Terrible master, without rival among the great gods!
In the tempest his weapons flash,
In his flames steep mountains are overthrown.

Marduk was generally represented armed with a kind of scimitar felling a winged dragon, a souvenir of his victory over Tiamat. In this way he could be seen in the *Esagil,* his famous temple in Babylon, where he was enthroned beside his spouse Zarpanit.

Each year on a fixed date the god's statue was carried solemnly through the immense crowd out of the Esagil and out of the city to a place in the country called the *Akitu* which was a sort of temple. Here it remained for several days. The ritual of this ceremony, which has been restored for us by Thureau-Dangin, comprised prayers chanted by the priests, magic ceremonies, purifications and sacrifices: the king himself came to receive investiture from Bel-Marduk. These festivals lasted no less than ten days. It seems that during them a mystery play was given in which were represented the death of the god, his resurrection and finally his marriage with the goddess.

Similar ceremonies, arranged in the same way, took place annually at Uruk in honour of Anu and Ishtar, and at Ur in honour of Nannar.

Asshur. But the day came when the might of Babylon faded before that of Nineveh. The national god of the Assyrians, Asshur, then took the first place. In order to make this substitution easier Asshur was identified with the ancient Babylonian god Anshar. Thus Asshur became 'king of all the gods, self-created, father of the gods, maker of the sky of Anu and of the underworld, author of mankind, who lives in the bright heavens, Lord of the gods, he who ordained men's fate...'

Asshur was above all a warrior-god who shared the bellicose instincts of his people. He accompanied their armies into battle, fought at their side, directed the soldiers' blows and rendered their arms victorious. Thus he received the first fruits of the booty and the vanquished became his subjects. Nor did he disdain to appear to his followers in order to stimulate their courage and strengthen their confidence. Such was that king of Lydia to whom he showed himself and said: 'Kiss the feet of the king of Asshur, Ashurbanipal, and in his name thou shalt surely triumph over thine enemies.'

Asshur is generally represented in the form of a winged disk, or mounted on a bull, or floating through the air. These are warrior representations. But he was not merely a warlike god. In his quality of supreme divinity he was also the great god of fertility. He is then represented surrounded by branches and his attribute is a female goat.

Asshur's principal consort was the goddess Ninlil.

THE SIDEREAL DIVINITIES

Sin. The moon-god occupied the chief place in the astral triad. Its other two members, Shamash the sun and Ishtar the planet Venus, were his children. Thus it was, in effect, from the night that light had emerged.

In his physical aspect Sin – who was venerated at Ur under the name of Nannar – was an old man with a long beard the colour of lapis-lazuli. He normally wore a turban. Every evening he got into his barque – which to mortals appeared in the form of a brilliant crescent moon – and navigated the vast spaces of the nocturnal sky. Some people, however, believed that the luminous crescent was Sin's weapon. But one day the crescent gave way to a disk which stood out in the sky like a gleaming crown. There could be no doubt that this was the god's own crown; and then Sin was called 'Lord of the Diadem'. These successive and regular transformations lent Sin a certain mystery. For this reason he was considered to be 'He whose deep heart no god can penetrate'.

Because he illuminated the night Sin was an enemy of evil-doers whose criminal enterprises were favoured by darkness. We have already seen how wicked spirits plotted against him. They had won to their cause even the god's children Shamash and Ishtar as well as Adad, the god of thunder. Their combined efforts succeeded in eclipsing Sin, and only Marduk's intervention re-established order.

Sin had other functions. It was he who measured time; for so Marduk had decided on the day of the creation.

> At the month's beginning to shine on earth
> Thou shalt show two horns to mark six days.
> On the seventh day divide the crown in two;
> On the fourteenth day, turn thy full face.

Sin was also full of wisdom. At the end of every month the gods came to consult him and he made decisions for them.

His wife was *Ningal,* 'the great Lady'. He was the father not only of Shamash and Ishtar but also of a son *Nusku,* the god of fire.

The Goddess Ishtar. Terracotta. Sumerian period. Louvre.

Shamash. Every morning the scorpion-men who inhabit the Mountain of the East and defend its approaches, open in the mountain's flank a great folding door. From it will spring, on his daily journey, Shamash, the sun-god. The god appears. Luminous rays seem to issue from his shoulders. In his hand he grasps an object which resembles the blade of a saw: is it a weapon or more simply the key to the Eastern Gate? With alert footstep he climbs the mountain and joins Bunene, his coachman, who is harnessing the chariot in which the god will take his place. In a dazzle of light Shamash begins slowly to mount the sky. When evening falls Shamash guides his chariot towards the great Mountain of the West. A gate opens and he penetrates the depths of the earth. The sun has disappeared. During the night Shamash pursues his subterranean course so that before dawn he shall have regained the Mountain of the East.

Vigour and courage were the distinctive qualities of this god who triumphed over the night and put the winter to flight. But above all he was the god of justice. His bursting light which chased away the shadows where crime throve made him the terror of the evil-doer: he 'breaks the horn of him who meditates evil'. How could one escape him? Not only did he see everything, but his rays were a vast net which caught all who committed iniquities. Thus he bore the title of 'Judge of the Heavens and the Earth', 'Sublime Judge of the Anunnaki', 'Lord of Judgment'. His temple in Babylon was called the 'House of the Judge of the World'. In his role of judge the god was represented seated on a throne, holding

Gilgamesh in conflict. The great Sumerian hero
is probably shown here wrestling with the celestial bull
which was sent against him by the goddess Ishtar after he had repulsed her
advances, the duplication of the figures being for the purposes of symmetry
and balance – a common device in Sumerian art.
Impression from a mother of emerald Akkadian cylinder seal.
c. 2340 to 2180 B.C.

Two scenes from the story of Gilgamesh. On the left Gilgamesh
and his friend the half man – half bull, Enkidu,
are shown in conflict with a lion, an animal which they loved to hunt
together, while on the right the hero is probably shown crossing the waters
of Death in the boat of Urshanabi in search of his dead companion.
Impression from an Akkadian cylinder seal. 2340 to 2180 B.C.

in his right hand the sceptre and the ring.

Shamash had another role. Like the later Greek Apollo, who
was also a sun-god, Shamash was the god of divination. Through
the intermediary of a soothsayer, the *baru,* he revealed to men the
secrets of the future. After he had offered sacrifice to Shamash
the soothsayer would observe the various shapes assumed by oil
poured on the water in the sacred tub, or examine the liver of the
sacrificial victim, or decipher what the gods had decreed from the
position of the stars, the movements of the planets, the appearance
of meteorites. It was especially at Sippar, where the sun-god was
particularly honoured, that the art of divination flourished.

There Shamash with his wife, *Aya,* was venerated. To the divine
couple two gods of abstract character were born: *Kittu* who was
justice, and *Misharu* who was law.

Ishtar. According to some, Ishtar was the daughter of Anu; according to others, of Sin. She called herself 'goddess of the morn and
goddess of the evening'. One of the most prominent figures in the
Assyro-Babylonian pantheon, Ishtar was the divine personification
of the planet Venus. While the Assyro-Babylonians made Ishtar a
goddess, the Arabs made her a god under the name *Athtar.*

The same complexity occurs in her functions, depending on
whether she was considered to be the daughter of Sin or of Anu.
In the former case she was a war-goddess, in the latter the goddess
of love.

The warrior Ishtar was the daughter of Sin and the sister of
Shamash. She was the 'Lady of Battles, valiant among goddesses'.
She retained this character in the forms in which she was worshipped by the Assyrians. Like Asshur she went on expeditions,
took part in battles 'covered with combat and arrayed in terror'.
She is represented standing on a chariot drawn by seven lions,
with a bow in her hands. She was particularly worshipped at
Nineveh and Arbela (Erbil). She was the sister of Ereshkigal,
queen of the underworld, and she helped greatly to people the
infernal regions; for she was the 'Star of Lamentation' who 'made
brothers who were on good terms quarrel among themselves, and
friends forget friendship'.

On the other hand at Erech, Ishtar, daughter of Anu, was above
all the goddess of love and voluptuousness, not indeed that her

character manifested much more tenderness. On every occasion
the goddess was irritable, violent and incapable of tolerating the
least obstacle to her wishes. 'If you do not create the celestial bull,'
she said to her father Anu, 'I shall break (something) open...the
dead will become more numerous than the living.' Finding that
the gates of the underworld did not open quickly enough for her
she threatened the porter:

> If you open not the gate that I may pass,
> I shall burst it in and smash the lock,
> I shall destroy the threshold and break the doorposts,
> I shall make the dead to rise and they will outnumber the living!

It was, however, she who roused amorous desire in all creatures.
As soon as she withdrew her influence:

> The bull refuses to cover the cow, the ass no longer approaches
>   the she-ass,
> In the street the man no longer approaches the maid-servant.

Sacred prostitution formed part of her cult and when she descended
to earth she was accompanied by 'courtesans, harlots and strum-
pets'. Her holy city Erech was called the 'town of the sacred courtesans'. Ishtar herself, moreover, was the 'courtesan of the gods'
and she was the first to experience the desires which she inspired.
Her lovers were legion and she chose them from all walks of life.
But woe to him whom Ishtar had honoured! The fickle goddess
treated her passing lovers cruelly, and the unhappy wretches usually
paid dearly for the favours heaped on them. Animals, enslaved
by love, lost their native vigour: they fell into traps laid by men
or were domesticated by them. 'Thou hast loved the lion, mighty
in strength', says the hero Gilgamesh to Ishtar, 'and thou hast
dug for him seven and seven pits! Thou hast loved the steed, proud
in battle, and destined him for the halter, the goad and the whip.'

Even for the gods Ishtar's love was fatal. In her youth the goddess
had loved Tammuz, god of the harvest, and – if we are to believe
Gilgamesh – this love caused the death of Tammuz. Ishtar was
overcome with grief and burst into lamentations over her dead
lover. In such a way, later, Aphrodite was to bewail the death
of Adonis.

In order to find Tammuz again and snatch him from his sad
abode, Ishtar conceived the audacious plan of descending into
the underworld, 'to journey towards that land without return,
towards that house from which he who enters does not come out
again'. She had the gates opened and penetrated the seven precincts,
at each gate stripping off one by one a piece of adornment or dress:
the great crown from her head, pendants from her ears, the necklace
from her throat, the jewels from her breast, her girdle adorned with
birthstones, the bracelets from her hands and from her feet; and
finally the garment which covered her nakedness. She arrived in
the presence of Ereshkigal, queen of the infernal regions. But
Ereshkigal called Namtaru, her messenger, and ordered him to
lock up Ishtar in the palace and to let loose against her the sixty
maladies. Thus Ishtar was a prisoner, and on earth there was
desolation and in the heavens great sorrow. Shamash and Sin,
her father, carried their grief to Ea. Ea, in order to deliver Ishtar,
thereupon created the effeminate Asushu-Namir and sent him to
the land of no return, instructed with magic words to restrain the
will of Ereshkigal. In vain the queen of the infernal regions strove
to resist. In vain did she attempt 'to enchant Asushu-Namir with
a great enchantment'. Ea's spell was mightier than her own, and
Ereshkigal had to set Ishtar free. Ishtar was sprinkled with the
water of life and, conducted by Namtaru, again passed through
the seven gates, recovering at each the adornment she had abandoned.

In spite of the violence of her character Ishtar's heart was not
a stranger to kindness. Mortals often experienced her benefactions.
Many a king owed his elevation to the throne to Ishtar's love and
the story of Sargon, King of Agade, related by himself, is significant.

'My mother was a priestess. I did not know my father. The
priestess, my mother, conceived me and gave birth to me in hiding.
She placed me in a basket made of reeds and closed the lid with
pitch. She put the basket in the river which was not high. The river
carried me away and brought me to Akki who was a man responsible for libations. Akki looked upon me with kindness and drew

Colossal human-headed winged bull from the palace of Sargon II
at Khorsabad. This awe-inspiring figure represents a benevolent genie
and was one of a pair which together guarded an entrance to the palace.
It wears the horned head-dress of divinity and is provided with five legs
as it was intended to be seen from both the front
and the side. Eighth century B.C.

Ningirsu, god of Lagash, clasping in one hand the eagle with
outstretched wings, his emblem, and in the other a club,
with which he seems to threaten the captives taken in his net.
Fragment of the Vulture Stela. Sumerian archaic art.
Beginning of the third millennium. Louvre.

Eagle-headed winged genie carrying a vessel of lustral water
and a pine-cone sprinkler – one of the benevolent genie who
accompanied men in their daily lives and protected them
from disease and evil forces. His long fringed robe is held at
the waist by a belt into which a dagger is thrust and he wears
thonged sandals on his feet.
Assyrian bas-relief in marble. 885 B.C.

me from the river. He adopted me as his child and brought me
up. He made me his gardener. It was while I was his gardener
that the goddess Ishtar loved me. Then I became king.' (Dhorme's
translation.)

Those whom she cherished Ishtar treated with maternal tenderness. Addressing Ashurbanipal she says:

My face covers thy face like a mother over the fruit of her womb,
I will place thee like a graven jewel between my breasts,
During the night will I give thee covering.
During the day I shall clothe thee,
Fear not, oh my little one, whom I have raised.

Sovereign of the world by virtue of love's omnipotence, Ishtar
was the most popular goddess in Assyria and Babylonia. Under
the name Astarte she was one of the great goddesses of Phoenicia
and bequeathed more than one of her traits to the Greek Aphrodite.

Ninurta. Ishtar completes the great triad of the astral deities. In
Sumer and Akkad, however, another god continued to be honoured
who was of much the same character and who has been identified
with the constellation Orion. His name, according to place, was
variously Ningirsu or Ninurta.

Ningirsu, who was worshipped at Lagash, was the son of Enlil.
Ninurta was similarly a part of the Enlil cycle. Ningirsu, patron
of a part of the city of Lagash, was not only concerned with irriga-
tion, as 'the god of fields and canals, who brings fertility', but was
also a war-god and this is the aspect which Ninurta retained, a
hunter and warrior. He was called the 'champion of the celestial
gods'. He was the 'strong one who destroys the wicked and the
enemy'. His weapon and attribute was a kind of club flanked by
two S-shaped snakes.

The warlike disposition of Ninurta caused a fearful coalition to
rise against him, in which the whole of nature joined. The very
stones took part in the struggle. Some ranged themselves on the
side of Ninurta while others went to swell the ranks of his enemies.
When Ninurta emerged victorious he did not forget his humble
allies. He blessed the stones which had remained faithful to him
and cursed the others. And that is why certain stones such as the
amethyst and lapis-lazuli shine with such glittering brilliance, are
valued by man and are reserved for noble usage while others are
trodden under foot in disdain.

Ningirsu's wife was the goddess Bau, daughter of Anu, she who
breathed into men the breath of life. Every year, on New Year's
Day, the solemn nuptials of Ningirsu and Bau were celebrated.
The goddess was ushered into the bridal chamber in the midst of
a cortège of worshippers who bore wedding gifts. To this divine
couple were born septuplet virgins. At other places and times
Bau's role was assumed by others, such as Nin-Karrak or Gula.

GODS OF THE STORM AND WINDS

We have already seen that the god of Nippur, Enlil, was the
god of the hurricane, 'Lord of the winds'. But when he became
Lord or *ba'al* of the earth, Enlil slowly lost this primitive character.

Adad. From the beginning of the second millennium the mastery
of the storm was conferred on a special divinity: Adad. Adad is
usually represented standing on a bull and grasping thunderbolts
in each hand; he is the god of lightning and the tempest. It is he
who lets loose the storm, makes the thunder growl and bends the
trees under the fury of the winds. Enveloped in black clouds he
roars with his mighty voice. While Bêl decreed the deluge Adad
executed his will, and the tumult rose to the very heavens.

But Adad's aspect was not always so terrifying. Adad, the tempest-
god, was also the god who brought the beneficent wind and with
it the welcome rains. He was the god of the inundation which
fertilises, he who each year caused the river to rise and cover the
earth with nourishing slime. Hence, when Bêl wished to send a
series of plagues to chastise men he first addressed Adad: 'From
on high Adad hoarded the rains. Below, the flood-waters were
stubborn and no longer rose in the springs. The abundance of the
fields diminished.'

Finally, Adad shared with Shamash the privilege of revealing
the future. He was also the 'Lord of Foresight'.

Mythological scene. Two winged deities wearing horned head-dresses and bearing vessels of lustral water stand on either side of a floating female figure wearing a tiara. Above her she supports a winged disk, the emblem of the god Asshur, while from two vases in the heavens two streams of water pour into two similar vases on the earth. Impression from a late Assyrian chalcedony cylinder seal. 990 to 600 B.C.

In his various functions Adad was associated with his companion, the goddess Shala.

FIRE GODS

May Gibil devour you! May Gibil catch you!
May Gibil kill you! May Gibil consume you!

Such was the imprecation pronounced by the wizard, the Ashipu, as he consigned to the flames the clay image of a sorcerer whose malignant charm he wished to break, or – infallible method of destroying spells – as he burned a peeled onion and a crushed date.

GIBIL, the divinity thus invoked, was the god of fire and was called the son of Anu.

Another fire-god was NUSKU whose attribute was a lamp shaped like a wooden clog. More especially he represented the sacred fire which consumed burnt offerings and carried their delectable fragrance up to the gods. Thus he was called 'Bêl's sublime messenger'. He was invoked during sacrifices:

Without thee, a banquet cannot be prepared in the temple,
Without thee, the great gods cannot breathe the incense.

Gibil and Nusku helped – and sometimes took the place of – Sin and Shamash in dispensing justice.

O mighty Nusku, warrior-god! He burns the wicked,
He orders and decrees, he is attentive to the smallest fault;
Equitable judge, he sees into the hearts of men,
He makes justice and law to shine forth.
O Gibil, the powerful, the roaring tempest,
Thou governor of gods and kings,
Thou sittest in judgment on the unjust judge.

WATER GODS

Enki (or Ea), god of the Apsu, was the principal divinity of the liquid elements. But he had a daughter, the goddess NANSHE who shared his functions. She was the goddess of springs and canals. Like her father she was particularly honoured in Eridu, the holy city, which was situated at the mouth of the Apsu. She was also worshipped at Lagash and each year, on a canal near the city, there was a procession of boats to escort the sacred barge in which the goddess rode. Nanshe's emblem was a vase in which a fish swam.

Finally, the rivers too were deified. They were invoked not only as the creators of all things but also as instruments of the gods' justice.

It is thou, O river, who judges man's judgment,
O great river, O river sublime, O river of the sanctuaries.

The god Shamash dictates his laws to Hammurabi. Top of the Stela of Hammurabi. About 2000 B.C. Louvre.

Ashur-bani-pal building a temple to a god. On his head the great Assyrian emperor bears the brick basket which marked the founder of a temple. The first great private collector of books known to history, it was in his library at Nineveh that were discovered the tablets containing the text of the story of Gilgamesh. Stone stele from Babylon. Seventh century B.C.

EARTH GODS

From remotest times the Earth-mother was worshipped under the names of Ga-Tum-Dug at Lagash, of Bau and Innini at Der and at Kish, or of Gula and of Ninkhursag.

All these divinities represented, like the Gaea of the Greeks, the great creative principle.

Later the specialised role of these earth divinities became more marked.

Over the harvest presided Nisaba, goddess of the grain, the Babylonian Ceres. She was the sister of Nanshe.

The vine had its own goddess: Geshtin.

But the chief vegetation god was Tammuz, who was probably originally a tree god.

Tammuz, or Dumuzi, to use a more original form of the name, was the son of Ningishzida, 'Lord of the wood of life', whose own father was Ninazu, 'Lord of Soothsaying by means of water'. He was loved by Ishtar but, for a mysterious and doubtless involuntary reason, this love caused his death. Like the ear of corn which the reaper's scythe cuts off in the glory of its yellow ripeness, Tammuz, the harvest-god, was ravished by death in the fullness of youth, and forced to descend into the underworld. Heartbroken by the death of her lover Ishtar bewailed her sorrow in bitter lamentations which she poured forth from the midst of a choir of weeping men and women. This tradition was perpetuated among the people and each year when the earth, sweltering under the summer sun, had lost its harvest mantle, the death of Tammuz was bewailed in funeral chants. Similarly at Byblos the 'passion' of Adonis was commemorated by public mourning.

Ishtar descended into the infernal regions to dispute with her sister Ereshkigal possession of the 'lover of her youth'. Tammuz returned to the abode of the gods and remained thenceforth at the gate of Anu where with his father Ningishzida he stood guardian.

Ashur-nazir-pal II accompanied by a genie. In this bas-relief the Assyrian emperor is shown followed by a winged, eagle-headed divinity who carries a lustral vase and a pine-cone sprinkler with which he makes a purificatory gesture over the king. Stone bas-relief, 883 to 859 B.C.

GODS CONCERNED WITH THE LIFE OF MAN

The Origin of Humanity: The Deluge. Whether man was moulded by Marduk with his own blood, whether he was born of the union of Marduk and the goddess Aruru, or whether – as they told at Eridu – he had been fashioned by the goddess Mami from clay mixed with the blood of a god whom Ea had slain, one point is clear: namely, that humanity was the work of divine hands – men were children of the gods.

Nevertheless the gods one day resolved to destroy the human race. The motive for this remains unexplained. Assembled in the town of Shuruppak, which is situated on the banks of the Euphrates, the great gods Anu, Enlil, Ninurta and Ennugi decided to drown the earth with a deluge. But Ea, who was also present, took pity on mankind. He confided the secret of the project to a reedhut. As Ea intended, the secret was overheard by an inhabitant of Shuruppak named Uta-Napishtim:

Man of Shuruppak, son of Ubar-Tutu,

Destroy thy house, build a vessel,
Leave thy riches, seek thy life,
Store in thy vessel the seeds of all of life.

Uta-Napishtim listened to Ea's advice and set to work without delay. He built a great ship a hundred and twenty cubits high. He loaded it with all he possessed in gold and silver. He took his family aboard and herded in his cattle, together with the animals and birds of the land. Meanwhile the hour appointed by Shamash had arrived. That evening the Lord of Shadows caused the rain to fall, a rain of filth. Uta-Napishtim hastened to board his vessel and make fast the door.

When dawn broke
A cloud black as night rose from heaven's foundation.
Within it Adad bellowed!
Shullat and Khanish march at the head,
Nergal tears away the mast.
He comes, Ninurta, he spurs the attack,

The Anunnaki are bearing torches,
Their brilliance lights up the land,
Adad's tumult reaches the skies,
All that is bright is changed into darkness.

The terror which spread through the universe reached the gods themselves. Seized with fear they sought refuge in the sky of Anu. They crouched like dogs on the ramparts and their burning lips quivered with fright. Ishtar 'cried out like a woman in labour'. She repented having supported, perhaps even provoked, the decision of the gods. She had not contemplated a chastisement so dreadful.

May that day become as mud,
That day when I spoke evil to the assembled gods,
For I spoke evil to the assembled gods,
In order that my people might perish, I commanded the battle.
I give birth to my people!
Like the spawn of fish they fill the sea!

But nothing could stop the scourge. 'Six days and six nights the winds were abroad and the deluge descended.' At last, on the dawn of the seventh day the evil wind grew peaceful, the sea became calm; the voices of men were stilled, 'and all mankind was changed into mud'.

At this spectacle Uta-Napishtim could not hold back his tears. Meanwhile his ship had come to rest on the summit of Mount Nisir, the only land which had emerged from the waves. Uta-Napishtim let loose a dove and then a swallow, but they came back to the ship, having found nowhere to alight. A raven, in his turn released, did not come back at all. Then Uta-Napishtim came out from his boat. He poured a libation and placed a burnt offering on the summit of the mountain. With joy the gods smelled the good odour of sacrifice. Only Enlil was enraged to see that some mortals had escaped the disaster. But Ea managed to appease him by carefully chosen words. In token of reconciliation Enlil took Uta-Napishtim and his wife by the hand. He touched them on the face and said:

Formerly Uta-Napishtim was a human being,
Now Uta-Napishtim and his wife will be like unto us, gods.

And he fixed their abode 'far away, at the mouth of the rivers', in an inviolable retreat.

Gods and Men. Numerous divinities presided over the various phases of human life. When a mother felt the first pains of labour Mami was invoked, she who had created the new race of men. BELIT-ILI, 'the Lady of the Gods', who then took the name NINTUD, or 'The Lady of Childbirth', also watched over the birth of the newly born whose destiny was determined, from the moment of his arrival in the world, by the goddess MAMMITU.

The entire course of human life was, moreover, regulated by the sovereign will of the gods, whose chief attribute was deciding the fates of men. We have already seen how highly the gods valued this privilege which fell successively to Anu, Enlil, Ea and Marduk. Although it was the supreme god who made the final decision, all could discuss it. At the beginning of every year, while on earth the festival of the Zagmuk was being celebrated, the gods assembled in the Upshukina, the Sanctuary of Fates. The king of the gods in the later Babylonian period, Bêl-Marduk, took his place on the throne. The other gods knelt with fear and respect before him. Removing from his bosom the Tablet of Fates, Bêl-Marduk confided it to his son Nabu, who wrote down on it what the gods had decided. Thus the fate of the country was fixed for the coming year.

These decisions naturally remained secret. Men could, however, receive warnings from the gods, either in dreams or by apparitions. Dreams were sent to men by the god ZAQAR, the messenger of Sin. If they were too obscure one consulted the goddess NANSHE, 'the interpreter of dreams'. Apparitions were less frequent and only occurred to people of importance. Thus it was that Gudea, who reigned at Lagash, undertook the construction of the temple of Ningirsu in that city on the formal order of the god who had appeared to him while he was asleep. 'In the midst of my dreaming, a man as tall as the sky, as big as the earth, who as to his head was a god, as to his arms was the divine bird Imdugud, as to his feet was the hurricane, to the right and left of whom crouched a lion, has ordered me to construct his house...'

Happiness and unhappiness came from the gods. It was they

The goddess Ishtar riding on a lion. 'The goddess of the morn and the goddess of the evening', Ishtar was the personification of the planet Venus and was both a goddess of love and of war. Here she is depicted in her role as warrior goddess as 'Lady of Battles', armed and riding on her sacred animal, the lion. On her headdress she wears a star. Bas-relief on a stone stele from Tell Ahmar. Eighth century B.C.

who sent disease, having for this purpose recourse to IRRA, an aspect of NERGAL, king of the underworld, and NAMTAR, a plague demon. Men's health, on the other hand, depended especially on the goddess NIN-KARRAK and on the goddess GULA. Both were thought to be daughters of Anu. Gula could at will inflict illness or restore health. She was called 'the Great Doctoress' and her symbol was a dog.

Morality was also under the control of a deity. We have seen that Shamash and Nusku were the gods of justice. The same role was shared by KADI, the goddess of Der who had at first symbolised the creative earth. Kadi's attribute was a snake with, sometimes, a human bust.

Intellectual activity was placed under the protection of NABU whose principal sanctuary was at Borsippa, near Babylon. Nabu was the son of Marduk. The prestige of his father was reflected on to him and in the end he took over some of the paternal power. We have already seen how on the day when destinies were determined it was Nabu who engraved the gods' decisions on the sacred tablets. But his role was not confined to that of a simple scribe: he could, at will, increase or diminish the number of days allotted to each mortal being, and from this he derived his importance. Nabu had been chosen as secretary of the assembled gods because he – and his wife TASHMETUM – had invented writing. For this reason he also presided over *belles-lettres*. His attribute – like that of his father Marduk – was the serpent-headed dragon, and additionally the chisel and engraving tablet.

Various other divinities presided over men's arts and crafts. We have seen that Ea was the patron of carpenters and goldsmiths. The latter also appealed to the god GUHKIN-BANDA, if we can

The famous stone lion of Babylon. Under its feet it tramples the body of a man. Too heavy to be removed by the archaeologists, the lion still stands among the ruins of the city. It probably dates from the first millennium B.C.

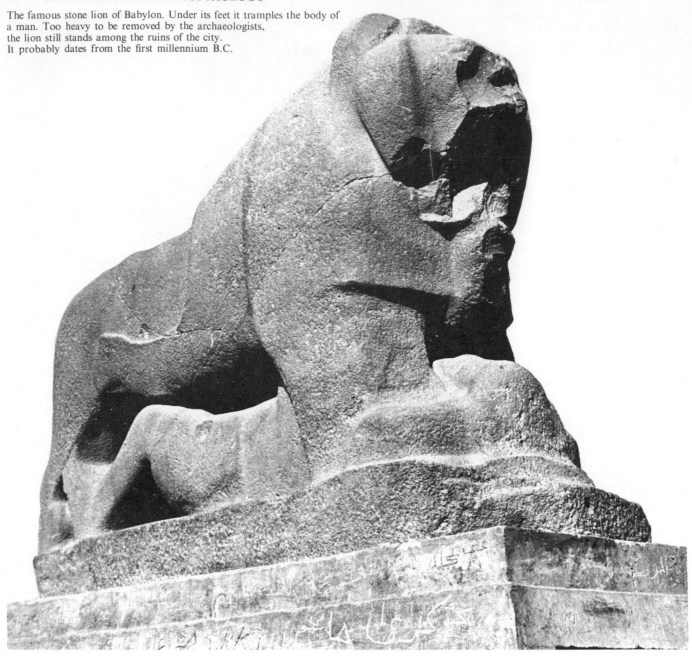

believe Ashurbanipal's statement: 'With the help of the god Guhkin-Banda I have made as an offering an artistic platter in bright gold.'

THE UNDERWORLD AND ITS DIVINITIES

Under the earth, beyond the abyss of the Apsu, lay the infernal dwelling-place to which men descended after death. It was the 'Land of no return', 'the house from which he who enters does not come out'. What hope was there to escape from this kingdom defended by seven-fold walls? To enter it a man had successively to penetrate seven gates, abandoning at each a part of his apparel. When the last gate had closed behind him he found himself naked and imprisoned for ever in the 'dwelling-place of the shadows'. The audacious Ishtar who had imprudently ventured into the land of no return was unable to escape, goddess though she was, and remained there a prisoner. To free her nothing less than the aid of Ea and the power of his magic incantations had been required. Sometimes the gods gave an especially privileged inhabitant of the underworld permission to come up for a moment into the light. Thus Enkidu, the companion of the hero Gilgamesh, was authorised to go and tell his friend what took place in the kingdom of the shadows. It was a sad picture. In these regions of eternal darkness the souls of the dead – *edimmu* – 'clad, like birds, in a garment of wings' are all jumbled together:

In the house of dust
Live lord and priest,

Live the wizard and the prophet...
Live those whom the great gods
Have anointed in the abyss.
Dusk is their nourishment
And their food is mud.

Only certain *edimmu*, especially favoured, had the right to a bed and fresh water.

As well as the souls of the dead the underworld also contained the 'captive gods' – Kingu and his accomplices who in the great civil war among the gods had taken the side of Tiamat and been vanquished by Marduk.

Over all this subterranean world reigned the goddess Ereshkigal, 'Princess of the great earth'. Originally she was sole sovereign. But one day the god NERGAL, 'Lord of the great dwelling' – who under another form bore the name Meshlamthea – invaded the infernal regions. With him were fourteen demons whom he posted at the different gates. To obtain peace Ereshkigal consented to take Nergal for her husband. 'Thou shalt be my husband', she said to him, 'and I shall be thy wife. I shall make thee ruler over the vast kingdom and place in thy hand the tablet of wisdom.' And so Nergal, who until then had been god of destruction and war, became the overlord of the dead. His symbol was a sword or a lion's head. To administer his commands he had Namtaru, god of the plague, 'who crouches by Nergal'. Among other infernal deities we meet BELILI, the sister of Tammuz, and the scribe BELIT-SERI.

Gilgamesh with two gods. In the centre, twin figures of the hero holding a gate-post stand on either side of a water-god with two streams of water flowing from his waist who stands in a shrine surrounded by water. This is possibly a representation of the water-god Ea in his dwelling, the House of the Apsu. On the left, a minor deity approaches in an attitude of worship. Impression from an Akkadian cylinder seal. 2340 to 2180 B.C.

THE GENII

Inferior to the gods but nevertheless participating in their nature and sharing certain prerogatives with them were the genii, the *utukku*. They were divided into two groups, the good and the evil. Even more than the gods they played a major role in the daily life of man.

The good genii, who were called *shedu* or *lamassu*, acted as guardian spirits. They defended the individual against evil powers, carried his homage to the gods and drew down on him divine favour. They could be seen standing before the gates of temples in the form of winged bulls with human heads. But their duty was not only to stand guard over sacred enclosures. Invisible but omnipresent they remained at a man's side, following him in the streets and into battle; for, as it was said, 'he who has no god when he walks in the street wears a headache like a garment'.

This was because men were constantly exposed to malignant forces, represented by the evil *utukku*. These were, firstly, the *edimmu* – the souls of the dead – who had not received burial or whose funeral rites had been neglected: they avenged themselves by tormenting the living. They could, to be sure, be appeased by the offer of a funeral repast, the *Kispu*, or by a libation of water. But there were other, more redoubtable *utukku* to be reckoned with. These evil genii issued from the lower world, the *arallu*, or emanated from the bile of Ea, and overwhelmed men with disease, inspired them to criminal acts, spread disunion among families, decimated the flocks. They were rightly compared with 'the storm which breaks loose with fury in the skies', or the 'rising wind which casts darkness over the bright day'. There was no way of appeasing them, 'for they heeded neither prayer nor supplication'. We have seen how they had no respect even for the gods and how they dared to attack Sin whose benevolent light they attempted to eclipse. Who precisely were these malevolent spirits? It is not known, only that 'they do not take wives and beget no children'. Seven of them were particularly dangerous. 'They were born in the Mountain of the West, they dwell in holes in the ground, they live among the ruin of the earth.' When they appeared to mortals it was in the form of terrifying creatures, as for example an apparition with a human body, the head of a lion bristling with horns, and feet armed with powerful claws. They could not be driven away except by incantations. The victim had recourse to the exorcist – the *ashipu* – who in Ea's name pronounced the liberating formula:

Evil *alu*, turn thy breast and depart!
O, inhabitant of the ruins, get thee to thy ruins;
For the great Lord Ea has sent me:

He has made his incantation fitting for my mouth,
He has given into my hand the cauldron for the Seven, according to the holy ordinances.

THE HEROES

Tradition retained the memory of legendary persons who had been in direct contact with the gods and whose adventures were of a mythical character. The most famous of these – omitting Uta-Napishtim, the hero of the deluge – were Etana, Adapa and above all Gilgamesh. If we wish to attribute a moral significance to these myths we can interpret them as men's efforts to rise above their wretched surroundings, conquer the heavens and achieve immortality.

Etana. In the days before there was a king on earth, when the 'sceptre, the diadem, the crown and the staff of office were placed before Anu in the heavens' the great Anunnaki, who determined men's fate, held counsel on the subject of the earth. The gods, especially Ishtar and Enlil, set about finding a king for men and, it seemed, chose Etana. All went well, until Etana complained that he had no heir. He addressed Shamash and said:

O my Lord, by your order let it come forth:
Grant me the herb of birth.
Tell me which is the herb of birth.
Set aside my shame, set for me a name.

Shamash, to whom Etana's libations and offerings of wild sheep had been agreeable, answered him: 'Take to the road and reach the mountain.'

Now this mountain had recently been the scene of a drama enacted by an eagle and a serpent. The two creatures lived side by side with their progeny. One day the eagle conceived the criminal design of eating the serpent's little ones. He accomplished the heinous crime in spite of the wise remonstrance of one of his little ones, 'young, but very intelligent', who put into him the fear of Shamash's wrath:

The net, the spell of Shamash would fall upon thee and seize thee.
He who trespasses on what is Shamash's, Shamash will punish him with his own hand.

And the serpent, in fact, brought his plaint before the god of justice, who said to him:

Take to the road and reach the mountain.
I will keep thee a buffalo.

Open his interior and pierce his belly!
Make thy habitation in his belly.
Birds of all kinds will descend from the sky.
The eagle will descend with them.
He will seize on the flesh.
When he comes inside the beast thou shalt clutch him by the
    wing:
Cut off his wings, his pinions, his claws,
Tear him and throw him into a ditch;
Let him die there from hunger and thirst!

And so it was done. Deceived by the serpent's stratagem, the eagle
fell into his power and was condemned to perish slowly in the ditch.

When Etana had come to the mountain he found the eagle in his
prison and, as Shamash had counselled him to do, he asked for the
herb which would give him a son. The eagle promised to procure
it for him as soon as he had regained his strength. For eight months
Etana brought food until the eagle was at last able to fly again.
He offered to carry Etana up to the very sky of Anu.

On my bosom place thy back,
In the feathers of my wings place thy hands,
Place thy flanks on my flanks,
And I shall carry thee to Anu's sky.

Either from curiosity, or ambition to seize the insignia of power, or,
more probably, in the hope of obtaining the wondrous herb, Etana
accepted; and the two companions soared into the air. At the end
of three double-hours the sea below looked to Etana no more than
'a small ditch in a garden'. The travellers reached the sky of Anu
without incident and prostrated themselves before the gods. But
the eagle wished to fly further until he reached Ishtar. For two
double-hours more they rose and Etana marvelled to see the earth
turn into a garden while the vast sea was like a basket. But at the
third double-hour he was seized by vertigo. In vain he cried to
the eagle: 'My friend, I can climb no higher into the sky! Stop!'
The fall was appalling. The eagle spun downwards with Etana and
the two imprudent ones crashed to the ground.

Adapa. In the holy city of Eridu, Adapa had been created by Ea to
reign among men. The god had given him great wisdom and extreme
prudence; only immortality, reserved for the gods, had been denied
him. Every day Adapa issued from the enclosure of Eridu, approached the bright harbour and, boarding his boat, sailed out on to the
broad sea to fish. One day while he was fishing the South Wind rose,
upset his boat and sent Adapa to the home of fishes. In a fury Adapa
broke the wings of the South Wind, and for seven days the wind
blew no more. Anu grew uneasy and, learning of the affair, summoned Adapa into his presence with the intention of offering him
the food of death.

But Ea, who watched over his protégé, taught him how to conciliate the gods who kept vigil at Anu's threshold, at the same time
warning him to accept from Anu neither food nor drink. Adapa
then put on a robe of mourning and, conducted by Ilabrat, Anu's
messenger, arrived at the gates of heaven. There he met the two
guardians, Tammuz and Ningishzida, who, seeing him, asked:
'Man, for whom dost thou wear a robe of mourning?' Adapa
answered as Ea had instructed him to do: 'On earth two gods have
perished and therefore do I wear mourning.' 'And who are these
gods?' they asked, and Adapa replied: 'Tammuz and Ningishzida.'
Delighted with this mark of respect Tammuz and Ningishzida
ushered Adapa into Anu's presence and interceded on his behalf.
The great god was appeased and, wishing in his turn to honour the
magnanimous Adapa he offered him the Food of Life. But Adapa
remembered Ea's warning and refused either to eat or drink. This
was how he lost the chance to become immortal.

Was he the victim of bad luck, or was it not that Ea, whom nothing
escaped, had foreseen Anu's offer and had not willed that Adapa –
and with him humanity – should acquire that immortality which
he had judged it best to deny him?

Gilgamesh. Of all the Assyro-Babylonian heroes the most famous
is certainly Gilgamesh whose figure and exploits have been im-
mortalised in a vast poem, the masterpiece of Babylonian literature,
and entitled, according to how it is interpreted, either as 'He who
discovered the source' or 'He who saw all'.

The chief text which we possess comes from the Library of
Ashurbanipal of Nineveh and dates from the seventh century B.C.
It comprises twelve cantos of about three hundred verses each.
The poem, however, is much more ancient, for a Babylonian
fragment of it has been preserved which goes back to the beginning
of the second millennium.

The hero of the poem – Gilgamesh – does not seem to have been
purely imaginary. It is generally agreed that he was a king of the
land of Sumer who reigned in the third millennium over the city of
Uruk or Erech in probable succession to the king Dumuzi. Among
the chiefs of these small Sumerian towns Gilgamesh doubtless
distinguished himself for his courage and the success of his enterprises. As happened in similar cases a legend grew up about him
and he became the central figure in a series of marvellous adventures
which form the material of the poem of which the following is a
résumé:

Over the ancient walled city of Erech, where Anu had his earthly
dwelling, 'Eanna the holy', there once reigned a wise but despotic
prince whose name was Gilgamesh. 'His two-thirds was a god, his
other third a man.' He spread consternation among local families,
taking daughters from their fathers, maidens from heroes, wives
from their husbands. The inhabitants of Erech complained to the
gods. The gods, too, were moved and spoke to Aruru the Great:
'Thou hast created Gilgamesh. Now create another man in his image
so that they shall fight each other and leave Erech in peace.' Aruru
took mud, cut it and from it fashioned in Anu's image the hero
Enkidu – who was also called Eabani. His body was covered with
hair; on his head his hair was like a woman's, 'growing like the
harvest'. He grew up in the desert among the wild beasts.

With gazelles he ate the grass,
With the cattle he quenched his thirst,
With the flocks his heart rejoiced to drink.

In order to defend his friends, the beasts, he filled in the trenches
dug by hunters, removed the nets they had spread and, as his
strength equalled an army of Anu, no one dared to venture into the
desert. It was decided to seize him. But how? Gilgamesh suggested
an expedient:
Go, my hunter, and take with thee a harlot. While he accompanies
his flock to the drinking trough, she – let her remove her robe. Let
him take his pleasure of her. He will see her and approach her.

Thus it was done. Posted near the drinking trough the hunter
and the harlot, after waiting for two days, saw Enkidu and his
familiar flock arrive. The girl exposed her bosom and drew off her
robe. Enkidu was overcome with passion and lay with her. When
he had his fill of pleasure he returned to his flock, but upon seeing
him the gazelles fled. 'The desert cattle shunned him.' Deprived
of his innocence Enkidu was no longer worthy to live in familiarity
with animals. In vain he tried to rejoin them. His knees betrayed
him, his body was as though paralysed. He returned and sat sadly
at the harlot's feet and she completed his enslavement by flattering
words.

Thou art beautiful, Enkidu, thou art like a god.
Why dost thou roam the desert with wild flocks?
Come! I shall lead thee to Erech within the walls,
Where Gilgamesh is perfect in strength
And, like a wild ox, has established himself over the people.

And without resistance Enkidu let himself be conducted to Erech.
Meanwhile Gilgamesh, in his palace, was disturbed by a dream:
in his sleep he had seen a man of prodigious strength with whom
he had vainly attempted to struggle. He went to find his mother
Ninsun who 'knew all knowledge' and confided to her his uneasiness.

My mother, I have seen a dream in the night:
Whilst there were stars in the heavens,
Someone swooped down upon me like an army of Anu;
I bore him and he was stronger than I,
His anger I repulsed violently, but I could not shake him off...
I overlaid him like a woman.
I laid him at thy feet:
Thou madest him measure himself with me.

Ninsun, who knew all knowledge, reassured her son. The dream
signified that Enkidu, who surpassed Gilgamesh in strength, would

The hero Gilgamesh holding a
lion that he has captured.
Bas-relief from Khorsabad.
Eighth century B.C. Louvre.

Gilgamesh watering a bull from a gushing vase. Cylinder seal. Clercq Collection.

Detail of the Ishtar Gate of Babylon. Dedicated to the goddess whose name it bears, this great double gate spanned the processional way linking the temple of Marduk with the palace of Nebuchadnezzar. It is decorated with bulls and dragons, the animals sacred to Adad and Marduk, in brown, white and yellow on a blue ground. Reconstruction in the Berlin Museum from the original glazed bricks. Between 604 and 561 B.C.

become his friend. And indeed when Enkidu presented himself at the palace, after a fierce wrestling bout, Gilgamesh welcomed him with friendliness and the two sat down side by side like brothers.

Enkidu became Gilgamesh's inseparable companion and led a royal existence. He was dressed in a magnificent robe, he slept in a well-made bed and sat in peace at Gilgamesh's left hand. The kings of the earth kissed his feet and the people of Erech acclaimed him with their voices. One night, however, Enkidu had a bad dream: a mysterious being with sombre visage and the claws of an eagle carried him above the clouds and cast him into the house of shadows where Nergal dwelt, 'the house from which he who enters does not come out'.

When day broke Enkidu recounted his dream to Gilgamesh and described the vision he had brought back from the nether world. Gilgamesh filled a pot of jet with honey, filled a pot of lapis-lazuli with butter and offered them as gifts to Shamash. The god advised Gilgamesh to go and fight Khumbaba the Strong, king of the Cedar Mountain.

As soon as she heard of the project Ninsun, the mother of Gilgamesh, dressed in her sacred ornaments and went up to the terrace of the palace. There she offered incense to Shamash and addressed him with a mother's tears.

'Why,' she asked, 'hast thou given my child a heart which does not sleep? And now thou hast touched him and he is going away by far-off paths towards Khumbaba. He faces a combat which he understands not; he undertakes a campaign which he does not understand.'

In vain the inhabitants of Erech attempted to restrain Gilgamesh by pointing out the perils of the enterprise. Khumbaba was a terrifying monster, and it required a march of twenty thousand hours to reach his retreat. In vain Enkidu himself showed his distaste for the expedition. Gilgamesh stubbornly insisted on carrying out his plan. He closed his ears to the advice of his elders, overcame Enkidu's hesitations and the two friends set out.

The itinerary of Gilgamesh and Enkidu has been widely discussed. For long it was believed that the Mountain of the Cedars was in Elam, in the neighbourhood of Susa in south-west Persia. But Virolleaud, on the strength of new fragments of the poem recently deciphered, has demonstrated that the mysterious Mountain of the Cedars was probably the Amanus, the mountain which separates Syria on the north-west from Asia Minor. So Gilgamesh's expedition, stripped of its legendary trimmings, simply commemorates the first expeditions of the inhabitants of Babylonia, who, lacking wood and stone in their own land, ascended the Euphrates valley in search of these materials which they finally found on the rocky and wooded slopes of the Amanus.

But to return to our heroes. After a long journey they arrived at the green mountain, mantled with its forest of cedar, which was the domain of Khumbaba. Enlil had placed Khumbaba there to keep the cedars intact. His voice was a tempest, his mouth was the mouth of the gods, his breath was a wind. 'Whoever cuts down his cedars is stricken with infirmity.' Enkidu again wished to dissuade Gilgamesh 'My friend,' he said, 'let us not go into the forest. My hands are weak and my ribs are paralysed.' But Gilgamesh led him on.

Winged human-headed genie. Shown in profile, the divinity wears a tall horned headdress and carries a vessel of lustral water and a pine-cone sprinkler. Probably one of a pair guarding a gateway or a king. It was said of the man who was not accompanied by such a benevolent genie that he 'wears a headache like a garment'. Assyrian bas-relief. *c.* eighth century B.C.

Two winged deities with a sacred tree. The two bearded figures wearing horned headdresses kneeling on either side of a stylised tree, towards which they stretch out protective hands, probably represent Enlil, or Bel, the god of the earth, or perhaps his twin guardian figures. Sacred trees, or trees of life, were particularly associated with the worship of Enlil. Bas-relief from Nimrud. *c.* 900 B.C.

Two winged female deities with a sacred tree. Holding a ring in one hand and extending the other towards a sacred tree, these two figures probably represent Ninlil, or Beltis, the consort of Enlil, or Bel, or her twin guardian figures. Ninlil, or Beltis, was a fertility goddess and, in this case, the stylised growing tree may represent her. Bas-relief from the north-west palace of Nimrud. *c.* 900 B.C.

The forest, covered with majestic and sweet-smelling cedars, was the dwelling of the gods and the sanctuary of Irnini, probably a form of Ishtar. Before the two heroes stretched its shadows, filled with delights and well-traced paths. The two friends took a path and soon came to an enclosure which marked the beginning of Khumbaba's domain. Gilgamesh called aloud upon the monster and challenged him. But the savage guardian of the forest refused to reply. Before the fight began Gilgamesh took care to consult the omens. He made an offering to the dead, chanted the funeral dirge, dug a trench into which he threw seed-corn and, climbing to the summit of the mountain, invoked Shamash: 'O Lord,' he said, 'send a dream for Enkidu.' And suddenly in the middle of the night Gilgamesh awoke and spoke to Enkidu who knelt, watching beside him. 'My friend,' he said to Enkidu, 'didst thou not call me? Why have I awakened? Has not a god passed by? Why is my flesh overwhelmed? Dreaming I saw the heavens cry out and the earth

Part of the great stele of Ur-Nammu, king of Ur. Above, on the left, the king pours a libation to the goddess Ningal while, on the right, he offers a similar libation to her consort Nannar – the moon-god Sin. The builder of the great ziggurat at Ur, Ur-Nammu is shown below with mason's tools on his shoulder following a god. Relief carving on stone. Second millennium B.C.

roar. In the darkness lightning flashed, fire burst forth; death fell like rain. Then the fire was extinguished...' Enkidu presumably interpreted the dream as an omen of victory, though the next part of the text is lost. He invoked the aid of the gods and went into battle. The gods let loose the elements against Khumbaba who confessed himself vanquished and was slain by Gilgamesh.

After his triumph Gilgamesh purified himself of his battle-stains, rearranged his hair and put on clean raiment. He fastened his robe and resumed his crown. The goddess Ishtar saw the hero and, struck by his beauty, spoke to him:

Come, Gilgamesh, be my lover!
Be my husband and I shall be thy wife!
I shall harness thee a chariot of lapis-lazuli and gold.
Come into our dwelling, in the perfume of the cedars.
When thou comest in our dwelling
They who sit on thrones will kiss thy feet,
Kings will prostrate themselves before thee, Lords and Princes...

But Gilgamesh roughly repelled the goddess. He well knew how inconstant she was and what wretched fate she reserved for her lovers when they had ceased to please her.

Come, I will reveal thy harlotry!
For Tammuz, lover of thy youth,
Year after year thou hast mourned.
The bird, the 'little gardener', the speckled one,
Thou hast loved him:
And struck him and broken his wing!
Thou hast loved the lion, mighty in strength:
And thou hast dug for him seven and seven pits.
Thou hast loved the steed, proud in battle,
And destined him for the halter, the goad and the whip.
Thou hast loved the shepherd:
To thee each day he sacrificed his kids;
Thou hast struck him and changed him into a leopard...
Me, too, wilt thou now love – and like them transform.

On hearing these harsh words Ishtar smouldered with rage. She rose to the skies, approached Anu, her father, and said: 'Gilgamesh has cursed me! Gilgamesh has recounted my shame...To chastise his impudence create a celestial bull to send against him!' Anu granted his daughter's request. He sent against Gilgamesh a furious

bull who was about to overthrow the hero when Enkidu rushed to his assistance, seized the beast by its tail and tore it to pieces. Then, seeing Ishtar on the walls of Erech, weeping in the midst of her sacred courtesans, he skinned off the right flank of the celestial bull and flung it derisively into the goddess's face, saying: 'And thou too, let me but catch thee – I shall do as much to thee.'

Gilgamesh removed the bull's vast horns, which could hold much oil, and reserved them for the ritual of anointing required by the cult of Lugal-banda for whom he had an especial veneration. After which the two friends, having washed their hands in the Euphrates, returned to Erech amidst the acclamations of the people who cried:

Gilgamesh is dazzling among men!
Gilgamesh is mighty among men!

Having accomplished their marvellous exploits our heroes rested. But the cruel Ishtar meditated her revenge. Enkidu was stricken with illness and for twelve days struggled against it. Thus was fulfilled the funereal dream which had disturbed him at the beginning of the poem. At dawn on the thirteenth day Enkidu expired in the arms of his friend. Gilgamesh bewailed him:

Enkidu, my friend, my little brother, who chased the tiger of the desert;
Together have we gone everywhere and climbed mountains:
What sleep has seized thee now?
Darkness has come over thee and thou hearest me not!

He felt his heart and his heart no longer beat. Suddenly seized with panic before the corpse Gilgamesh rushed from his palace and fled through the countryside. Those whom he met said to him:

Why is thy strength devoured? Why is thy face lowered?
Thy heart is in a sorry state; thy features are cast down.
And there is sorrow in thy bowels;
Sadness and mourning burn thy visage.

And Gilgamesh answered them:

Why should I not flee through the land?
Enkidu, my friend, my little brother, who chased the panther of the desert,
My friend who with me killed lions,
My friend who faced with me all difficulties,

His fate has overtaken him.
Six days and six nights have I wept over him.
Then was I afraid of death and I fled through the land.
My friend whom I loved has become like unto mud.
And I, must I too, lie down like him and never rise again?

So it was the fear of death which made Gilgamesh flee.

But where could he discover the secret of how to escape this inevitable fate? Finally he thought of going to consult Uta-Napishtim, that fortunate man who, having survived the deluge, had received from the gods the gift of immortality. To reach him the road was long and dangerous. To Gilgamesh that mattered not: he would face all perils.

If I meet lions and am afraid,
I shall raise my head and call upon Sin;
To Ishtar, courtesan of the gods, my prayers shall rise.

First he reached Mount Mashu. It was here that every evening the sun sought repose. The gates of the mountain were guarded by scorpion-men whose heads touched the terrace of the gods and whose breasts reached the netherworld. 'Their dazzling brilliance overthrew mountains.'

Seeing them Gilgamesh felt his face grow dark with fear and horror. Nevertheless he recovered his courage and bowed before them. A scorpion-man, who had recognised in Gilgamesh the flesh of the gods, obligingly indicated the route, and the hero strode forward into the depths of the mountain. For eleven double-hours he marched through impenetrable darkness. Finally, at the twelfth double-hour, the light again shone, and Gilgamesh found himself in a wonderful garden which lay beside the sea. Before him rose the tree of the gods whose fruits, magnificent to behold, were borne on branches of lapis-lazuli. The ground was strewn with precious stones. This place of delights was the dwelling of the goddess Siduri Sabitu (that is, the inn-keeper) 'who lives at the edge of the sea'. At the sight of the hero, dressed in the skin of a wild animal, Siduri took fright and locked herself in her house. But Gilgamesh threatened to break the bolt and smash in the door. The goddess then consented to listen to him. When he had told her the object of his journey she first pointed out that it was useless.

O Gilgamesh, why dost thou run in all directions?
The life thou seekest thou shalt never find.
When the gods created man
They gave him Death.
Life they kept in their own hands.

Let Gilgamesh, then, be satisfied with earthly joys.

Fill thy belly,
Night and day rejoice,
Make every day a festival!
Put on lavish raiment,
Let thy head be washed! Wash thee with water,
Consider the child who grasps thy hand,
Let thy wife rejoice on thy bosom!

Moreover, to what perils would he not expose himself if he persisted in his design:

O Gilgamesh! There has never been a way,
And no one since the days of old has passed the sea.
The way is hard and the road is rough,
And deep are the waters of Death which close the entrance.
Where, then, Gilgamesh, shalt thou pass over the sea?
When thou reachest the waters of Death, what shalt thou do?

Being, however, unable to overcome the hero's stubbornness Siduri advised him to seek Urshanabi, Uta-Napishtim's boatman, who alone could guide him on this difficult voyage.

Urshanabi bade Gilgamesh cut in the forest a hundred and twenty poles each sixty cubits long. After that he invited him on board his boat. They reached the waters of Death which surrounded the paradise of Uta-Napishtim and defended its approaches. Woe to him who touched these waters! But thanks to Urshanabi's foresight Gilgamesh avoided their deadly contact. He threw away each pole after having used it only once. With the one hundred and twentieth pole the crossing was accomplished.

Gilgamesh found Uta-Napishtim and explained his desire for immortality. But 'he who had found everlasting life' urged upon him death's inescapable necessity.

'Do we make a house to last for ever? Does the river rise for ever? No one knows the face of death. Mammitu who created fate decides, with the Anunnaki, the fates. They determine life and death and they never make known the days when death will come!'

If, after the deluge, he himself had become immortal the privilege was due to the benevolence of a god. And to prove to Gilgamesh the force of destiny he proposed an experiment. Since sleep is the image of death let Gilgamesh not go to bed for six days and seven nights. Alas! Gilgamesh had scarcely sat down before he was asleep! Uta-Napishtim said with contempt to his wife:

Behold the strong man who desired everlasting life!
Sleep, like a hurricane, breaks over him.

So Gilgamesh returned home and retained his mortal state. Before he departed, however, Uta-Napishtim at his wife's request revealed to Gilgamesh a wondrous secret: at the bottom of the ocean there was a prickly plant – 'like the bramble its thorn pricks the hand, but its name is "the-old-man-becomes-young" and he who eats of it regains his youth.' Gilgamesh at once attached heavy stones to his feet, plunged into the ocean, gathered the plant which pricked his hand and, removing the stones, rose again and regained Urshanabi's boat. His journey would not have been useless. But alas! during his return journey he bathed in a fountain of fresh water; when a snake, attracted by the odour of the plant, stole the magic branch. Then Gilgamesh sat down and wept.

Doubly disappointed, Gilgamesh regained Erech with its enclosure. Still haunted by the fear of death he evoked the shade of Enkidu, to learn from him the 'law of the world'; but Enkidu could only describe to his friend the mournful condition of those who are everlastingly imprisoned in the sombre kingdom of Nergal. And it is upon this disheartening vision that the adventures of Gilgamesh close.

THE GODS OF ELAM

In the mountainous country east of Babylonia lay the land of Elam – which was once, in the fourth millennium B.C., the scene of a flourishing civilisation whose chief centre was the city of Susa.

This civilisation was closely related to that of the land of Sumer and their religions had much in common. Unless they had a common origin – which some have suggested – their similarity of religious belief can be simply explained by their propinquity.

The chief divinity of the Elamites was IN-SHUSHINAK, 'He of Susa' who was not only, as his name seems to indicate, Susa's local god, but was also considered the 'Sovereign of the Gods', 'Master of heaven and earth', 'Maker of the Universe'. These are the same titles which in Babylon were given to supreme gods. IN-SHUSHINAK is a personal name rather than an indication of origin.

It is not easy to identify In-Shushinak exactly, but it is generally agreed that he corresponded to Ninurta, 'the champion of the celestial gods', or even Adad, god of lightning and the tempest. We must not forget that these two divinities had, as well as their terrible aspect, a more beneficent function: they were gods of the welcome rain and fruitful flood and, hence, gods of fertility. In-Shushinak must without doubt have also shared this double nature.

Among the other divinities who peopled the Elamite pantheon and who, since we know scarcely more than their names, can only be enumerated are: KIRIRISHA, the sovereign goddess whose spouse was the god KHUMBAM who is identified with the Babylonian Marduk; LAGAMAL, described as the son of Ea; NAH-HUNTE, the sun who, like Shamash, was at the same time god of light and of justice; TESHUB, god of the tempest, who was, moreover, worshipped throughout Western Asia; NARUTI, whom we only know from an offering presented to the deity by the *ishakku* of Susa.

These national deities were later joined by the gods and goddesses of Sumer and Akkad who may have been imported into Elam when it fell under the hegemony of the rulers of Agade, Ur and Lagash; or else may have been introduced when the Elamites extended their domination over Babylonia.

PHOENICIAN MYTHOLOGY

INTRODUCTION

The Phoenicians were a part of the Canaanite world which was formed at the dawn of history by Semitic immigration into the territories between the Mediterranean and the Syrian desert. The mythology of the Phoenicians is thus largely derived from a background common to a more widely extended ethnic group. We know much less about it than about the mythology of the Egyptians or the Assyro-Babylonians. In the last few decades, however, such progress has been made, thanks to excavations at Byblos and Ras Shamrah, that our sources of information have been much enlarged.

At the moment our sources consist of four groups of texts.

The most ancient go back to the times of the Old Kingdom in Egypt, that is to say to the beginning of the third millennium B.C. They were discovered by Pierre Montet in central Phoenicia, in the ruins of Gubla, the Byblos of the Greeks, to-day Jebeil, a little village of the Lebanon Republic, north of Beirut. They are of especial value when studied in conjunction with Egyptian texts of various periods and the illustrations on contemporary monuments.

The second group of Phoenician mythological texts comes from Schaeffer and Chenet's excavation in the ruins of Ugarit, a town which was a little to the north of the Phoenicia of classical authors, a place which to-day is called Ras Shamrah. They are very valuable documents, written in the first half of the fourteenth century B.C., discovered in 1929 and the years following, transcribed and translated by Virolleaud in the review *Syria* and the subject of a brilliant commentary by R. Dussaud in the *Revue de l'histoire des religions*.

The third group consists of certain inscriptions and illustrations on monuments, of the literary works of Philo of Byblos, of Damascius, Mochus, the Bible and of Assyrian and Egyptian texts.

One cannot overlook the mythology peculiar to Carthage, Phoenicia's principal colony. Carthaginian documents thus form the fourth and last of these groups which we shall now consider in turn.

BYBLOS, AT THE BEGINNING OF THE THIRD MILLENNIUM

In the days of the first Egyptian dynasties Byblos was a small town on a hill beside the sea. It did a lively trade in the wood of the neighbourhood. The Egyptians came to Byblos in search of the timber they required for the construction of sea-going ships, the masts decorated with streamers which rose before their temples, the hewn planks they used in making furniture and coffins. From Byblos they also brought back the resin which was so important in embalming. Many documents bear witness to these economic relations, which were non-existent between Egypt and any other towns on the Phoenician coast. The result was an exchange of myths between Egypt and Byblos.

The chief deity of Byblos was a goddess. She was probably already known under the title of Ba'alat, that is 'the Lady (of Byblos)'. On a cylinder seal, engraved at Byblos itself for a prince whose name has not come down to us, she is represented seated, dressed in a tight robe with shoulder straps, wearing her hair in the Egyptian manner, her head surmounted by a disk between two horns. Thus she resembles the goddess Hathor, who was venerated on the banks of the Nile.

Statuette of Ba'al from Ras Shamrah. Ba'al, or 'Lord', was a title conferred on a number of gods by the Phoenicians. At Ras Shamrah it was given to Hadad, the god of the tempest, portrayed here as a young warrior with his left arm outstretched to wield his lightning spear. In his right hand he would have held a club. Copper inlaid and overlaid with gold and silver. Fourteenth century B.C. Louvre.

An Egyptian bas-relief, discovered by Renan and preserved in the Louvre, portrays her welcoming and embracing a Pharaoh. From one of the horns above her face is suspended a uraeus which poises its head against that of the uraeus ornamenting the brow of the king.

Another bas-relief in the museum of Beirut has two symmetrical scenes in each of which a king of some dynasty between the fifth and the eleventh – probably one of the Pepis – kneels and presents two vases to a divinity. In one scene it is the Lady of Byblos; in the other a lion-headed god, who, like the goddess, is designated by the epithet: 'Beloved of Hathor'.

From the time of the twelfth dynasty, relations between Egypt and Byblos became such that the Lady of Byblos was finally equated with Hathor. Henceforth she seems eager to copy the Egyptian manner of attitude and costume. For example, the stela of Yehaw-melek, during the Achaemenian Empire, shows the Lady of Byblos wearing the head-dress of the goddess Hathor of Ptolemaic times – a vulture skin surmounted by a mortier.

According to the cylinder seal already mentioned there existed in Byblos a great god who was assimilated to the Egyptian sun-god Ra. He was distinguished by two epithets which were not used in Egypt: he was called 'Ra, of Foreign Lands' and 'Ra, who is on Pharaoh's Lake'.

His son was the god of Byblos, to whom the cylinder gives the Egyptian name of Ruti, that is to say, 'He who resembles a Lion'. It is he whom we have already seen on the bas-relief with symmetrical scenes, depicted with a human body and a lion's head.

The cylinder seal gives us the name of a fourth divinity: Hay-Tau of Nega, of whom the prince calls himself the well-loved.

Nega is mentioned several times in Egyptian texts. It was either the territory between northern Lebanon and the sea, which later formed the district of Byblos, or else merely the region of Nahr Ibrahim, five miles to the south of Jebeil, which became the centre of the cult of Adonis. It was a wooded region where grew various species of conifers, junipers and a tree with red wood called the *mer*. The god of Nega, Hay-Tau, a prototype of Adonis, was the spirit of forest vegetation. At some period he became metamorphosed into a tree.

The Egyptians adopted Hay-Tau and identified him with their Osiris, according to the legend recounted by Plutarch which has been referred to in the section on Egyptian mythology. The resin of the conifers was the tears of Osiris; and, if the coffins of Egyptian priests were by preference made of resinous wood, that was because the priests had become 'Osirises'. The pyramid texts mention the god Hay-Tau of Nega three times, with whom the Pharaoh is

Head of a god from Djabboul in Syria. Possibly a representation of El, 'the Father of Men', the god is portrayed wearing a helmet adorned with four superimposed rows of bull's horns – the emblems of divinity. The supreme god of the Semitic pantheon, El was worshipped throughout Syria alongside the local gods, or 'Ba'als', one of his titles, indeed, being 'the Bull' – an appellation which probably signified his strength.

Clay tablet inscribed with the different signs of the alphabetic cuneiform script in which the mythological texts of Ras Shamrah were set down. Discovered in a library in the former city of Ugarit (now Ras Shamrah), the texts recount the stories concerning El, Ba'al and Asherat and the other gods and goddesses of the Phoenician religion and the legends involving mortals such as Keret and Danel. The tablet is the earliest known alphabet. Fourteenth century B.C.

identified in his tomb. It is requested, moreover, that the dead king shall not be treated like Osiris who is changed into a tree in Nega.

An Egyptian document long before Plutarch, the Story of the Two Brothers, shows another form of Hay-Tau's introduction into Egyptian mythology. The Egyptian hero is called Ba-Tau. His brother had wished to kill him. He therefore fled to the Valley of the Pine, very likely the Valley of Nahr Ibrahim, and placed his heart on the topmost branch of the pine. Egyptian soldiers came to carry off his wife. She had the tree cut down and immediately Ba-Tau died. He came to life again four years later when his brother found the heart. He transformed himself into a bull and returned to Egypt, carrying his brother on his back. The identification of Ba-Tau with Hay-Tau was for the Egyptians especially clear because the god of Nega, in the hieroglyphic texts, was associated with a bull. We shall see that in Phoenician mythology, as the Ras Shamrah texts present it, the bull is frequently associated with gods.

THE LEGENDS OF RAS SHAMRAH

The cuneiform tablets of Ras Shamrah reveal in the fourteenth century B.C. mythological material of a tradition which was already ancient and which, moreover, was to continue, though not without modifications, until the end of paganism, since echoes of it are found in the works of Philo of Byblos.

The basis of this mythology was the cult of the elements and of natural phenomena. In it, all the divinities have clearly been transformed into human shape and are arranged in a strict hierarchy.

At the head of the pantheon stood El, the great god who from remote times was honoured among all the western Semites. He governed the entire land of Canaan. He made the rivers flow into the abyss of the ocean and thus assured the fertility of the earth. As 'father of years', for he regulated their course, and as 'the king', El dwelt in a pavilion near the shore where rivers flow into the sea. He was honoured under various titles. The most important of these seems to have been 'Bull' or 'Bull-El'; not that he was identified with an animal, though in certain cases he was thus represented. But the idea of power and strength was symbolised among the Canaanites by the bull, which was also the symbol or animal-attribute of other divinities.

After El the greatest god was Ba'al. He was often El's enemy. He was less ancient than El in Phoenician mythology. Ba'al did not appear before the arrival of the Phoenicians on the Mediterranean coast when they emigrated from the Negeb, south of Palestine, where they had previously lived. Ba'al, in the Ras Shamrah texts, is the same god as Ba'al Tsaphon, a name which can be translated 'Lord of the North'. He is the same god as Ba'al Lebanon, 'Lord of Lebanon', later venerated in all the places of cult in the Lebanon Mountains, in the attitude popularised by the images of the Heliopolitan Jupiter.

But, as in all the other cases where a Canaanite divinity was called Ba'al, the name was never a proper name. It was an appellation that hid the god's true name, which was known only to the initiated. Like the name of the god of Israel it could, apparently, be pronounced only in exceptional cases which were laid down by tradition. Ba'al, in the Ras Shamrah texts, is Hadad, god of the atmosphere, of clouds and the tempest. His voice sounded in the clouds, he wielded the thunderbolt, he dispensed rain.

This god did not, like El, exist before the birth of the gods. He had a mother, the goddess Asherat-of-the-Sea. His consort also is Asherat, but it is impossible to say whether she is the same goddess or one of her hypostases. In Ugarit, the ancient city whose ruins to-day bear the name Ras Shamrah, she was many times represented on the stelae erected in his temple.

After 1350 B.C. we see him on a stela with the general traits of the god Sutekh – a type created by the Egyptians to represent foreign gods. This stela indicates the influence of the Pharaoh in Phoenicia, an influence of which we were already aware thanks to the famous diplomatic correspondence called the 'Letters of el Amarna'.

Elsewhere, under the influence of the Hittites who disputed the control of Upper Syria with the Egyptians, the same god, wearing a pointed helmet adorned with the symbolic horns which the Sumerians reserved for the head-dress of their gods, thrusts his spear into the earth and the shaft of his spear appears to simulate the lightning's zigzag.

A famous cylinder seal in the Boston Museum, though not

Funeral stele from Marash in Anatolia. The scribe Tarhunpiyas is portrayed standing on the knees of a seated woman, probably a mother goddess, who clasps the lower part of his body in her arms. He holds – or is connected to – the figure of a falcon.

The Ba'al Tsaphon. Stela from Ras Shamrah. Fourteenth century B.C. Louvre.

actually of Phoenician origin, represents Ba'al Hadad. Not only has he overthrown a man with his lance, but behind him there is a representation of his animal attribute, the bull. This representation was traditional among the western Semites. At the beginning of the second millennium in the Semitic colonies of Asia Minor, Hadad, armed with a thunderbolt and standing on a bull, faces a god who holds a spear with its point lowered towards a man stretched at his feet.

Mot, one of the sons of El, was the spirit of the harvest. He ruled the countryside when the ground lay dry beneath the burning sun, when the corn had reached maturity. The plains on which it never rains were the domains of Mot, the divine son. He was the god El's favourite son.

At the time of the harvest Mot was sacrificed by the goddess Anat, but he did not remain dead for long. Almost immediately he was reborn and his reign seemed scarcely to have been interrupted. But he was to be vanquished in a combat with the son of Ba'al at the beginning of the rainy season and abandoned by El his father, who himself had determined that such should be the unfortunate Mot's fate.

Aleyin, Mot's opponent, was the son of Ba'al. As with Mot, his relationship and dependence upon his father was close. Indeed it seems that he was merely another concept of Ba'al with the special function of maintaining the water supply. Most of the rivers in Phoenicia had divine names which were connected with the cycle of Aleyin. Aleyin, the spirit of springs, fostered vegetation which relied upon the season of the rains. He was called the 'Ba'al of the Earth', 'the House of Water'. Perhaps it was he who was honoured later with those monuments called 'Memnonia' erected at the mouths of most rivers in Phoenicia, temples where mourning rites were celebrated.

Aleyin, 'he who rode the clouds', was accompanied by seven companions and a troop of eight wild boars.

The goddess Asherat-of-the-Sea was called 'Mother of the Gods' and was said to have seventy children. She was also 'Creator of the Gods', and 'In Wisdom the Mistress of the Gods'. She was El's counsellor and the mother of Ba'al. Asherat, consort of Ba'al, may be merely a hypostasis of Ashtart. There was also an Asherat of Tyre.

Ashtart (in Greek Astarte) and Elat, whose names occur together in a list of sacrifices, are only rarely mentioned in the Ras Shamrah texts.

Ashtart of the Sky of Ba'al was the most beautiful of heavenly bodies, the planet Venus.

Elat is the feminine form of the name El. There was a goddess Elat of the Sidonians.

The virgin Anat was the daughter of Ba'al and the sister of Aleyin. She was above all a divinity of bellicose temperament. We see her proceeding to the ritual murder of the god Môt. Later she finds herself obliged to ask her father's aid to put an end to the life of the harvest-god. The role which El had assigned to her was that of perpetuating the life of the gods – not in giving them life but in procuring for them the means of preserving it, especially by being responsible for constant sacrifices.

The Hyksos introduced her into Egypt. At Avaris she was honoured as the consort of a god sometimes called Ba'al, sometimes Sutekh. Her cult continued to flourish after the expulsion of the Hyksos.

As a daughter of the rain-god and sister of the water-god, Anat also played a part in fostering vegetation. She sprinkled the earth with dew; for the dew, like the rain, is the 'fat of the earth'.

At Ugarit great care was taken to ensure that the dead were supplied with water. Wells, cisterns covered with a flagstone pierced with a hole, gutters and jars sunk into the ground, provided reservoirs of water not only for those buried in the cemetery but also for those who had perished far from home. For the latter, funeral rites were piously performed and gifts deposited in the tombs which they would never occupy; for their souls could return to the land of their fathers to receive offerings and sacrifices.

Qadesh, the 'Holy', whose animal-attribute was the lion in Egyptian documents, was only an epithet of the goddess Anat. By this name she was the consort of the god Amurru, god of the 'West', who in Egyptian texts was given the name Reshef. They appeared together in the sacrifice of the ass at harvest time.

Offerings and Sacrifices. To nourish the gods, who like mortals were obliged to eat, one offered them bread and wine on a golden table.

Come, give them drink. Put bread upon the table, bread. And pour wine into the cups. In the golden goblet the blood of trees.

They were also offered a great variety of sacrifices, many of which are mentioned in the Bible. There were, for instance, expiatory sacrifices. When Anat reproaches Mot for the death of her brother Aleyin, Mot answers her:

End panel of the sarcophagus of king Ahiram of Byblos. Four mourning women with their upper garments loosed and their breasts bare are shown performing a ritual dance. In addition, the first two lacerate their breasts—a mourning rite known from the Ba'al myth of Ras Shamrah – while the other two tear their hair or pour dust upon it. Though Ahiram reigned in the early tenth century B.C., the sarcophagus in which he was interred probably dates from three centuries earlier. Limestone.

I am Aleyin, son of Ba'al. Make ready, then, the sacrifice. I am the lamb which is made ready with pure wheat to be sacrificed in expiation.

Animals offered in sacrifice were the ox, the sheep, the ram, the calf, the lamb. No female animal is mentioned, at least in the ceremonies which accompanied the consecration of a temple.

A special sacrifice at the season of the harvest, to reawaken the spirit of the vine which the ass, nibbling the leaves, might have eaten, shows Qadesh and Amurru – in other words, Anat and Aleyin – intervening. Asherat-of-the-Sea gives them the following order:

Tie up the ass, bind the stallion. Make ready the vine-shoots with silvery leaves – of vivid green. Remove the she-asses from the vine.

Qadesh and Amurru obey. They tie up the ass, bind the stallion. They make ready the vine with silvery leaves, of vivid green. They remove the she-asses from the vine.

Qadesh and Amurru cross their hands. Asherat installs the ass on the high place. The stallion on the ... of the high place.

Qadesh seizes them, Amurru embraces them – when the morning star appears before the sanctuary of the virgin Anat. Then the sailor protects the sailor of Tsapuna.

The struggle between Aleyin and Mot. One of the poems of Ras Shamrah presents the two vegetation-gods and tells of their struggle which recurs every year.

The part of this poem which has been preserved begins at the moment when Aleyin, son of Ba'al, has just died. Asherat, his grandmother, and Ba'al, his father, are deeply distressed.

Latpon, one of the sons of the god El, goes to find his father in the tent he inhabits where 'the rivers meet the sea', to ask that the dead god be given a successor. El addresses Asherat-of-the-Sea and begs her to designate one of her sons.

Here part of the text is missing. Later the goddess Anat demands that Mot give her back her brother. She sets her dogs on the murderer's flocks, seizes him and puts him to death.

Sharrupa protecting king Tuthaliya IV. The god is shown over life-size to emphasize his divine character and wears a tall, multi-horned head-dress and a short kilt together with a sword. He embraces the king with his left arm – a gesture denoting honour and protection. To the right and left, above, are divine ideograms. Relief in the rock shrine of Yazilikaya near Hattusa, the former capital of the Hittite Empire.

King Sulumeli and the weather-god. The bearded weather-god appears twice on this Hittite relief from Malatya. On the left he is seen riding in a chariot drawn by two bulls while in the centre he receives a libation from the king. Dressed in a horned head-dress and short tunic, he holds a thunderbolt in his left hand and brandishes a boomerang in his right. The king holds the royal staff. Tenth century B.C.

She seizes Mot, the son divine. With her sickle she cleaves him. With her flail she beats him. With fire she grills him. With her mill she grinds him. In the fields she scatters him. To consume his leaven, so that he no longer withholds his share (of the crop).

When Mot, the divine son, has perished, then Aleyin, son of Ba'al, is alive. The rains fall in abundance, rivers overflow, floods threaten. El orders Anat to inquire into the situation. Anat addresses the goddess Sapas, one of El's daughters, who is called the 'Torch of the Gods'. Sapas departs in search of Aleyin.

Finally Ba'al intervenes when, at the end of seven years, Mot threatens Aleyin with the seven chastisements of which he himself has been a victim. Aleyin takes up the challenge and the goddess Sapas announces Mot's downfall.

'Listen well, Mot, O son of the Gods! Behold, thou shalt do battle with Aleyin, son of Ba'al. Behold, thy father, Shor-El, will not listen to thee! May he tear away the gates of thy dwelling-place! May he overthrow the throne of thy royalty! May he break the sceptre of thy sovereignty!'

Mot, vanquished, descends into the underworld. Aleyin is re-established in his own, and his triumph is the subject of another poem.

The death of Ba'al and the death of Aleyin. Ba'al was hunting in the desert, probably the desert of Qadesh, when he suddenly found himself face to face with strange creatures, as big as wild bulls. El had created them to bar Ba'al's way, and Amat Asherat, whom El had banished to the desert, had brought them into the world.

The battle was merciless and at first Ba'al had the advantage. Finally, however, he succumbed and fell like a bull.

Anat soon arrived to undertake the burial of him whom the legend here calls her son. She dug a grave, transformed part of the desert into a garden and, after announcing the death of the god, descended with him into the tomb, accompanied by the sun-goddess who remained there until she became surfeited with the tears which she drank as though they were wine.

Aleyin also died. Anat bore him on her shoulders as far as the Mountain of the North. There she offered perfume to the deities of the underworld, then six sacrificial bulls, rams, stags, ibex and asses, in order that Aleyin should have enough to eat during his six months in the underworld. Finally she sent an announcement to El saying that he and his wife Asherat could rejoice since Ba'al and Aleyin were dead.

El and his wife rejoiced, but as Aleyin fulfilled an indispensable role they set about seeking someone to replace him.

Then Anat appeared again and accused the god Mot of responsibility for her brother's death.

The temple of Ba'al. Another poem of ancient origin which describes the construction of the Temple of Ba'al is purely mythical in substance and contains no mortals.

Though Ba'al was the owner of all space it was better that he, like other divinities, should possess a dwelling less vast as a place of prayer.

Ba'al has not a temple like a god; neither a sacred enclosure like a son of Asherat.

Before beginning the construction, the authorisation of El had to be obtained, without which all work would be in vain. To make sure of El's benevolence he was presented with a golden throne and a golden table covered with offerings. It was the work of Hiyon, the divine craftsman, who with his bellows and tongs 'melted silver, plated gold' and fashioned images of bulls in precious metals to decorate the future sanctuary.

Asherat-of-the-Sea undertook to present the request to El. Then to Latpon – the god who shared with her the gift of wisdom – she gave orders to begin work.

Latpon El Dped answered: 'I shall labour, I, the magician of Asherat. I shall work, I who perceive. Behold, Amat Asherat fashions the bricks. A house shall be constructed for Ba'al, for he is a god; and a holy enclosure, for he is a son of Asherat.'

Later the goddess urges Latpon to rest.

And the Lady Asherat-of-the-Sea, of all the gods Mistress in Wisdom, said: 'Rest from thy toil, for thou art of great age. Rest, because of thy lungs … And delight also in his rain.'

Ba'al himself took part in the work. With the lightning – 'his earthly saw' – he felled cedars for the roof of his dwelling. A message sent to Ba'al's son, Aleyin, shows that the erection of the holiest part of the edifice was reserved for him.

'Build a chapel of gold and silver. It will be the chapel of the pure. I shall watch over them.'

Ba'al was finally installed, and Anat offered to him the sacrifice of a bull. Then two brothers, Kusor and Hasisu, appeared and proposed to install windows in the temple.

And Kusor-and-Hasisu said: 'Listen, Aleyin, son of Ba'al, mark our words, O Rider of the Clouds. Behold, I shall put a sky-light in the sanctuaries, a window in the middle of the temples.'

But this did not suit Aleyin who retorted:

'Thou shalt place no sky-light in the sanctuaries, nor window in the middle of the temples.'

The argument was not settled; they had to appeal to a higher divinity, Ba'al, or perhaps even to the supreme god, El. Then Aleyin proposed a compromise.

'I myself shall place them. Kusor, the mariner, Kusor, son of the law (?), he shall open the window in sanctuaries, the sky-light in the middle of temples. And Ba'al shall open a fissure in the clouds – above the (face) of Kusor-and-Hasisu.'

Thenceforth the waters above would no longer spill from the heavens entirely by hazard and a deluge need be feared no more. Ba'al would let the rain fall only when Kusor opened the windows of the temple. Kusor became the regulator of the seasons, as Philo teaches us. Kusor also possessed the art of incantation and sooth-saying. He was the inventor of mechanical devices and of the fishing boat.

The Epic of Keret. In the texts of Ras Shamrah Phoenician mytho-logy is not exclusively occupied with gods. There are also legends in which mortals appear, together with gods and with god-like heroes who have commerce with the daughters of men.

Keret was a son of the supreme god, El, and the soldier of the goddess Sapas. He was also king of Sidon. El, his father, ordered him to resist an invasion conducted by Etrah or Terah, a moon-god.

Allied with the enemy were the people of Zabulon – a tribe which was later to form part of the people of Israel and occupy the country between Carmel and the Lake of Galilee. Also with the enemy were the Koserites, who are mentioned in the lists of enemy towns inscribed on Egyptian vases at the end of the eleventh dynasty.

Far from hastening to obey El's orders, Keret shut himself up in his chamber and burst into tears. But in dreaming he regained his confidence: he dreamed that he would be the father of a son. This decided him to execute the orders he had received, but before he departed on the campaign he ascended a migdol, sat on the parapet of the tower and there, raising a hand to the sky, offered in sacrifice wine in a silver cup, honey in a golden vase, and the blood of a bird and of a lamb.

He then returned to the town and made arrangements for six months' food supplies for the population. But Terah had already occupied five towns and was attempting to cut the territory of the Phoenicians in two. The battle took place in the Negeb to the south of Palestine. The vanquished were obliged to emigrate: some did so in a body, others in small groups. Keret does not seem to have emerged victorious from the struggle. When he returned to Sidon he bought a wife and paid for her in gold and silver. By this wife he had a son, beautiful as Ashtart and gracious as Anat. This son was a prodigy: he had scarcely been born before he cried out: 'I hate the enemy!' He demanded justice for the widow, protection for the orphan and assistance against the plunderer.

Danel is another mythological hero. He was versed in the art of divination and his daughter knew all the secrets of astrology. His memory was preserved and, it seems, it is to Danel that the prophet Ezekiel compares the king of Tyre when he says to him: 'Thou art wiser than Daniel, no secrets are hidden from thee.' (XXVIII. 3.)

Poem of the birth of the gracious and fair gods. This myth, like the Epic of Keret, reminded the Phoenicians in mythological form of their land of origin, the Negeb, from where, via what was later called the Philistine coast, they reached, towards the beginning of the third millennium, Tyre, Sidon, Gubla and Arvad. In the fourteenth century B.C. they had not yet been driven by the Philistines from the coast near Egypt and they continued to use the trade routes of the Negeb.

This poem, in its essential features, has survived in a sort of mnemonic for the use of reciters during a religious ceremony which seems to have accompanied sacrifices made towards the end of winter.

Mot-and-Shur is then very tired. Dussaud, following Jeremiah II. 21, sees Mot as the spirit of the withering vine when it has the aspect of dead wood, in this hyphenated form of the god's name.

Mot-and-Shur sits down, holding in his hand a sceptre of sterility, holding in his hand a sceptre of unfruitfulness.

This is the moment in the vineyard when the vine is pruned, the shoots are tied and the terraces made ready. Among the sacrifices

Hittite war god. The vigorous young god strides forward grasping an axe in his right hand with a curved sword thrust into his belt.
On his head he wears a pointed helmet with cheek and neck flaps, its plume falling to his elbow. His short kilt is fastened by a sash which falls to his knee. His feet are bare.
Relief from the inside of the King's Gate at Hattusa.
Fourteenth century B.C. Ankara Museum.

for the occasion was that of cooking a kid in the milk of its mother, a Canaanite custom which Mosaic law condemned and formally forbade.

To this fertility rite, a rite of procreation was added in which El, the supreme god, took direct part in order to create the gods 'gracious and fair'.

El, the sun-god, advanced along the shore, on the banks of the abyss. The celebrants called upon Mot lamenting. Then they called upon the 'Mother' – probably Asherat-of-the-Sea. El plunged into the waves.

The hands of El reach out like the sea. And the hands of El reach out like the waves. El stretches his hand like the sea. El stretches his hand like the waves.

With this the god obtained two objects which he put in his house. El placed the wave in the sky, and when it fell again as rain upon the earth it bent Mot's sceptre and his hands began nervously to tremble.

When El had made his wives fruitful, they accused themselves of Mot's misfortunes.

O Mot, Mot, it is we who made thy sceptre to bend, we who caused thy hand to tremble.

The narrative then says:

El leaned over their lips; then he raised his voice and said: 'Behold, their lips are sweet as a bunch of grapes.'

The continuation concerns the ritual of divine marriage. After having recounted that,

Mythical animal. This two-headed winged animal with the head and body of a lion surmounted by a second, human head wearing a tall head-dress is probably derived from the sphinxes of Egypt which were taken over by the Hittites and put to a similar use as protective images. The shape of the head-dress on the human head is reminiscent of the white crown of Upper Egypt. Bas-relief, 1050 to 850 B.C. Ankara Museum.

In the kiss and the conception, in the embrace...She...and she bore Sahar and Salem ('the Dawn' and 'the Evening'),

the principal actor says:

Send to El this message: 'My wife, O El, has given birth.'

El asks:

'To whom has she given birth?'

And the answer is:

'Sahar and Salem are born to me.'

Then follows the birth, under the same conditions, of five gracious gods, and finally of Sib'ani ('the seventh') whose father is called Etrah, perhaps the same personage as the moon-god Terah who is mentioned in the poem of Keret.

The myth thus takes on an historical interest. It takes us to the south of Palestine, to the Negeb, a region which was in Palaeolithic times, as recent research has shown, already populated. It shows the Phoenicians building one of the towns which would be among the most important in the land of the Philistines, and contracting an alliance with the desert Bedouins in order to ensure safe passage towards the Aelanitic gulf. The mother of Sib'ani lived in the desert for seven years, in order to purify herself, and at the end of the seven years she returned and asked for food and drink.

Set down in its present form in the thirteenth or fourteenth century B.C., this poem was already evidence of a distant past. A fortunate discovery made in 1932 at Byblos gives us further evidence: the carved scabbard of a gold dagger corroborates pictorially what is known by the texts of journeys to Ophir. The episodes depicted take place before a king, mounted on a mule. One, in the desert, shows an attack from behind on a lion who is busy seizing a gazelle. In the land of monkeys we see a servant leading a dog-faced baboon. Finally, since to reach this far-off region it was necessary to cross the sea, the goldsmith has suggested the idea of this journey by carving a fish.

PHOENICIAN GODS OF THE FIRST MILLENNIUM B.C.

In the first millennium B.C. every town in Phoenicia honoured its Ba'al – that is, its 'Lord', its 'Master', who was the proprietor of the soil and supreme ruler of its inhabitants. Instead of a Ba'al the deity honoured could be a Ba'alat, a 'Lady'. In certain regions there also existed Ba'alim: the Ba'al Tsaphon, 'Lord of the North' whom we have met in the myths of Ras Shamrah; the Ba'al Shamim, 'Lord of the Skies' of the Bible; the Ba'al Lebanon, 'Lord of Lebanon'.

The real name of the divinity is almost never known. As in Israel, one avoided pronouncing it, though perhaps for different reasons. In Phoenicia the object was to prevent strangers from discovering it lest, in their turn, they invoked the god, drew his benevolence upon themselves and succeeded by diverting his interest in turning him from his own people.

The meeting of the gods. In the centre the divine couple greet one another, the Weather-god of heaven, on the left, standing on the backs of two mountain gods while Hepat, the sun-goddess of Arinna, rides on her sacred animal, the lion. Behind her is their son, Surruma, also standing on a lion, followed by two goddesses above their emblem, a two-headed eagle. On the far left is the weather-god of Hattusa. Relief from the rock shrine of Yazilikaya. Thirteenth century B.C.

From the earliest times Gubla had had a Ba'alat as its chief divinity. She was identified with the Egyptian Hathor and for the Greeks she was a form of Astarte.

Berytus also worshipped a 'Lady', a nymph whom the god Adonis wooed, but a marine Ba'al was more fortunate than he.

The Ba'al of Tyre was a solar god in origin. Later, like the other divinities of Phoenician ports, he added to his primitive characteristics the characteristics of a marine deity. He was known under the title of Melkart, 'God of the City'. The Greeks identified him with Heracles.

Sidon venerated Eshmun, who became a god of health and was equated by the Greeks with Asclepius. The same town also worshipped an Ashtart in honour of whom King Solomon built a sanctuary in Jerusalem. Kings and queens were priests and priestesses of this lascivious goddess, whose cult was practised in grottoes in the place which is to-day called Maghdusheh.

Of the Phoenician divinities of this epoch we know only the adventures of one, to whom the Greeks gave the name Adonis. Details of the story were collected in the fifth century B.C. by the poet Panyasis.

The Myth of Adonis. Adonis is the direct successor of Hay-Tau of Nega and he replaced the two vegetation gods Aleyin and Mot of the Ugarit poems.

Born of a tree into which his mother had transformed herself, Adonis was of an extraordinary beauty. At his birth Aphrodite put him a coffer which she confided to the goddess of the underworld, Persephone. When later she came to reclaim the coffer she found that Persephone had already opened it, beheld the great beauty of the child and refused to give him up. The dispute between the two goddesses was brought before Zeus, who decided that Adonis should

spend half the year on earth and half in the underworld.

According to other legends, Aphrodite fell deeply in love with the young god. She feared that a tragic fate would befall him and tried to discourage his passion for the chase. Adonis persisted in hunting and was killed by a wild boar or by a bear.

Adonis was an agricultural divinity and a vegetation spirit who, like Aleyin, was manifest in the seed of corn. His name, Adonis, is only known in Greek texts. It is a Hellenised form of the Semitic word *adoni*, 'my Lord, my master', which was ceaselessly repeated by Phoenician women in their lamentations during the god's festivals. In the Bible Ezekiel calls him Tammuz, the name of the Mesopotamian vegetation and corn-god. His actual Phoenician character was revealed only in the sixth century of our era by Damascius: Adonis is Eshmun.

The cult of Adonis was common to all Phoenicia, but it was in the territory of Byblos that it was celebrated with the greatest pomp.

Halfway between Byblos and Baalbek, near the source of the Nahr Ibrahim which the Greeks called the River Adonis, was the village of Aphaca, to-day called Afka. There, on a site which modern travellers all praise for its extraordinary charm, rose a sanctuary to Ashtart which was destroyed by the Emperor Constantine.

From the terrace of the sanctuary one sees the impressive circle of tall cliffs and the river, springing from a grotto, as it splashes tumultuously from cascade to cascade between verdant and wooded banks until at last it plunges into the depths of the gorge where the god perished.

At Ghineh one of the monuments erected in honour of Adonis still exists. Sculptured in the rock, the god grasps a spear in his hand and is on the watch for the animal which is about to attack him. The goddess, meanwhile, sits in an attitude of deep affliction.

It was believed that every year Adonis returned to such places,

Procession of gods. Twelve running warrior gods bearing curved swords are shown on this Hittite relief at Yazilikaya near Hattusa. They are identically dressed in tall, ribbed head-dresses and short belted tunics and on their feet wear the shoes with upturned toes characteristic of a mountain people. The Hittites had a large and varied pantheon of a 'thousand gods and goddesses'. The names of these particular gods and the part they played in their religion, however, is not yet known.

there to be mortally wounded. The waters then would change to blood: a phenomenon due to the particles of red haematite which become detached from the rocks during certain natural conditions such as the season of high waters.

Festivals of Adonis. The *Adonia*, as the Greeks called the annual festivals which commemorated the death of Adonis, were the most beautiful of Phoenician festivals and were celebrated immediately after the harvest. Saglio described them in outline as follows:

'It seems that nothing was lacking which normally took place at funerals: neither the oiling and toilet of the dead, nor the exhibition of the body, funeral offerings and communal repasts. Images of Adonis in wax and terracotta were placed before the entrance or on the terraces of houses. Women crowded round them or carried them through the town, wailing and beating their breasts with every sign of the deepest grief. They danced and chanted dirges to the strident sound of short flutes – called *giggros* or *giggras* – which the Phoenicians use for their funeral ceremonies.' This picture must be completed by Theocritus's description of the festival celebrated with oriental pomp at Alexandria in the palace of Arsinoe, wife of Ptolemy Philadelphus. Under an arbour of greenery in which cupids flutter, the beautiful adolescent Adonis lies on a silver bed, covered with rich purple tissue. Venus is beside him. Around him are arranged vases full of perfumes, fruits, honey, cakes, and finally silver baskets containing what were called 'gardens of Adonis'. It was the custom to sow in vessels, normally not so valuable as the vases found in Arsinoe's palace, but in earthenware pots, in bottoms of cups, sherds, sometimes in baskets, all kinds of plants which germinate and grow rapidly, such as fennel, barley, wheat, and especially lettuce, which played a part in the legend of Adonis. (It was said that Venus had laid the body of her lover on a bed of lettuce.) These plants grew in a few days under the influence of the June sun, but, having no roots, faded and withered immediately. They were thus a symbol of the ephemeral existence of Adonis. These little artificial gardens were displayed with images of the god during the pomp and ceremony of the *Adonia*; afterwards they were thrown into the sea or into fountains.

Lucian mentions a joyful rite which was added to the ancient lamentations to celebrate the resurrection and ascension of Adonis.

The Works of Philo. Towards the end of the first century of our era, Philo undertook to demonstrate that Greek mythology was based on Phoenician mythology, which itself can be explained by the history of the first generation of human beings. Philo's authority was a rather mysterious Phoenician writer named Sanchuniathon. Among the fragments of Philo's works which have survived we can distinguish a cosmogony, a primitive history and the history of the Uranus group.

The *Cosmogony* of Philo is a combination of traditional elements over which 'troubled and windy air or a breath of wind and dark chaos' presides as ruling principle. Thus it was for many centuries; then, 'the breathing air became enamoured of its own principles and made a mingling and this union was called Desire. This was the principle of creation of all things, but the breath knew not its own creation and from embracing itself produced Mot. Some say that this was slime and others a rotting of aquatic composition. From it came all the germs of all created things and it was the origin of everything.'

This conception of spontaneous creation was accompanied by the idea of a cosmic egg, borrowed from Egypt. Then, by means of evolution, beings were differentiated and those beings who were to have intelligence finally became conscious of themselves.

Greek authors mention other Phoenician cosmogonies. One of these, attributed to the philosopher Eudemus, has in the beginning Time – then Desire and Darkness. 'From the union of these two first principles were born Aer (air) and Aura (breath). Aer represented pure intelligence and Aura the first living creature proceeding therefrom by movement. This couple then produced the cosmic Egg, in conformity with the intelligible spirit.'

According to Damascius, in the sixth century A.D., the first principle of the Phoenicians was 'cosmic Time which contained all things within it'. For Mochus, in the second century A.D., there was in the beginning a double principle: Aether and Air. Then came the Wind and afterwards the two winds Lips and Notos; later Oulomos (the Ages) and still later Chousor, the Opener, and the Egg.

'The air was illuminated', Philo continues, 'due to the flaming of the earth and sea; and winds were formed and clouds. And there was a vast downpouring of waters and floods from the sky. And when, after the sun's heat, all things were separated and left their appointed place to meet in the air and there collide, thunder and lightning resulted. At the sound of the thunder the intelligent animals awoke and took fright at the noise and wandered over the earth and in the sea, as males and females.'

Philo's *Primitive History* is an account of the progress of civilisation and religion.

The first generations deified the products of the earth, considered them to be gods and worshipped them, 'for from the earth they drew their substance, they and those who followed them and all those who had been before them; and they made libations and ritual aspersions'. When a plant died there was lamentation, and also at the birth or death of an animal.

Progress was attributed to Aeon, who discovered edible fruits. From the race of Aeon and Protogonos, both sons of Kolpia and his wife Baau, issued Genos and Genea, who were the first inhabitants of Phoenicia. 'There was a drought and they lifted their hands to the sun in the sky. For they considered the sun to be a god and the sole lord of the sky. They named him Beelsamin, which to the Phoenicians means "Lord of the Sky", or to the Greeks "Zeus".'

The invention of fire was due to mortal offspring of the same race named Light, Fire and Flame. 'They found fire by rubbing sticks of wood together and taught others to do likewise.'

This important step in civilisation was followed by the appearance of giants. Their names – Cassios, Lebanon, Antilebanon and Brathy – were given to the mountains over which they ruled. It seems that these giants must be considered the inventors of burning incense; for all these mountains were renowned for their fragrant woods.

In the meanwhile men's morals had become so licentious that 'children took the name of their mothers; for women in these days would give themselves to the firstcomer'. One of these children of an unknown father was Hapsouranios, who was said to live in Tyre. He was the inventor of huts built of rushes and papyrus. His brother Ousoos was the first to make garments from animal skins. 'The rains came and with them violent winds so that the trees which grew at Tyre brushed together and caught fire, and the forest was consumed. Ousoos took a tree, stripped it of its branches and was the first who dared to venture out to sea. He consecrated two stelae, one to Fire and one to Wind, and worshipped them and sprinkled them with libations of the blood of beasts which he had killed in the chase.'

Hypsouranios and Ousoos were deified after death. Their stelae were worshipped: every year festivals were held in their honour.

Two of their descendants invented hunting and fishing. Later two brothers invented iron and the manner of working it. 'One of them, Kusor, practised the arts of magic formulas, incantation and divination...he invented the fish-hook and bait, the fishing-line and fishing-boat, and he was the first man who learned to navigate.' This Kusor, whom we have already met in the myth of the temple of Ba'al at Ugarit, was identified by Philo and by Herodotus with the Greek god Hephaestus.

He, whom the people of Byblos called the greatest of gods, discovered how to 'add to houses courtyards, porches and cellars' and thus to turn them into luxurious dwellings. The same period saw the beginning of hunting with hounds. A little later pastoral life developed: Amynos and Magos taught the people how to live in villages and tend flocks.

Then came the discovery of salt by Misor and Sydyk. A descendant of Misor's, Taautos, whom the Egyptians called Thoth, invented the first written characters. The Cabeiri, descendants of Sydyk, perfected navigation.

Finally 'others discovered the use of herbs and simples and a remedy for the bite of poisonous animals'.

In this primitive history the actors follow one another and the various inventions are made, so to speak, without particular sequence or connection. Philo's *History of the Uranides* has a more logical sequence. In it Philo treats the gods as ordinary mortals who take part in a series of adventures from which result the creation of royalty, the foundation of the first town, the invention of the plough and the cultivation of wheat, the institution of votive sacrifices and of human sacrifices, the construction of temples, the transition from free love to polygamy and finally monogamy.

Uranus, the Sky, had a sister Ge (or Gaea), the Earth. Their father Hypsistos (Elioun, the All Highest) 'having ended his life in a struggle against ferocious beasts, was deified, and his children offered sacrifices and libations to him'.

When Uranus had succeeded to his father's authority, he took his sister Ge in marriage and they had four children. Uranus had numerous other children by other wives. Ge was distressed by his infidelity and tormented with jealousy, so that they finally separated. When, however, the fancy took him, Uranus would approach his wife with violence and many times he attempted to destroy the children she had borne him. Ge defended herself as best she could. When Cronus (El), one of her sons, had become a man he declared war upon his father in order to avenge his mother. Hermes Trismegistus, secretary and adviser to Cronus, harangued his master's allies with magic words and the struggle ended in the overthrow of Uranus, whose authority passed to Cronus. During the battle Uranus' favourite concubine, who was pregnant to him, fell into the hands of Cronus, who gave her as a wife to Dagon. Uranus' son whom she bore received the name Demarus. He was to become the father of Melkart, the god of Tyre.

Cronus surrounded his house with a wall and founded Byblos, the first city. Fearing the schemes of his brother Atlas, he buried him, on the advice of Hermes, in the depths of the earth. He killed his own son, against whom he harboured suspicions, and cut off the head of his own daughter 'so that all the gods stood stupefied before the decrees of Cronus'.

In those days the descendants of the Cabeiri had perfected ships. They disembarked on the coast near Mount Cassios and there consecrated a temple.

Uranus had long since fled, but he still planned to avenge himself on his son. He sent three of his daughters – Ashtart, Rhea and Dione – to kill Cronus by treachery. Cronus seduced them and made them his wives 'although they were sisters'. Uranus did not admit defeat. He sent against his son Hour and Destiny together with other allies. These, too, Cronus seduced and kept at his side.

By Ashtart, Cronus had seven daughters and two sons, Pothos and Eros. Rhea presented him with seven children, the youngest of whom was recognised as a god from the moment of his birth.

Sydyk married one of Ashtart's daughters, who bore Asclepius. Demarus begat Melkart, identified with Heracles, and to Pontus was born Poseidon and Sidon. She was endowed with a wondrous voice and invented the chanting of hymns. In these days Dagon made the first plough and began the cultivation of grain.

Because of Uranus the war continued. Pontus, the father of Sidon, put Demarus to flight. Demarus was the first to make a vow to offer sacrifice to the gods if they helped him to escape from the critical situation in which he found himself. In the thirty-second year of his reign Cronus caught his father in an ambush and cut off his sexual organs. The spirit of Uranus was dispersed: the blood of his severed genitals flowed in the water of springs and rivers.

In the following period we meet the divinities of the Phoenician towns. Cronus – that is to say the Phoenicians themselves – undertakes long voyages.

Cronus decided that Ashtart, Demarus and Adod should rule over the country. 'Ashtart placed on her head a bull's head as a royal insignia. While travelling the world she found an aerolith which she brought back to Tyre to consecrate on the holy island.

'...Cronus also made a tour of the world. He made his daughter Athene sovereign of Attica. There was famine and plague and Cronus offered his own son in sacrifice to his father Uranus. He circumcised himself and forced his allies to do likewise. Shortly afterwards he deified another child whom Rhea had borne him and who had died. He was named Moûth, and the Phoenicians called him Death and Pluto.

'Cronus gave the city of Byblos to the goddess Baltis, who is Dione. He gave Berytus to Poseidon and to the Cabeiri, who were either hunters or fishermen, and deified the remains of Pontus there. Previously the god Taaut (the Egyptian Thoth), who had taken on the outward appearance of Cronus, Dagon and all the other gods combined, had drawn the sacred characters of writing.

'Taaut also designed the insignia of royalty for Cronus: four eyes, two in front and two behind, two opened and two closed; on his shoulders four wings, two spread in flight, two hanging limp. The eyes were a symbol to show that Cronus slept while he watched and watched while he slept. The wings on his shoulders meant that he flew while at rest and rested in flight. The other gods each had two wings on their shoulders to indicate that they flew with Cronus. The god El also had two wings on his head, one for pure intelligence, the other for feeling.

The entrance to the temple of Ba'al at Thuburbo Majus near Carthage. Ba'al-Hammon, the Phoenician sky – and fertility-god, was the chief god of Carthage, Phoenicia's principal colony, and it was doubtless to the same Ba'al that the temple in the Roman city of Thuburbo Majus was dedicated – the Romans confusing the god with the African god Jupiter Ammon.
The god was normally associated with the great goddess of Carthage, Tanit.

Ashtar was known by various names, including Astarte, Ishtar (to the Babylonians), Ashtoreth (to the Hebrews), and when the great city of Carthage was founded she became known as Tanit. The Phoenicians adopted her as the protective deity of the city which was to become their greatest glory. She is symbolically represented in this stele found at Dougga in Tunis – not far from the site of ancient Carthage.

'Cronus, having arrived in the land of the South, gave all Egypt to the god Taaut to be his kingdom.'

THE GODS OF CARTHAGE

In the trading posts and colonies which the Phoenicians founded on the coasts of Africa and on the islands of the Mediterranean the gods were those of Phoenicia.

At Carthage, their chief foundation, Ba'al-Hammon was worshipped. He was a dignified old man with a beard, and his head was embellished with ram's horns. He sat on a high-backed throne and rested his hands on the heads of two rams which formed the arms of the seat. Ba'al-Hammon was a sky-god and a god of fertility; the Romans confused him with the African god Jupiter Ammon.

Carthage also honoured, with Eshmun and Adonis, the god Bes, who was a frightening dwarf with bow-legs and prominent belly. Bes was also known in Egypt and western Asia, where images of him were widely spread.

The great goddess of Carthage, normally associated with Ba'al-Hammon in inscriptions, was called Tanit. She was described as the 'face of Ba'al'. On numerous little stelae, designed to commemorate sacrifices, Tanit is represented by a symbol the meaning of which has not yet been determined. Some think it is a degenerated human figure in outline, others a primitive representation of an altar. This 'symbol of Tanit', of which one example is known in Phoenicia, is in the form of a truncated cone surmounted by a disk. Sometimes between the disk and the truncated cone is inscribed a horizontal line the two ends of which turn up at right angles.

Another symbol, equally common on Carthaginian stelae, is the open hand – a gesture of propitiation.

THE HITTITE GODS

The mythology of the Hittites has not yet been studied in all its details, but in the chaos of the pantheon where the 'thousand gods and goddesses' dwell, one can distinguish groups of extremely varied origin: ancient indigenous gods worshipped before the advent of the Indo-European Hittites, Irbitiga, Kalhisapi, Teteshapi and Wasezzel; Luwian divinities such as Santa, Tarhunza and Wandu; Hurrian divinities like Teshup and Hepat; gods of Babylon and Assyria, who are less easy to recognise because their names can also represent Hittite names in consequence of the system of allography (or name substitution) adopted by the Hittites.

Thus the Sumerian name Ishkur, adopted as an ideogram in Akkad for the god Hadad, and the number X, a name of the same god, were utilised by the Hittites for the still unknown name of their god who presided over tempests and beneficial rainfall, as Ishkur and Adad did, as Teshub did in Hurrian lands, or Hadad did in Canaan.

At the head of the Hittite pantheon can be distinguished the divine couple, symbolising vital forces, which is common to all Asian peoples. In the thirteenth century B.C. this couple can be seen leading a long procession of other gods on the rocks at Yazilikaya, a mile and a half from the ruins of Hattusa, the capital of the empire.

We shall mention only two of the Hittite myths: that of the Great Serpent and that of Telepinu.

The Great Serpent had dared to attack the weather-god. The god demanded that he be brought to justice. Inar, a god who had come southward with the Indo-European Hittites, prepared a great feast and invited the serpent with his family to eat and drink. The serpent and his children, having drunk to satiety, were unable to go back into their hole, and were exterminated.

Telepinu had vanished and all life withdrew from the earth. Fire was extinguished, the gods died of hunger in their sanctuaries, animals perished in their stables, the trees lost their leaves and the fields their verdure. The Sun gave a festival. His divine guests could not eat their fill nor could they quench their thirst. The weather-god explained the situation to them: his son, Telepinu, was angry and had gone no one knew where, taking all his goods with him. All the gods, great and small, set about searching for the fugitive. Twice the eagle vainly explored the entire land. Then, on the orders of the Lady of the gods, the bee flew off with instructions that if she found Telepinu she should 'sting him in the hands and feet to make him reappear'.

Telepinu returned, and at once life resumed its normal course.

GREEK MYTHOLOGY

It is now known that well before the peoples whom we know as the Greeks had emerged from primitive barbarism there existed in the basin of the Aegean Sea a Mediterranean civilisation which had its centre in Crete. Aegean civilisation, which had already made tentative beginnings in the third millennium, reached its apogee towards the sixteenth century B.C. when it spread to continental Greece, starting in Argolis (Mycenae). It was destroyed in the twelfth century by the Dorian invasions.

In Aegean civilisation, religion naturally had its place. But the only silent documents which archaeology has yet furnished are insufficient to allow an exact estimate of its character and elements. As with all peoples the first form Aegean religion took was fetishism—the worship of sacred stones, the cult of pillars, the cult of weapons (particularly the double-axe), the cult of trees and animals.

Later, when an anthropomorphic conception of divinity had arisen, the Cretan pantheon was formed and myths were created. We find survivals of such myths in a great many Greek legends; for instance, the birth of Zeus in Crete, Europa and the bull, Cretans brought by Apollo to Delphi to be priests of his cult, the Minotaur, etc. When they moved to continental Greece, however, the Aegean divinities took on a Hellenic aspect beneath which their original physiognomy disappeared. Thus what we know about the Aegean pantheon is reduced to very little.

THE AEGEAN PANTHEON

The Great Goddess. The chief deity of the Aegeans was – like that of many Asiatic cults – feminine. She was the *Great Goddess,* the *Universal Mother,* in whom were united all the attributes and functions of divinity. Above all she symbolised fertility, and her influence extended over plants and animals as well as humans. All the universe was her domain. As celestial goddess she regulated the course of the heavenly bodies and controlled the alternating seasons. On earth she caused the products of the soil to flourish, gave men riches, protected them in battle and at sea guided them on their adventurous voyages. She killed or tamed fierce beasts; and finally she also reigned over the underworld: mistress of life, she was also sovereign of death.

The Great Goddess is represented, depending on the epoch, either crouching or standing. Sometimes she is nude, sometimes dressed like a Cretan woman. In the latter case she wears a flounced skirt and her bosom is either entirely bare or covered with a corsage which leaves her breasts exposed. Her head-dress varies: the hair may be free, knotted with a simple fillet; it may be covered either by a sort of turban decorated with flowers or aigrettes, or by a conical tiara in the Oriental manner, or, again, by a very tall tiara in the shape of a topless cone.

Although the type is always the same and only the attributes and details of dress vary, it is questionable if a single divinity is concerned or if, on the contrary, these various representations do not depict distinct goddesses, each having her own character. The procreative goddess with broad hips who presses her raised arms to heavy breasts – could she be the same as the virgin warrior who advances, escorted by a lion, striking the ground with her spear? Could the vegetation-goddess whom we see sitting under the sacred

The Protectress of Athens. Perhaps the most characteristically Greek of all the Olympians, Athene is also the most positively identified as having developed from an archaic local cult. The daughter of Zeus, according to the Greeks, she sprang fully armed from his brow. Warrior goddess, patroness of the arts, and the personification of intelligence, she was a deity much revered and respected. Her formidable character is well caught in this striking bronze statue of the fifth century B.C.

Head of a Cycladic idol. This simple head depicts a deity of the early Mediterranean civilisation which grew up in the islands of the Aegean in the third millennium B.C. The Cyclades, the islands round Delos, were once, according to ancient tradition, inhabited by the Carians (a people of Asia Minor) who were later driven out by Minos, King of Crete. Though some four thousand years old, this head bears a striking resemblance to some modern sculpture. Third millennium B.C.

Cretan rhyton, or ritual vase, in the shape of a bull's head. The bull played an important part in Cretan mythology being the emblem of the Great God who was associated with the Great Goddess in the religion of the Aegean. Survivals of these Cretan legends are found in the legends of Greece. Black steatite with inlay of tridacna shell and rock crystal, and horns of gilded wood. From Cnossos, c. 1500 B.C.

tree, receiving from her priestesses the first fruits and flowers, be the same as the sea-goddess who is carried across the waves in a boat, or the earth-goddess around whom serpents intertwine?

What was the name of the mother-goddess of the Aegeans? Here again in the absence of documentation we are left to conjecture. It seems that she was worshipped in Crete under the vocable *Rhea*. At least this was the name later associated with the ancient Cretan divinity in the cult of Zeus. Zeus was made her son, a tradition revived, as we shall see, by Hesiod in his *Theogony*.

Two other names of Cretan goddesses have been preserved: *Dictynna* and *Britomartis*. In their legends the Greeks applied the two names to the same divinity.

Dictynna, whom the Greeks called the 'goddess of the nets', was perhaps the goddess of Mount Dicte, a mountain in Crete which was later said to be the birthplace of Zeus. She would, then, be the mother-goddess.

Britomartis means 'the sweet virgin', a denomination which

could not very well be applied to the Great Mother of the universe.

According to the Greek legend, Britomartis was a young virgin huntress who pursued wild beasts in the forests of Crete. She was said to be the daughter of Zeus. Minos saw her and was captivated by her beauty. He offered her his love, but was refused. He then attempted violence but Britomartis fled and, after a race which lasted no less than nine months, in order finally to escape Minos she flung herself off a high rock into the sea. She fell into the nets of a fisherman and for that reason received the name Dictynna. Artemis, in reward for her chastity, raised her to the rank of the immortals and thenceforth she appeared during the night to navigators. The Greeks made the assimilation even closer and called Dictynna-Britomartis the Cretan Artemis.

The God. With the Great Goddess the Aegeans associated a god. It would seem that this god, at least originally, was, in imitation of the cults of Western Asia, subordinate to the goddess; but though we are informed of the relationship between Tammuz and Ishtar, between Attis and Cybele, and between Adonis and Astarte, no indication has yet come to light with regard to the relationship between the Aegean god and goddess.

A celestial divinity, like the goddess with whom he was associated, the Aegean god bore the epithet *Asterius* (the 'starry'). He is found again under the name Asterion, king of Crete, who married Europa after her adventure with Zeus. Afterwards he was assimilated with Zeus himself, whose legend was thus enriched with the older Cretan contributions.

The peculiarity of the Cretan god was the mingling of animal and human features which composed his nature. The bull, as in many Asiatic religions, had been adopted since the earliest ages as the Aegean symbol of strength and creative energy. It later became the emblem of the Great God, and as such played an important part in Cretan legends. It even became incorporated in the divine nature: Minotaur is analogous to the bull-god of the Elamites and to the Enki of the Sumerians, who was also 'the savage bull of the sky and the earth'.

The bull-god was not the only aspect under which the Cretan god appeared. Besides the *Minotaur* there was also *Minos*. Therefore the god was also conceived in human form, and it was thus that he sometimes appeared to his worshippers in all his terrifying majesty.

But whether we are concerned with Minos or the Minotaur we know them only through the modifications they underwent when Hellenised. We shall therefore only mention them here in passing and reserve a later occasion to discuss them at greater length, when we meet them again in the heroic legends of classical Greece.

THE MYTHOLOGY OF CLASSICAL GREECE

INTRODUCTION

Greek Theogonies. The Greek pantheon was established as early as the Homeric epoch. The many divinities of which it was composed generally appear in the *Iliad* and the *Odyssey* with their characteristic physiognomy, their traditional attributes and their own time-honoured legends. But the poet tells us nothing of their origin or their past. At the most he mentions that Zeus is the son of Cronus and says incidentally that Ocean and his spouse Tethys were the creators of gods and living beings.

It was only later that the Greeks felt the need to provide their gods with a genealogy and a history. Hesiod's poem, the *Theogony*, written in about the eighth century B.C., is the oldest Greek attempt at mythological classification. While recounting the origin of the gods, recalling their chief adventures and establishing their relationships, he also claims to explain the formation of the universe. The poem is thus as much a cosmogony as a theogony. A reflection of popular beliefs, the *Theogony* of Hesiod had, in Greece, a kind of official recognition.

From the sixth century B.C., however, until the beginning of the Christian era other theogonies were elaborated under the influence of Orphic doctrines; and these theogonies departed widely from the traditions of Hesiod. But the Orphic theogonies, known only to the initiated, were never popular. In addition they were too intermingled with foreign contributions, notably Asiatic, to be specifically Greek in character. We shall therefore merely give a summary of their principal features, having first given Hesiod's version of the origins of the world.

THE FORMATION OF THE WORLD AND THE BIRTH OF THE GODS

Chaos and Gaea. In the beginning, Hesiod says, there was Chaos, vast and dark. Then appeared Gaea, the deep-breasted earth, and finally Eros, 'the love which softens hearts', whose fructifying influence would thenceforth preside over the formation of beings and things.

From Chaos were born Erebus and Night who, uniting, gave birth in their turn to Ether and Hemera, the day.

On her part Gaea first bore Uranus, the sky crowned with stars, 'whom she made her equal in grandeur, so that he entirely covered her.' Then she created the high mountains and Pontus, 'the sterile sea', with its harmonious waves.

The abduction of Europa – one of the legends originating in Crete which were later incorporated into the mythology of Greece. The daughter of Phoenix, or Agenor, the king of Phoenicia, she is seated on the back of a bull – in reality Zeus in disguise – who plunges into the waves to carry her off to Crete. She later gave birth there to Minos, Rhad-amanthys and Sarpedon. Terracotta from Tanagra in the archaic style.

Gold funerary mask of a Mycenean prince. Mycenae, on the mainland of Greece, was an offshoot of the early Mediterranean civilisation which flourished in the Aegean basin before the arrival of the Greeks. This mask dates from the time of its apogee. It was discovered by Schliemann in one of the royal graves of the citadel and believed by him to be the mask of Agamemnon. It predates Homer's king, however, by several centuries. Sixteenth century B.C.

Hermes Kriophoros, the Ram-bearer. Probably a very ancient divinity of the Pelasgians (the pre-Hellenic Aegean inhabitants of Greece), Hermes is shown in this archaic statuette carrying out his original functions as protector of flocks and herds. After the Dorian invasion he lost much of his prestige, his functions being taken over by Apollo Nomius, while he himself became the son of Zeus and the messenger of the gods. *c.* sixth century B.C.

Cronus seated on his throne. The youngest son of Uranus, the starlit sky, and Gaea, the earth, Cronus castrated his father at the instigation of his mother and became the head of a new dynasty. By his sister Rhea he was the father of Hades, Poseidon, Zeus, Hestia, Demeter and Hera. The later Greeks read Cronus as Chronos and thought of him as Time. Roman statue.

Frescoes in the palace at Cnossos in Crete. Cnossos, in the north of the island, was the capital of the pre-Hellenic Aegean civilisation which had its centre in Crete. Its palace was decorated with numerous frescoes showing scenes from daily life. Here two superimposed rows of youths wearing ceremonial loin-cloths and carrying vases are probably taking part in some religious rite – the clouds above them indicating that they are in the open air. Fifteenth century B.C.

Uranus and Gaea: The Uranus group. The universe had been formed. It remained to be peopled. Gaea united with her son Uranus and produced the first race – the Titans. There were twelve of them, six male and six female: Oceanus, Coeus, Hyperion, Crius, Iapetus, Cronus; Theia, Rhea, Mnemosyne, Phoebe, Tethys and Themis.

Uranus and Gaea then gave birth to the Cyclopes: Brontes, Steropes and Arges, 'who resembled the other gods but had only one eye in the middle of their forehead'. Finally they bore three monsters: Cottus, Briareus and Gyges. 'From their shoulders sprang a hundred invincible arms and above these powerful limbs rose fifty heads attached to their backs'. For this reason they were called the Hecatoncheires or the Centimanes.

Uranus could only regard his offspring with horror, and as soon as they were born he shut them up in the depths of the earth. Gaea at first mourned, but afterwards grew angry and meditated terrible vengeance against her husband. From her bosom she drew forth gleaming steel, fashioned a sharp sickle or *harpe* and explained to her children the plan she had made. All of them hesitated, struck with horror. Only the astute Cronus, her last-born, volunteered to support his mother. When evening fell Uranus, accompanied by Night, came as usual to rejoin his wife. While he unsuspectingly slept, Cronus, who with his mother's aid lay in hiding, armed himself with the sickle, mutilated his father atrociously and cast the bleeding genitals into the sea. From the terrible wound black blood dropped and the drops, seeping into the earth, gave birth to the redoubtable Furies, to monstrous giants and to the ash-tree nymphs, the Meliae. As for the debris which floated on the surface of the waves, it broke into a white foam from which was born a young goddess, Aphrodite, 'who was first carried towards the divine Cythera and thence as far as Cyprus surrounded with waves'.

The Character of the First Gods. Such are the first divine figures and the first drama they underwent. Some of the actors are, it is true, rather vague and ill-defined.

The Chaos of Hesiod, the name of which comes from a Greek root meaning 'to gape', simply designates open space. Only later,

Statue of the goddess Hera.
The wife of Zeus and, as such,
the chief feminine deity of
Olympus, Hera presided over all
phases of feminine existence and
was above all the goddess of
marriage and maternity. Her chief
sanctuary was at Samos, where she
was believed to have been born,
and it was here that this over-
lifesize statue was discovered.
It was dedicated to the goddess by
Cheramyes and was originally
painted. Marble. *c.* 560 B.C.

The Minotaur. The Cretan
bull-god appeared in
Greek mythology as the offspring
of Pasiphaë, the wife of Minos,
King of Crete, and a bull.
Half human and half bull, it is
depicted in this archaic statuette as
a man with a bull's head and
upraised arms. the Minotaur fed
exclusively on human flesh and
lived in a palace called the
Labyrinth. It was finally killed by
Theseus. Bronze. *c.* eighth
century B.C.

Head of Gaea. Probably the great deity of the early Greeks,
Gaea represented the earth and was worshipped as the universal
mother who had created the universe and borne both the first
race of gods and the first humans. She was later superseded by
other divinities but continued
to preside over marriages and oaths and be honoured as a prophetess.
She had a number of sanctuaries.

because of a false derivation from a word meaning 'to pour', was
Chaos considered to mean the confused and unorganised mass of
the elements scattered through space. Chaos is moreover a pure
cosmic principle devoid of god-like characteristics.

The same may be said of Hesiod's Eros, who has nothing in
common with the Eros whom we shall meet in later legends. Here
Eros has only a metaphysical significance: he represents the force
of attraction which causes beings to come together.

Uranus, son and husband of Gaea, is the starlit sky. It may be
pointed out that he received no cult in Greece. This conception
of the sky and the earth, considered as two primordial divinities,
is common to all Indo-European peoples. In the Rig-Veda the
sky and the earth were already called 'the immortal couple' and
the 'two grandparents of the world'.

Gaea. The only divinity with well-defined features is Gaea, the
earth. According to Hesiod it seems likely that Gaea, from whom
all things issued, had been the great deity of the primitive Greeks.
Like the Aegeans and like the peoples of Asia, the Greeks must
doubtless have originally worshipped the Earth in whom they beheld
the mother-goddess. This is again confirmed by the Homeric hymn
in which the poet says: 'I shall sing of Gaea, universal mother,
firmly founded, the oldest of divinities.'

Gaea, 'the deep-breasted', whose soil nourishes all that exists,
and by whose benevolence men are blessed with fair children and
all the pleasant fruits of earth, was thus at one time the supreme
goddess whose majesty was acknowledged not only by men but by
the gods themselves. Later, when the victorious dynasty of the
Olympians was established, Gaea's prestige was not lessened. It
was still she whom the gods invoked when they made oaths: 'I

swear by Gaea and the vast sky above her,' Hera proclaims when,
in the *Iliad*, she answers Zeus' accusations.

Gaea the omnipotent not only created the universe and bore
the first race of the gods, but also gave birth to the human race.
Thus in the myth of Erichthonius she draws him forth from her own
bosom and offers him to Athene: he was the first inhabitant of Attica.

The power of Gaea was also manifest in her gift of foretelling the
future. The Oracle of Delphi, before it passed into Apollo's hands,
had originally belonged to Gaea.

Later, as other divinities rose in the estimation of men, the role
of Gaea gradually became less important. Her cult, however, always
continued in Greece. She presided over marriages and was honoured
as pre-eminent among prophetesses. At Patras the sick came to
consult her. She was particularly venerated at Aegae, at Delphi
and at Olympia. She had sanctuaries at Dodona, Tegea, Sparta
and at Athens, near the Areopagus. She was offered first fruits
and grain; but when she was invoked as the guardian of the sanctity
of oaths a black ewe was immolated in her honour. She was commonly represented in the form of a gigantic woman.

The Titans. The Titans, who formed the first divine race, had for
the most part no very clearly defined personality. The etymology
of their name which Hesiod gives (from a word meaning 'to stretch
out', because they had stretched out their hand against their father)
is fanciful. Their name probably derives from a Cretan word which
meant 'king'.

In Greece the Titans were honoured as the ancestors of men.
To them was attributed the invention of the arts and of magic.

Cyclopes and Hecatoncheires. In Hesiod the Cyclopes were storm
genii, as their names indicate: Brontes, thunder; Steropes, lightning;
Arges, thunderbolt.

As for the Hecatoncheires or Centimanes – the 'hundred-handed' –
their names are sufficient to characterise them. They, too, were
three in number: Cottus, the Furious; Briareus, the Vigorous;
Gyges, the Big-limbed.

The Tholos at Delphi. Situated on the lower slopes of Mount Parnassus, Delphi was the most ancient and sacred sanctuary in Greece. Its famous oracle was presided over by Apollo and drew worshippers from far and near. The Tholos is one a number of buildings standing in a precinct dedicated to Athene – the only deity apart from Apollo to have her own temple at Delphi. Pentelic marble. Beginning of the fourth century B.C.

Titans, Cyclopes and Hecatoncheires symbolised the tumultuous forces of nature.

Orphic Cosmogonies. To the above primitive and popular cosmogony followers of Orphism opposed other explanations of the origin of things. They claimed as their authority the apocryphal writings attributed to Orpheus which seem actually to have been written by a priest named Onomacritus. The philosophic and scientific pre-occupations which all these systems reflect, the subtleties in which they delight, and the many abstractions which they employ, remove them from the realm of the primitive. They are metaphysical systems rather than mythology.

Taken as a whole this is roughly what they come to: the first principle was Cronus, or Time, from which came Chaos, which symbolised the infinite, and Ether, which symbolised the finite.

Chaos was surrounded by Night, which formed the enveloping cover under which, by the creative action of the Ether, cosmic matter was slowly organised. This finally assumed the shape of an egg of which Night formed the shell.

In the centre of this gigantic egg, whose upper section formed the vault of the sky and whose lower section was the earth, was born the first being, Phanes – the Light. It was Phanes who, by union with Night, created Heaven and Earth. It was he also who engendered Zeus.

We shall not dwell longer on this brief summary of Orphic doctrine; for we shall meet it again when we come to the god Dionysus, who became the supreme god of Orphism. Meanwhile Hesiod continues to recount the fate of the second divine dynasty.

CRONUS: THE BIRTH OF ZEUS: THE COMING OF THE OLYMPIANS

The Reign of Cronus. When Uranus was reduced to impotence, Cronus liberated his brothers, the Titans – with the exception of the Cyclopes and the Hecatoncheires – and became chief of the new dynasty.

Under his reign the work of creation continued. Night gave birth to Doom (Moros), to black Ker (Moera) and to Death; then to Sleep and his retinue of Dreams. She then bore bantering Gaiety (Momus) and wailing Misery (Oizus), and the Hesperides who guarded the golden apples beyond the Ocean. Then came the Fates: Clotho, Lachesis and Atropos, who when a mortal was born apportioned his share of good and evil. Night also bore Nemesis, fearful to mortals, Fraud, Incontinence, Old Age and Eris (Strife) who in turn gave birth to Sorrow, Forgetfulness and Hunger, to Disease, Combat, Murder, Battles, Massacres, Quarrels, Lies and Equivocations, to Injustice and Oaths.

Pontus, the sea, united with Gaea, the earth, to produce Nereus the Truthful, Thaumas the Monstrous, Phorcys the Intrepid and pretty-cheeked Ceto and Eurybia with the heart of steel.

To Nereus and Doris, daughter of the Ocean, were born fifty daughters, the Nereids. To Thaumas and Electra were born Iris, the rainbow, and the Harpies with their fair tresses. By Phorcys Ceto bore the Graeae (the Old Ones) who came into the world with white hair, and the Gorgons who lived beyond the Ocean in the land of the Hesperides.

The Titans also begot children either with their sisters or with nymphs.

Oceanus and Tethys had three thousand sons, the Rivers, and three thousand daughters, the Water Nymphs, plus Metis (Wisdom), Tyche (Fortune), and Styx (the Infernal River). To Hyperion and Theia were born Helios (the Sun), Selene (the Moon) and Eos (the Dawn). Coeus and Phoebe engendered Leto and Asteria. By Eurybia Crius had: Astraeus, Pallas and Perses. By the Oceanid Clymene or, according to others, by Asia, Iapetus fathered Atlas, Menoetius, Epimetheus and Prometheus. Finally Cronus married his sister Rhea, who gave him three daughters: Hestia, Demeter and Hera; and three sons: Hades, Poseidon and Zeus.

Typhon. In her fury that Zeus had given birth to Athene alone and unaided, Hera prayed that she too might bear a child unaided and produced the monster Typhon. Her son is confused with another Typhoeus, or Typhon, the son of Gaea and Tartarus, the lower half of whose body was composed of coiled serpents and whose wings blotted out the sun. Detail from a red-figured vase.

But whether it was that he feared, as it seems an oracle had predicted, that he would be supplanted by one of his children, or whether he had agreed with his older brothers, the Titans, to leave no posterity, Cronus swallowed each of his children as it was born.

The Birth and Childhood of Zeus. Rhea, his wife, was overwhelmed with boundless grief. She asked herself in despair if she were condemned to see all her progeny thus disappear. When the time approached for her to give birth to Zeus she beseeched her own parents, Uranus and Gaea, to help her save this child. On their advice she went to Crete and there, in a deep cavern under the thick forests of Mount Aegeum, she brought forth her son. Gaea took the new-born baby and undertook to bring it up. Meanwhile Rhea wrapped up an enormous stone in swaddling clothes and presented it to the unsuspecting Cronus, who swallowed it at once.

Meanwhile Gaea had carried her grandson to Mount Ida (others say to Mount Dicte) and given him for safe keeping into the hands of the nymphs Adrasteia and Ida, daughters of Melisseus, king of Crete. The two nymphs surrounded the young god with care and attention. They put him in a golden cradle and to amuse him Adrasteia presented him with a ball composed of hoops of gold. So that Cronus should not hear the baby crying the Curetes executed around the cradle warlike dances, beating their bronze shields with their swords.

Who exactly were these Curetes? In primitive times there had been a tribe of this name settled in Aetolia. On the other hand the Greeks gave them the epithet *Gegeneis* (children of the earth) or *Imbrogeneis* (children of the rain), so they may have been earth-spirits. Herodotus, however, calls them Phoenicians, followers of Cadmus, who had settled in Crete. Others say they came from Phrygia. Probably the Curetes were Cretan priests devoted to the orgiastic cult of the great goddess Rhea. They were distinguished by their half-warrior, half-sacredotal character. To increase their prestige the first among them were deified and thus became the

sacred Curetes, the protectors of Zeus. They had temples, in Messina notably, and – which tends to confirm their earth-spirit origin – they were invoked in making oaths. The Curetes appear many times in the mythological history of Greece; on Hera's orders they spirited away at birth the young Epaphus, son of Zeus and Io, and were in consequence put to death by Zeus.

Thus sheltered from his father's cruelty the young Zeus grew up in the forests of Ida. For a wet-nurse he was given the goat Amaltheia. She was a wondrous animal whose aspect terrified even the immortals. In gratitude Zeus later placed her among the constellations and from her hide, which no arrow could pierce, he made the redoubtable aegis. To the nymphs he gave one of her horns, conferring upon it the marvellous property of refilling itself inexhaustibly with whatever food or drink was wished for; this was the horn of plenty (cornucopia). According to certain authors Amaltheia was the wife of Melisseus and suckled the young god with her milk. Others make her a nymph who simply watched over the child Zeus, claiming that the god was fed on ambrosia and nectar brought to him by doves and an eagle. And if Adrasteia and Ida are called daughters of Melisseus (from the Greek *melissa*, a bee) was this not because the bees of Ida brought their scented honey to the divine child?

The oracle which had predicted to Cronus that he would one day be overthrown by one of his sons had not lied. As soon as Zeus had reached manhood he planned to punish his father. Apollodorus tells us that he summoned to his aid Metis, daughter of Oceanus. Metis gave Cronus a draught that made him vomit up the stone and with it the gods, his own children, whom he had swallowed. Vanquished by the might of Zeus, Cronus was driven from the sky and cast to the very depths of the universe and there enchained in the region which stretches beneath the earth and the fruitless sea. This at least is what Homer says; according to others Cronus was sent to the ends of the earth to dwell in bliss, or plunged into mysterious slumber in distant Thule.

The creation of Man. In the presence of the gods of Olympus (Poseidon, Hermes, Hera, Zeus, Apollo) Prometheus prepares to animate the body of the first man whom he has just fashioned. Bas-relief from a sarcophagus in the National Museum, Naples.

To bear witness to his victory Zeus placed the stone Cronus had disgorged in divine Pytho, at the foot of Parnassus, 'to be one day in the eyes of mortals a monument to these wonders'.

This famous stone was for long preserved at Delphi within the walls of the tomb of Neoptolemus. The era of the Olympians now began.

The Revolt of the Titans. The Titans, with the exception of Oceanus, were jealous of the new gods and wished to reconquer the kingdom of which they had been dispossessed. Then the terrible struggle began. From their stronghold on Mount Othrys the Titans launched furious attacks upon Olympus. For ten years the outcome of the war remained doubtful. Zeus descended into Tartarus where, guarded by the monster Campe, the Hecatoncheires and the Cyclopes were kept prisoners. He set them free and made them his allies. The Cyclopes gave him the thunderbolt and the Hecatoncheires put their invincible arms at his service. Seizing in their enormous arms great boulders, they crushed the Titans. 'Sea and earth resounded with the horrifying clamour and the shaken firmament groaned aloud.' Zeus, too, was unable to curb his warlike rage and joined in the fray. From the heights of Olympus, Hesiod tells us, from the heights of the heavens he hurled thunder and lightning. With unwearying hand he flung bolt after bolt, and the air was rent with sound and fury. The fertile earth shuddered and burned; vast forests flamed and all things melted and boiled: the River Ocean, the immense sea and the entire earth. Around the infernal Titans arose stifling mists and blazing air; their bold glances were blinded by flashes of lightning. The fire even reached Chaos, and from what the eye could behold and the ear distinguish one would have said that sky and earth were confounded, the earth shaken on its very foundations, the sky crashing down from its heights. Such was the mighty uproar of this battle among the gods!

In spite of their pride and courage the Titans were finally defeated and, bound with chains, cast into the abysmal depths of the earth – as far below its surface as is the earth itself from the sky. 'It is there among impenetrable shadows and foul vapours, at the very end of the world, that the Titans, by the will of the king of the heavens, are buried.'

The War of the Giants. Zeus had scarcely put down this dangerous revolt when he was forced to undergo a new struggle, this time against the Giants. The Giants had sprung from the blood of the mutilated Uranus and were not only distinguished for their size. For these monstrous sons of the Earth had legs like serpents and their feet were formed of reptiles' heads. At the instant that they emerged from the entrails of the ground at Phlegra, in the peninsula of Pallene, they appeared in glittering armour grasping enormous spears. Porphyrion and Alcyoneus were their leaders. They at once attacked Olympus, whose mass dominated the plain of Phlegra on the west. Islands, rivers, mountains, all gave way before them. 'While one,' says Claudian, 'with vigorous arm shook Mount Oeta of Thessaly in the air, another balanced the summits of Mount Pangaea in his powerful hand. One armed himself with the ice of Mount Athos, another seized Ossa and lifted it, while still another tore up Rhodope...From everywhere the horrible din echoed.' To reach the heights of Olympus the giants piled the surrounding mountains one upon another, Ossa on Pelion. But grouped around Zeus the gods – with the exception of Demeter who took no part in the struggle – stood their ground before the assailants. Apollo struck down Ephialtes. Clytius fell under the blows of Hecate or Hephaestus. The impetuous Ares pierced Pelorus and Mimas with his sword. Poseidon pursued Polybutes across the sea, flung the island of Nisyros on top of him and buried him.

The gods alone, however, could not triumph, for the oracle had declared that the sons of Gaea would succumb only to the blows of a mortal. This mortal was Hercules (Gk. Heracles), with whom Dionysus was sometimes associated. While Dionysus struck down Rhaetos (or Eurytus), Hercules attacked Alcyoneus. At first the giant resisted his blows. Hercules was astonished, but Athene revealed to him that Alcyoneus was invulnerable as long as he stood

Typhoeus or perhaps Typhon. The monster's three human torsos terminate in the triple body of a dragon. He holds birds and sparks of fire in his hands. Sculpture in porous limestone from the Hecatompedon. Period of Solon.

on the soil which had given him birth. The hero then seized the giant in his arms and carried him away from the territory of Pallene and at once slew him. Porphyrion wished to avenge his brother, but Zeus inspired in him a sudden passion for Hera. While the giant pursued Hera, Hercules pierced him with a deadly arrow. From that moment the defeat of the giants was assured. In vain Pallas and Enceladus attempted to struggle against Athene; one after the other they were overcome. With the skin of Pallas Athene fashioned the aegis. As for Enceladus, she buried him under the island of Sicily. And even today when the giant turns over, the entire island quakes.

Typhoeus. Gaea, however, could not resign herself to the defeat of her children. Against Zeus she raised up a final monster, Typhoeus, whom she had borne to Tartarus. He was a terrifying creature whose hands worked ceaselessly and whose feet were never still. From his shoulders sprang a hundred horrible dragons' heads, each with a darting black tongue and eyes which spurted searing flame. From his thighs emerged innumerable vipers; his body was covered with feathers; thick bristles sprouted from his head and cheeks. He was taller than the tallest mountain. At sight of Typhoeus the gods were seized with fear and fled as far as Egypt. Only Zeus stood firm before the monster; but entwined in the myriad coils of the serpents he fell into the hands of Typhoeus who cut the tendons of his hands and feet and imprisoned him in his den in Cilicia. Rescued by Hermes, Zeus renewed the struggle. With his thunderbolts he overwhelmed Typhoeus, who fled to Sicily, where under Etna the god crushed him.

Thus in the first ages of the world, when the elements were not yet mastered and matter was still rebellious, there occurred terrifying cataclysms which threatened to overthrow everything. The ground writhed and trembled, the mountains crumbled or split apart to belch forth enormous boulders and molten stone, rivers broke from their courses, the seas rose and engulfed the earth. But the divine wisdom, regulator of the universe, finally imposed its will over all these disorderly elements. The earth became firm, the volcanoes subsided, the now well-behaved rivers again irrigated the plains and the tumultuous sea no longer tossed its waves beyond the sands of its shores. Harmony was born anew and man, reassured, gave thanks to the god whose might had triumphed over the forces of evil.

The defeat of Typhoeus assured the final and lasting supremacy of Zeus. From then on no serious adversary dared to measure his strength with this god who had vanquished all the powers of evil. His reign, established by triple victory, would never be seriously disturbed; and among the Olympians Zeus maintained his rank of uncontested master of gods and men.

THE ORIGINS OF HUMANITY

Prometheus. The Titan Iapetus was the father of four sons. Their mother, according to Hesiod, was the Oceanid Clymene; according to Aeschylus, she was Themis. Two of these sons, Menoetius and Atlas, were punished by Zeus, doubtless for having taken part in the revolt of the Titans. Menoetius was plunged into darkest Erebus, in punishment for 'his wickedness and boundless audacity'. As for Atlas, he was condemned to stand for ever, before the Hesperides on the edge of the world, and to bear upon his shoulders the vault of the heavens. The other two – Prometheus (who foresees) and Epimetheus (who reflects after the event) – had a different fate and played an important role in the legendary history of the origins of humanity.

In view of the unchallengeable might of the Olympians, Prometheus' only weapon was cunning. During the revolt of the Titans he had kept a prudent neutrality and had even made overtures to Zeus when it seemed likely that the war would be won by him. Thus Prometheus had been admitted into Olympus and the circle of the Immortals. But he entertained a silent grudge against the destroyers of his race and revenged himself by favouring mortals to the detriment of the gods.

He had, perhaps, other reasons for his interest in the human race; for a tradition – rather late, it is true – said that Prometheus was the creator of mankind. It was he who with earth and water – some said with his own tears – had fashioned the body of the first man into which Athene breathed soul and life. In Phocis the author

Pausanias saw bits of hardened clay which had the odour of human skin and which were plainly the residue of the slime employed by Prometheus.

But it seems that this creation took place only after the earlier race of man had been destroyed in the deluge. Current opinion actually attributed to mankind an older and nobler origin. 'Men and gods,' says Pindar, 'we are of the same family; we owe the breath of life to the same mother.'

The Four Ages of Man. The first men, who were contemporaries of Cronus, enjoyed complete happiness. It was the Golden Age. Hesiod says: 'They lived like gods, free from worry and fatigue; old age did not afflict them; they rejoiced in continual festivity.' Their lot did not include immortality, but at least 'they died as though overcome by sweet slumber. All the blessings of the world were theirs: the fruitful earth gave forth its treasures unbidden. At their death, men of the Golden Age became benevolent genii, 'protectors and tutelary guardians of the living'.

After the Golden Age came the Silver Age, during which lived a race of feeble and inept men who obeyed their mothers all their lives (i.e. it was a matriarchal age). They were also agriculturalists, Hesiod says.

The men of the Bronze Age were robust as ash trees and delighted only in oaths and warlike exploits. 'Their pitiless hearts were as hard as steel; their might was untameable, their arms invincible.' They ended by mutually cutting each other's throats. From this generation, however, dated the discovery of the first metals and the first attempts at civilisation.

After the Bronze Age Hesiod places the Heroic Age, peopled by the valiant warriors who fought before Thebes and under the walls of Troy. But the more widespread opinion was that after the Bronze Age came the Iron Age – the contemporary age, a period of misery and crime 'when men respect neither their vows, nor justice, nor virtue'.

Thus they explained the progressive degeneration of mankind.

The Theft of Fire: Pandora. As long as Cronus had reigned, gods and men had lived on terms of mutual understanding. Hesiod says: 'In those days meals were taken in common; men and the immortal gods sat down together.' Everything changed with the coming of the Olympians. Over men Zeus asserted his divine supremacy. A meeting of gods and men was held at Sicyon to determine which portion of victims offered in sacrifice was owed to the gods. Prometheus, who was in charge of the partition, laid out an enormous ox which he had cut up in his own way. He arranged the flesh, the entrails and the most succulent morsels in the skin and placed them on one side; on the other side he perfidiously laid the fleshless bones which he had covered with a rich layer of fat. Zeus, who was invited to take first choice, chose the bones; but when he had removed the white, gleaming fat and discovered nothing but the animal's bones he fell into a rage. In his anger he withheld fire from the unfortunate race who lived on earth. But the astute Prometheus went to the island of Lemnos, where Hephaestus kept his forges. There he stole a brand of the holy fire which he enclosed in a hollow stalk and carried back to men. Another version of the story claims that he lighted his torch at the wheel of the sun.

Outraged by the theft, Zeus sent a fresh calamity to men. He ordered Hephaestus to fashion clay and water into a body, to give it vital force and human voice, and to make therefrom a virgin whose dazzling beauty would equal that of the immortal goddesses. All the divinities heaped their especial gifts on this new creature, who received the name of Pandora. Hermes, however, put perfidy into Pandora's heart and lies into her mouth. After which Zeus sent her as a gift to Epimetheus. Although his brother Prometheus had warned him against accepting any gift from the ruler of Olympus, the imprudent Epimetheus was enchanted by Pandora's beauty, welcomed her, and made a place for her among men. Unhappy imprudence! For Pandora brought in her arms a great vase – which is incorrectly called 'Pandora's Box'. She raised its lid, and the terrible afflictions with which the vase had been filled escaped and spread over the earth. Hope alone did not fly away. Thus, with the arrival of the first woman, misery made its appearance on earth.

The Deluge: Deucalion and Pyrrha. Zeus' rage, however, was not appeased. In his anger he resolved to annihilate the human race

The Poseidon of Artemision. Discovered in the sea off Cape Artemision, this great bronze statue shows the god of the sea hurling his trident–the sign of his sovereigny. After the shipwreck of the Persian fleet off the Cape in 480 B.C. the god was worshipped as Poseidon Soter (the Saviour), a title normally reserved for Zeus, and this may explain the similarity of the pose to that of Zeus hurling his thunderbolt which has sometimes led to the statue being described as the latter. *c.* 460 B.C.

by burying it beneath the waves of a deluge. But once again Prometheus was on guard. He warned his son Deucalion who, with his wife Pyrrha, daughter of Epimetheus and Pandora, then reigned in Thessaly. On the advice of his father, Deucalion constructed an ark and with his wife went aboard. For nine days and nine nights they floated on the waters. On the tenth day the downpour ceased and the two survivors disembarked on the crest of Mount Othrys or Mount Parnassus. Deucalion offered up sacrifice to Zeus Phyxius (protector of fugitives) and the god, touched by his piety, promised to grant him his first wish. Deucalion asked Zeus to renew the human race.

Another legend says that Deucalion and Pyrrha, having gone to Delphi, addressed their prayers to Themis. 'Veil your heads,' replied the goddess, 'remove the girdles of your robes and cast behind you the bones of your first ancestor.' Stricken at first with astonishment, Deucalion and Pyrrha at last solved the mystery of this ambiguous command. They veiled their heads and walked across the plain, throwing over their shoulders stones torn from the earth – for were they not descendants of Gaea, the earth, and were not the rocks her very bones? The stones which Deucalion threw were changed into men, those that Pyrrha cast were transformed into women.

The human race was renewed and Zeus recovered from his anger. Deucalion was regarded as the father of the Hellenes, the first king and founder of towns and temples. It was he, they said, who built the temple of Olympian Zeus at Athens, and nearby the temple his tomb was pointed out. In Cynos, however, they also boasted of having the tomb of Deucalion and his wife Pyrrha.

Ganymede and the eagle.
The son of king Tros is being
snatched up to Olympus by an
eagle, or by Zeus in that shape, to
become the cup-bearer of the gods–
their choice having fallen on him
on account of his great beauty.
There he was made immortal and
dispensed nectar from a golden
bowl – a function formerly
performed by Zeus' daughter
Hebe. Hellenistic sculpture.

The Torture of Prometheus. Although peace had been concluded
between Zeus and mankind, Prometheus had to pay cruelly for
his trickery and thefts. At the command of Zeus, Hephaestus,
assisted by Kratos and Bia, seized and bound Prometheus with
indestructible chains to one of the crests of Mount Caucasus.
There, 'an eagle with outstretched wings, sent by Zeus, fed upon
his immortal liver; as much as the winged monster devoured
during the day, that much grew again during the night'. In spite
of the torture the Titan persisted in his attitude of revolt. Disdaining
complaints and humiliating prayers he never ceased to defy the lord
of Olympus and to express his hatred in violent outbursts. For was
he not in possession of a secret which dangerously concerned the
future of Zeus himself?

Finally after thirty years of suffering – others say thirty thousand
years – he was with Zeus' permission rescued by the divine Hercules,
who slew the eagle and broke the prisoner's chains. Prometheus
then revealed to Zeus his famous secret and warned him that
if he continued to pay court to Thetis, daughter of Nereus, he would
run the risk of seeing a son born who would dethrone him. Not
wishing to chance the same misadventure that had befallen his
father and his grandfather, Zeus abandoned his amorous enterprise
and allowed Thetis to marry a mortal, Peleus.

Prometheus, however, could not acquire divine immortality
unless some immortal consented to exchange destinies with him.
Now the centaur Chiron, whom Hercules had struck with a poisoned
arrow, was in despair lest his wound never healed. To put an end
to his suffering Chiron begged to be allowed to descend into Hades
in the place of Prometheus. Zeus consented, and from then on the

son of Iapetus took his permanent place on Olympus. And the
Athenians, who saw in Prometheus the benefactor of mankind
and the father of all the arts and sciences, raised an altar to him in
the gardens of the Academy.

OLYMPUS

Mount Olympus. On the confines of Thessaly and Macedonia.
along the shores of the Aegean Sea from which it is separated only
by a narrow littoral, rises the chain of Olympus. While on the north
the mountain group descends to the plain by a series of gentle
hills, the south face – that which the Greeks saw – falls precipitously
and the mountain offers the aspect of a rocky cliff. Above a sort of
monster plateau. itself steeply flanked which serves as a base, Mount
Olympus soars in one sweep up to more than nine thousand feet.
Down its sheer slopes, covered with dark woods, tumble numerous
torrents which dig deep furrows. rather like the folds of a garment.
Thus the poets called it 'Olympus of the innumerable folds'. The
line of the mountain peaks is rounded into a kind of amphitheatre
and the upper tiers of rock, formed by the heaping up of huge
boulders round which cling shreds of cloud, look like gigantic
seats arranged there for the use of supernatural beings.

The mariner who sailed into the gulf of Therme (today the gulf
of Salonica) would feel himself filled with religious awe when he
perceived against the hard blue line of sky the lofty profile of Mount
Olympus. Everything concurred to reveal to him the fearful majesty
of the gods. In the first place he had no doubt that Olympus was the
highest mountain in the world. Then he would remember that the

The peaks of Olympus. The throne of Zeus and the seats of the gods.

The gods on Olympus. Poseidon, Apollo, Artemis. Frieze from the Parthenon, Pentelic marble. Acropolis Museum, Athens.

narrow Vale of Tempe, which separates Olympus from Ossa and cradles under its willows and plane-trees the peaceful stream of Peneus, had been hollowed out by Zeus during his struggle with the Titans. Finally he would scarcely dare raise his eyes towards the summits; for he knew that up there, behind the veil of clouds which hid them from mortal regard, dwelt the almighty gods. Bending over his oars he would repeat the words of old Homer who, speaking of Olympus, had said: 'Never is it swept by the winds nor touched by snow; a purer air surrounds it, a white clarity envelops it and the gods there taste of a happiness which lasts as long as their eternal lives.'

Actually when the sons of Cronus drew lots for the partition of the empire of the world, Zeus received as his share the sublime regions of the Ether, Poseidon the tumultuous sea, and Hades the sombre depths of the earth. But it was agreed that Olympus should be held in common by all the gods and that there they should make their dwelling-place.

The Gods on Olympus. Assembled on Olympus, the gods formed a society with its own laws and hierarchy. First came the twelve great gods and goddesses: Zeus, Poseidon, Hephaestus, Hermes, Ares and Apollo; Hera, Athene, Artemis, Hestia, Aphrodite and Demeter. Beside them were ranged other divinities, some of whom did not relinquish pride of place to the great twelve. Such were Helios, Selene, Leto, Dione, Dionysus, Themis and Eos. Then, of a lower rank, forming as it were the courtiers of the Olympians and sworn to their service, came: the Horae, the Moerae, Nemesis, the Graces, the Muses, Iris, Hebe, Ganymede. It must be pointed out that Hades, although a brother of Zeus, did not frequent Olympus and, with the goddesses Persephone and Hecate, remained in his subterranean empire.

Over this society Zeus reigned as sovereign ruler. If at times the gods were tempted by rebellious impulses they were quickly reduced to obedience. In Homer we see how Zeus speaks to them: 'Let no god, let no goddess attempt to curb my will ... or I shall seize him and cast him into darkest Tartarus. Then will he recognise how much mightier am I than all the gods! Come, then, try it, O gods! And you will discover with whom you have to deal. Hang from the heavens a golden chain and attach yourselves all, gods and goddesses, to it, and no matter how hard you strive, you will not drag Zeus in his supreme wisdom from the sky down to earth. But when, afterwards, I begin to pull I shall draw you, you and the earth and the sea together, I shall draw you up and roll the chain around the summit of Olympus and you will all remain there suspended in the air.' Without quite carrying out this threat Zeus nevertheless inflicted severe penalties on gods who had displeased him. For instance he would make them serve as slaves to mortals; such was the fate of Poseidon and Apollo. Therefore the gods did not resist him and even the irascible Hera counselled prudence. 'Foolish that we are to lose our tempers with Zeus ... He sits apart and neither worries nor is disturbed; for he boasts of being incontestably superior to the immortal gods in might and power. So resign yourselves.'

Above the gods, however, and above Zeus himself hovered a supreme power to whom all were subject: Moros, or Destiny. Son of the Night, Moros, invisible and dark like his mother, prepared his decrees in the shadows and extended his inescapable dominion over all. Zeus himself could not set aside his decisions and had to submit to them like the humblest mortal. He had, moreover, no desire to set aside the decisions of Destiny; for, being himself Supreme Wisdom, he was not unaware that in upsetting the destined course of events he would introduce confusion into the universe it was his mission to govern. Thus, even when it was a matter of saving the life of his own son Sarpedon, the hour of whose death the Fates had marked down, Zeus preferred to bow his head and let what was ordained be fulfilled.

The days of the gods passed in merrymaking and laughter. Sometimes, when they intervened in the affairs of men whose quarrels they enthusiastically adopted, the gods would disagree. But these passing storms did not affect the normal serenity of Olympus.

Seated around their golden tables the gods dined on celestial nectar and ambrosia, and savoured the rising fragrance of fatted cattle which mortals burned in their honour on their altars below. Even when Zeus called them together in counsel on the topmost peak of Olympus where he resided, the fair Hebe would move among them pouring nectar, and the golden cups would pass from hand to hand.

While they drank, Apollo would delight them with the harmony of his lyre and the Muses would sing in turn in their sweet voices.

Finally, 'when the brilliant torch of the sun had disappeared the gods would take their leave and return to the dwelling Hephaestus had built with wondrous cunning for each of them, there to rest and repose'.

If the gods' daily life resembled that of men it was because, at least in appearance, their natures were not dissimilar. Their bodies were like mortal bodies, but superior in stature, strength and beauty. Ares' body, stretched on the ground, covered a length of seven plethra – well over two hundred yards – and when Hera from the heights of Olympus swore by the Styx, she could touch the earth with one hand and with the other reach the seas.

In the case of the gods, however, blood was replaced by a more fluid substance, the ichor, which rendered the body imperishable and incorruptible. This did not prevent the gods from being vulnerable to weapons used by men. But their wounds, no matter how painful, always healed and their bodies retained eternal youth.

Another privilege which the gods enjoyed was the power of metamorphosis, to change themselves if they wished into animals or even to take on the aspect of inanimate objects.

Like mortals the gods were subject to human passions. They were accessible to love, hate, anger, even to envy. They cruelly punished all who aroused their enmity, but showered favours on those who revered and honoured them with gifts.

ZEUS

The very name Zeus, in which the Sanskrit root *dyaus* and the Latin *dies* (the day) are found, evokes the idea of the luminous sky. Originally, then, Zeus was the god of the sky and of atmospheric phenomena. He was lord of the winds, of the clouds, of rain both destructive and beneficial, of the thunder. He resided in the ether, the upper part of the air, and on mountain tops. He was literally the All-high. Hence he was worshipped in elevated spots such as Mount Lycaeus in Arcadia, Mount Apesas in Argolis, Parnassus and Hymettus in Attica, Helicon in Boeotia, Pelion in Thessaly, Olympus in Macedonia, Pangaea in Thrace, Ida in Crete and so forth.

His Attributes. Later Zeus took on a moral personality and became the supreme god who united in himself all the attributes of divinity. He was omnipotent, he saw everything and knew everything. Thus he was the fountainhead of all divination, whether he spoke oracularly in person as on Olympus and at Dodona, or whether he had recourse as at Delphi to the intermediary of Apollo, his prophet. A wise sovereign, he ordained all according to the law of Fate with which his own will was merged. To mortals he dispensed good and evil; he was, moreover, kind and compassionate. Though he chastised the wicked he was capable of pity. He averted threatening dangers (*Alexikakos*); he protected the weak, the indigent, the fugitive and, in general, all suppliants (*Milichios*). His solicitude also extended to the family as god of the hearth (*Ephestios*), of marriage (*Gamelios*), of friendship (*Philios*), and of the peoples' assemblies (*Agoraios*). Finally he was the protector-god of all Greece – Panhellenic Zeus.

His Cult. The most famous sanctuary of Zeus was that of Dodona, in Epirus. It was also the oldest, dating back to the Pelasgians. People came there from all parts of Greece to consult the oracle of a sacred oak whose rustling and murmurs were regarded as the words of Zeus himself. On the origin of this oracle Herodotus, who claims to have heard it from the lips of the priestesses of Dodona, says: 'Two black doves flew from Thebes in Egypt, one to Libya and the other to Dodona. The latter, alighting in an oak tree, began to speak in a human voice and to say that an oracle of Zeus should be founded in this place. The people of Dodona believed that they had received an order coming from the gods, and on the dove's advice founded the oracle.' The interpretation of the oracles of Dodona was entrusted to a college of priests, the Selli, a name which was undoubtedly none other than that of the former inhabitants of the country. These priests practised asceticism, slept on the ground and never washed their feet. To the Selli were later added three priestesses, called the Peleiades. They were more especially attached to the service of the goddess Dione, who was venerated at Dodona at the side of Zeus, here taking over the role of Hera. Dione was a Pelasgian divinity and, according to Hesiod, the daughter of Oceanus and Tethys. She was said to be mother of Aphrodite.

Among Zeus' other sanctuaries must be mentioned that of Mount Lycaeus in Arcadia on the summit of which was a mound of earth, fronted by two columns with engraved eagles. Here, it was said, human sacrifice was once practised. The root from which the word Lycaeus was formed (it means 'light') reveals that Zeus was here originally a solar deity.

Finally there was the celebrated temple of Olympus with its famous statue of the god sculptured by Phidias. It rose on a richly ornamented pedestal which was about ten yards high and seven yards wide. The statue itself was more than thirteen yards in height. Seated on a throne of bronze, gold, ivory and ebony, the god held in his right hand a crowned Victory while his left hand rested on a sceptre surmounted by an eagle. He was dressed in a golden mantle strewn with flowers. On his brow there was an olive wreath and his countenance, framed by a long beard, wore an expression of serene majesty.

Representations. The Olympian Zeus of Phidias represented the ideal which inspired subsequent artists. The god was normally depicted as a man in the fullness of maturity, of robust body, grave countenance and with broad forehead jutting out above deeply set eyes. His face is framed by thick waving hair and a finely curled beard. Except in primitive images he is rarely nude. He usually wears a long mantle which leaves his chest and right arm free. His attributes are the sceptre in his left hand, in his right hand the thunderbolt and at his feet the eagle. Often on his brow he wears a crown of oak-leaves.

The Marriages of Zeus. Before marrying Hera and associating her officially with his sovereignty, Zeus, among whose many functions that of procreation was pre-eminent, had contracted numerous unions.

His first wife was Metis (Wisdom) who, says Hesiod, 'knew more things than all the gods and men put together'. But Gaea and Uranus warned Zeus that if he had children by Metis they would be more powerful than he, and dethrone him. So, when Metis was about to give birth to Athene, Zeus, in order to forestall the danger, swallowed the mother and with her the unborn baby. By avoiding the risk of an embarrassing posterity in this manner he also now embodied supreme Wisdom – a double benefit.

Next he married Themis, daughter of Uranus and Gaea. Themis was the Law which regulates both physical and moral order. It is not surprising, then, that her children should be: the Horae or Seasons; Eunomia (Wise Legislation); Dike (Justice); Eirene (Peace), and finally the Fates or Moerae who were also said to be the daughters of Night. Even when she was replaced by Hera, Themis continued to remain near Zeus as an adviser, and she was always revered on Olympus.

Another Titaness, Mnemosyne, was the wife of Zeus. The god stayed nine nights with her, and when her time had come Mnemosyne gave birth to nine daughters, who were the Muses.

Zeus was also enamoured of Demeter, but the goddess repulsed his advances. He changed himself into a bull and violated her, and from this union was born Kore, also called Persephone.

The Oceanid Eurynome was also among Zeus' wives and was the mother of the three Graces or Charites.

Zeus and Hera. And then Zeus married Hera. Actually their relationship was already long established. In the days when Cronus

The marriage of Poseidon and Amphitrite. Poseidon and Amphitrite are seated in a carriage drawn by two Tritons one of whom plays a conch-shell and the other a lyre. Behind them follow a procession of Tritons and Nereids. The daughter of Oceanus or Nereus, Amphitrite at first fled from Poseidon but was later brought back by a dolphin to become his wife. Frieze from an altar in the temple of Neptune at Rome.

still reigned, the young goddess grew up in the island of Euboea under the care of her nurse Macris. Zeus came to her one day and bore her to Mount Cithaeron on the confines of Attica and Boeotia, where he lay with her. Another legend places the first encounter between Zeus and Hera in the region of the Hesperides, while at Cnossus in Crete, near the river Theris, they also pointed out the exact spot where the marriage of the divine couple was consummated. Pausanias relates the adventure differently. In order not to awaken his sister's suspicions Zeus came to her in the form of a cuckoo. It was winter and the bird seemed to be frozen with the cold. Touched by pity, the young goddess warmed the cuckoo by holding it against her breast. Zeus then reassumed his natural form and attempted to take advantage of the situation. Hera resisted at first and gave way only after Zeus had promised to marry her. The marriage, solemnly celebrated on Olympus, did not, however, put an end to Zeus' amorous enterprises. Braving Hera's jealousy and ignoring the misfortunes which this jealousy could bring upon its victims, Zeus continued enthusiastically to pursue goddesses and mortal women.

Zeus and the Titanesses. Zeus was not always successful. Thus, on the advice of Prometheus, he freely renounced Thetis for fear of begetting by her a son who would dethrone him. Nor could he overcome the resistance of the nymph Asteria, daughter of Coeus and Phoebe, who in order to escape him changed herself into a quail and threw herself into the sea where she became a floating island called, at first, Ortygia, and later Delos.

Leto was less shy than her sister Asteria and surrendered to Zeus' seductions. In this way she earned Hera's enmity and, as we shall later see, it was only after many misadventures that she was finally able to bring into the world her two children: Apollo and Artemis.

Maia, daughter of Atlas and Pleione, was more adroit and succeeded in evading Hera's jealous eye. She lived in Arcadia on Mount Cyllene. 'Escaping from the crowd of happy immortals,' says the Homeric hymn, 'Maia of the fair tresses lived in the depths of a dark cavern. It was here that the son of Cronus lay all night with the nymph whilst sweet sleep held alabaster-limbed Hera, sleep who thus deceives immortals and feeble men alike.' Maia gave birth to Hermes.

It was said that another daughter of Atlas, Electra, bore Zeus Harmonia – whom Hesiod, however, calls the daughter of Ares and Aphrodite – and Dardanus. Finally a third daughter of Atlas, Taygete, was pursued by Zeus. According to some accounts she was protected by Artemis, who turned her into a hind and only later restored her to her original form. In gratitude Taygete consecrated to the goddess a hind whose horns she had gilded and which we shall meet again during the labours of Hercules. According to other accounts Taygete submitted to Zeus and gave birth to Lacedaemon.

Zeus, 'The Father of gods and men'. He was the supreme god of the Greeks, the protector of laws and morals and the dispenser of good and evil. After defeating his father Cronus, he reigned supreme over the gods of Olympus and was the father of Athene, Artemis, Apollo, Ares and Dionysus and of innumerable other children by nymphs and mortals. His most famous sanctuary was at Dodona.
Greek sculpture, fourth century, B.C.

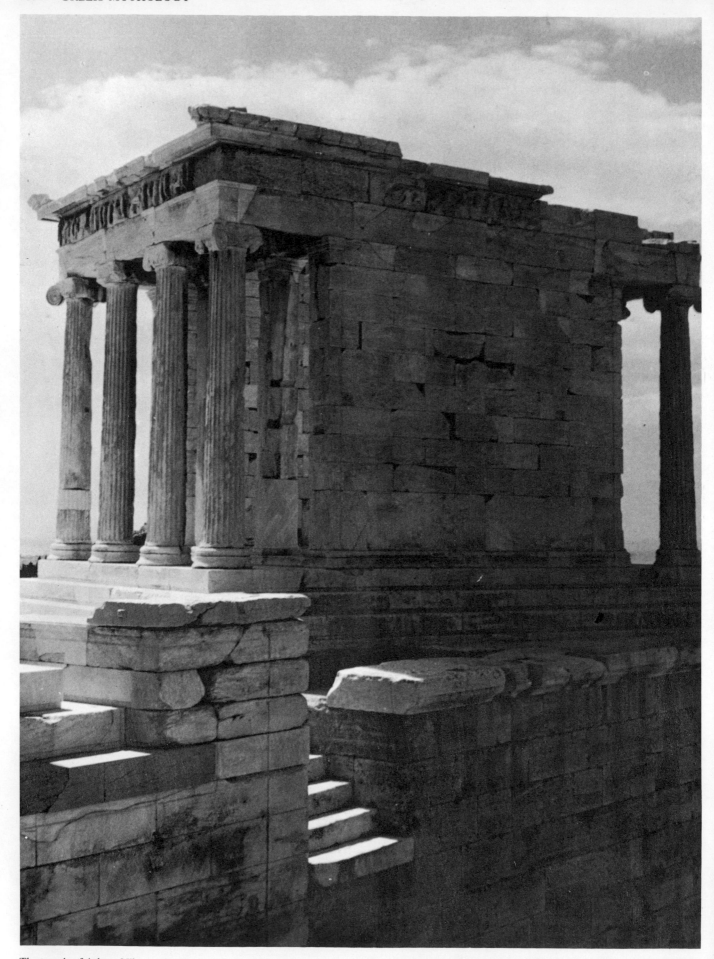

The temple of Athene Nike on the Acropolis of Athens. This little temple is the smallest of the three temples dedicated to the goddess Athene on the Acropolis of Athens. It was demolished by the Turks in the seventeenth century and built into a bastion but has since been reconstructed from the original blocks. The goddess was worshipped here in her role of bringer of victory. The frieze depicts the Battle of Plataea. Third quarter of the fifth century B.C.

Zeus and the Nymphs. Among the nymphs loved by Zeus must also be mentioned Aegina and Antiope, the daughters of the river-god Asopus. The former had been carried off by Zeus who, assuming the shape of an eagle or a flame, had borne her to the island of Oenone or Oenopia, where she gave birth to Acacus. Asopus set out in search of them. From Sisyphus he discovered the name of his daughter's ravisher and the place where she had hidden herself. He was on the point of finding her when Zeus struck him with a thunderbolt and forced him to return to his river-bed. Others relate how Asopus surprised the two lovers: to protect Aegina from the paternal fury Zeus changed her into an island and himself into a rock.

As for Antiope – who, according to Pausanias, was not the daughter of Asopus but of Nycteus – Zeus approached her in the form of a satyr and surprised her when she was asleep. To hide her shame Antiope fled to Sicyon, where she married the king, Epopeus. Her father Nycteus killed himself with despair, but before he died he charged his brother Lycus to avenge his honour. Lycus seized Sicyon, put Epopeus to death and brought Antiope back, a prisoner. At Eleuthere Antiope gave birth to twins, Amphion and Zethus, whom she exposed on Mount Cithaeron and who later figured among the chief heroes of Theban legend.

The nymph Callisto was a daughter of Lycaon. She was a companion of Artemis and had made a vow of chastity. But Zeus was captivated by her extraordinary beauty. One day while the nymph was reposing in the woods Zeus presented himself to her in the form of Artemis. The young virgin welcomed him unsuspectingly, and when she realised her mistake it was already too late. She tried to hide her shame, but Artemis discovered what had occurred when one day she saw Callisto bathing with her companions. In order to shield the nymph from the rage of the goddess, Zeus changed Callisto into a bear. But Artemis pierced her with her arrows and she died giving birth to a son, Arcas, who was the ancestor of the Arcadians. As for Callisto, she was transformed into a constellation and became the Great Bear.

A similar adventure overtook Mera, daughter of Praetus. Mera too was a follower of Artemis and was also killed by the goddess for having given herself to Zeus. Before dying she gave birth to Locri, ancestor of the Locrians.

Zeus and Mortal Women. The first mortal woman whom Zeus loved was Niobe, daughter of Phoroneus and the nymph Laodice. She gave birth to Argos, founder of the city of that name. The same Phoroneus, son of Inachus, had a sister named Io who, in the former Heraeum, between Mycenae and Tiryns, exercised the functions of priestess of Hera. Zeus fell in love with her. In order to lie with her he took the form of a cloud. In spite of this stratagem Hera's suspicions were aroused. Zeus pleaded innocence and, in order to put his wife off the scent, changed his mistress into a white heifer. Hera pretended to be deceived and asked him for the heifer as a gift. Once it was in her possession she placed the animal under the care of Argus Panoptes – 'who sees all'. This Argus, son of Arestor, was a giant of redoubtable strength: he had once killed a bull which was ravaging Arcadia, and slain Echidna, daughter of Tartarus and Gaea. In addition he had one hundred eyes, of which fifty remained open while the other fifty closed in sleep. Zeus, however, ordered the cunning Hermes to set Io free. Hermes succeeded in charming the giant to sleep with the sound of his flute, and cut off

Athene overpowering the giant Enceladus. Both a warrior-goddess and the goddess of the arts of peace and of learning, Athene is shown here taking part in the battle of the gods and giants. Her emblem, the screech-owl, appears above her left arm. Detail from a Greek amphora.

Head of Hera. This head is all that remains of a colossal cult group from the goddess's temple at Olympia which showed her seated on her throne with her husband Zeus standing armed beside her. Her hair is held by a narrow hairband while she wears a crown of leaves and blossoms on her head. The statue was originally painted, the goddess's hair being reddish-yellow and her hairband dark red. Grey limestone. *c.* 600 B.C.

Leto with Apollo and Artemis. According to ancient tradition, Leto was the wife of Zeus before he married Hera. The daughter of the Titans Coeus and Phoebe, she bore him the twins Apollo and Artemis, the latter preceding her brother into the world by a day. It was only later that Leto was made a mistress of Zeus and a victim of Hera's jealousy. Her wistful expression betrays her sufferings.

The Bath of Hera. Ludovisi Relief. Believed to be the remains of a monumental bed sculptured by Polycletus for the Heraeum at Argos (fifth century B.C.). The goddess, attended by two nymphs, emerges from the spring of Canathus. This bas-relief was long believed to represent the birth of Aphrodite. Terme Museum, Rome.

Interior of the temple of Hera at Paestum. Founded by Doric speaking colonists *c.* 600 B.C., Paestum (or Posidonia) in southern Italy possesses some of the most imposing ruins of the Hellenistic world. Of its three Greek temples the second temple of Hera (illustrated below) is not only the finest but is also the best-preserved Greek temple outside Attica. Built in the fifth century B.C. in the Doric style, it was for long believed to be a temple of Poseidon.

The warrior Athene from the temple of Aegina. Although archaic
this statue already suggests the Athene of classical art. Munich Museum.

Archaic Head of Athene, helmeted. On the reverse side, the owl. A four drachma piece. Athens. Fifth century B.C.

his head. To honour Argus, who had served her, Hera distributed his eyes over the tail of her favourite bird, the peacock, whose plumage was thenceforth so brilliant. As for the unfortunate heifer, Hera sent a gad-fly to torture her. Driven mad by the stinging insect, Io fled across the world. She swam the Thracian Bosphorus, crossed the Ionian Sea which took her name and, having ranged Asia Minor, finally reached Egypt where, by a simple touch of the hand, Zeus restored her to her human form. She then bore a son, Epaphus – child of 'the touch'. But Hera was not disarmed. She ordered the Curetes to abduct the child. They obeyed and for this reason were slain by Zeus. Io at last found her child in Syria and returned to Egypt where she married the king, Telegonus. In later days Io became confused with the Egyptian goddess Isis and her son Epaphus with Apis.

At Argos reigned Acrisius who had but one daughter, Danae. An oracle had told Acrisius that one day his daughter would bring into the world a son by whose hands he would perish. Acrisius thereupon had a chamber of bronze built underground – or some say a tower – and in it locked Danae with her nurse. But Zeus, who had been attracted by the girl's charms, found a way to enter the chamber in the form of a shower of gold and frequently visited Danae. The result was the birth of a son, Perseus. Acrisius was terrified when he learned of this miraculous birth, and shut up both mother and child in a chest which he cast into the sea. Tossed by the waves, the chest was finally carried to the island of Seriphus where a fisherman, one Dictys, brother of King Polydectes, caught it in his nets. Danae and Perseus were thus saved. We shall see, when we come to Perseus, how this romantic adventure continued.

More terrible still was Hera's jealousy of and the vengeance she took on another of Zeus' loves, Semele, daughter of Cadmus. When she learned of the relationship between her husband and this mortal girl Hera came to her rival in disguise and suggested that Semele ask her lover to appear before her in all the brilliance of his majesty. Zeus tried in vain to dissuade Semele from making such an unreasonable demand. Semele insisted. The god gave in, and visited her in his chariot of glory, surrounded by lightning and thunder. The sight of the great god in all his dazzling splendour was too much for mortal eyes and Semele perished, consumed by celestial flames. Zeus gathered up the child she bore in her womb and enclosed it in his own thigh until the day set for its birth: it was to be Dionysus.

The rape of Europa had less tragic consequences. Daughter of Phoenix or of Agenor, King of Phoenicia, and of Telephassa, the young Europa was playing one day at the water's edge, gathering flowers with her companions. Her attention was caught by the sight of a bull with glistening hide who browsed peacefully among her father's herd. His air, gentle and at the same time majestic,

struck her. She did not suspect that this bull was none other than the master of the gods, Zeus himself, who had assumed this shape in order to deceive the girl of whom he had become enamoured. Trustingly Europa approached and caressed the animal, who very gallantly knelt before her. She climbed playfully on to his mighty back, and began to wreathe flowers around his powerful horns. Suddenly the bull reared to his feet, at a bound sprang into the waves, and carried the weeping virgin across the vast sea. They finally reached the southern coast of Crete, at Gortyna. In the days of Theophrastus the plane tree under which Zeus made the young Phoenician his mistress was still pointed out. Because it had witnessed and sheltered the divine union this tree received the privilege of retaining its foliage in all seasons. Europa gave birth to Minos, Rhadamanthys and Sarpedon. All three were adopted by the King of Crete, Asterius, who subsequently became Europa's husband.

Although it was within his province to guard the sanctity of marriage, Zeus on occasion did not hesitate to pay court to married women. Thus he fell in love with Leda, the wife of Tyndareus. One evening when the young woman was bathing in a pool she saw floating majestically towards her a swan of dazzling whiteness. It was Zeus. The same night Leda also lay with her own husband; afterwards she bore Pollux and Helen, children of Zeus; and Castor and Clytemnestra, children of Tyndareus.

In order to seduce Alcmene, Zeus employed another stratagem. He wished, Hesiod says, 'to produce a son who would one day be a powerful protector for gods and men alike', and he had set his heart on the wife of the Theban chief, Amphitryon. But as he knew she was virtuous and incorruptible he took advantage of Amphitryon's absence to assume Amphitryon's own appearance. Alcmene welcomed Zeus in this disguise exactly as though he were her actual husband. When the real Amphitryon returned a few hours later he was surprised by his wife's lack of enthusiasm while she, in her turn, was astonished that he had so quickly forgotten the marks of tenderness she had so recently bestowed upon him. The mystery was finally cleared up by the soothsayer Teiresias. From the double union twins were born: Hercules, son of Zeus; and Iphicles, son of Amphitryon.

Such were the more memorable of Zeus' love affairs. But many more were attributed to him and his progeny was enormous.

By him the Oceanid Pluto had Tantalus. The Danaid Anaxithea and Hesione had, respectively, Olenus, founder of Olenus in Achaia, and Orchomenus, king of the city of the same name in Boeotia. Orchomenus' own daughter, Elara, was also loved by Zeus who, to protect her from Hera's jealousy, hid her under the earth, where she gave birth to the giant Tityus. Zeus also loved Neaera, who bore Aegle. He carried off Protogenia, daughter of Deucalion, from her husband Locre and she bore him a son, Opuns. Another daughter of Deucalion, Thyia, was also loved by Zeus; and he changed himself into a pigeon in order to seduce a young nymph of Achaia named Phthia.

Among the other mistresses of Zeus were Thalia, daughter of Hephaestus, who became the mother of the Palici; Thymbris who bore a son, Pan; Dia, wife of Ixion, whom Zeus seduced in the shape of a horse and who became the mother of Pirithous; finally, in Crete, Carme, who gave birth to Britomartis; and Cassiopeia, whose son Atymnius was honoured at Gortyna with Europa.

One could prolong the list, which was enriched by the regional pride of various provinces of Greece or even small towns, eager to give themselves a divine ancestor. We have seen, in fact, how a number of Zeus' offspring became the ancestors of a tribe or the founders of cities. But some of these unions of the god can be explained in other ways. Some are solar myths: for instance the union of Zeus, god of the luminous ether, with Leto and Leda, who seem to have been deities of the night. Others are merely allegorical accounts of historical facts: the Phoenician Europa brought to Crete by a bull could represent the contribution of Asiatic civilisation to that of Crete, symbolised by the bull-god. Finally others are the romanticised expression of great natural phenomena: in the shower of gold which penetrates to the subterranean Danae it is easy to recognise the rays of the sun which germinate the seed buried in the ground.

In attributing to Zeus all these adventures, the Greeks then were not guilty of irreverence towards their god. They were only translating the emotions they felt in face of nature's great mysteries into gracious and poetic form. Or else, more naïvely, they were creating for themselves a noble ancestry.

HERA

The name Hera was once believed to be connected with the Latin root *herus* (master) and with an old Greek word which meant 'earth'. Today, however, it is agreed that Hera is related to the Sanskrit *svar* (the Sky). Hera was then originally queen of the sky, the celestial virgin (hence her epithet Parthenia), and at first quite independent of Zeus. Their marriage was arranged afterwards, in order to explain the fusion of two cults which had at first been distinct. Some authorities even see in the hostility of Hera towards her husband a vestige of the resistance which the worshippers of Hera opposed to the rival cult of Zeus. Others interpret the noisy quarrels of the divine couple as a mythological translation of storms or the 'struggle of the meteors and atmospheric disturbances in revolt against the sky'.

Her Functions. Hera, however, soon lost her cosmic character and retained only her moral attributes. She was thought of as Woman deified. She presided over all phases of feminine existence. Thus Temenus, son of Pelasgus, consecrated at Stymphalus three temples to her: the first to the child-goddess, the second to the wife-goddess, the third to the widow-goddess. But primarily she was the goddess of marriage (*Gamelia*) and maternity. She represented the idealised type of wife.

Representations. Hera was depicted as a young woman, fully developed, of a chaste and rather severe beauty. Her forehead is normally crowned with a diadem or with a high crown of cylindrical shape, the *polos*. She wears a long tunic or *chiton* and is enveloped in a veil which adds to her bearing of nobility, reserved and full of modesty. Her attributes are a sceptre surmounted by a cuckoo (in allusion to the circumstances of her nuptials) and a pomegranate, symbol of conjugal love and fruitfulness. The bird sacred to her is the peacock, whose spangled plumage recalls the stars in the vault of heaven – and testifies to the service of hundred-eyed Argus.

Her Cult. Like Zeus, Hera was venerated on the summits of mountains. In Greece the chief centre of her cult was Argos. Here she had five or six temples, the oldest of which had been built by Phoroneus. It was the Heraeum at Argos which housed the famous statue of Hera in gold and ivory by Polycletus. The goddess was represented seated on a throne, her brow crowned by a diadem on which were depicted the Horae and the Graces. In her left hand she held a pomegranate and in her right a sceptre surmounted by

a cuckoo. Near her stood her daughter Hebe. Hera also possessed sanctuaries at Mycenae, Olympus, Sparta, in Attica, Boeotia and Euboea. She was particularly venerated in Crete and at Samos where stood the greatest of her temples, which was built, it was said, by the Argonauts.

The Legend of Hera. Hera was the oldest daughter of Cronus and Rhea, born, according to the Samians, on the isle of Samos, on the banks of the river Imbrasos near a waterwillow which could still be seen in the days of Pausanias. She had been brought up, according to some, by Macris or by the daughters of the river Asterion; according to others, by the Horae or Seasons. Her childhood was spent on the isle of Euboea and we have seen how her brother Zeus found her there and made her his wife. From then on Hera was associated with Zeus' sovereignty and became the chief feminine deity of Olympus. She sat on a golden throne beside her husband, and when she entered the assembly of the gods all rose in homage to her. On Olympus her marriage to Zeus had been the occasion of great rejoicing. All the Immortals had taken part in the procession and the Fates themselves had chanted the hymeneal chorus.

But Hera's happiness was not unclouded. She had given Zeus four children: the gracious Hebe, Ilithyia, mother of birth-pangs, the impetuous Ares, and the skilful Hephaestus. Her fidelity to her husband was exemplary. He, on the other hand, was constantly unfaithful.

It was not that she was lacking in charm. She took great care of her beauty. Every year she went to bathe in the spring Canathus at Nauplia and in these marvellous waters each time renewed her virginity. The 'white-armed goddess' was irresistible when she anointed her lovely body with an oil whose sweetness was such that it filled the whole earth and sky with its fragrance. When she had arranged her divine tresses, when she had pinned to her breast with golden clasps the robe Athene had woven for her with such art, put on her ear-rings, exquisitely worked and set with precious clusters of three drops, and draped from her head a glorious veil white as the sun, Zeus himself, seeing her thus arrayed, cried: 'Never has love for goddess or mortal woman so flooded my senses and filled my heart!'

Hera would never have lacked suitors had she wished them. Ixion, King of the Lapithae, when invited to dine with the gods, had only to turn his eyes towards her to be inflamed with irresistible desire. In the madness of his passion he even embraced a cloud which Zeus had shaped to resemble Hera. Ixion was chastised for his insolence: he was bound to a fiery wheel which whirled him perpetually through the sky.

Hera, proud of her own virtue, did not endure the continual faithlessness of her husband without protest. Shortly after her marriage she left Olympus in vexation and returned to the isle of Euboea. In order to bring her back again Zeus employed a pleasant stratagem. He had a veiled statue carried around in a chariot and let it be everywhere known that this was the new fiancée of the master of the gods. In a transport of jealousy and wounded pride Hera arrested the chariot, lacerated the robes of her supposed rival and, discovering the trick her husband had played on her, returned somewhat crestfallen to Olympus.

The renewed infidelities of Zeus incited her to avenge herself physically on his person. One day, assisted by Poseidon, Apollo and Athene, she succeeded in binding him with thongs. It would have been the end of Zeus' power had not Thetis summoned to his rescue the hundred-armed giant whom the gods called Briareus and men called Aegaeon. 'Proud of his glory, he sat beside the son of Cronus; and the gods were struck with terror and did not enchain Zeus.'

Hera considered it equally outrageous that Zeus alone and unaided had given birth to Athene. In her rage she invoked the earth and the vast heavens and the Titans imprisoned in Tartarus, and implored their favour so that she, too, might bear unaided a child 'who should be in no way inferior in strength to Zeus'. Her wishes were granted and when her time came she gave birth 'not to a son who resembled gods or men, but to the frightful, the terrible Typhon, scourge of mankind'. This monster is confused with Typhoeus, son of Gaea and Tartarus, against whom Zeus had had so hard a struggle.

Hera was roughly punished for these vain attempts to revolt. One day Zeus beat and bruised her, and when Hephaestus tried to defend his mother Zeus seized his too-zealous son by one foot and flung him from the heights of Olympus. On another occasion Zeus attached an anvil to each of Hera's ankles, bound her hands with bracelets of unbreakable gold and suspended her from the sky, surrounded by clouds.

Though Hera was forced to submit she could at least vent her fury on her rivals. She caused Semele's death, for a long time persecuted Io, and tried to prevent the confinement of Leto and of Alcmene. She was equally remorseless towards the children of her rivals and towards their families. Hercules was her victim, and Ino, Semele's sister, was cruelly punished for having cared for the infant Dionysus.

The vindictive temper of the goddess was not only displayed when her conjugal honour was at stake. Because Antigone, daughter of Laomedon, had boasted of having hair more beautiful than Hera's, Hera turned her locks into serpents. Because they had treated a wooden statue of the goddess with contempt the daughters of Proetus, Lysippe and Iphianassa, were stricken with leprosy and madness. They went raging half-nude through the Peloponnese and were only cured by the costly intervention of the seer Melampus. Melampus demanded as the price of his services a third of Proetus' kingdom. Proetus at first refused; but his daughters' madness became worse. He went again to Melampus, who raised his price and insisted on a second third of the kingdom for his brother Bias. Proetus consented, and from Hera Melampus obtained the two girls' restoration to health. Another tradition, to be sure, attributes the madness of Proetus' daughters to the anger of Dionysus.

Finally Hera never forgave the Trojan Paris for having preferred Aphrodite on the occasion of the famous beauty contest on Mount Ida, and her rancour was only satisfied when the entire Trojan race had been annihilated.

ATHENE

Of the many derivations proposed for the name of Athene (or Athena) none is really satisfactory. The Sanskrit *vadh* (to strike) and *adh* (hill) have been suggested, as well as the Greek for 'flower' and 'nurse'! The poetic epithet *Pallas* frequently joined to the name Athene comes either from the Greek 'to strike' or more probably from the Greek 'girl'.

Her Character and Functions. Although certain scholars have seen in Athene a personification of moisture, analogous to the Hindu Sarasvati, it seems more probable that she was in origin a storm- and lightning-goddess. Hence her normal attribute, the aegis – which in primitive times signified the stormy night – and her epithet as a goddess 'of the brilliant eyes'. She would thus be analogous to the Vedic goddess Vach. But Athene very quickly lost this meteorological character.

Her functions were many: she was venerated among the great divinities in her quality of warrior-goddess, as goddess of the arts of peace and as goddess of prudent intelligence.

To Athene the warrior – her oldest manifestation – belong the epithets *Promachos* ('who fights in the foremost ranks') and *Alalcomeneis* ('who repulses the enemy'). She was the protectress of towns and the guardian of acropolises.

The pacific Athene protected various industries. She was pre-eminently the *Ergane,* or working woman, and was the patron of architects and sculptors, as well as of spinners and weavers. She also protected horses (*Hippia*) and oxen (*Boarmia*). The olive tree owed to her its fruit. Her wisdom, which earned her the epithet *Pronoia* (the Foreseeing), made her the counsellor-goddess (*Boulaia*) and the goddess of the Assembly (*Agoraia*). Athene's emblem was the owl.

Her Cult. Though she was honoured throughout Greece Athene was the object of an especial cult in Athens. On the Acropolis she had, besides the Parthenon, two other temples: the temple of Athene Nike and the Erechtheum.

The chief festivals of the cult of Athene were: the *Arrephoria,* in the course of which two little girls of noble family, from seven to eleven years old, descended from the Acropolis to deposit in an underground chamber near the sanctuary of Aphrodite mysterious objects which they carried in a basket; the *Scirophoria,* when priests and priestesses walked in solemn procession under a vast parasol (*sciron*); and finally the *Panathenaea* which dated from the days

Athene Parthenos. This statue reproduces, with a slight variation in posture, the celebrated Athene of Phidias. Athens Museum.

of Theseus and consisted of a solemn procession to the Acropolis in which was carried to the goddess a *peplos* made by the most skilled workmen in Athens. Taking part were not only priests and magistrates but also girls carrying baskets, old men bearing olive branches and young men on horseback. During the Panathenaea were held races, gymnastic games, regattas and contests of music, singing and dancing.

Representations. The oldest representations of Athene were the *palladia*. Originally the palladia were stones which were said to have fallen from the sky and to which protective power was attributed. Later these stones were replaced by statues in wood (*xoana*) which had the same celestial origin. In them the goddess was depicted with her body sheathed in tight draperies, and in her hands she held a shield and spear. The most celebrated statue of the warrior Athene was that of the Parthenon, the work of Phidias. The goddess, standing, wore a long chiton; her head was helmeted, her breast covered with the aegis, her right hand rested against a spear and in her left hand she held a winged victory.

The Birth of Athene. When Zeus swallowed his wife Metis she had been about to give birth to a child. Shortly afterwards Zeus was tortured by an intolerable headache. To cure him Hephaestus – some said Prometheus – split open his skull with a bronze axe and from the gaping wound, shouting a triumphant cry of victory, sprang Athene – 'fully armed and brandishing a sharp javelin'. At the sight all the Immortals were struck with astonishment and filled with awe. 'Great Olympus was profoundly shaken by the dash and impetuosity of the bright-eyed goddess. The earth echoed with a terrible sound, the sea trembled and its dark waves rose . . .'

In Crete they said that the goddess had been hidden in a cloud and that it was by striking this cloud with his head that Zeus had caused Athene to emerge. The event was supposed to have taken place near Cnossus beside a stream, the Triton: whence the epithet Tritogeneia (born of Triton) often given to Athene. It was also explained by making her the daughter of Poseidon and of Lake Tritonis. Finally some said that Athene's father was the giant Pallas whom she had killed because he wished to ravish her. But these various relationships were dubious and it was generally agreed that Athene was the daughter of Zeus, engendered by the god himself.

This birth, in which she had played no part, infuriated Hera who, in reprisal, gave unassisted birth to the monster Typhon.

Athene was Zeus' favourite child. His preference for her was marked and his indulgence towards her so extreme that it aroused the jealousy of the other gods.

'Thou hast fathered,' says Ares to Zeus, 'a rash and foolish daughter who delights only in guilty acts. All the other gods who live on Olympus obey thee and each of us submits to thy will. But she, thou never curbest neither by word nor deed; she does as she pleases.'

Athene, the Warrior Goddess. The manner in which Athene made her first appearance revealed her warlike proclivities. And, indeed, she delighted above all in battle. We have seen her taking part in the war against the giants, killing Pallas and hurling her chariot against Enceladus whom she finally crushed under the island of Sicily. We find her again, equally belligerent and ardent, in the battles which raged beneath the ramparts of Troy. Not satisfied with stimulating the ardour of the Greeks – whom she favoured – she entered the skirmish herself. She put on her head a helmet of gold with jutting crest 'vast enough to cover the foot-soldiers of a hundred towns'. Over her shoulder she slung the aegis which she had fashioned, according to some, from the skin of the giant Pallas or which – as was more generally held – was made from the hide of the goat Amaltheia. Zeus had used it for the first time during the war with the Titans and afterwards presented it to his daughter. It was a sort of cuirass or breastplate, fringed and bordered with snakes and bearing in the centre the horrifying head of the Gorgon. Thus armed, Athene mounted on to the chariot of Diomedes, seized the whip and reins herself, and flung the horses against Ares, whom she stretched on the ground with a blow of her spear.

The memory of Athene's warlike prowess was perpetuated in Libya in annual festivals during which girls, divided into two camps, would stage a furious battle with sticks and stones.

Athene, Protectress of Heroes. Herself a warrior, Athene protected the brave and valorous. When Hercules, a victim of Hera's hostility, undertook his arduous labours Athene stood at his side to help and comfort him. It was she who gave him the brazen cymbals whose sound frightened the birds of Lake Stymphalus. It was she who escorted him when he brought Cerberus from the underworld. Finally it was she who, after his death, welcomed him on the threshold of Olympus. And so, when Hercules won the golden apples of the Hesperides, he offered them in homage to this tutelary goddess.

In the same way Athene also guided Perseus on his expedition against the Gorgons. As the hero dared not look into the terrifying face of the Medusa she guided his arm so that he could strike the monster. In gratitude Perseus afterwards gave Athene the Gorgon's head which she placed on her shield. Athene's part in the adventures of Perseus was so active that certain traditions say that she herself killed the Medusa by striking her during her sleep. This theory gave rise to several legends; for instance, that the battle between Athene and the Gorgon was the result of a beauty contest; and that the goddess gathered up the blood of her victim and made a gift of it either to Asclepius or to Erichthonius – blood which had issued from the left vein brought death, blood from the right vein restored life.

Athene was also kindly disposed towards Bellerophon: she appeared to him in a dream and gave him a golden bridle, thanks to which he was able to tame the horse Pegasus.

Finally she protected Odysseus successfully against all the perils which assailed him on his return from Troy, and in the guise of the sage Mentor she guided young Telemachus during his efforts to find his father again.

Athene's Chastity. On all these occasions when Athene came to the aid of heroes it was because they were worthy of her esteem, not because of any amorous attraction. Athene was a striking exception to Olympian society because of her absolute chastity. In spite of calumny and insinuations about supposed relations with Helios, Hephaestus and even Hercules, her heart remained insensitive to the pangs of love and she defended her virginity fiercely. Woe to anyone who wounded her modesty!

One day when she was bathing with the nymph Chariclo, Teiresias by chance beheld her. He was guilty of no more than involuntary indiscretion. Athene, nevertheless, punished him by depriving him of his sight. In spite of her companion's plea for pity she refused to revoke her decision, but to soften the harshness of the punishment she conferred upon the unhappy Teiresias the gift of foretelling the future.

Hephaestus became enamoured of Athene. One day when the goddess came to see him about making a suit of armour for her he attempted to violate her. Athene fled, pursued by the limping god. He caught up with her, but she defended herself so effectively that Hephaestus was unable to accomplish his criminal design and, instead, scattered his seed on the earth, which shortly afterwards gave birth to a son, Erichthonius. The child was found by Athene, who brought him up unknown to the other gods. She enclosed the infant in a basket which she confided to the daughters of Cecrops, forbidding them to open it. One of the sisters, Pandrosos, obeyed; the other two, Herse and Aglauros, could not control their curiosity. But the moment they opened the basket they fled in terror; for around the infant a serpent was coiled. They were stricken with madness by Athene, and flung themselves off the top of the Acropolis. Erichthonius grew to maturity and became king of Athens, where he established the solemn cult of Athene.

The Quarrel between Athene and Poseidon. Previously the goddess had already shown particular benevolence to the land of Athens. In the days of King Cecrops a dispute had arisen between her and Poseidon for the possession of Attica. To affirm his rights Poseidon struck the rock of the Acropolis with his trident and a salt water spring gushed forth. According to another tradition it was a horse which appeared under Poseidon's trident. Athene, in her turn, caused an olive tree to sprout on the Acropolis, a tree which could be seen in the time of Pericles, still alive in spite of having been burned by the Persians during the invasion of Xerxes. Asked to settle the dispute the gods, on the evidence of Cecrops, pronounced in favour of Athene.

The Gifts of Athene. Athene was as benevolent in peace as she was redoubtable in war, and rendered valuable service to mankind. She taught the people of Cyrene the art of taming horses. She showed Erichthonius how to harness the first war chariots. She was present while Jason's companions were building the ship *Argo*. Her skill was revealed in the humblest handicrafts: she invented the potter's wheel and made the first vases. But above all she excelled in woman's work. The art of weaving cloth and embellishing it with wonderful embroidery had no secrets from her. The Immortals relied on her skill and it was she who embroidered Hera's veil. She was jealous of her accomplishments and allowed no one to surpass her.

In Lydia there lived a girl named Arachne who was renowned for her skill in handling needle and spindle. One day she dared to challenge the goddess to compete with her. Athene arrived in the guise of an old woman and asked Arachne to withdraw her impious challenge. Arachne refused. Athene reassumed her divine form and accepted the challenge. Arachne at once drew threads across her loom and with cunning hand guided the shuttle through the taut netting. As a subject, she had chosen to weave the loves of the gods. When she had finished she submitted her work to Athene for examination. The goddess tried in vain to discover any imperfection in it. Furious at her failure and unwilling to admit defeat, Athene changed Arachne into a spider and condemned her eternally to spin, and to draw from her own body the thread with which to weave her web.

Although Athene's activities were chiefly concerned with useful work she was not averse to artistic creation. Certain traditions originating in Boeotia attributed to her the invention of the flute. They said that the goddess had thought of blowing into a stag's horn, pierced with holes, in order to imitate the plaintive whistling sound made by the Gorgon when Perseus cut its throat. But in Athens it was said that Athene had not persevered with her musical efforts because the Olympians had laughed at her when she blew out her cheeks and pursed her lips. So she had contemptuously tossed the flute aside and pronounced a curse against any person who picked it up. The satyr Marsyas, who dared to take possession of the instrument, was cruelly punished for his imprudence.

Athene also at times filled the role of goddess of health: everyone knew how the architect Mnesicles who, while working on the construction of the Propylaea, had fallen and was in danger of death, had been miraculously healed by Athene who was called for this reason Hygieia.

Athene extended her protection not only to individuals but also to entire cities. She was symbolised by the *Palladia* or statues of herself which had, it was claimed, fallen from heaven. The possession of a palladium was a pledge of security. Athens guarded one jealously in the Erechtheum. When Danaus fled from Egypt he was careful not to forget his palladium which he carried to Lindus in the isle of Rhodes. The most celebrated palladium was that of Troy which Zeus had presented to King Dardanus. According to others it had been made by Athene herself: heartbroken at having accidentally killed young Pallas, her playmate and the the daughter of Tritonis, her foster-father, Athene carved from a tree trunk a statue reproducing the features of Pallas which she left with Zeus. Later Electra, whom Zeus seduced, took refuge behind this palladium. Zeus tossed it away and it fell on the land of Ilium, where Ilus had a temple built for it. When the Greeks laid siege to Troy they realised that they would never be victorious so long as the city retained its palladium. Diomedes and Odysseus therefore decided to steal the precious idol, and its theft spread discouragement among the Trojans. It was said, to be sure, that Dardanus had taken the precaution of exposing to the faithful only a copy of the palladium, and had carefully concealed the original in the adytum – or innermost sanctuary – of the temple. Thus it was the replica that the Greeks had stolen. As for the genuine palladium, it was taken after the fall of Troy to Italy by Aeneas. But it did not remain there. After many vicissitudes it was brought back to Amphissa in Locris, where it could be seen and venerated by all.

APOLLO

The etymology of the word Apollo is uncertain. A connection has been suggested between the name and an old Greek verb which means 'to repel or set aside', and also an ancient form of a verb meaning 'to destroy'. (In the latter case Apollo would be the 'destroyer', as he appears to be in the *Iliad*.) A relationship between Apollo and the English word apple which would make of him a primitive apple-tree god is equally unsatisfactory.

Origin, Character and Functions. The same uncertainty surrounds Apollo's origin. Some authorities believe that he came from Asia and was either a Hittite god, a Hellenic double of the Arab god Hobal, or a god of Lycia. Others, because of his close relations with the Hyperboreans, think that he was a Nordic divinity, brought by the Greeks from the North in the course of their migrations. It is difficult to decide between these two opposing schools of thought because, though both advance plausible arguments, neither can actually prove its case.

Apollo. Originally a sun-god or god of the light, whence his titles 'Phoebus' (the brilliant) and 'Chrysocomes' (of the golden locks), Apollo was also a pastoral and musician-god and a god of prophecy. His oracle at Delphi, where he had his chief shrine, was famous. He was the son of Zeus and Leto and the twin brother of Artemis. Statue in Parian marble from the island of Lemnos, *c.* 480 B.C.

Artemis, the virgin-huntress. The goddess of the chase and of forests, Artemis loved the pleasures of the hunt in the woods and glades of Arcadia accompanied by her band of nymphs. Like her twin brother Apollo she could dispense sudden death with her arrows but though implacable towards those who aroused her anger she could be benevolent towards those who honoured her. Greek statue from Pompeii.

The Ephesian Artemis, a fertility goddess of Asia Minor. Sometimes confused with the virgin goddess of the Greeks, she was in fact an Ionian deity of completely different character.

Apollo and Marsyas. Emboldened by the praise that he had received for his playing, the satyr Marsyas had challenged Apollo to a musical contest, the winner to inflict whatever punishment he wished on the loser. Apollo is seated on the left listening to the satyr who is playing on the flute. Marsyas was defeated and flayed with the knife held by the servant in the centre. Bas-relief from the pedestal of the statue of the goddess Leto by Praxiteles. *c.* 366 B.C.

Artemis Bendis. Dressed in her saffron hunting tunic and buskins and with a hooded cape fastened over her shoulders, the goddess receives a torch which had been passed from horseman to horseman in the annual race held in her honour at the Piraeus. In addition to her role as goddess of the chase, Artemis was also a moon-goddess and she has here taken over a rite belonging to another moon-goddess, the Thracian Bendis. Relief sculpture, fourth century B.C.

Artemis causes Actaeon to be devoured by his hounds. Metope from Temple E, Selinus. National Museum, Palermo.

The Erechtheum and the Parthenon from the west. Both these temples were dedicated to the goddess Athene – the Parthenon to Athene Parthenos and the Erechtheum to Athene Polias. The Parthenon, the masterpiece of the Doric style, was commenced in 447 B.C., dedicated in 438 B.C. and completed in 432 B.C. The Erectheum was built some decades later in the Ionic style on the most sacred spot on the Acropolis. In the precinct before it grew Athene's olive tree.

The difficulty is that the legend of Apollo and his functions reveal divergences which are sometimes even contradictory. How is it, for example, that this pre-eminently Greek god was, in the *Iliad*, the ally of the Trojans – that is to say, the Asiatics? And if he was in fact of Asiatic origin, how can we explain his retreat in the Vale of Tempe and among the Hyperboreans? In this it is tempting to see a return of the god to the land of his origin.

As to his functions, they are so multiple and complex that it is often hard to connect one with another.

Apollo was first of all a god of the light, a sun-god – without, however, being the sun itself, which was represented by a special divinity, Helios. From this arose his epithets: Phoebus, the 'brilliant'; Xanthus, the 'fair'; Chrysocomes, 'of the golden locks'; as such he delighted in 'high places, the frowning peaks of high mountains, wave-lapped, beetling promontories'. This god of the light was the son of Latona or Leto – probably a double of the Asiatic Lada – who was undoubtedly a divinity of the night.

As a solar god Apollo made the fruits of the earth to ripen, and at Delos and Delphi the first crops were therefore consecrated to him. In addition he protected the crops by destroying the mice which infested the fields (*Apollo Smintheus*) and drove off the locusts which devastated the harvest (*Apollo Parnopius*).

Because the sun is murderous with its rays which strike like darts, and at the same time beneficent because of its prophylactic powers, Apollo was thought of as an archer-god who shot his arrows from afar (*Hecatebolos*) as the god of sudden death; but also as a healer-god who drove away illness (*Alexikakos*). In this latter function he had apparently supplanted a primitive deity Paeon (the healer) whose name is closely related to the divinity whom Homer calls the physician of the gods, Paeëon.

Apollo was also the god of divination and prophecy. Without speaking of the many early oracles he possessed in Asia Minor, at Thymbra, Clarus, Grynia, Didymus, all over Greece he had sanctuaries where men came to consult him and where he pronounced judgment through the intermediary of priestesses, the Sibyls. Famous were those of Tegyra, near Orchomenus, and of Thebes in Boeotia, over which presided Teiresias' own daughter, Manto.

At Thebes in the days of Pausanias the stone from which the priestess delivered her oracles could still be seen. It was called the Seat of Manto. Manto was afterwards led to Delphi, where she devoted herself to the cult of Apollo. The god, it was said, sent her to Asia Minor to found the oracle of Clarus.

But of all the sanctuaries of Apollo the most celebrated was that of Delphi, situated in a deep cavern from which emanated prophetic vapours. The priestess, or Pythia, sat on a tripod placed on the threshold of the cavern. Soon, under the god's influence, she would fall into a trance and, possessed by prophetic delirium, begin to pour forth broken phrases and obscure words which were then interpreted by the priest and members of the sacred counsel of Delphi.

This role of prophecy conferred on a sun-god is surprising in view of the fact that in Greece divination was reserved for underworld divinities. It is a fact, however, that Apollo ousted them all little by little. We must then assume that he already possessed this function when he came to Greece; and we cannot fail to notice his resemblance in this respect to the Assyro-Babylonian sun-god Shamash, who also had the gift of prophecy – an argument in favour of Apollo's being of Asiatic origin.

But there are other aspects of the sun-god which are not easy to relate to the above.

For Apollo was also a shepherd-god (*Nomius*) whose mission it was to protect the flocks. We shall see later that flocks are often associated with Apollo. His epithet, Lycian – unless it simply signifies that he was of Lycian origin – can clearly be derived from the root *lux*, light, and would then be a qualifying epithet for a solar-deity. But 'Lycian' is also related to the Greek word meaning wolf. Apollo could then have primitively been a wolf-god (as Reinach conjectured) or else a god who killed wolves (*Lukoktonos*) – both equally applicable to a rural divinity. Apollo Nomius may be linked with Apollo Carneios (the ram-god of the Dorians) who was also a pastoral divinity.

Apollo is a musician-god as well, the god of song and the lyre. This is how Homer shows him when he described the gods listening to 'the sound of the gracious lyre which Apollo held'.

He is also a builder and a colonising-god who, as Callimachus

Hermes resting. Greek bronze. National Museum, Naples.

Hermes Psychopompus leads Eurydice to Orpheus. Attic bas-relief. Villa Albani, Rome.

Hermes and the infant Dionysus. The messenger of the gods rests on his journey to the nymphs of Nysa to whose care he is to entrust his little half-brother Dionysus on the orders of Zeus. In his right hand he held a bunch of grapes with which to amuse the child. Originally thought to be Praxiteles' original of *c.* 330 B.C., the statue, which was found in the temple of Hera at Olympia is now believed to be a later copy. Parian marble.

says, 'delights in the constructions of towns of which he himself lays the foundations'.

So many varying functions lead one to suspect that in Apollo there were many personalities, and the problem of his origin would be clarified by considering him to be a solar-god from Asia who was merged with a pastoral-god, the chief god of the Dorians, who came from the north of Greece.

Representations. In spite of his multiple character Apollo always appears as a single type in the representations which were made of him. He was depicted as a young man of idealised beauty, with a vigorous body, a broad chest and slim hips. His beardless face with its delicate features is surmounted by a high forehead and thick, long hair which sometimes falls freely behind him, sometimes is knotted on top or at the nape of his neck so that only a few curls fall to his shoulders. He is generally nude or wears only a chlamys thrown over his shoulder. Sometimes, particularly when he is

represented as a musician, he wears a long tunic with loose folds.

His attributes are the bow, the quiver, the shepherd's crook, the lyre. The animals which are sacred to him are the swan, the vulture, the crow, the cock, the hawk, the cicada, the wolf and the serpent. His favourite plants are the laurel, the palm, the olive and the tamarisk.

The Birth of Apollo. According to the oldest traditions Apollo's mother, Leto, daughter of Coeus and Phoebe, was the wife of Zeus before Zeus was married to Hera. This is how she appears in the *Iliad* where, like her son – and doubtless because of her Asiatic origin – she protects the Trojans. Hesiod also depicts her in the same role and represents her as enveloped in a veil of sombre hue, a garment natural to a goddess of the night. Only later was Leto made a mistress of Zeus and a victim of Hera's jealousy; and it is chiefly the history of her misfortunes which enriches her legend.

When Leto was pregnant with the twins Zeus had given her she wandered the earth in search of a place to give birth to them. But she was pursued by Hera's jealous fury and ranged Attica, Euboea, Thrace and the islands of the Aegean sea, begging in vain of each of these countries to receive her. All feared the anger of Hera and all 'were seized with dread and terror' and none dared receive her. But Leto at last found shelter. It will be remembered that Leto's sister, Asteria, had been changed into a quail because she had resisted the ardours of Zeus, then into the floating isle of Ortygia. On the promise that Apollo would erect a splendid temple on its stony and barren soil, the isle of Ortygia consented to receive Leto. Hera, however, had sworn that her rival would only give birth in a place where the sun's rays never penetrated. In order that this vow should not be broken Poseidon raised the waves like a dome over the isle of Ortygia which, at the same time, he anchored to the depths of the sea with four pillars. After the birth of Apollo, Ortygia changed its name to Delos – 'the Brilliant'.

No longer able to prevent the birth she loathed, Hera attempted at least to delay it. While all the other Immortals hastened to Delos to be with Leto, Hera kept Ilithyia, the goddess of childbirth, behind. During nine days and nine nights Leto was the victim of atrocious suffering. Finally Iris was dispatched to Olympus and succeeded in fetching Ilithyia. Then, says a Homeric hymn to Apollo, 'Leto clasped a palm-tree in her arms, pressed the soft ground with her knees, and the earth beneath her smiled and the child leapt into the light. All the goddesses cried out with joy. Then, O Phoebus, the goddesses washed thee in sweet water, limpid and pure, and they gave thee for swaddling clothes a white veil of tissue, light and fresh, which they tied with a golden girdle'.

Leto, at the same time, gave birth to a daughter, Artemis.

Due to the similarity of names the birth of Apollo is sometimes placed in the sacred grove of Ortygia, in the neighbourhood of Ephesus.

Leto's tribulations did not end with the birth of Apollo. For fear of Hera she left Delos in haste and went to Asia Minor, to the land which later became Lycia. There one day she paused at the edge of a pool. She wished to quench her thirst but was prevented from doing so by rude shepherds who stirred the water to make it muddy. Leto punished them by turning them into frogs.

The Childhood of Apollo: The Serpent Python. Unlike other children Apollo was not nourished on his mother's milk. Themis put nectar and sweet ambrosia to his lips. Immediately the new-born baby threw off his swaddling clothes and was endowed with manly vigour, which he proved without delay in doing battle with the serpent Python.

This monster was a female dragon which the earth had given birth to and which had acted as nurse to Typhon. Hera, who was resolved to exterminate her rival, sent Python against Leto at the moment of Apollo's birth. But thanks to Poseidon, who had hidden Leto's retreat among the waves, Leto was saved and the serpent Python returned to its lair on the wooded slopes of Parnassus. Now, four days after his birth, Apollo set forth in search of a place to establish his sanctuary. Armed with the arrows which Hephaestus had forged for him, he descended from the heights of Olympus, crossed Pieria, Euboea, Boeotia, and arrived in the valley of Crissa. On the treacherous advice of the nymph Telphousa, who reigned over this region and wished to retain her position, Apollo wandered into the savage gorge of Parnassus which was the serpent Python's lair. The serpent saw the god and sprang at him. But Apollo let fly an arrow. 'Torn with cruel pain the monster lies shuddering: he rolls in the sand. He plunges into the forest and twists on the ground, now here, now there, until the moment when, with poisonous breath, he exhales his life in a torrent of blood.' Apollo contemptuously pushed his victim aside with one foot and said: 'Now rot where you lie.' And in memory of the occasion the spot where this dramatic encounter took place was called by the name *Pytho* – from the Greek 'to rot'. It was later changed to Delphi. As for Telphousa, the god punished her treachery by smothering her under a rock.

In order to purify himself from the stains he had got when killing the serpent, Apollo exiled himself to Thessaly, in the Vale of Tempe. When his period of expiation was concluded he returned to Delphi, his head crowned with sacred laurel, and escorted by a procession of priests, chanting hymns of triumph.

The memory of these events was perpetuated at Delphi by the festival of the *Septeria* (or Veneration) which was celebrated every nine years. An adolescent youth, chosen from among the nobility, represented Apollo. Accompanied by other young folk he would go and set on fire a wooden hut which symbolised the dragon's lair. At the close of the Septeria the same youths would make a pilgrimage to the Vale of Tempe, practise expiatory rites and return to Delphi carrying sacred laurel.

The Foundation of Delphi. Delphi was in fact Apollo's chosen land. Soon after his victory over the serpent Python he built an altar in harsh Pytho, in the midst of a sacred grove. The place was deserted and Apollo was wondering where he would find priests for his new cult when he perceived in the distance on the dark sea a ship manned by some Cretans. Immediately assuming the form of a dolphin, he sped after the ship and leapt on to the deck, to the great terror of the sailors, who were even more terrified when their ship suddenly ceased to obey the oars and, deviating from its course, rounded the Peloponnese, entered the Gulf of Corinth and ran aground on the shores of Crissa. Apollo then reassumed his his divine appearance and told the Cretans his will. 'From now on none of you will again return to your pleasant city. You will see your rich dwellings and your cherished wives no more; but you will guard my temple. You will know the designs of the immortal gods and, by their will, you will be perpetually honoured. You will have in abundance all that the illustrious tribes of men bring to me. And since you first beheld me on the dark sea in the shape of a dolphin, you shall invoke me by the name of the Delphinian.' Such was the origin of Delphi. The same episode explains the role of Apollo as god of navigation and marine expeditions, particularly colonisation.

But Apollo did not always remain at Delphi. Every year at the end of autumn he went away, beyond the Rhipaei mountains where the impetuous Boreas reigned, towards the mysterious land of the Hyperboreans. There, under a sky eternally bright, lived a happy and virtuous race of men devoted to the cult of Apollo. Leto herself, they said, was a native of this blessed land, which she had left in the guise of a she-wolf to come to Delos. With the return of the good weather Apollo would come to Delphi again in a chariot drawn by white swans or monstrous griffins. Some placed this annual exile of the god in Lycia.

The Exploits of Apollo. Apollo, the celestial archer whose arrows were long-ranged and infallible, was distinguished for many exploits. He fought against the Aloadae, Ephialtes and Otus. These two giants, sons of Aloeus or Poseidon, aspired to the hands of Hera and Artemis, and repeating the audacious attempt of the Titans to scale Olympus, piled Pelion on Ossa to achieve their daring objective. They would have succeeded had not Apollo struck them down with his arrows. It is true that another tradition attributes the death of the Aloadae to Artemis. Apollo, in the same way, slew the giant Tityus who had dared to assail the honour of Leto, his mother.

The god was no less ruthless towards mortals. In Phocis there was a man of extraordinary strength named Phorbas, chief of the Phlegyians. He would lie in wait beside the road which led to the temple of Delphi and force the passing pilgrims to fight with him. Having vanquished them he would then put them painfully to death. Apollo, disguised as an athlete, appeared one day and felled Phorbas with a mighty blow of the fist. Apollo even measured his strength against Hercules. Hercules had come to Delphi, but, not obtaining from the Pythia the oracle he hoped for, he seized the sacred tripod and carried it away. Apollo hastened after him, overtook him and prepared to fight it out. It required the intervention of Zeus himself to put an end to the combat. Zeus obliged Hercules to restore the tripod and reconciled the two adversaries. Apollo, indeed, tolerated no insult to his person or his cult. The archer Eurytus, who had dared to challenge him, perished for his presumption; and because Agamemnon at Troy had gravely offended his priest Chryses, Apollo for nine days let fly his exterminating arrows against the Greek army, sending innumerable warriors to the kingdom of Hades.

Among the Olympians Apollo enjoyed especial consideration. When he entered, the assembly of the gods all rose in sign of respect. Leto, his mother, would relieve him of bow and quiver, which she would hang from a golden nail. Zeus would welcome his son and give him nectar in a golden cup. The Immortals would then resume their places. Leto was proud to have borne this illustrious son who wielded the redoubtable bow.

Only the cunning Hermes dared to play tricks on his half-brother; we shall see later how he stole Apollo's heifers.

Apollo's Servitude. In spite of the marked favour which the master of the gods showed him, Apollo twice aroused the wrath of Zeus. The first time was when Apollo took part in the plot which Hera formed against her husband and which failed thanks to Thetis. In fury Zeus condemned Apollo, together with Poseidon, to go to Troy, there to enter the service of King Laomedon for a year. While Poseidon worked on the construction of the Trojan ramparts, Apollo pastured the royal oxen on the slopes and in the wooded gorges of Mount Ida. When the year had run its course Laomedon refused to pay the two gods the wages which had been agreed upon and even threatened to cut off their ears. In revenge Apollo spread plague through the country and Poseidon summoned a a monster from the sea which killed men in the fields.

The second time Apollo incurred his father's anger was when, in order to avenge the murder of his son, Asclepius, whom Zeus had struck with a thunderbolt, Apollo killed the Cyclopes who had made the thunderbolt. Zeus punished him by sending him to serve Admetus, king of Pherae. Apollo tended his mares and ewes. He showed devotion to his mortal master, helped him to get married and even saved his life. These two episodes demonstrate the pastoral character of Apollo Nomius.

was the most important of musician-gods. Attracted by the divine music, the fallow deer and hinds would come to frisk, and even the savage beasts of the forest joined in. Did Apollo invent the lyre? According to some he did; though it seems more likely that he received the instrument from Hermes.

Apollo would have it that no instrument could compare in beauty with the lyre or the cithara. One day while strolling on Mount Tmolus he was challenged to a musical contest by the satyr Marsyas,

While he watched his flocks Apollo would play his lyre, for he who had acquired a remarkable virtuosity on the flute which Athene had once cast aside. A jury was constituted among whom sat the Muse and Midas, king of Phrygia. When the tournament was finished Apollo was declared the victor. Only Midas voted for Marsyas. The god punished Midas by bestowing upon him a pair of ass's ears. As for his unfortunate rival, he attached him to a tree trunk, flayed him alive and suspended his body at the entrance of a cavern which could be seen in the neighbourhood of Celaenae in Phrygia. According to other traditions the contest took place between Apollo and Pan.

The Loves of Apollo. It would seem that a god endowed with all the charms of youth, strength and grace would find few to resist him. Indeed the amorous adventures of Apollo were numerous; but several of them were singularly unfortunate – his mistresses were unwilling and the dénouements were tragic.

To be sure, he was loved by the Oceanid Melia, whom he made mother of Ismenius, by Corycia who gave him a son Lycoreus, and by Acacallis, mother of Phylacides and Philandros; but he tried in vain to seduce Daphne. This nymph, daughter of the river Peneius, was as chaste as she was beautiful. When she refused to submit to Apollo he attempted to ravish her; but she fled. He overtook her and she already felt the eager arms of the god around her when she called upon the venerable Gaea to aid her. Immediately the earth gaped open. Daphne disappeared, and in her place a laurel tree sprang from the ground. Apollo made it the plant sacred to him.

The nymph Cyrene, who was said to be the daughter of King Hypseus, was a huntress. Apollo saw her one day on the wooded slopes of Mount Pelion, wrestling with a lion. Charmed by her beauty and courage, he carried her away in a golden chariot to Libya, where she gave birth to Aristaeus.

Nor did all mortal women submit to Apollo's desires. There was Castalia, a girl of Delphi, who, in order to escape the god's pursuit, threw herself into the fountain which afterwards took her name.

Acacallis – who must not be confused with the nymph of the same name – and Chione were loved simultaneously by Hermes and Apollo. Chione, daughter of Daedalion, had Autolycus by Hermes and Philammon by Apollo. Very proud of the beauty of her sons she had the imprudence to scoff at the barrenness of Artemis, who in punishment pierced her with arrows. Acacallis, also called Deione, was the daughter of Minos. Her father had sent her to Libya, where she knew Apollo. She had two sons by him, Amphithemis or Garamas and Miletus. When Miletus was born his mother, for fear of Minos, had him carried into a forest where, thanks to Apollo's protection, the wolves took care of the newly born babe who grew up among them. Shepherds discovered him and removed him from this savage existence. Later Miletus aroused the suspicions of Minos and fled to Asia Minor, where he founded the town of Miletus. Less fortunate was Linus, Apollo's son by Psamathe, daughter of Crotopus, King of Argos. Linus had been exposed by his mother, who wished to conceal his birth, and he was devoured by dogs. At the news Psamathe was overcome with grief and betrayed herself. Her father had her put to death. Apollo immediately struck the city of Argos with a terrible plague which only ceased when Crotopus was exiled. This Linus, who died in infancy, is not the musician hero whom Apollo had by Urania.

The adventure of Apollo and Coronis had a tragic sequence. Coronis, daughter of Phlegyas, King of the Lapiths, had yielded to Apollo and conceived a son. When she was on the point of becoming a mother she married the Arcadian Ischys. A crow, that Apollo had left with Coronis to watch over her, came at once to tell Apollo of the girl's infidelity. In his rage Apollo cursed the crow, whose plumage suddenly turned black, and put Coronis and Ischys to death. According to others he let Artemis avenge him. The two bodies were placed on the funeral pyre and the body of Coronis was already half consumed when Apollo arrived and tore from the flames the child who was about to be born. The child became the god of medicine, Asclepius. When Phlegyas learned who was responsible for the tragedy he marched on Delphi and burnt the temple of Apollo. But he perished under the blows of the god and was thrown into Tartarus, where he was cruelly tortured for his sacrilege.

One day while gathering flowers on the slopes of the Acropolis, Creusa, daughter of Erechtheus and Praxithea, was surprised by Apollo. She lay with him in a neighbouring cavern. Here she later gave birth to a son, Ion. Apollo sent Hermes to fetch the child and bring him to Delphi, where he entered the service of the temple. Meanwhile Creusa had married Xuthus, but their union remained childless. The couple came to Delphi, where the oracle proclaimed that the first being whom they beheld would be their son. As they emerged from the temple the first person they encountered was the young Ion. Xuthus adopted him. Creusa, jealous, attempted to poison Ion, and Ion himself tried to kill Creusa. The Pythia herself cleared up the misunderstanding and revealed to Creusa and Ion that they were mother and son. Athene also told Xuthus the truth, and from Apollo Xuthus received the promise that he would become the father of two sons, Dorus and Achaeus who, with Ion, were the ancestors of the Greek race.

By Thyria Apollo had a son Cycnus, a youth of rare beauty who was attached by a tender affection to his companion of the chase, Phylius. When Phylius abandoned him, Cycnus in despair threw himself into Lake Canopus. Thyria, his mother, threw herself in after him; and Apollo changed them both into swans.

By a certain Cyrene, sometimes also called Asteria, Apollo had another son, Idmon, whom he endowed with the gift of foreseeing the future. When he was invited to take part in the expedition of the Argonauts, Idmon foresaw that he would die in the course of

the voyage. He went, nevertheless, and was in fact killed by the bite of a snake.

Evadne bore Apollo Iamus, a celebrated soothsayer and chief of the family of the Iamidae at Olympia.

Divination naturally plays an important role in the legends of Apollo. Thus, when Apollo fell in love with Cassandra, daughter of King Priam, he conferred upon her the gift of foretelling the future on her promising to yield herself to him. But Cassandra refused to fulfil her part of the bargain. Apollo then begged a single kiss. In this way he breathed into her mouth and, though he left her with the power of foretelling the future, he took from her the power of persuasion so that from then onwards no one would believe what Cassandra predicted.

Several youths were also loved by Apollo. Such was Cyparissus, whom the god changed into a cypress because the young man was heartbroken at having carelessly killed a favourite stag. Such also was Hyacinthus, son of Amyclas, King of Laconia. Now Hyacinthus was loved not only by Apollo but also by Boreas and Zephyrus. One day when Hyacinthus and Apollo were throwing the discus, Boreas and Zephyrus jealously directed the discus which Apollo had just thrown so that it struck Hyacinthus on the head and immediately killed him. From the blood which gushed from the wound sprang the flower which bears his name, the hyacinth. In memory of this sad event they celebrated annually in Laconia the festival of the *Hyacinthia*, which began with funeral offerings and lamentations and ended with songs of joy in honour of the young hero who had become immortal.

THE RETINUE OF APOLLO

The Muses. In his aspect of god of music, Apollo's habitual companions were the Muses. Thus he was called *Apollo Musagetes*.

Originally the Muses, like the Nymphs, seem to have been deities of springs. Afterwards they became goddesses of memory, and then of poetic inspiration.

This number varied. The first Muses worshipped on Mount Helicon were three in number: Melete, Mneme and Aoide. There were also three at Sicyon, as well as at Delphi, where their names – Nete, Mese and Hypate – personified the three strings of the lyre. There were seven Muses in Lesbos and in Sicily, eight for the Pythagoreans and in primitive Athens. It was finally agreed that there were nine Muses: Clio, Euterpe, Thalia, Melpomene, Terpsichore, Erato, Polyhymnia, Urania and Calliope.

Functions. The Muses were for long merged in an indissoluble choir which presided over music and poetry in general. It was only later that a special province was assigned to each.

Clio thus became the Muse of History. Her attributes were the heroic trumpet and the clepsydra.

Euterpe presided over flute-playing and her attribute was the flute.

Thalia, who was at first considered a bucolic Muse, became the Muse of Comedy. In her hands she carried the shepherd's staff and the comic mask.

Melpomene was the Muse of Tragedy. Her attributes were the tragic mask and also the club of Hercules.

Terpsichore, whose attribute was the cithara, was the Muse of Lyric Poetry and of the Dance.

Erato was the Muse of Love Poetry.

Polyhymnia, after having been the Muse of heroic hymns, became the Muse of Mimic Art. She was represented in an attitude of meditation with a finger on her mouth.

Urania was the Muse of Astronomy and her attributes were the celestial globe and a compass.

Calliope, who was first in rank among her sisters, was considered in turn to be the Muse of Epic Poetry and Eloquence. Her attributes were the stylus and tablets.

Places of Cult and Representations. The cult of the Muses originated in Thrace, or more precisely in Pieria, as their oldest sanctuary testifies. It was established at Libethrum on the eastern slopes of Olympus, whence it spread to Boeotia where, around Helicon, the centres of the cult were the towns of Ascra and Thespiae. At Thespiae festivals in honour of the Muses were celebrated every five years and included poetic contests. In the rest of Greece the cult

The punishment of Ixion. Invited to Olympus by Zeus, Ixion, the king of the Lapithae, had cast eyes upon Hera and was deceived by Zeus into embracing a cloud made in her image. Here he stands before her, grasped by Ares and Hermes, awaiting his punishment. Zeus condemned him to be scourged by Hermes and he was then bound to a fiery wheel which rolled him ceaselessly through the sky. Detail from a red-figured vase.

of the Muses was no less fervent. In Athens a hill near the Acropolis was consecrated to them and they were worshipped on the banks of the Ilissus. At Delphi they were venerated with Apollo. The Muses also had sanctuaries at Sparta, Troezen, Sicyon, Olympus, in the islands and in several towns in Magna Graecia.

Their former character of spring nymphs explains why numerous fountains were sacred to the Muses.

Offerings to the Muses consisted of grains of wheat kneaded with honey. Libations were poured to them of water, milk and honey.

The Muses are represented as young women with faces smiling, grave or thoughtful, according to their function. They are dressed in long floating robes, covered by a mantle. Urania and Clio are normally depicted sitting. They are otherwise distinguished by their individual attributes.

The Legend of the Muses. As to the origin of the Muses traditions vary. According to Mimnermus and Alcman they were born of Uranus and Gaea; they were also said to be daughters of Pierus and Antiope or else the nymph Pimplea, of Zeus and the Arcadian nymph Neda, of Apollo and so forth. Hesiod's opinion was, however, generally accepted, and he called them the daughters of Zeus and the Titaness Mnemosyne (or Memory).

It was told how after the defeat of the Titans the gods had asked Zeus to create divinities who were capable of celebrating the victory of the Olympians. The master of the gods then went to Pieria, where he shared Mnemosyne's couch for nine consecutive nights. When her time had come Mnemosyne gave birth to nine daughters who formed the choir of the Muses.

Although the Muses often frequented Olympus, where they added gaiety to the feasts of the Immortals with their singing, they preferred to dwell on Helicon, a high mountain in Boeotia whose wooded slopes were covered with fragrant plants which had the property of depriving snakes of their venom. Here numerous springs

caused an agreeable freshness: the most celebrated were Aganippe and Hippocrene, which gushed forth under the hoof of Pegasus. Both had the virtue of conferring poetic inspiration on those who drank their waters. On the tender greensward which bordered these fountains the Muses 'with tireless feet would trace the graceful figures of a dance, full of charm, while they displayed the harmony of their brilliant voices', and when they were tired they would restore the freshness of their complexions in the azure waters of Hippocrene. When night came they would abandon the summits of Helicon and, wrapped in a thick cloud, draw near the habitations of men, who could then hear the melodious sound of their voices.

The Muses also liked to visit Parnassus in Phocis where they shared the company of Apollo. From the flank of this mountain came forth a spring, the fountain Castalia, which was sacred to them and whose waters also gave poetic inspiration. This fountain which, they said, communicated with the Cephisus – which also had its source on Parnassus – was regarded as a mouth of the River Styx. The waters of Castalia were used in purification rites in the temple at Delphi, and they were given to the Pythia to drink. The Muses, indeed, were closely connected with the cult of Apollo and as well as being patrons of poetry were guardians of the oracle of Delphi. They themselves, moreover, had the gift of prophecy: 'they said that which is, what will be, and what has been'. It was they who taught Aristaeus the art of divination.

But their legend is chiefly concerned with them as goddesses of song. Hesiod shows us the Muses on Olympus charming the great soul of Zeus. 'Their tireless voices flow from their mouths in sweet accents, and this bewitching harmony as it spreads afar brings smiles to their father's palace, their father who wields the thunderbolt.'

Like all goddesses the Muses were easily offended and harshly punished anyone who dared compete with them.

When the Thracian Bard Thamyris boasted that he surpassed

Hephaestus returns to Olympus. Detail from an Attic crater. Louvre.

even the Muses, they struck him blind and dumb.

Pierus, King of Emathia in Macedonia, had nine daughters, the Pierides, who dared to challenge the Muses for the prize of poetry. They were changed into magpies by Apollo and the Muses took over their name.

Finally, the Sirens paid dearly for their presumption. Having issued a challenge to the Muses they were vanquished in spite of the irresistible sweetness of their voices, and in consequence were deprived of their wings.

Originally the Muses were represented as virgins of the strictest chastity. They had taken shelter one day with Pyreneos, King of Daulis in Phocis, when the king attempted to violate them. The Muses then took their wings and flew away. Pyreneos tried to follow them, but he fell from the top of his palace and was killed.

Later numerous love-affairs were attributed to the Muses.

Calliope was not only loved by Apollo, by whom she had two sons, Hymenaeus and Ialemus; she also married Oeagrus, to whom she bore Orpheus, the celebrated singer of Thrace.

Melpomene lay with the river-god Achelous and became the mother of the Sirens.

Euterpe – others say it was Calliope or Terpsichore – had by Strymon, the river-god of Thrace, a son Rhesus who was slain during the Trojan war by Odysseus and Diomedes; for an oracle had said that if the horses of Rhesus drank the waters of the Xanthus Troy would become impregnable.

Clio, having reproached Aphrodite for her passion for Adonis, was punished by Aphrodite, who roused in her heart an irresistible love for Pierus, King of Macedonia. By him Clio had Hyacinthus, whose unfortunate history we have already read.

Thalia gave birth to the Corybantes after lying with Apollo.

By Amphimarus, the musician, Urania had Linus, who was also said to be the son of Apollo and Calliope or Terpsichore. To Linus was attributed the invention of melody and rhythm. It was told how he challenged Apollo to a song contest and how Apollo killed him. Linus had a statue on Helicon where he was honoured as an equal of the Muses. Thebes claimed to possess his tomb.

Finally, Thamyris was supposed to be the son of Erato, and Triptolemus the son of Polyhymnia.

ARTEMIS

The etymology of the name Artemis is obscure and gives us no precise indication of her character. The laws of phonetic derivation are against connecting the name with the world for 'bear', and 'quail' has been suggested in memory of her birth in the isle of Ortygia. The adjective meaning 'safe and sound' has also been proposed, which would make Artemis 'she who heals sickness'. But none of the etymologies take into consideration the goddess's complex character in which, it would seem, different divinities are merged, as in the case of Apollo.

Character and Functions. The primitive Artemis, probably a replica of *Apollo Nomius*, was an agricultural deity, worshipped especially in Arcadia. She was the goddess of the chase and of forests (*Agrotera*). Her symbol was a she-bear, which suggests that she was originally confused with Callisto, who was later made her companion. One is tempted to connect the Arcadian Artemis with Artio, the Celtic goddess of Berne, whose symbol was also a she-bear.

From the beginning Artemis was associated with Apollo and could not fail to participate in his nature: thus she is also a divinity of the light (Phoebe), though of the moon's light. Similarly, her lunar character gradually became less marked, as the appearance of a special moon-goddess, Selene, testifies. In her aspect of light-goddess she has the same functions as Apollo. Like him armed with bow and quiver, she bore the epithet *Apollousa*, the destructress; or *Iocheaira*, who liked to let fly with arrows, strike down mortals with her fearful darts, and assail their flocks with deadly disease. Like Apollo she was the deity of sudden death, though it was usually women whom she struck. She was, however, equally benevolent and brought prosperity to those who honoured her.

In her capacity of moon-goddess Artemis presided over childbirth, jointly with Ilithyia.

Finally Artemis was likened to other divinities who had no connection with her, such as the moon-goddess of Tauris, as a result of confusion caused by the epithet *Tauropolos* which Artemis had in certain towns like Samos, Amphipolis and Icarus. She was also compared to the Cretan goddess Britomartis, and to Hecate, a Thracian divinity who was at the same time a moon-goddess and a goddess of the underworld. There is even less connection between the Greek Artemis and the Artemis or Diana of Ephesus, a personification of fecundity, one of the forms of the Great Mother-goddess of the Orient.

Artemis, particularly venerated in Arcadia, was worshipped throughout Greece, notably in the Peloponnese, at Sparta, at Caryae in Laconia, at Athens, Aegina, Olympia and Delos, where the laurel was consecrated to her and where Hyperborean girls brought their offerings to her. She was revered, too, in Crete, Asia Minor and Magna Graecia.

Representations. Although the lunar character of Artemis is sometimes recalled on coins by a torch held in her hand, or by the moon and the stars which surround her head, sculptors have chiefly emphasised her rural aspect. She appears to us as a young virgin, slim and supple, with narrow hips and regular features. Her beauty is a little severe, with her hair drawn back or partly gathered in a knot on her head. She wears a short tunic which does not fall below her knees: this is, in fact, the Dorian chiton which has been turned up and the folds retained by a girdle. Her feet are shod with the cothurnus or laced buskin. She is usually accompanied by a hind or a dog.

Very different is the appearance of the crowned Artemis of Ephesus, whose body is tightly sheathed in a robe covered with animal heads which leaves her bosom with its multiple breasts exposed: a striking image of a fertility-goddess who has nothing to do with the Greek Artemis.

The Legend of Artemis. Artemis was occasionally presented as the daughter of Zeus and Demeter or Persephone; or else of Dionysus and Isis. But according to the tradition general among the Greeks she was the daughter of Leto, and Apollo's twin sister.

She was born, they said, on the sixth day of the month of Thargelion – a day before her brother – on the isle of Ortygia which only took the name Delos after the birth of Apollo. She shared the vicissitudes which marked the childhood of her brother, accompanying him on his expedition against the serpent Python and during his exile in Thessaly. Then she chose Arcadia for her favourite place of abode. In this savage and mountainous region, where torrents tumbled down the woody slopes and plunged through narrow gorges, Artemis, accompanied by sixty young Oceanids and twenty nymphs appointed to the care of her pack of swift hounds gave herself to the pleasures of the chase. As soon as she was born she had, in fact, gone to find her father Zeus and, embracing his knees, begged from him, not ornaments or jewellery, but a short tunic, hunting boots, a bow and a quiver full of arrows.

As skilled as her brother, 'on the shady mountainside, on the wind-lashed mountain tops, she bends her bow of sparkling gold and lets fly her deadly arrows'.

When she had tired of tracking wild beasts or pursuing the light-footed roebuck she would pause beside the clear waters of a fountain and bathe with her companions until the freshness of the waters had assuaged her fatigue.

In this rude, out-door existence there was no place for love. To the virgin huntress even the legitimate joys of marriage were repugnant, and she made of chastity a strict law which she imposed on her companions. Woe to the nymphs who had joined Artemis' band and then so far forgot their duty as to taste of forbidden pleasures! Even were she a victim of some god's trickery she was nonetheless cruelly chastised. The unfortunate Callisto, who had been approached by Zeus in the guise of the goddess herself and seduced, fell beneath Artemis' arrows when her disgrace became known.

Woe, also, to the imprudent man who gave way to his curiosity! Actaeon, son of Aristaeus and Autonoë, was himself a passionate huntsman. One day with his hounds he was chasing a stag when he came to the valley of Gargaphia, near the fountain Parthenius, where at that moment Artemis and her companions happened to be bathing. Ravished by the beauty of the goddess, Actaeon paused to contemplate her. He was observed. Enraged that a mortal should have seen her in her nakedness, Artemis changed Actaeon into a stag and set his own pack on him. The hounds tore Actaeon to pieces and devoured him.

But on one occasion, it would seem, Artemis' own heart was stirred by the hunter Orion. Perhaps she might even have married him had not Apollo intervened. One day when Orion, a strong swimmer, was bathing in the sea, he had swum far from shore and had nearly vanished on the horizon when Apollo challenged his sister to hit the scarcely perceptible point which, far out to sea, moved on the surface of the waves. Artemis, not realising that the distant object was Orion, accepted the challenge, bent her bow and shot an arrow. It pierced the temple of him she loved. Did Apollo wish to safeguard his sister's honour, or was he motivated by secret jealousy? Certain traditions do, indeed, claim that he had ravished Artemis on his own altar at Delos. But we prefer to believe in the intact purity of the goddess.

Elsewhere it was told that Orion perished for having dared to touch the goddess one day when they were hunting together in the island of Chios. Artemis summoned a deadly scorpion from the earth which stung Orion on the heel.

This version agrees better with what we know of the dark and vindictive character of Artemis. When Apollo punished Tityus for the outrage done to Leto, his mother, Artemis seconded him. To her also the death of the Aloadae was sometimes attributed: the two giants having attempted to violate her, Artemis turned herself into a white doe and got between them in such a way that, trying to strike the beast with their javelins, they ran each other through instead.

We have seen how Artemis killed Chione whom her brother loved, because Chione was vain of her children's beauty. Niobe was punished still more harshly. Daughter of Tantalus, Niobe had six sons and six daughters by her husband Amphion. In her maternal pride she dared to disparage Leto, who had brought only two children into the world. To punish this insolence Apollo and Artemis struck down all twelve of Niobe's children with their arrows and Niobe, heartbroken, at last persuaded Zeus to change her into a rock.

The slightest negligence towards Artemis was apt to be punished. Admetus, who had omitted to offer sacrifice to the goddess on his marriage, had when he entered the bridal chamber the disagreeable surprise of finding it full of snakes. Oeneus, who reigned at Calydon in Aetolia, forgot to consecrate the first fruits of his crop to Artemis: his territory was ravaged by a prodigious boar and, in the course of the adventures which accompanied and followed the capture of the monster, his whole family perished.

Votive relief to Asclepius and Hygieia. The god of health is seated on the left with his daughter Hygieia standing before him. On the right a family lead a sacrificial bull to the altar. Patients would spend the night on the skin of the sacrificed animal in one of the god's sanctuaries after observing special purificatory rites of a religious and medical nature. Cures were marked by ex-votos such as this.

It was also for offending the goddess, either by killing a stag in a wood that was sacred to her or by boasting that he was a more skilled hunter than she, that Agamemnon was wind-bound in the port of Aulis, together with the Greek fleet. He could obtain the return of favourable winds only by immolating to Artemis his own daughter, Iphigenia. But the goddess took pity on the innocent victim and snatched Iphigenia away at the moment of sacrifice, bearing her to Tauris where she was made a priestess of Artemis' cult.

In the Tauric Chersonese there existed, in fact, a local divinity who was later identified with the Hellenic Artemis and who was honoured by blood sacrifices. All strangers who were shipwrecked on the coasts of Tauris were sacrificed to her. Iphigenia presided over the sacrifices. One day her brother Orestes approached these inhospitable shores. He was condemned to death, but he revealed himself to his sister and together they fled, carrying with them the statue of the goddess, which was deposited in the town of Brauron in Attica and later transferred to a sanctuary on the Acropolis in Athens. It was venerated under the name of *Artemis Brauronia*, the bear being sacred to her. It was told a tame bear which wandered freely through the villages of Attica one day lacerated a girl with its claws. It was killed by the girl's brothers. Artemis in anger at once sent a deadly plague to Athens. The oracle, when consulted, replied that the scourge would cease only if the inhabitants consecrated their daughters to Artemis. And so, every five years, a procession of little girls from five to ten years old, dressed in saffron-coloured robes, would wend its way solemnly to the temple of Artemis.

The town of Limnaion in Laconia also gloried in the possession of the true Taurian Artemis. The statue had been found standing upright in the middle of a thicket – for this reason it was called Artemis Orthia (the upright) – and the discovery had been accompanied among the inhabitants of Limnaion and the neighbouring villages by an outbreak of madness, murders and epidemics. They succeeded in appeasing the bloodthirsty goddess by human sacrifices, later replaced by the flagellation of youths in front of the statue of Artemis. The statue was carried by the priestess, and it became heavier whenever the zeal of those performing the flagellation slackened.

We should be wrong, however, to consider the daughter of Leto only under this rough and barbarous aspect. Though she loved to roam the mountains and the valleys, she also permitted herself more gentle amusements. She was the sister of Apollo, god of the cithara, and she too was a musician-goddess: song and dancing were pleasing to *Artemis Hymnia*. 'When the chase has rejoiced her heart she unbends her bow and enters the vast dwelling-place of her brother in the rich land of Delphi and joins the lovely choir of the Muses and the Graces. There she hangs up her bow and arrows and, dressed in gracious style, leads and directs the choir.'

Artemis of Ephesus and the Amazons. We have said above that by a rather strange confusion the name of Artemis had been given to a fertility-goddess particularly venerated at Ephesus. The origin of this cult was said to go back to the Amazons, a mythical people of female warriors who had come from the region of the Caucasus to settle in Cappadocia on the banks of the Thermodon. There the Amazons founded a state whose capital was Themiscyra and which was ruled over by a queen. Men were not admitted. Once a year the Amazons would go to their neighbours the Gargarensians to form temporary unions. Of the children which resulted therefrom they would keep only the girls who, from infancy, were trained for the chase and for war. The ancient Greeks derived their name from *mazos*, 'breast', and '*a*', 'no', and explained that they removed their right breast in order to draw the bow more easily. But, apart from the fact that no trace of such mutilation is ever seen in representations of the Amazons, the peculiar aspect of Artemis of Ephesus, their great goddess, suggests that the prefix '*a*' has, on the contrary, an augmentative value.

To the Amazons was attributed the foundation of many towns: Smyrna, Ephesus, Cyme, Myrina and Paphos. From Cappadocia they reached the islands, landed at Lesbos and Samothrace, and had even penetrated Boeotia and Attica. The motive for this invasion of Attica was to avenge the abduction or the abandonment – one does not know exactly which – of Antiope by Theseus. Antiope was the sister of the Amazon queen, Hippolyta. In Athens they used to show the tombs of the Amazons who had perished in the course of the war, and every year the Athenians offered sacrifices to the *manes* of their enemies. The Amazons also fought in Lycia against Bellerophon, and against Hercules, who slew Hippolyta, their queen. During the Trojan war they came to the aid of Troy and saw their young queen, Penthesileia, fall beneath the blows of Achilles. It was also told how they sent an expedition against the isle of Leuce in the Black Sea, where they were put to flight by the shade

Hephaestus and the Cyclopes forging the shield of Achilles. Antique bas-relief. Rome. To the left, Athene, to the right, Hera.

of Achilles, whose sanctuary they were about to sack. By their warlike habits and their horror of men the Amazons offer some resemblance to the Greek Artemis, which is doubtless the reason why their great goddess was given the same name.

HERMES

As in the case of the other Greek gods, many etymologies have been proposed for the name Hermes. Some suggest a connection with the Vedic Sarameya, derived from Sarama, god of the storm or of the dawn; others relate Hermes to a Greek word which conveys the idea of movement; still others – thinking of the early representations of the god – suggest the word for 'stone' or 'rock', and also the verb which means 'to protect'.

Character and Functions. Certain details of Hermes' legend suggest that he was either a god of the twilight or of the wind. Such are his birth, his theft of Apollo's heifers – analogous to the cows of the Vedic Indra, which personified the clouds – the myth of his slaying Argus, later thought to explain the epithet *Argephontes*, a probable deformation of *Argeiphantes*, 'he makes the sky clear'. It is, however, more probable that Hermes was a very ancient Pelasgian divinity. of Thracian origin, who was particularly honoured by the shepherds of Arcadia and whose mission was to watch over their flocks and protect their huts. From this doubtless arose the Greek habit of placing at the doors of houses a more or less crude image of this god. The Dorian invasion lessened the prestige of Hermes. Apollo Nomius took his place, and the primitive Hermes of the shepherds and of animal fertility took on another character.

Hermes was above all thought of as the god of travellers, whom he guided on their perilous ways. His images were placed where country roads branched and at crossroads in towns. It is without doubt a natural extension of this role that Hermes was also charged with conducting the souls of the dead to the underworld. Unless, indeed, this *Hermes Psychopompus* (conductor of souls), who is sometimes differentiated from the celestial Hermes, was not a substitute for some older subterranean divinity, a kind of *Zeus Plutos*.

Since in primitive times voyages were scarcely undertaken except for commerical purposes, Hermes was consequently the god of commerce, the god of profit – lawful and unlawful – and the god of games of chance. And, since buying and selling require much discussion, and the art of the trader is to overcome the buyer's hesitation by subtle and persuasive words, Hermes became the god of eloquence, the god *Logios*.

To these various functions Hermes added that of being the messenger of Zeus. This is how he appears in Homer, where he is qualified with the epithet *Diactoros* (the messenger). He comes to earth ceaselessly with orders from the king of the gods and undertakes the most delicate missions. In Hesiod, Hermes is the god who brings to men's hearts the impressions and sentiments which Zeus has inspired.

This indefatigable runner could scarcely fail to be honoured by athletes. Thus he had the epithet *Agonios*, 'who presides over contests', especially in Boeotia. His statue stood at the entrance to the stadium at Olympia, and to him was attributed the invention of pugilism and racing.

Representations. The classic aspect of Hermes is that of an athlete-god. In primitive times he had been represented as a mature man with a thick, long beard, his hair bound with a fillet and falling in curls to his shoulders. Afterwards he became the idealised type of the *ephebe* or young gymnast, with lithe and graceful body. His hair is short and crisp, his features fine; he carries his head slightly inclined as though listening with friendly interest. His nervous and supple body is largely exposed by the chlamys tossed over his shoulder or wound round his left arm. He often wears a round, winged hat – a *petasus* – and on his feet there are winged sandals. In his hand he holds a winged staff around which serpents are entwined; this is the *caduceus*.

The Theft of Apollo's Heifers. Hermes, son of Zeus and Maia, was born in the depths of a cave on Mount Cyllene in Arcadia. On the very day of his birth Hermes displayed his mischievous humour by stealing the cattle which had been confided to the care of Apollo. Sneaking furtively from his cradle, the infant god climbed the mountains of Pieria, where he found the divine herd. From it he separated fifty lowing heifers which he drove before him under cover of the night to the banks of the Alpheus. He made them walk backwards so that their hoofmarks should not betray the direction they had taken. He himself had cautiously put enormous sandals of tamarisk and myrtle twigs on his delicate feet. Before shutting up the heifers in a cavern he picked out two of the fattest and, having ingeniously produced fire by rubbing twigs of laurel together, he roasted them, dividing the flesh into twelve equal portions in honour of the twelve great gods. After which he regained the heights of

Cyllene, re-entered his cave through the keyhole, 'like vapour or a breath of autumn', and crawled into his cradle again. On the following day Apollo noticed the disappearance of his heifers. He grasped – by divination – what had occurred and went at once to Cyllene, where Hermes stubbornly denied all knowledge of the theft. Apollo seized the infant in his arms and carried him to the tribunal of Zeus on Olympus. The master of the gods could not but laugh at the cunning of his new-born child but, as he also cherished Apollo, he instructed Hermes to return the heifers. 'The two handsome sons of Zeus then hastened to sandy Pylus, near the ford of the Alpheus, and they reached the fields and the tall stable where the objects of the theft had been shut in at nightfall.'

The Invention of the Lyre. Reconciliation between the two gods was completed by the gift Hermes made to Apollo of a musical instrument he had ingeniously devised. When he had set out on his nocturnal adventure, Hermes found a tortoise in his path. He picked it up and, with a bright chisel, emptied the shell. Around it he stretched oxhide with the aid of reeds and arranged over a bridge seven strings made from sheep gut which then gave out harmonious sounds. It was the first lyre.

When Apollo, still annoyed by the theft of his heifers continued bitterly to reproach him, Hermes struck the strings of the instrument he had just fashioned. Apollo was charmed by the sound and his anger died – 'while the delightful sound of the divine music penetrated his senses, a sweet desire took possession of him'. Hermes guessed that Apollo coveted the lyre and spontaneously gave it to him. In exchange Apollo gave Hermes a bright whip or a golden wand – a prototype of the caduceus – and entrusted him with the care of the celestial herd. From then on Apollo became the god of music and Hermes the protector of flocks and herds. The friendship of the two gods was never broken. On many occasions Hermes was of service to Apollo and, in particular, took charge at their birth of several of Apollo's children.

The Good Offices of Hermes. In spite of his malicious pranks Hermes won the sympathy of all the gods. Even the vindictive Hera forgot her jealousy where Hermes was concerned. Alone among the illegitimate children of Zeus, the son of Maia found favour with her and the august goddess even consented to suckle him.

Hermes was always willing to be helpful, and his ingenuity made him a valuable ally. During the war against the giants he put on the helmet of Hades – which made him invisible – and killed the giant Hippolytus. We have already seen how he freed Zeus, when Zeus was a prisoner of Typhoeus. He restored Zeus' strength by replacing the nerves which the giant had cut. During Zeus' amorous adventures, Hermes' aid was invaluable: he put the giant Argus to sleep with the sound of his flute and then, in order to free Io, killed him. When Dionysus was born it was Hermes who carried the child to Orchomenus and delivered him into the hands of Ino, Semele's sister. Zeus moreover made him his messenger. In order rapidly to cross the celestial spaces Hermes wore winged sandals which bore him 'over the watery sea or over the vast earth like a breath of wind'. To aid his flight he sometimes added wings to his hat.

When Ares fell into the hands of the Aloadae and was kept captive for thirteen months without anyone's knowing the place of his captivity, it was Hermes who finally discovered his prison and set him free. Again it was Hermes who, with the help of Iris, found in the abode of Tantalus the golden dog Pandareus had stolen from Zeus.

Hermes' protection was also extended to heroes: when Perseus faltered he restored his courage, and he accompanied Hercules during his descent to the underworld.

Hermes was a benefactor of mankind, and protected their flocks, guided them on their voyages, presided over their business affairs and inspired in them melodious speech and eloquence. Often he also took a direct part in their affairs. He plunged the Greeks into deep slumber with the aid of his magic wand 'with which he made drowsy the eyes of mortals or, if he so desired, roused them from sleep'. In doing this he made it possible for Priam to bring the body of his son Hector back into the walls of Troy. He gave Odysseus a magic plant which made him immune to the enchantments of Circe. We even see him one day, when the Euboeans were preparing to attack the city of Tanagra, put himself at the head of the youths of that city in order to repel the invaders.

Hermes, as we have seen, was also concerned with the underworld; for it was he who conducted the souls of the dead to their final dwelling-place. For this reason he was called *Psychopompus*.

Homer shows us the souls of Penelope's suitors slain by Odysseus as they fly after Hermes, rustling like bats, until they reach the 'fields of asphodel where dwell the phantoms of those who are no longer'. Hermes could also lead back the souls of the dead into the world of light. When Tantalus cut his own son into pieces and served them as a feast for the gods, Hermes, on the instructions of Zeus, re-assembled the pieces and restored the young man to life. Hermes also accompanied Orpheus on his search for Eurydice.

The Sons of Hermes. Hermes, like the other gods, had many amorous adventures. Among the goddesses he was, it appears, the lover of Persephone, Hecate and Aphrodite. Among nymphs, whom he pursued in the shady depths of forests, his conquests were wider. By them he had a numerous progeny among whom it is sufficient to mention: Saon, son of the nymph Phene, who colonised Samothrace; Polydorus, son of the Thessalian nymph Polymele; Daphnis, the beautiful and unhappy shepherd of Sicily, who was born in the neighbourhood of Etna; and above all Pan, the rustic god of Arcadia. While tending the flocks of Dryops on the slopes of Mount Cyllene, Hermes saw Dryops' daughter and loved her. She brought into the world a son who was covered with hair and had the horns and feet of a goat. In horror she abandoned him, but Hermes picked him up, wrapped him in the skin of a hare and then carried him to Olympus where the gods delighted in the spectacle. According to another tradition, Pan was the son of a mortal, Penelope, whom Hermes came to in the guise of a he-goat.

Among the mortals whom Hermes loved were Acacallis, daughter of Minos, whom he made mother of Cydon, founder of the Cretan town of Cydonia, and Chione, who also bore him a son, Autolycus. Autolycus received from his father the gift of rendering what he touched invisible. In this way he was able to commit numerous thefts until one day Sisyphus, whose oxen he had stolen, caught him. Another son of Hermes was Myrtilus, who was killed by Pelops: the god avenged himself on the murderer's descendants.

ARES

Should we, with Max Muller, connect the name Ares – like Mars – with the Sanskrit root *mar*, from which derive the Vedic *maruts*, storm-divinities? Or with the Greek root which means 'carry away, destroy'? Both hypotheses are equally ingenious and equally uncertain.

Character and Representations. Ares originated in Thrace. He was always thought of by the Greeks with more terror than sympathy, and his role was strictly limited. He was simply the god of war, of blind, brutal courage, of bloody rage and carnage. Hypotheses which would make him primitively a fertility-god or a solar deity seem to be unfounded.

Actually we know little more about this god than what the poets tell us. He was, however, honoured throughout Greece and his cult was particularly developed in Thrace and Scythia. He had a temple in Athens. Olympia honoured him under the name Ares-Hippios, and Sparta under that of Ares-Enyalius (the warlike). A spring was consecrated to him near Thebes, beneath the temple of Apollo.

In Greek sculpture Ares was not represented by any especially fixed type. We scarcely know him except from vase paintings. At first he was depicted as a bearded warrior wearing a helmet with a tall crest and dressed in heavy armour. Later he appears as a young man, almost nude, who has retained little of his warlike attributes except the spear and helmet.

The Rages of Ares. 'Of all the gods who live on Olympus', says Zeus in the *Iliad* to Ares, 'thou art the most odious to me; for thou enjoyest nothing but strife, war and battles. Thou hast the obstinate and unmanageable disposition of thy mother Hera, whom I can scarcely control with my words.'

In expressing these unfriendly sentiments to his son, the master of the gods exactly defines the character of Ares, 'a furious god, by nature wicked and fickle', who in the immortal society of Olympus found, it seems, very little sympathy.

As god of war it was natural that he enjoyed fighting. Mounted

The blinding of Polyphemus. Odysseus and two of his companions drive a sharpened stake into the eye of the sleeping Cyclops who had been keeping them prisoner on their return journey from Troy in order to devour them. Though the Cyclopes traditionally only had one eye in the middle of their foreheads, the artist has depicted Polyphemus as having two in the normal manner. Black-figured Boeotian skyphos, second quarter of the sixth century B.C.

on a chariot drawn by swift horses with golden brow-bands, clad in bronze armour and grasping in his hands an enormous spear, Ares ranged the battlefield, striking deadly blows on all sides. His two squires, Deimos (Fear) and Phobos (Fright) – sometimes said to be his sons – accompanied him, together with Eris (Strife), 'insatiable in her fury', Enyo, 'destroyer of cities', and the Keres, sombre divinities, eager to drink the black blood of the dying.

Though none disputed his warlike ardour, Ares was disliked not only for his perpetual thirst for blood and slaughter which made him the 'scourge of mortals', but for his brutality and blind violence. It was in this, especially, that he differed from Athene who, as a warrior-goddess, represented cool and intelligent courage. Ares and Athene were thus constantly opposed. Many times they encountered each other on the plains of Ilium where they fought on opposite sides. The very sight of Athene set Ares in a rage. 'Why, then, shameless fly, dost thine insatiable audacity enflame the war between the gods? What ardour carries thee away? I think that to-day thou shalt pay for all thou hast done to me!' With these words he struck the terrible aegis which even the thunderbolt of Zeus could not break. Athene, drawing back, took up a stone which was lying on the plain: a black stone, rugged and enormous, which men of past ages had put there to serve as a boundary stone for the field. She hurled it at the neck of the impetuous Ares. His knees gave way and when he fell his body covered seven acres. Dust soiled his hair and about him his armour jangled. Pallas Athene smiled and, glorying in her exploit, addressed to him winged words: 'Vain fool! Hast thou not yet learned how superior my strength is to thine?'

Indeed the impetuous Ares, contrary to what one might expect, rarely emerged victorious from combat. Nor was it only the immortal gods who got the better of him. Otus and Ephialtes, the two Aloadae, succeeded in binding and keeping him captive for thirteen months. When he challenged Hercules, who had just killed his son Cycnus, Ares was wounded by the hero and forced to return groaning to Olympus. According to others, Zeus, who did not wish to see his two sons quarrel, put an end to the fight by dropping a thunderbolt between the two combatants.

The Loves of Ares. He was scarcely more happy in his love affairs. Impressed by the glamour of the handsome warrior whom she doubtless compared with Hephaestus, her ill-favoured husband, Aphrodite fell in love with Ares. The sentiment was quickly reciprocated. Ares took unscrupulous advantage of Hephaestus' absence to dishonour the marital couch; but Helios, who had observed the two lovers, reported the business to the smith-god. Although a deceived husband is usually an object of ridicule, Hephaestus was able to parry the laughter by an ingenious artifice. Secretly he forged a net so fine that it could not be seen, but so strong that it could not be broken. He arranged this net above the couch where the lovers normally frolicked, and pretended to leave for Lemnos.

'As soon as Ares saw the industrious Hephaestus depart he directed his steps towards the dwelling-place of the illustrious god, burning with love for Cytheraea of the fair crown. She was seated. He took her hand and said, "Come, my dear, let us lie on the couch of Hephaestus, for thy good man has gone to Lemnos, the land of the barbarous-tongued Sintians."' Thus he spoke, and his words were pleasing to the goddess. Soon they fell asleep and the invisible net of the ingenious Hephaestus spread over them. Then the limping god, who had retraced his steps, cried out in a terrible voice to all the gods:

'"Zeus and ye Immortals! Come in haste and see this intolerable thing, worthy of your laughter. Because I am lame Aphrodite despises me. She loves the fatal Ares because he is agile and handsome. See them both, asleep on my couch. Soon they will no longer care to sleep; for these cords will keep them bound together until Zeus returns the gifts I made him in order to obtain this impudent wench who cannot restrain her lust!"'

Then the gods gathered together in the palace of bronze and from their throats rose roars of uncontrollable laughter which threw Ares and Aphrodite into a state of extreme confusion. Hephaestus at last consented to free the two guilty ones when Ares promised to pay him the price of the adultery. The guilty wife fled to Paphos in the island of Cyprus and the seducer retired into the mountains of Thrace. From the union of Ares and Aphrodite a daughter was born, Harmonia, who later became the wife of Cadmus, King of Thebes.

Whether Ares had other misadventures of this nature is unknown, but he had little luck with his children.

By the nymph Aglauros Ares had a daughter, Alcippe. One day

Aphrodite of Cyrene. Inspired by Hesiod's account of the goddess' birth, this statue from Cyrene in Libya shows Aphrodite, 'the foam-born', freshly risen from the sea in the act of wringing out her hair. A dolphin frolics by her feet. The goddess of love was worshipped throughout the Greek world, her cult reaching as far West as Italy and Sicily. Early Hellenistic original, or possibly a Roman copy.

Halirrhothius, son of Poseidon, ravished her and Ares killed him. For this murder Poseidon summoned him before the tribunal of the twelve great gods, which met on a hill situated in front of the Acropolis in Athens. Ares was acquitted. In memory of this event the hill received the name of the Areopagus, and afterwards criminal cases continued to be judged there.

Among the other children of Ares who came to unhappy ends it is sufficient to mention: Phlegyas, son of Chryse, who was killed by Apollo; Diomedes, King of the Bistones of Thrace, who was put to death by Hercules; Cycnus, son of Pelopeia or of Pyrene, who was also killed by Hercules: cruel and belligerent like his father, Cycnus used to attack travellers in the region of Tempe and use their bones for building a temple to his father. He challenged Hercules, who struck him down and, into the bargain, wounded Ares himself, who had tried to defend his son. Some genealogies say that the unhappy Meleager, son of Oeneus and Althaea, was also the son of Ares.

Having seduced Harpina, daughter of the river-god Asopus, Ares had by her a son, Oenomaus, who reigned near Olympia, and himself had a daughter, Hippodameia. Since an oracle had predicted that he would be killed by his son-in-law, Oenomaus, in order to get rid of her suitors, announced that he would give his daughter only to the man who beat him in a chariot race. He was certain he would always win, because Ares his father had made him a gift of winged steeds. Pelops, however, carried away the prize, thanks to a treacherous ruse of Hippodameia herself, and Oenomaus found death in defeat.

Finally, among mortal women who were loved by Ares, there was Aerope, daughter of Cepheus, who died in giving birth to a son, Aeropus. However, thanks to the intervention of Ares, the new-born babe was able miraculously to suckle at the breast of his deceased mother.

HEPHAESTUS

Origin, Function and Representations. Whether we see in the name Hephaestus the Greek form of the Sanskrit *Yavishtha* (the very young), an epithet of Agni, the Vedic god of fire, or whether we derive it from the Greek words for 'hearth' and 'to kindle', there is no doubt that Hephaestus was, from remotest times, the personification of terrestrial fire, of which volcanoes were the most terrifying manifestation.

Thus the cult of Hephaestus, who was perhaps an Asiatic divinity, a native of Lycia, first arose on the volcanic island of Lemnos. From there it was brought to Attica and, with the colonisations, introduced into Sicily.

It is possible that in primitive times Hephaestus personified celestial fire and that he had thus been a thunder-god; his limping gait would then symbolise the zigzag of the lightning. If fire is of celestial origin then there is no reason why Hephaestus should not have such a character.

The fire which he represents is not, however, the destroying element, but rather the beneficent element which permits men to work metal and foster civilisation. Thus Hephaestus appears as the divine blacksmith, the artisan-god, the demiurge who has created admirable works and taught men the mechanical arts.

That is why Hephaestus – who was at first depicted as a beardless young man – was afterwards traditionally represented as a robust smith, with bearded face, powerful neck and hairy chest. His short and sleeveless chiton leaves his right shoulder bare; on his head he wears a conical bonnet and in his hands he grasps a hammer and tongs.

The Birth of Hephaestus. Although Hesiod's genealogy claims that Hephaestus was, like Typhon, born by Hera alone, it was generally admitted that he was the son of Hera and Zeus. At most one was sometimes given to understand that he was conceived before the official marriage of the two deities and that Hera had invented this legend of a miraculous birth in order to conceal her shame.

In contrast with the other Immortals, who were distinguished by beauty and the symmetry of their bodies, Hephaestus was ill-made and lame in both legs. His feet were twisted. His stumbling gait and dislocated hip aroused the 'unquenchable laughter of the Immortals' when he walked among them.

His Misadventures. Contrary to what was often said Hephaestus' infirmity was not the result of an accident. He was lame from birth. Homer, in fact, recounts that Hera, ashamed of the ugliness of her son, tried to hide him from the Immortals 'because he was lame'. She threw him from the heights of Olympus into the sea, where he was taken in by Thetis, daughter of Nereus, and Eurynome, daughter of the old Ocean. For nine years he remained concealed in their deep grotto, 'forging a thousand ingenious objects for the two nymphs', and at the same time preparing a cunning revenge. One day Hera received a gift from her son, a golden throne artistically wrought. She sat on it with delight, but when she tried to rise again she was suddenly gripped by invisible bands. The Immortals tried in vain to extricate her from the throne. Only Hephaestus was capable of releasing her, but he refused to leave the depths of the Ocean. Ares tried to drag him up by force, but was put to flight by Hephaestus who threw burning brands at him. Dionysus was more successful: he made Hephaestus drunk and, while he was drunk, perched him astride a mule and thus brought him back to Olympus. But they still had to meet his demands: Hephaestus refused to set Hera free unless they gave him the loveliest of the goddesses, Aphrodite – though some say Athene – for a bride. According to another tradition the reason why Hephaestus bound up Hera was to make her tell him the secret of his birth.

From then on there was peace between Hera and her son. Indeed, forgetting his former rancour, Hephaestus at the peril of his life attempted to defend his mother when she was beaten by Zeus. Irritated by his son, Zeus seized him by one foot and flung him from the courts of heaven. All day long he tumbled through space and, at sunset, fell more dead than alive on to the island of Lemnos, where the Sintians gathered him up.

The Blacksmith of Olympus. Under this graceless exterior, however, lurked a subtle and inventive spirit. Hephaestus excelled in the art of working metals. On Olympus he built palaces for the gods. For himself he constructed a 'sparkling dwelling of glittering and incorruptible bronze'. In it he had his workshop. There he could be seen beside the flaming furnaces, bathed in sweat, bustling about his bellows, poking the fires under twenty crucibles at a time, or hammering out the molten metal on an enormous anvil. When some god came to visit him, the gigantic blacksmith would pause to sponge his face, his hands, his powerful neck and hairy chest. He would put on a tunic and, leaning against a heavy staff, reach his gleaming throne. In order to steady his unsure footsteps – for his frail legs supported his massive body with difficulty – he had even fashioned two golden statues which resembled living girls. They had been endowed with movement and hastened to his side to aid him as he walked.

The Earthly Dwellings of Hephaestus. Homer placed the workshop of Hephaestus on Olympus. But the fire-god also haunted the earth, where he maintained various underground places of residence. He had done his apprenticeship as a blacksmith in the isle of Naxos and it was said that he unsuccessfully disputed the possession of the island with Dionysus. If so, understanding between the two gods was quickly re-established, and they always remained on excellent terms. Often the Sileni and the Satyrs helped Hephaestus in his work. To initiate him in the art of the forge Hera, it was said, had confided Hephaestus to the dwarf Cedalion, whose identity is rather mysterious. Some call him the son, others the father of Hephaestus. All that is known is that he always remained attached to the fire-god and followed him to Lemnos when Hephaestus set up an establishment there.

Hephaestus, indeed, had never forgotten the welcome the Sintians had given him on the occasion of his fall from Olympus and, in gratitude, settled in this volcanic island. His presence there was attested by the flaming vapours which escaped from Mount Moschylus to the accompanying sound of dull rumbling. This was the sound of the divine blacksmith's hammers from the workshop he had set up in the bowels of the mountain. Beside him worked the faithful Cedalion from whom he was never separated, except on the occasion when he lent him as a guide to the blind giant Orion who wished to be conducted to the West in order to recover his eyesight. Hephaestus was also helped by the Cabeiri, who were probably his sons. One tradition says Prometheus came to Lemnos to steal the divine fire which he then gave to mankind.

Marine Aphrodite. Possibly as the result of her birth, Aphrodite was also worshipped as a goddess of the sea and of seafaring in addition to her chief role of goddess of love and fertility. As Aphrodite Euploia she gave prosperous voyages and as Aphrodite Galenaia, fair weather, her shrine as a marine goddess being at Hermione. Of her numerous other sanctuaries the most famous were at Paphos, Cythera and Corinth. Late first century B.C.

The Judgment of Paris. Hermes leads the three contending goddesses into the presence of Paris who is seated on the left guarding his father's flocks and playing the lyre. Behind the messenger of the gods in his winged sandals comes Athene, armed with her helmet and spear, followed by Hera, with her staff, and Aphrodite, who is accompanied by Erotes and carries a dove. Detail from a red-figured kylix by Herron.

Later on Hephaestus emigrated to Sicily. At first we find him in the volcanic archipelago of the Lipari Islands. He it doubtless was, mysterious and obliging blacksmith, who at night wrought the metal which was left in the evening on the edge of a crevasse and found there again next morning wondrously worked. Subterranean ramifications connected the Lipari Islands with Mount Etna in Sicily, where Hephaestus finally settled. He dislodged an indigenous demon called Adranus. In Etna Hephaestus also acted as a gaoler to Typhoeus who, it will be remembered, had been crushed under this mountain by Zeus. Earthquakes and eruptions of lava were due to the convulsions of this monster when he attempted to break from his prison. But he could not escape, for Hephaestus had placed on his head heavy anvils on which he energetically hammered bronze and iron. When sailors skirted the coasts of Sicily and saw long streamers of smoke escaping from the crest of Etna they had no doubt that it was Hephaestus lighting his forge. The god was helped in his task by the Palici, twins whom he had had by the Oceanid Etna (though others say that the Palici were sons of Zeus and the nymph Aethalia, daughter of Hephaestus). The giant Cyclopes also assisted him.

His Works. The activity of Hephaestus was prodigious and only equalled by his skill. He was ceaselessly employed on some work of great delicacy. As well as the palaces on Olympus with their bronze trimmings, he fashioned Zeus' golden throne, sceptre and thunderbolts, the fearful aegis, the winged chariot of Helios, the arrows of Apollo and Artemis, Demeter's sickle, Hercules' cuirass, the arms of Peleus, the armour of Achilles, the necklace which Harmonia, wife of Cadmus, wore for her nuptials, Ariadne's diadem, Agamemnon's sceptre, the hypogeum or underground chamber of Oenopion. Nor should one forget the golden goblet which Zeus offered to Aphrodite, a vase given by Dionysus to Ariadne, the *harpe* of Perseus and Adonis' hunting equipment. To Hephaestus were also attributed such works of wonder as the tripods with golden wheels which rolled of their own accord into the assembly of the gods, the bronze bulls whose nostrils spurted forth flame, the golden and silver dogs of Alcinous' palace, and even the giant Talos 'that man of bronze' whose duty it was to guard the Cretan tree and prevent its being approached.

Nothing was impossible to him. When Zeus, in order to punish men, decided to create the first woman, Pandora, it was to Hephaestus that he turned. He ordered Hephaestus to mould the body of a woman with water and clay, to give it life and a human voice, and to form from it a virgin of ravishing beauty. To perfect his work Hephaestus encircled Pandora's brow with a golden crown which he himself had engraved.

On many other occasions Hephaestus gave assistance to Zeus. He split his skull with an axe in order that Athene might spring out. On his orders he bound Prometheus to the Caucasus. Doubtless he remembered the harsh lesson his father had given him when he had dared to cross Zeus' will. For this reason Hephaestus would pacify the other gods on Olympus, and especially Hera, when they were angry with Zeus. To all he preached submission: 'Have patience, O my mother, and, in spite of thy sorrow, be resigned so that I shall not see thee struck before my eyes. No matter how distressing this would be I could not come to thine aid; for it is hard to oppose the master of Olympus.' And all these quarrels spoiled the joy of living. 'The finest feast is without pleasure when discord triumphs.'

His Loves. Hephaestus was addicted to all pleasures. In spite of his ugliness he became the husband of Aphrodite. The position was not without its compensations, nor without its risks: his wife was continually unfaithful to him, especially with Ares. We have already seen with what spirit Hephaestus avenged himself by imprisoning the two lovers in a net and exposing them thus to the laughter of the Olympians. This misadventure did not prevent Hephaestus himself from aspiring to the love of the wise Athene. But the goddess successfully resisted him and he tried in vain to ravish her in the plain of Marathon. Certain legends say that Hephaestus' passion for Athene dated from the very moment of her birth. Before he struck Zeus with the axe which would liberate Athene from his head, Hephaestus had demanded the hand of the virgin who was about to appear. Zeus, they said, consented; but Athene herself refused to keep her father's promise. Must one see in these pursuits and evasions a symbol of the rivalry between these two working-gods, or an antagonism between celestial fire (Athene) and terrestrial fire (Hephaestus)? It is more probable that their histories are mingled simply because both were patrons of men's work and hence frequently associated.

Hephaestus was also said to have married the beautiful Charis and Aglaia, one of the Graces. By Cabeiro, daughter of Proteus, he was the father of the Cabeiri. The Oceanid Etna bore him twins, the Palici, the Dioscuri of Sicily; though another tradition says that they were sons of Zeus and the nymph Aethalia, daughter of Hephaestus. To escape Hera's vengeance Aethalia begged the earth to conceal her until the day of her delivery. Her prayers were granted and when her time came the two children sprang from the earth, whence their name: 'They who return to the light'. Two small lakes at the foot of Etna, always full of boiling sulphur water, marked the place where they had appeared. Their temple was there, and there they delivered oracles.

Among the other sons of Hephaestus may be mentioned Ardalus, Palaemon, Pylius – who cared for Philoctetes in Lemnos – and Periphetes who, like his father, was lame – which did not, however, prevent him from attacking travellers on the outskirts of Epidaurus and slaying them with his brazen club. He was killed by Theseus.

The Companions of Hephaestus. We have seen that Hephaestus was aided in his work by a certain number of subterranean divinities or fire genii. The best known were the Cyclopes, who assisted him at the forges under Etna. The first Cyclopes who appear in Greek mythology were the three sons of Uranus and Gaea: Arges, Steropes and Brontes. It may be remembered how after their father had cast them into Tartarus they were delivered by Zeus, whom they helped in his struggle against the Titans. Apart from thunder, the thunderbolt and the lightning which they gave Zeus, they presented Hades with a bronze helmet and Poseidon with a trident. They were put to death by Apollo, who took his vengeance on them for the death of his son Asclepius.

These earlier Cyclopes had nothing in common with the Cyclopes whom Homer introduces us to in the *Odyssey*. The latter were men of gigantic stature and repellent ugliness with their single eye in the middle of their forehead, who inhabited the south-west coast of Sicily. Given to a pastoral existence, they were gross and ill-mannered, living in isolated caverns, slaughtering and devouring any strangers who approached their shores. The best known among them was Polyphemus, who took Odysseus and his companions prisoner. In order to escape, the Greek hero made Polyphemus drunk and put out his single eye by means of a sharpened, burning stake; Odysseus and his companions then escaped from the cavern by tying themselves under the bellies of rams. Before this misfortune Polyphemus had fallen in love with the Nereid Galatea. He paid court to her by sending her a daily present of a bear or an elephant. To this inelegant suitor Galatea preferred the shepherd Acis, son of the nymph Symoethis. Jealous of this rival Polyphemus crushed him beneath a rock, and Acis was changed by the gods into a river.

When tradition made Mount Etna the abode of Hephaestus he was given the Cyclopes as companions. They borrowed their features from the Cyclopes of Hesiod and Homer. They were, says Callimachus, 'enormous giants, as big as mountains, and their single eye, under a bushy eyebrow, glittered menacingly. Some made the vast bellows roar, others, laboriously raising one by one their heavy hammers, struck great blows at the molten bronze and iron they drew from the furnace.' Their number was not stated. Among the names which were given to them we find those of Brontes, Steropes, Acamas and Pyracmon.

At Lemnos the Cyclopes were replaced by the Cabeiri, divinities whose origin and nature have remained rather mysterious especially since they occur in various regions with quite distinct characters. The Cabeiri of Lemnos, said to be the sons of Hephaestus, were benevolent genii, underground smiths evidently associated with the volcanic nature of the island's structure. At Samothrace the Cabeiri were a kind of inferior god, sworn to the service of the great gods of the island; tradition made them the sons of Zeus and Calliope. At Thebes in Boeotia the Cabeiri appear to have been associated with the cult of Demeter and Kore, since their temple was situated near a grove sacred to these two goddesses. In Thessaly they spoke of a Cabeire who was put to death by his two brothers and buried at the foot of Olympus. Finally we find Cabeiri at Pergamus in Phoenicia, and Herodotus believed he recognised them in Egypt. From all this it would seem that the Cabeiri, whose name has been compared with the Phoenician *qabirim,* 'the powerful', were in primitive times underground spirits, originating in Phrygia, who in the volcanic islands naturally took on the character of fire genii. They were reputed to be the first metal-workers.

The Greeks, however, recognised other metallurgical genii who, without being directly concerned with the cult of Hephaestus, must be mentioned here.

In the forests of Phrygian Ida there lived cunning magicians called the Dactyls. Originally there were three of them: Celmis, Damnameneus and the powerful Acmon, 'who in the caves of the mountains was the first to practise the art of Hephaestus, and

The Themis of Rhamnus. National Museum, Athens.

Oceanus. The father of the three thousand Oceanids and the three thousand rivers, Oceanus is portrayed as a vigorous middle-aged man with marine animals in his hair in this antique bronze. Originally conceived as one of the great elemental forces which had helped form the world, Oceanus was believed to encircle the entire universe with his waters from which rose the sun and the stars. His importance diminished in the later stages of Greek culture.

who knew how to work blue iron, casting it into the burning furnace'. Later their number increased. From Phrygia they went to Crete where they taught the inhabitants the use of iron and how to work metals. To them was also attributed the discovery of arithmetic and the letters of the alphabet.

Genii who also played a civilising role but afterwards assumed a malignant character were the Telchines, said to be the sons of Poseidon and Thalassa, though another tradition makes them Poseidon's guardians. The centre of their cult was the Isle of Rhodes, whence they spread to Crete and Boeotia. They were great metal-workers, as the names of three of them suggest: Chryson, Argyron and Chalcon. They forged the first statues of the gods, and among their works were the sickle of Cronus and the trident of Poseidon. But they were feared for their enchantments. They could cast the evil eye and, by sprinkling the ground with the waters of the Styx mixed with sulphur, they blighted the harvest and killed the flocks.

APHRODITE

Origin and Character. Though the primitive Greeks certainly had a goddess of love it would seem she was not Aphrodite. We must not be misled by the legend which arose later to justify an etymology based on a sort of pun which connects her name with the Greek word for 'foam'. In reality the name Aphrodite seems to be of oriental origin, probably Phoenician, like the goddess herself –

sister of the Assyro-Babylonian Ishtar and the Syro-Phoenician Astarte. From Phoenicia the cult of Aphrodite passed to Cythera, a Phoenician trading-post, and to Cyprus (whence the epithets Cytheraean and Cyprian which the goddess has in Homer); then it spread throughout Greece and even reached Sicily.

In origin Aphrodite was – like the great Asiatic goddesses – obviously a fertility goddess whose domain embraced all nature, vegetable and animal as well as human. Afterwards she became the goddess of love in its noblest aspect as well as in its most degraded.

Aphrodite Urania, or the celestial Aphrodite, was the goddess of pure and ideal love. Aphrodite Genetrix or Nymphia favoured and protected marriage: unmarried girls and widows prayed to her in order to obtain husbands. Aphrodite Pandemos (common) or Aphrodite Porne (courtesan) was the goddess of lust and venal love, the patroness of prostitutes. Under the influence of her legend Aphrodite later became a marine deity (Pelagia, Pontia).

Cult and Representations. The chief centres of the cult of Aphrodite were Paphos in Cyprus and Cythera in Crete. Among her most famous sanctuaries were the temple of Cnidus in Caria and the temple on the Isle of Cos. Aphrodite Pandemos was venerated at Thebes, where a statue of the goddess could be seen, made, they said, of the battering-rams of the ships which had brought Cadmus to Greece. In Athens there was a temple of Aphrodite Hetaera, in which the goddess was represented sitting on a he-goat. She was venerated at Abydos, at Ephesus and above all at Corinth, where the prostitutes of the town were her veritable priestesses. Aphrodite Genetrix was worshipped at Sparta and at Naupactus. Aphrodite Urania had temples at Sicyon, Argos and Athens. Finally the marine Aphrodite Pelagia was especially honoured at Hermione. In Thessaly they venerated an Aphrodite Anosia (the impious) in memory of the murder of the courtesan Lais by the wives of the region. In Sicily Aphrodite had a celebrated temple on Mount Eryx.

The representations of Aphrodite vary according to the character in which she was envisaged.

At Sicyon they venerated an ivory-adorned statue in which the goddess was crowned by a *polos*. Nobility and modesty characterised this statue, which evidently depicted Aphrodite Urania or Genetrix.

The note of sensuality is emphasised in the later effigies of Aphrodite. Indeed, the models whom the sculptors employed were often courtesans like Cratina, Phryne or Cambyse, the mistress of Alexander. Such were the nude Aphrodites of Praxiteles which, it is said, shocked the piety of the inhabitants of Cos. The Aphrodite which was honoured at Cnidos was particularly voluptuous.

Hesiod's myth of the birth of Aphrodite inspired the various types of Aphrodite *anadyomene* – i.e., rising from the waters – like the celebrated Aphrodite (or Venus) de Medici, and the Aphrodites at the bath so popular in statuary.

A type rather different from the preceding is Aphrodite the Warrior, represented armed and wearing a helmet. She was particularly venerated at Sparta. She is an echo of the warrior Ishtar of Babylonia.

The Birth of Aphrodite. Homer describes Aphrodite as the daughter of Zeus and Dione – a rather vague divinity who was said to be the daughter of Oceanus and Tethys and of whom we know only that she was closely associated with the cult of Zeus at Dodona. Even her name, which is merely the feminine form of Zeus, suggests her lack of defined personality. Popular imagination could scacely be satisfied with so poor a legend, and the Homeric tradition was thus supplanted by another, richer in popular appeal.

When, at the instigation of his mother, Gaea, the audacious Cronus had castrated his father, Uranus, he cast the severed genitals into the sea. They floated on the surface of the waters, producing a white foam from which rose Aphrodite. Carried on the moist breath of Zephyrus, the West Wind, across the tumultuous sea, the goddess was borne along the coast of Cythera and finally landed on the shores of Cyprus. She was greeted by the Horae, who dressed her richly, adorned her with precious jewels and conducted her to the assembly of the Immortals. Beside her walked Love and Himeros, tender Desire. When they saw her the gods were struck with admiration for such beauty and each, says the poet, 'wished in his heart to take her as a wife and lead her to his abode'.

It was natural that they should be moved; for Aphrodite was the essence of feminine beauty. From her gleaming fair hair to her silvery feet everything about her was pure charm and harmony. To be sure Hera and Athene were also very lovely, but the haughty beauty of Hera imposed respect and the severe beauty of Athene arrested desire. Aphrodite exuded an aura of seduction. To the perfection of her figure and the purity of her features she added the grace which attracted and conquered. 'On her sweet face she always wore an amiable smile.'

The Judgment of Paris. One can imagine that the other goddesses did not accept the presence on Olympus of this redoubtable rival without resentment. They were determined to dispute the prize of beauty with her. Now, to the nuptials of Thetis and Peleus all the Immortals had been invited except Eris, or Discord. Infuriated by the omission, Eris tossed into the hall where the guests were gathered a golden apple with this inscription: *For the fairest.* Hera, Athene and Aphrodite all three claimed it. To settle the affair Zeus ordered them to submit the argument to the judgment of a mortal. Choice fell upon one Paris, son of King Priam of Troy. Hermes then conducted the three goddesses to Phrygia where Paris was tending his father's flocks on the slopes of Mount Ida. Paris was acutely embarrassed and tried to refuse, but he had to submit to the will of Zeus, expressed by Hermes. One by one the three goddesses appeared before him and attempted to influence his decision by reinforcing the power of their charms with alluring promises. 'If you award the prize to me,' said Hera, 'I shall make you lord over all Asia.' Athene promised to see that the young shepherd was always victorious in battle. Aphrodite, who could offer neither sceptres nor victories, merely loosened the clasps by which her tunic was fastened and unknotted her girdle; then she promised to give Paris the most beautiful of mortal women. The verdict was then delivered, and the shepherd of Mount Ida awarded the coveted apple to Aphrodite. In this way Paris won possession of Helen, wife of Menelaus; but neither Hera nor Athene forgave him the wound to their pride, and avenged themselves cruelly by delivering his country, his family and his people to devastation and making sure that he, too, fell beneath the blows of the Greeks.

But from that time Aphrodite's supremacy remained uncontested. Even Hera, when she wished to recapture her husband's wayward love, did not hesitate to run to her former rival to borrow the magic girdle which was endowed with the power of enslaving the hearts of gods and men alike. It was a girdle wondrously worked and cunningly embroidered. It contained every seduction, Homer tells us – love and desire and sweet dalliance – which enthrals the heart of even the wisest.

Goddess of love, Aphrodite was mistress of seductive conversation, 'gracious laughter, sweet deceits, the charms and delights of love.' This was her empire, though, like the other gods, she sometimes espoused the quarrels of mankind. On such occasions she too threw herself into the fray and we see her defending the Trojans and taking part in the battles which raged beneath the walls of Ilium with, it may be added, little success. One day when she had come to the aid of her son Aeneas and was shielding him from the Greek arrows with a fold of her sparkling veil, Diomedes recognised her. Well aware that she was a divinity without courage, he attacked her, and with the point of his spear lightly wounded her delicate hand. Aphrodite retired hastily to Olympus, regarded mockingly by Athene who said: 'Doubtless the Cyprian has been persuading some Greek woman to fight for her dearly beloved Trojans, and while she was caressing the woman a golden clasp has scratched her delicate hand!' Aphrodite complained bitterly to the father of the gods. Zeus smiled and said to her: 'You, my child, were not meant to concern yourself with matters of war. Go, attend to the sweet tasks of love.'

The Loves of Aphrodite. Aphrodite's beauty had stirred all the gods; but it was Hephaestus, the ugliest and most graceless among them, who obtained her for a wife. Such an ill-matched union could not be happy, and even on Olympus Aphrodite found those to console her, among others Ares, with whom she was surprised by her husband, and Hermes who, it seemed, was more adroit. Aphrodite, moreover, took a wicked delight in rousing the passionate desires of the Immortals and launching them on amorous adventures. With the exception of Athene, Artemis and Hestia, all came under her influence. The master of the gods himself yielded to her power.

'She distracts the mind of Zeus, deceives his prudent soul, and sends him chasing after mortal women.'

To avenge himself 'Zeus, in his turn, inspired in Aphrodite the sweet desire to lie with a mortal man'. And so the goddess was seized by an irresistible passion for the Trojan Anchises, whose beauty rivalled that of the gods. One day when Anchises was pasturing his flocks on Mount Ida Aphrodite came to join him. First she had visited her sanctuary at Paphos where the Graces had anointed her body with fragrant and incorruptible oil and adorned her in her most precious jewels. 'Her veil was more dazzling than flame, she wore bracelets and ear-rings, round her throat there were golden necklaces, her delicate bosom shone like the moon.' While she climbed the slopes of Mount Ida shaggy wolves, bristling lions and agile panthers frisked around her; 'at this spectacle she rejoiced and instilled love in their hearts'.

When she came to Anchises she explained that she was the daughter of Otreus, King of Phrygia, and confessed her desire to become his spouse. Without further ado Anchises conducted Aphrodite to his well-prepared couch, covered with the skins of bears and lions. And there 'a mortal man, by the will of the gods and destiny, slept with an immortal goddess without knowing who she was'.

Upon awaking Aphrodite appeared before Anchises in all her divine splendour. The shepherd beheld her in terror, fearing the premature old age with which a man who has lain with an immortal goddess is stricken. But Aphrodite reassured him and promised him a son who would be like a god. She asked of him only that he should never reveal the name of the child's mother. The child was later the pious Aeneas.

Anchises was not the only mortal loved by Aphrodite. The Phoenicians who frequented the isles of the Aegean and the ports of the Peloponnese had brought with them the tale of the love of their own goddess Astarte for Adonis. The Greeks naturally retold it of Aphrodite, and the story of Aphrodite and Adonis was one of the episodes most often treated by poets and artists.

Among Aphrodite's favourites must be mentioned Phaethon, son of Eos and Cephalus, who was carried off as a child by the goddess and became 'the nocturnal guardian of her sacred temples'. There was also Cinyras, sometimes described as the father of Myrrha – and consequently of Adonis. He was usually regarded as the founder of the cult of Aphrodite in the island of Cyprus over which he reigned.

In this same island of Cyprus, in Amathus, there lived a sculptor named Pygmalion. Passionately devoted to his art, Pygmalion was only happy in the silent world of statues which his chisel had created. His misanthropy was attributed to the disgust he felt at the conduct of the Propoetides. These were girls in Amathus who rashly denied the divinity of Aphrodite. To punish them Aphrodite inspired in them such immodesty that, losing all sense of shame, they would prostitute themselves to all comers. In the end they were turned into rocks. Thus Pygmalion shunned the society of women, but nonetheless fervently venerated Aphrodite. Now it came about that he made an ivory statue of a woman of such extraordinary beauty that he fell in love with it. Alas! the cold image did not respond to his transports of love. Aphrodite took pity on this singular lover. One day while pressing the inert statue in his arms Pygmalion felt the ivory suddenly moving; his kisses were returned. The statue was miraculously alive.

This prodigy is only an example of the sovereign power of Aphrodite over all creation. Throughout all nature she spread her lifebringing joy: at her appearance, Lucretius says, 'the heavens are assuaged and pour forth torrents of light; the waves of the sea smile on her'. Aphrodite, however, was also the terrifying divinity who filled women's hearts with the frenzy of passion. Unhappy were they whom Aphrodite chose for her victims; such would betray their own fathers like Medea or Ariadne. They would abandon their homes, like Helen, to follow a stranger. They would be overcome, like Myrrha or Phaedra, with incestuous desires, or, like Pasiphaë, be torn by monstrous and bestial passions.

The same Aphrodite nevertheless protected legitimate unions and figured among the divinities who presided over the sanctity of marriage. Spartan mothers offered a sacrifice to her when their daughters were married. It was she who cared for the daughters of Pandareus, Merope and Cleothera, after the death of their parents, fed them on milk and honey and delectable wine and, when they had grown up, asked the almighty Zeus that their nuptials should be blessed. Had it depended on Aphrodite alone, Merope and Cleothera would have become happy and respected wives; but the two unfortunate young women, at the moment of their marriage, were carried off by the Harpies and made into followers of the odious Furies.

Hermaphroditus. Among Aphrodite's children were Harmonia, a daughter, whom she bore to Ares and who married Cadmus, and a son, Hermaphroditus, whose father was Hermes.

To conceal his birth Aphrodite immediately confided Hermaphroditus to the nymphs of Mount Ida who brought him up in the forests. At the age of fifteen he was a wild and savage youth whose chief pleasure was to hunt in the wooded mountains. One day in Caria he arrived at the banks of a limpid lake whose freshness tempted him to bathe. The nymph Salmacis who ruled the lake saw him and was enamoured of his beauty. She told him so, and in vain the shy youth attempted to repulse her. Salmacis threw her arms around him and covered him with kisses. He continued to resist and the nymph cried out: 'Cruel youth! You struggle in vain. O ye gods! Grant that nothing may ever separate him from me, or me from him!' Immediately their two bodies were united and became as one. 'In their double form they are neither man nor woman; they seem to have no sex yet to be of both sexes.'

In consequence of this event the waters of the lake received the property of causing those who bathed therein to lose their virility. This was in accomplishment of the final wish that Hermaphroditus had pronounced just before Salmacis drew him down into the depths of the water.

Some have interpreted this strange fable as a survival of the cult of the Bearded Aphrodite of Cyprus.

THE RETINUE OF APHRODITE

Eros. Among Aphrodite's normal companions the most important was Eros. Unknown in Homeric times, he appears in Hesiod's *Theogony* as the son of Erebus and the Night. His role was to co-ordinate the elements which constitute the universe. It is he who 'brings harmony to chaos', and permits life to develop. This primitive deity, a semi-abstract personification of cosmic force, has little resemblance to the traditional Eros whose physiognomy was only developed in later times.

About his origin there is little agreement. Some say his mother was the goddess Ilithyia; others say he was born to Iris and Zephyrus. Sometimes he is supposed to have been born before Aphrodite, whom he and the Horae welcomed on the shores of Cyprus. Sometimes – and this was the most widespread tradition – he was considered to be the son of Aphrodite. As to his father, the ancients hesitated between Ares, Hermes and Zeus.

Eros was the youngest of the gods; he was a winged child, gracious though rebellious, whose pranks and caprices caused much suffering among men and gods. He was armed with a bow and arrows whose prick stirred the fires of passion in all hearts. In his malice he respected not even his own mother, and Aphrodite sometimes had to punish him by taking away his wings and quiver. Normally, however, he was her zealous servant. He helped with her toilet and accompanied her abroad. While the goddess lingered in the arms of Ares, Eros amused himself by handling the war-god's heavy weapons and trying on his helmet with its gleaming plume. In much the same way we see him later playing with the weapons of Hercules.

This cruel and charming young god who delighted in torturing men and gods, who, according to Anacreon, repaid hospitality offered to him by an artfully released dart, was himself sometimes a victim of the passions he inspired in others. This is illustrated by the charming tale of Psyche, although the story is of late invention and more philosophical than mythological.

Eros and Psyche. Psyche (in Greek the word means 'soul') was a princess of such remarkable beauty that Aphrodite herself was jealous of her. She instructed her son Eros to punish the audacious mortal. Shortly afterwards an oracle commanded Psyche's father, under threat of terrifying calamities, to conduct his daughter to the summit of a mountain where she would become the prey of a monster. Trembling but resigned, Psyche was awaiting on a solitary rock the fulfilment of the oracle, when suddenly she felt herself gently lifted in the arms of Zephyrus, who carried her to a magnifi-

cent palace. When night fell Psyche was on the verge of sleep when a mysterious being joined her in the darkness, explaining that he was the husband for whom she was destined. She could not see his features, but his voice was soft and his conversation full of tenderness. Before the return of dawn the strange visitor disappeared, first making Psyche swear never to attempt to see his face. In spite of the oddness of the adventure, Psyche was not discontented with her new life; in the palace nothing she could desire was lacking except the constant presence of her delightful husband, who only came to visit her during the dark hours of night. Her happiness could have continued in this way had not her sisters – who were devoured by envy – sown the seeds of suspicion in her heart. 'If your husband,' they said, 'is afraid to let you see his face it is because he must really be some hideous monster.' They nagged her so much that one night Psyche, in spite of her promise, rose from the couch she shared with her husband, stealthily lighted a lamp and held it above the mysterious face. Instead of a fearful monster she beheld the most charming person in the world – Eros himself. At the foot of the couch lay his bow and arrows. In her delight Psyche, in order to study her husband's features more closely, held the lamp nearer. A drop of scalding oil fell on the god's bare shoulder. He awakened at once, reproached Psyche for her lack of faith and immediately vanished.

The palace vanished at the same time, and poor Psyche found herself on the lonely rock again in the midst of terrifying solitude. At first she considered suicide and threw herself into a nearby river; but the waters bore her gently to the opposite bank. From then on she was pursued by Aphrodite's anger and submitted to a series of terrible ordeals. She succeeded, however, in overcoming them one by one, thanks to mysterious assistance. She even had to descend into the underworld. Finally, touched by the repentance of his unhappy spouse, whom he had never ceased to love and protect, Eros went to Zeus and implored permission for Psyche to rejoin him. Zeus consented and conferred immortality on Psyche. Aphrodite forgot her rancour, and the wedding of the two lovers was celebrated on Olympus with great rejoicing.

At the side of Eros other divinities were often seen, of which the chief were Himeros and Pothos, both personifications of amorous desire.

The Graces. Aphrodite's retinue was usually completed by the Graces. Though sometimes said to be the daughters of Helios and Aegle, the Graces were more generally considered to have been born to the Oceanid Eurynome and fathered by Zeus. They were smiling divinities whose presence spread joy not only throughout the external world but also in the hearts of men. 'With you,' Pindar says to them, 'all becomes sweetness and charm.' Their number and their names often varied. According to epochs and regions they were called: Charis and Pasithea (by Homer); in Sparta, Cleia and Phaenna; Hegemone and Auxo in Athens. But the most widely accepted tradition fixed their number as three and their names as Aglaia, Euphrosyne and Thalia. They were Aphrodite's companions and attended to her toilet. The goddess made use of their services when she wished to adorn herself in all her seductions.

With the return of Spring the Graces delighted in mingling with the nymphs, forming with them groups of dancers who tripped the ground with nimble step. This was because these divinities – in whom some have seen a personification of the sun's rays, but who were originally nature-goddesses – also presided over the budding of plant-life and the ripening of fruits. Aglaia was 'the brilliant'. Thalia was 'she who brought flowers'. The joy which results from the sun's blessings is revealed in Euphrosyne's name: 'she who rejoices the heart'. In origin as well as function the Graces were closely connected with Apollo: hence they often form part of his retinue.

They were also considered to be the goddesses of gratitude. Thus their mother was sometimes said to be Lethe (oblivion) because gratitude is quickly forgotten.

The most celebrated sanctuary of the Graces was at Orchomenus in Boeotia, where they were worshipped in the form of aeroliths or meteorites. They also had two sanctuaries in Athens.

The Graces were at first clad in long chitons and wore crowns. However, from the end of the fourth century B.C. they were represented as three nude young women holding one another by the shoulder.

POSEIDON

Character and Function. Although Poseidon's dominion was the sea, he held his own appointed position among the great gods on Olympus.

Far from being a Libyan importation, as Herodotus claims, he was actually a very ancient Pelasgian deity, older even than Zeus. His province, later confined to the waters, was in primitive times much wider.

The etymology which the ancients gave his name, connecting it with 'drink' and 'river', is doubtful. The name Poseidon seems rather to derive from the root meaning 'to be master' which is found again in the Latin *potens*.

It is not impossible that this primitive Poseidon, this sovereign 'master', had once been a celestial god, as his attribute, the trident – probably a symbol for the thunderbolt – seems to indicate. Though supplanted by Zeus, Poseidon continued to exercise his empire over the entire earth, as is proved by those struggles he had with other divinities who contested with him the supremacy of various parts of Greece, and also by the titles Homer gives him, such as *Enosichthon* – 'earth-shaker'. Poseidon was, indeed, the god of earthquakes. Even when his sphere was more narrowly confined to the sea Poseidon retained his character of a great god: he remained the equal of the celestial Zeus, the Zeus Elalios (marine), whose power extended over the whole physical universe.

As a personification of the watery element Poseidon was always considered a god of fecundity and vegetation.

Cult and Representations. Poseidon was a national god of the Ionians of the Peloponnese, who brought him with them when they emigrated from Asia, and was particularly worshipped in this part of Greece. At Sparta he was even called *Genethlios*, the creator. But his cult was spread throughout Greece, especially in maritime towns. In Corinth, Rhodes and Taenarus he actually succeeded in supplanting the local divinity.

Animals which were sacred to him were the horse, symbol of gushing springs, and the bull, emblem either of his power to fertilise or of his impetuosity. In the course of certain festivals dedicated to Poseidon and called Taureia, black bulls were thrown into the waves.

In the same way horse races were celebrated in honour of Poseidon. This custom originated in Thessaly where the god, they said, had created the horse with a blow of his trident.

In the art of classical antiquity Poseidon very much resembles Zeus: he has a similar majesty when he is depicted standing, his chest bare, grasping his trident. But normally his features are less serene and, with his thick beard and disorderly hair, reveal a care-worn expression.

The Legend of Poseidon. Poseidon was a son of Cronus and Rhea. He shared the fate of his brothers and sisters, and at birth was swallowed by his father. He was disgorged with the others when Zeus, on the advice of Metis, gave Cronus the draught which made him vomit up his children. According to another tradition Rhea managed to shelter Poseidon from his father's voracity by giving Cronus a young foal to swallow, meanwhile hiding her son in the midst of a flock of lambs near Mantinea. Poseidon was then confided to a nurse named Arne and grew up without his father's knowledge. It was also said that Rhea gave Poseidon to Capheira, a daughter of Oceanus who, with the aid of the Telchines, brought him up in Rhodes.

When Zeus fought the Titans and the Giants, Poseidon fought at his side and killed the giant Polybutes by hurling at him a fragment of cliff torn from the island of Cos, which later became the islet of Nisyros. After their common victory the paternal heritage was, as we remember, divided into three parts: Zeus took the vast heavens, Hades the murky underworld, and Poseidon obtained the immense sea.

Although he was the equal of Zeus by birth and dignity Poseidon was nevertheless subject to his brother's sovereign power. The sea-god complained and grumbled at times. Once he went so far as to conspire with Hera and Athene to dethrone Zeus. Zeus was the stronger and Poseidon was forced to pay for his attempted revolt by spending a year in the service of the haughty Laomedon, for whom he constructed the walls of Troy.

Poseidon's empire, however, was not unworthy of his ambitions.

He was master not only of the sea but of the lakes and rivers. In a sense even the earth belonged to him, since it was sustained by his waters and he could shake it at will. Indeed, during the war with the Giants he split mountains with his trident and rolled them into the sea to make the first islands. And it was he who, in the days when Thessaly was merely a huge lake, had cleared the road for the River Peneius by splitting the mass of Mount Ossa in two.

Poseidon's thirst for possession was so keen that he often found himself in conflict with the other gods.

We have already mentioned the dispute he had with Athene for the possession of Attica, a dispute which ended to Athene's advantage. Out of spite Poseidon flooded Attica. Nor could he win Troezen from the same goddess; Zeus awarded it to them in common.

Poseidon was no more fortunate with Hera, with whom he contested the dominion of Argolis. The decision was submitted to the judgment of the river-god Inachus, assisted by the rivers Asterion and Cephissus. It was unfavourable to Poseidon, who avenged himself by drying up the three rivers and with them Argolis.

There was also a contest between Poseidon and Helios over the isthmus of Corinth. Briareus, chosen to arbitrate, awarded the Corinthian Acropolis to Helios and left the rest of the isthmus to Poseidon. This was the origin of the cult in which Poseidon was honoured in the isthmus of Corinth; during his festivals the celebrated Isthmian Games were held.

Finally Poseidon unsuccessfully disputed Aegina with Zeus, and Naxos with Dionysus. He had to cede the territory of Delphi, which until then he had held in common with Gaea, to Apollo, receiving in exchange the island of Calauria.

On the other hand no one ever disputed Poseidon's rule over the sea. He established his abode in the depths of the Aegean Sea where 'there had been built for him a magnificent palace, glittering with gold, which would endure for ever'. When he left the palace he would harness to his chariot swift steeds with golden manes and shod with bronze. Clad in golden armour he would seize a cunningly wrought whip in his hand and hurl his chariot across the watery plain. Around him would frolic sea monsters, come up from the abysmal depths to render homage to their sovereign. The joyful sea would open before him as his chariot flew lightly across waves which did not even so much as wet the bronze axle. More often, however, the appearance of Poseidon was accompanied by wild tempests, a manifestation of the god's furious rage.

Amphitrite. Poseidon's wife was Amphitrite who was in origin the feminine personification of the sea. She was a daughter of Oceanus or of Nereus. Poseidon picked her out one day when she was dancing with her sisters on the isle of Naxos. When he asked for her hand in marriage Amphitrite at first refused and fled to Atlas. Poseidon sent a dolphin to look for her. The dolphin discovered where she had taken refuge and brought her back to his master; as a reward Poseidon placed him among the constellations.

From then on Amphitrite shared Poseidon's kingdom. We see her at her husband's side on the divine chariot drawn by tritons blowing conch-shells. In her hand she sometimes holds the trident, insignia of Poseidon's sovereignty.

From the union of Poseidon and Amphitrite were born a son, Triton, and two daughters: Rhode, who gave her name to the island of Rhodes and was the mother of the Heliades; and Benthesicyme, who settled in Ethiopia.

Amphitrite was an accommodating wife and patiently put up with her husband's frequent infidelity. Only once did she show jealousy: this was with regard to Scylla, who was originally a nymph of rare beauty. Enraged by the love Poseidon showed her, Amphitrite threw magic herbs in the pool where Scylla used to bathe, and the nymph was changed into a frightful monster. Her metamorphosis is sometimes attributed to Circe.

The Loves of Poseidon. Of Poseidon's innumerable mistresses we shall mention only the principal ones.

Among the goddesses there was Gaea, whom he made mother of the fearful giant Antaeus. There was Demeter, who changed herself into a mare in order to escape him. But Poseidon took the form of a stallion and from their union was born – apart from a daughter whose name remains mysterious (perhaps it was Despoena) – the wild horse, Arion, whose right feet were

Hebe. Detail from an antique vase painting. Ruvo, Italy.

those of a man and who was endowed with the power of speech.

It was also in the shape of a horse – though others say a bird – that Poseidon succeeded in seducing Medusa, in the very temple of Athene. Infuriated by this profanation, Athene turned Medusa's hair into snakes. When Perseus decapitated Medusa, the blood which escaped from the wound gave birth to Chrysaor and the horse Pegasus.

By Alcyone, one of the Pleiades, Poseidon had a daughter, Aethusa, who was loved by Apollo, and two sons: Hyperenor and Hyrieus. The latter reigned in Boeotia and by the blessing of the gods became father of the giant Orion, of whom we shall speak later.

By the harpy Celaeno, Poseidon had two sons: Lycus, who reigned over the Fortunate Isles, and Eurypylus, who distinguished himself at the siege of Troy and took part in the expedition of the Argonauts.

Another Eurypylus, who reigned over the isle of Cos and was killed by Hercules, and the Argonaut Ancaeus were born to Poseidon and Astypalaea, sister of Europa.

Chione, daughter of Boreas, was seduced by Poseidon and had a son, Eumolpus. To hide her shame she threw the child into the sea; but Poseidon saved it and carried it to Ethiopia where he confided it to his daughter Benthesicyme, who later became Eumolpus' mother-in-law.

Aethra was the daughter of Pittheus, King of Troezen. Athene ordered her in a dream to go to the isle of Sphaeria and there on the tomb of Sphaerus to offer a sacrifice. Aethra was surprised in the temple by Poseidon and ravished. She afterwards married Aegeus and became the mother of Theseus.

Because of her great beauty Theophane, daughter of Bisaltes, was besieged by suitors. To protect her from their attentions Poseidon, who loved her himself, carried her to the isle of Crinissa (Crumissa). The suitors followed her. Poseidon then turned her into a ewe, the inhabitants of the island into sheep, and himself into a ram. Theophane gave birth to the famous ram with the golden fleece.

Alope, daughter of Cercyon, had a son by Poseidon. She exposed him, after having covered him with a rich robe. The infant was suckled by a mare and found by herdsmen who carried him to Cercyon. Cercyon at once recognised the rich robe and discovered his daughter's disgrace. He condemned her to perpetual imprisonment and once more exposed the infant. But the faithful mare again came to suckle him. For this reason he was named Hippothous. Later, when Cercyon was slain by Theseus, Hippothous mounted the throne of his grandfather.

For having plundered a grove sacred to Demeter, Erysichthon, King of Thessaly, was afflicted with insatiable hunger. To appease it he was obliged to sell everything he possessed. At the end of his resources he finally put his own daughter Mestra up for sale. Now Poseidon loved Mestra and granted her the gift of metamorphosis, so that each time she was able to escape her purchasers. This stratagem allowed Erysichthon to sell his daughter over and over again, until at last the ruse was discovered and he had no alternative but to devour himself.

During the drought in Argolis which was the result of Poseidon's fury with Inachus, Danaus sent his daughters in search of water. One of them, Amymone, carelessly wounded a sleeping satyr who then leapt at her. Others say that Amymone was surprised by the satyr while she herself was asleep. In either case Poseidon arrived, put the satyr to flight and rescued Amymone, whose favours he then enjoyed. In gratitude the god struck a rock with his trident and the springs of Lerna gushed forth. By this union Amymone had a son, Nauplius, who later founded Nauplia and was swallowed by the waves for having blasphemed the gods. The origin of the fountain of Pirene, near Corinth, was also connected with a legend of Poseidon. By the nymph Pirene, daughter of Achelous or Asopus, the god had two sons who perished miserably. Pirene was inconsolable and could not stop weeping; it was her tears which gave birth to the celebrated fountain.

The nymph Tyro, daughter of Salmoneus and Acidice, had conceived a passion for the river Enipeus. Poseidon, who loved her, despaired of moving her heart. One day when Tyro was strolling along the banks of the Enipeus Poseidon assumed the appearance of the river-god and approached her. The nymph was deceived by this disguise and yielded. She bore two sons, Pelias and Neleus, whom she exposed. They were found by shepherds and brought up

among herds of horses. Meanwhile Tyro had married Cretheus, King of Iolcus, and was ill-treated by Sidero, her mother-in-law. When Pelias and Neleus returned to their mother they killed the wicked Sidero.

The Posterity of Poseidon. Among Poseidon's numerous offspring we shall limit ourselves to mentioning a few names:

Euphemus, son of Europa, who received from his father the power of walking on the waters and who was the second pilot during the expedition of the Argonauts.

Halirrhothius, son of the nymph Euryte, who was put to death by Ares for having ravished his daughter Alcippe. This murder gave rise to a quarrel between Ares and Poseidon, to settle which the tribunal of the Areopagus was instituted at Athens.

Evadne, daughter of Pitane, who at her birth was confided to Aepytus, King of Phoesane in Arcadia, and who afterwards bore a son to Apollo, Iamus.

The Molionids, twin sons of Molione, who were born of a silver egg and who so resembled each other that later tradition said they had but a single body with two heads, four arms and four legs. It was they who commanded the troops of Augias against Hercules who, moreover, killed them.

Cycnus, son of Calyce or Harpale, who was exposed on the seashore at birth and taken in by fishermen. Later, he became king of Colonae in the Troad, and by his first wife, Procleia, had two children, Tenes and Hemithea. His second wife, Phylonome, conceived a passion for her stepson Tenes but, unable to seduce him, slandered him to his father. Cycnus had Tenes and his sister Hemithea locked up in a chest and set them adrift on the sea. But the two young people were saved by Poseidon, and Tenes, landing at Tenedos, became its king. When Cycnus learned the truth he killed Phylonome and went to join his son. Both fought in the Trojan ranks against the Greeks and perished by the hand of Achilles. Since Cycnus was invulnerable, Achilles strangled him with the strap which secured his helmet; but when he attempted to despoil him of his arms the body of Cycnus changed into a swan.

Finally we mention a certain number of monstrous and malignant beings who were also among Poseidon's progeny.

Amycus, born of the nymph Melia, reigned in Bithynia. He was of prodigious strength and challenged all strangers who approached his kingdom to a fatal boxing match. When the Argonauts arrived in Bithynia he at once defied them, but Pollux accepted the challenge and killed him.

The Aloadae were children of Poseidon by Iphimedeia, wife of Aloeus. They were twin brothers, Ephialtes and Otus, who each year grew so fast that at the age of nine they were nearly twenty yards high. We have seen how they attempted to scale Olympus, kept Ares captive for thirteen months and finally perished either beneath Apollo's blows or through a stratagem of Artemis'. They were thrown into Tartarus for their crimes and there bound, back to back, to a column by means of a chain made of interlaced serpents. To them were attributed the foundation of Ascra and the institution of the cult of the Muses on Mount Helicon.

Cercyon, son of a daughter of Amphictyon, lived in Eleusis. He forced all travellers to wrestle with him and he killed the vanquished. Only Theseus succeeded in beating him, and put him to death. Cercyon was the father of Alope, who was herself loved by Poseidon.

Another son of Poseidon's was also killed by Theseus. This was the brigand Sinis, who lived in the Isthmus of Corinth. He submitted all passers-by to an odious torture: he tied them to the tops of two pine-trees which he had bent down. When the trees were released the victims were torn asunder. Theseus made him suffer the same torture.

No less cruel was the King of Egypt, Busiris, son of Poseidon and Anippe. When drought devastated his kingdom Busiris consulted a soothsayer of Cyprus, who declared that the scourge would cease only if each year he immolated a stranger. Busiris began by immolating the soothsayer and continued this bloody practice until the day when Hercules arrived in Egypt and was chosen as a victim. They were about to cut his throat when Hercules burst from the chains which bound him and killed Busiris and his attendants. From that day human sacrifice was no longer practised in Egypt.

To this list of monsters may be added the Cyclops Polyphemus, son of Poseidon and the nymph Thoösa.

In this monstrous progeny attributed to Poseidon may perhaps be seen a survival of the impression of terror felt by primitive men at the rages of the stormy sea. Similarly it was said that Poseidon often summoned up fearful monsters against his enemies. He sent such a monster to ravage the Troad to revenge himself on Laomedon; another, at the prayers of the Nereids, desolated Ethiopia in order to punish the pride of Cassiopeia, mother of Andromeda. He sent a wild bull to devastate the plain of Marathon and a dragon which caused the death of the son of Theseus, Hippolytus.

HESTIA

Character and Functions. The Greek word 'hestia' means the hearth, the place in the house where the fire was maintained. The difficulty which primitive man experienced in procuring fire easily explains why he tended it with care and also venerated it. Moreover it was around the hearth that the family gathered. When one of its members departed to found a new family he took with him a parcel of fire from his parents' hearth, which thus symbolised the continuity of the family. When families began to form groups in towns, each town had its communal hearth where the public fire was maintained. Finally the fire of the *hestia* was used in sacrifices. For these various reasons the *hestia*, like the Vedic Agni, very early took on a sacred character. This character was afterwards personified in a deity who took the actual name of the object she symbolised.

Hestia, then, was, like Hephaestus, a fire-divinity. But while Hephaestus represented the fiery element in its celestial and sub-terranean manifestations, Hestia symbolised the household fire – fire, as it were, domesticated. Hence the homely and social character of this goddess, whose province was to protect not only the house and the family but also the city. Later Hestia, by analogy, represented the fire in the centre of the earth and the earth itself; but this conception was less mythological than philosophical.

Hestia was venerated in all Greek towns; she had her altar in every prytaneum – or Public Hearth. The Hestia of Delphi was the object of an especial cult, because Delphi was believed to occupy the centre of the universe and its hearth was therefore the common hearth of all Greece. Temples of Hestia were characterised by their circular form.

Representations of Hestia are rare. Glaucus of Argos sculptured one for Olympia. There was also a very celebrated one in Paros. The goddess was depicted sometimes seated, sometimes standing, but always in an attitude of immobility.

Hestia did not spring, like the other divinities, from popular imagination, and legends about her are few.

According to Hesiod – for Homer, before him, did not know of the goddess Hestia – she was the first child born to Cronus and Rhea. Thus she was the oldest of the Olympians and always maintained her precedence. Men understood this well and when they offered sacrifices consecrated the first morsels of the victims to Hestia and in festivals poured her the first and last libations. On Olympus Hestia's dignity was unquestioned and her rights as the eldest were recognised. She seems to have taken little advantage of this and played a minor role in Olympian drama. 'In the dwelling of the gods,' says Plato, 'Hestia alone maintains repose.' We only know of her that both Poseidon and Apollo sought her hand in marriage. She would have neither one nor the other. In order to put an end to their attentions she placed herself under Zeus' protection and made a solemn vow, touching the head of the master of the gods, to remain a virgin for ever. Zeus accepted her vow and 'instead of marriage offered her a handsome recompense: seated in the midst of the celestial dwelling-place she receives the richest part of sacrifices, and among men she is of all the deities the most venerated'.

Hestia thus shared with Athene and Artemis the prerogative of chastity. She was one of those over whom Aphrodite never succeeded in exercising her power.

THE LESSER GODS OF OLYMPUS

Olympian society was made in the image of human society and beneath the great gods there were lesser gods who held various positions.

Themis. Of these Themis may be said to be the most important. She was the daughter of Uranus and Gaea and belonged to the race of Titans which the Olympians had supplanted. Far from sharing the disgrace of her brothers, however, Themis never ceased to be honoured on Olympus. Indeed, at the beginning of his reign Zeus had chosen her for his wife. The Moerae, they said, had brought her to Zeus from the far-off regions where Uranus dwelt. Later, when Hera became the wife of Zeus, Themis remained at his side to offer counsel and service. It seems that Hera took no offence at this; when Hera arrived in the assembly of the gods it was from the hand of Themis that she received the cup of nectar.

Themis' mission on Olympus was not only to maintain order but also to regulate the ceremonial; she invited the gods to forgather and prepared their feasts.

She was moreover helpful and obliging. It was she, they said, who had received the infant Zeus from Rhea when Rhea wished to shelter him from the voracity of his father, Cronus. Later she presided over the laborious birth of Apollo and Artemis. It was also said that she made Apollo a present of the oracle at Delphi which she had inherited from her mother, Gaea.

On earth her province was also extensive; above all she was the goddess of justice. She protected the just – whence her epithet *Soteira* – the protectress – and punished the guilty. In her name and according to her advice judges gave their verdicts. Themis was also goddess of wisdom and was called *Euboulos*, the good counsellor; under this title she presided over public assemblies. Finally, since she was the interpreter of the gods' will, she had the gift of delivering oracles. It was she who, after the deluge, suggested to Deucalion the means of re-peopling the earth. We have just seen that she once owned the oracle of Delphi.

From her union with Zeus Themis had several children: the Horae, and the Moerae or Fates. The Hesperides were also sometimes said to be her daughters.

The cult of Themis was spread throughout Greece; a temple was consecrated to her in the citadel of Athens. She also had sanctuaries at Troezen, Tanagra, Olympia and at Thebes, where she was worshipped with Zeus Agoraios.

She is represented as a woman of grave countenance and austere features. Her attribute is a pair of scales.

Iris. Pontus and Gaea had had, among other children, a son Thaumas who united with Electra, daughter of Oceanus and Tethys. From this union were born the Harpies and Iris. On Olympus Iris, who to the ancients personified the rainbow, was the messenger of the gods. She was assigned in particular to the service of Zeus. When Zeus had an order to give another Immortal, Iris delivered it. If he wished to make his will known to men, Iris flew lightly down to earth where she either borrowed mortal shape or appeared in her divine form. In her divine form she wore a long, full tunic, her hair encircled by a bandeau, and in her hand held the caduceus. She could be recognised by the golden wings attached to her shoulders. Occasionally, like Hermes, she wore winged sandals. Sometimes she cleaved the air as swiftly as the wind, at others glided down the rainbow which bridged sky and earth. She sped through the waters with equal ease. When Zeus sent her in search of the marine-goddess Thetis, Homer tells us how she dived into the dark waves between Samos and the cliffs of Imbros, making the gulf itself groan aloud. Even the underworld opened before Iris when, at the command of Zeus, she went to refill her golden cup with the waters of the Styx by which the Immortals bound themselves with fearful oaths.

Iris was devoted to Zeus but even more so to Hera. She not only delivered Hera's messages but also effected her vengeance, such as the time when she went to Sicily and, in the guise of Beroe, set fire to Aeneas' fleet. Iris also fulfilled the role of Hera's faithful servant. She prepared Hera's bath, helped with her toilet, and night and day stood at the foot of her mistress's throne, never falling asleep or even loosening her girdle or sandals.

She also waited on the other gods. When they returned to Olympus in their chariots she would unharness steeds and give them nectar and ambrosia. When Aphrodite was wounded by Diomedes, Iris 'took the overwhelmed goddess and led her away from the battle', helped her to mount the chariot of Ares, and took the reins and whip into her own hands.

Even mortals experienced her good nature. When she heard Achilles bitterly complain that the flames of the pyre were slow in consuming the body of Patroclus she immediately went to find the Winds – who had just foregathered in the dwelling of the violent

Odysseus forces Circe to restore his companions to human form. Polychrome funerary urn. Fourth century B.C. Orvieto Museum.

Zephyrus for a solemn feast – and begged Boreas and Zephyrus to come and fan the funeral pyre.

Some said that this same Zephyrus was the husband of Iris and claimed that Eros was the fruit of their union.

On earth Iris was particularly honoured at Delos, where she was offered dried figs and cakes of wheat and honey.

Hebe. Hebe was worshipped by the Greeks as the goddess of youth. She had an altar in the Cynosarges at Athens. At Phlius a grove of cypresses which possessed the right of asylum was sacred to her. She also had a sanctuary at Sicyon.

She was the daughter of Zeus and Hera. She had the gift of eternal youth and represented the deified type of young maiden who in the primitive family was devoted to domestic occupations. Thus on Olympus she performed many duties.

She assisted her brother Ares to dress, bathed him and clad him in magnificent robes. When her mother Hera wished to go forth from Olympus, Hebe prepared the chariot, 'rapidly fixing the curved wheels to the iron axle, tying to the end of the shaft a handsome golden yoke to which she attached reins of gold'. But her chief duty was to hand around nectar and ambrosia to the gods during their feasts. She would move among them, bearing the ewer with the divine draught with which she would fill their goblets. It was claimed that as a result of a fall in which Hebe exposed herself to the eyes of all in a rather indecent posture, she lost her job and was replaced by Ganymede.

When Hercules, having at last appeased Hera's wrath, was admitted on his death to Olympus with the rank of a god, he was given the gracious Hebe for a wife. They had two children, Alexiares and Anicetus.

Ganymede. In primitive times Ganymede seems to have been conceived as the deity responsible for sprinkling the earth with heaven's rain. He is compared with the Vedic *Soma* who, like him, was ravished by Indra – and changed into a sparrow-hawk. Ancient astronomers identified him with Aquarius, the Water-carrier.

The Horae and the god Pan. Votive bas-relief. Capitol Museum, Rome.

Ganymede was venerated at Sicyon and at Phlius conjointly with Hebe.

He is depicted as an adolescent in a Phrygian cap and a mantle thrown back over his shoulders, either seated beside Zeus or carried through the air by an eagle.

In spite of the honorary position he occupied on Olympus, Ganymede was not of divine birth, being the son of Tros, King of Phrygia, and of Callirrhoe. At least this was the general opinion, although some said his father was Laomedon, Ilus, Assaracus or even Erichthonius. He was distinguished among mortals for his extraordinary beauty. Zeus was charmed and, wishing to make him his favourite, had him swept up by an eagle from the plains of the Troad and brought to Olympus. It was also said that Zeus himself took the form of an eagle in order to carry off the fair adolescent. The abduction of Ganymede took place, according to various versions, in either Mysia, Harpagia, on Phrygian Ida or on the promontory of Dardanus.

To recompense Tros for the loss of his son Zeus presented him with magnificent steeds, 'swift as the storm'.

On Olympus Ganymede became the cup-bearer of the gods and rejoiced the eye of all by his beauty.

The Horae. The Greek word from which the Horae derive their name signifies a period of time which can be applied equally to the year, the seasons, and the hours of the day. These different meanings influenced the successive conceptions of the Horae.

First the Horae were divinities of a meteorological character whose function was limited to showering the earth with life-giving rain. They encouraged the blossoming and ripening of fruits and therefore symbolised spring and summer. Afterwards they presided over the order of nature and the succession of the seasons, with whom in the end they were confused.

The number of the Horae varied. The Athenians venerated two: Thallo, who brought the flowers; and Carpo, who brought the fruits. Hesiod counted three Horae: Eunomia, Dike and Irene. Then their number became four and, according to the classification of Hyginus, as many as ten or eleven.

Their sphere of influence soon became moral as well as physical.

Guardians of the order of nature, they also watched over the moral order: Eunomia saw that the laws were observed; Dike attended to justice, Irene to peace. According to Hesiod's expression 'they mellowed the behaviour of men'. Finally they were regarded as the protectors of youth.

The Horae were honoured at Athens, Argos, Olympia and particularly at Corinth.

They are depicted as young maidens, holding in their hands the products of the various seasons: a branch in flower, an ear of corn, a vine stock.

Even before their number was determined and their names decided, the Horae had their appointed occupations on Olympus. In particular it was their duty to guard the gates of heaven, which they opened or closed to the passage of the Immortals by removing or replacing a thick cloud. This is how they appear in the Homeric poems, where we can also see them harnessing Hera's chariot with the celestial steeds which they fed with ambrosia.

Later their character became definite: it was known that their number was three, that their names were Eunomia, Dike and Irene, and that they were the daughters of Zeus and Themis. They were charming maidens with lovely hair, golden diadems and a light footstep. On Olympus they loved to dance in company with the Graces, and thus formed part of the retinue of Aphrodite, whom they adorned with their own hands.

When Zeus to man's perdition sent Pandora down to earth the Horae enhanced her attractions by embellishing her hair with floral garlands.

On many occasions they demonstrated their tenderness towards childhood and youth. It was they who nurtured Hera. It was they again who swaddled Hermes at his birth and wove garlands to shelter him. They received Dionysus when he emerged from the thigh of Zeus. Thallo, the Athenian Hora, was venerated by youthful athletes in the temple of Agraulos.

The adventures which were related of them sometimes appear to arise from confusion with other divinities. For example, it was told that the Hora of springtime had been loved by Zephyrus, to whom she bore a son, Carpos; but the tale seems to apply rather to Chloris, the Flora of the Latins. In the same way Pausanias makes

Boreas abducting Oreithyia. Detail of an Attic hydria. Fifth century B.C. Vatican Museum, Rome.

Irene the mother of Plutus because in Athens there was a statue of Irene with Plutus in her arms; nothing, however, authorises such a relationship. Of Carpo, one of the two Athenian Horae, it was said that she fell in love with young Camillus, son of the river-god Maeander, and that in despair she drowned herself in the waters of the river, whereupon Zeus changed her into fruit.

SIDEREAL AND METEOROLOGICAL GODS

By his sister Theia (or by Euryphaessa) the Titan Hyperion, son of Uranus and Gaea, had three children: Helios, the sun; Selene, the moon; and Eos, the dawn.

HELIOS

Although the Greeks considered Apollo to be the god of solar light, the sun itself was personified by a special divinity, Helios. In Greece the cult of Helios was very ancient and was practised throughout the land, at Elis, at Apollonia, on the Acropolis of Corinth, at Argos, at Troezen, on Cape Taenarum, at Athens, in Thrace and finally, and especially, in the island of Rhodes which was sacred to him. In Rhodes could be seen the colossal statue of Helios, the renowned work of the sculptor Chares. It was about thirty yards high, and ships in full sail could pass between the god's legs.

It was related that Helios was drowned in the ocean by his uncles, the Titans, and then raised to the sky, where he became the luminous sun.

Every morning Helios emerged in the east from a swamp formed by the river-ocean in the far-off land of the Ethiopians. To his golden chariot, which Hephaestus had fashioned, the Horae harnessed the winged horses. They were of dazzling white, their nostrils breathed forth flame and their names were Lampon, Phaethon, Chronos, Aethon, Astrope, Bronte, Pyroeis, Eous and Phlegon. The god then took the reins and climbed the vault of heaven. 'Drawn in his swift chariot, he sheds light on gods and men alike; the formidable flash of his eyes pierces his golden helmet;

sparkling rays glint from his breast; his brilliant helmet gives forth a dazzling splendour; his body is draped in shining gauze whipped by the wind.'

At midday Helios reached the highest point of his course and began to descend towards the West, arriving at the end of the day in the land of the Hesperides, where he seemed to plunge into the Ocean. In reality, there he found a barque or a golden cup, made by Hephaestus, in which his mother, wife and children were awaiting him. He would sail all night and in the morning regain his point of departure.

The abode of Helios was also said to be on the isle of Aeaea where his children Aeëtes and Circe lived. Again it was said that his horses rested on the islands of the Blessed, at the western extremity of the earth, where they browsed on a magic herb.

Helios possessed other domains on earth. When the gods had divided up the world Helios was absent and was forgotten. He complained about this to Zeus and obtained an island which was just beginning to emerge from the waves. He called it Rhodes after the nymph Rhode, whom he loved.

A dispute arose one day between Helios and Poseidon for the possession of the Isthmus of Corinth. The giant Briareus, who was chosen to arbitrate, awarded the Isthmus to Poseidon but gave Acrocorinth to Helios, who later relinquished it to Aphrodite.

As well as his horses, Helios owned on the isle of Thrinacia seven herds of oxen and seven flocks of ewes with beautiful fleece, each herd and flock being of fifty head. This number always remained constant, like the three hundred and fifty days and three hundred and fifty nights of the primitive year. Two daughters of the god, Phaetusa and Lampetia, guarded these animals. When Odysseus and his companions landed on the isle of Thrinacia the men, in spite of their chief's warning, laid hands on the sacred cattle. 'Chasing before them the handsome broadbrowed heifers which grazed not far from the azure-prowed vessel, they cut their throats, then cut up the flesh in morsels which they fixed to their skewers.' When Helios was told by Lampetia what had occurred he complained to the gods and threatened to shut himself up in the kingdom of Hades and shed his light on the dead. Zeus calmed him by promising to strike these foolish mortals with a thunderbolt.

The Chimaera. Etruscan Bronze. Archaeological Museum, Florence.

Odysseus and the Sirens. Perched on rock or fluttering overhead, the three sirens seek to lure Odysseus and his companions to their deaths with their melodious voices. Forewarned by Circe, Odysseus has had himself securely bound to the mast of his ship while his companions row on, their ears stopped with bees-wax, unable to hear the sirens' song. Detail from a Greek red-figured stamnos from Vulci. Early fifth century B.C.

As god of light Helios saw everything and knew everything. Of him it could be said what Pindar said of Apollo: 'He is the god who plumbs all hearts, the infallible, whom neither mortals nor immortals can deceive either by action or in their most secret thoughts.' Similarly the Assyro-Babylonian sun-god Shamash was also the god who discovered the crimes of the wicked. Nothing escaped Helios. It was he who informed Demeter of the rape of her daughter. It was he who revealed Aphrodite's unfaithfulness to Hephaestus.

Aphrodite avenged herself by inspiring in Helios a burning passion for Leucothea, daughter of Orchamos, King of Babylon, and Eurynome. Having assumed the appearance of the venerable Eurynome, Helios was about to approach the young maiden, who received him without suspicion. But Clytie, Leucothea's sister, who had herself enjoyed the favours of the god, was jealous of Leucothea's happiness. She informed Orchamos, who condemned his daughter to be buried alive. Helios came in haste, but his rays could not 'bring back living warmth into the frozen limbs of his mistress'. Incapable of restoring her to life, he changed her into an incense shrub. As for Clytie, she realised that the god was now indifferent to her love and, according to Ovid, died of despair. 'Exposed to the weather's inclemency, night and day she slept naked on the ground; for nine days without food or water she could quench her thirst only with the dew and her own tears. . . Her body at last took root in the soil; a mortal pallor spread over her and her limbs changed into a colourless stalk; her head became a flower bright as the violet, and in spite of the root which held her fast to the ground she turned her face towards Helios whom she never ceased to worship.' She is the heliotrope.

Helios also loved the nymph Anaxibia, but she fled from him and took refuge in the temple of Artemis Orthia and disappeared. Helios was unable to find her and rose up into the sky; the place took the name of Anatolius, which means ascension.

Helios had numerous wives as well: the Oceanid Perse, by whom he had two sons, Aeëtes and Perses, and two daughters, Circe and Pasiphaë; Neaera, who bore him Phaetusa and Lampetia, the guardians of his flocks; the nymph Rhode, by whom he had seven sons, the Heliads, and one daughter, Electryone. The Heliads were distinguished for their intelligence and to them was attributed the perfecting of naval architecture as well as the division of the day into hours. One of them, Tenagis, was outstandingly learned and finally aroused the jealousy of his brothers, who murdered him. After the murder they dispersed among the islands in the neighbourhood of Rhodes.

Among the wives of Helios were also Gaea, who gave him a son, Achelous; Iphinoë (or Iphiboë) or Naupiadame, mother of Augeias; finally Clymene, wife of Merops, King of the Ethiopians, by whom he had seven daughters – who were also called the Heliads – and one son, Phaethon.

Phaethon. One day Phaethon had a dispute with Epahus, son of Zeus and Io, who had thrown doubts on his divine origin. Phaethon was mortified and went to his mother to complain. In order to reassure him, she advised him to go to Helios himself and ask for confirmation of his divine birth. Phaethon obeyed and begged Helios to accord him a favour which would prove to all eyes that he was indeed the son of Helios. The god gave his promise and swore it by the Styx, which made the oath irrevocable. Phaethon then demanded permission to drive the sun's chariot for one day. In vain Helios tried to dissuade the presumptuous youth from this insane project. Phaethon insisted and Helios was bound by his oath; he had, therefore, to confide the sun's impetuous steeds to Phaethon. The horses, no longer restrained by the firm hand of their usual driver, rushed wildly through space, carrying the unhappy Phaethon, who had lost all control over them, on their mad career. The chariot came too near the earth; the rivers dried up and the soil began to burn. The universe would have been destroyed by flame had not Zeus struck the rash youth with a thunderbolt and sent him tumbling into the waters of the Eridanus. Phaethon was buried by the nymphs. His sisters, the Heliads, came to weep beside his tomb and were changed into poplar trees. Their tears became the amber which was gathered in abundance on the banks of the Eridanus.

Circe. A daughter of Helios was equally celebrated in the mythological annals of Greece: Circe. Because she lived in the west of the isle of Aeaea some have tried to see in Circe a moon-goddess. But more probably she was a goddess of love – of degrading love – comparable to the Babylonian Ishtar who was so roughly treated by Gilgamesh.

Circe was above all known for her evil spells and enchantments. Married to the king of the Sarmatians, she poisoned her husband and went to live in the isle of Aeaea where she built herself a magnificent palace. She cast a spell over all who landed on the island and, by means of magic potions, turned them into animals. Thus she changed Odysseus' companions into swine. Odysseus alone escaped their fate, thanks to a herb, *moly*, which Hermes had given him. Better still, he forced the sorceress to restore his companions to their human form. Nevertheless he spent a year with Circe, forgetting his wife and his country. Circe, it was said, was slain by Telemachus, who had married her daughter, Cassiphone.

SELENE

Selene, who was also called Mene, was the sister of Helios, and with her golden crown illuminated the shadowy night. Every evening, beginning her journey when her brother had finished his, the divine Selene of the broad wings, 'after bathing her lovely body in the Ocean, clad herself in splendid robes and rose in the sky on her chariot drawn by shining steeds'. Sometimes we also see her mounted on a horse, a mule or even a bull.

Although she was generally considered to be the daughter of Hyperion and Theia (or Euryphaessa) her father was sometimes said to be Helios or even Zeus.

Her beauty attracted the love of Zeus, who made her mother of three daughters: Pandia, 'remarkable for her beauty among the Immortals'; Erse, the dew; and Nemea. It was claimed that the Nemean Lion was also born to Zeus and Selene, and that it fell from the moon on to the earth.

Selene was loved by Pan, who took the shape of a white ram and drew her into the depths of a wood in Arcadia.

Selene and Endymion. The best-known legend of Selene was that of her love for Endymion. The story was told differently in Elis and in Caria. According to the Elians, Endymion was a king of Elis whose tomb was still shown at Olympia and to whom Selene bore fifty daughters. According to the Carian tradition Endymion was a young prince who, hunting on Mount Latmus one day, lay down to rest in a cool grotto where he fell asleep. Selene saw him and, captivated by his beauty, stole a kiss while he slept. Endymion asked Zeus to grant him immortality and eternal youth; Zeus consented on condition that he remained eternally asleep.

Another tradition explains this eternal sleep as a punishment inflicted by Zeus on Endymion who, on his admission to Olympus, had been rash enough to aspire to Hera's love.

Be this as it may, Selene came faithfully night after night silently to contemplate her sleeping lover. Thus the rays of the amorous moon come to caress the sleep of mortals.

EOS

The third child of the Titans, Hyperion and Theia, was Eos (Aurora), the rosy-fingered dawn with the snowy eyelids. It was she who brought the first glimmer of day to men. Every morning at dawn she slipped from the couch of her husband, Tithonus, and

emerging from the ocean rose into the sky. Sometimes she appeared as a winged goddess tilting an urn from which fell the morning dew. Sometimes she was mounted on the horse Pegasus and bore in her hands a torch. Most often saffron-robed Eos rode on a purple chariot drawn by two horses.

It was only later that Eos was distinguished from Hemera, goddess of the day; originally she was represented as accompanying her brother Helios during his whole journey.

Eos at first united with the Titan Astraeus, to whom she bore the winds, Boreas, Zephyrus, Eurus, Notus and various astral bodies.

Eos was young and lovely and made to awaken desire. She was loved by Ares, which earned her the enmity of Aphrodite. To avenge herself, Aphrodite inspired Eos with love for numerous mortals.

She conceived a passion for the giant Orion, whom she carried off and kept with her, to the great annoyance of the gods. Artemis finally killed him by accident in the isle of Ortygia.

Eos and Tithonus. Then Aphrodite filled the heart of Eos with love for Tithonus, one of Laomedon's sons. Wishing to be bound to her new husband for eternity, Eos begged Zeus to confer immortality on him; but, alas, she had forgotten to ask at the same time for perpetual youth! As the years passed the young and handsome lover of former days became an old man with wrinkled brow. In vain Eos fed him on the celestial ambrosia which rendered the flesh incorruptible; old age gave way to decrepitude. The goddess then shut Tithonus up in a chamber where the impotent old man remained in solitude until the day when the gods took pity and changed him into a cicada.

Eos and Cephalus. Meanwhile the inconstant Eos sought consolation among other mortals. There was Cleitus, grandson of the soothsayer Melampus, for whom she obtained the favour of being admitted into Olympus. There was Cephalus, son of Hermes, or of Deion, King of Phocis, whose fate was more tragic. Cephalus had just married Procris, whom he dearly loved, when Eos saw him hunting on Mount Hymettus and carried him off to Syria. Far from responding to the goddess's love, Cephalus thought only of his beloved Procris. Not unnaturally irritated, Eos filled him with doubts about his wife's fidelity and advised him to test her. Cephalus then approached Procris in disguise and, offering her rich jewels, tried to seduce her. Procris repelled him at first, but finally the temptation was too strong for her. Cephalus revealed his identity and drove her away. The unhappy Procris retired to Euboea and put herself under the protection of Artemis. Artemis – or some say it was Minos – gave her a dog who never lost the scent and a javelin which never missed its mark, and sent her back in disguise to Cephalus. This time Cephalus, offered the dog and the javelin, was himself tempted and, in fact, made the same mistake his wife had previously made. The couple then became reconciled. But Procris still feared that her husband might be unfaithful to her and followed him when he went hunting, spying on him without his suspecting it. One day when Procris was hidden in a thicket Cephalus heard a rustling sound. Thinking it was some wild beast, he threw the javelin which never missed its mark. Procris was slain and Cephalus was summoned before the Areopagus, which banished him from Athens. He went to Thebes, where he visited Amphitryon, and then retired to an island which was named Cephallenia after him. According to another version of the story Cephalus was inconsolable at the death of Procris and threw himself from the promontory of Leucas into the sea.

The Offspring of Eos. By her marriage with Tithonus, Eos had two sons: Memnon and Emathion. Emathion reigned over Arabia and was killed by Hercules. Memnon was King of Ethiopia and went to Troy with an army of Ethiopians and Susians to assist Priam. He was 'the most handsome warrior who appeared before Troy'. Having killed Antilochus, son of Nestor, he was himself killed by Achilles. Eos obtained immortality for him; nevertheless she never ceased to weep each morning for her dearly beloved son, and it was her tears which formed the dew. It seems likely that this hero represents some former Asiatic divinity. Memnon, indeed, was reputed to have founded Susa – where his tomb was – and to have built the walls of Babylon. He was also venerated in Egypt: the colossal statue at Thebes was called the statue of Memnon.

Among the other sons of Eos must be mentioned Phaethon, son of Tithonus (or of Cephalus) who was carried off by Aphrodite to be the guardian of her temple. He is thus connected with the planet Venus, of which two other sons of Eos, Phosphorus and Hesperus, represent the planet's double aspect of morning star and evening star.

Phosphorus was the son of Astraeus; with a torch in his hand he could be seen in the guise of a winged spirit flying through the air before his mother's chariot.

Hesperus, 'the most splendid star which shines in the firmament', was sometimes said to be the son of Atlas. Hesperus' own children were: Daedalion, who in despair at the death of his daughter Chione threw himself from the heights of Parnassus and was changed by Apollo into a sparrow-hawk; and Ceyx, who married Alcyone. Ceyx and Alcyone were both turned into birds for having dared to compare themselves to Zeus and Hera. Another version is that when Ceyx perished in a shipwreck Alcyone threw herself in despair into the sea and Thetis changed the couple into halcyons or king-fishers.

The Hesperides. Hesperus was also said to be father of the Hesperides; though others said they were daughters of Night and Erebus, or of Phorcys and Ceto, or of Zeus and Themis. The Hesperides were three or four in number: Aegle, Erytheis, Hespera, Hestia or Arethusa. Their abode was beyond the river-ocean, at the extreme western limits of the world, where they personified the clouds gilded by the setting sun. They lived in a wondrous garden and guarded the golden apples which grew there. Since, however, the Greeks had two identical words for 'apple' and for 'flock of sheep', it has been wondered if the Hesperides were not rather guardians of the celestial flocks which in Indo-European mythology symbolised clouds.

ORION: THE PLEIADES: THE HYADES

The constellations of Orion, the Pleiades and the Hyades, occupied a particular place in Greek mythology.

Orion. Orion was a giant of Boeotia famous for his beauty. He was variously described as the son of Mother Earth, of Poseidon and Euryale, and of Hyrieus, King of Hyria in Boeotia. One day when Zeus, Hermes and Poseidon were travelling together on earth they were handsomely received by Hyrieus. In gratitude for his hospitality they promised to grant whatever he asked for. Hyrieus asked for a son. The three gods then took the hide of a heifer, urinated on it and buried it. Nine months later Orion emerged from the ground. This singular mode of procreation seems to arise from a play on words, Orion and urine being similar also in Greek. Orion was of such gigantic stature that he could walk on the bottom of the sea without wetting his head. He was endowed with prodigious strength and was a passionate hunter. He followed his favourite sport accompanied by his dog Sirius. He had married Side who, because she boasted that she was more beautiful than Hera, was cast by that goddess into Tartarus. Afterwards Orion fell in love with Merope, daughter of Oenopion, ruler of Chios. He rid the island of all its savage beasts in vain: he was rejected by Oenopion. Orion therefore took Merope by violence. Her father then implored the aid of Dionysus, who plunged Orion into deep slumber; while Orion slept, Oenopion put out his eyes. The giant, however, discovered from an oracle that he could regain his sight if he travelled towards the sun. He went to Lemnos, where Hephaestus gave him his son Cedalion for a guide. When his sight was restored Orion sailed on to Crete, where he went hunting with Artemis. We have seen that he was carried off by Eos. The end of Orion was attributed to Artemis, though there are various versions of how it occurred. Some said she struck him down on the isle of Ortygia after Eos had carried him off, others that she shot him by accident at Apollo's instigation, or that she caused his death by a scorpion's sting after he had attempted to ravish her, or, again, because he boasted of having destroyed all the wild beasts in Crete. Asclepius attempted to resuscitate Orion, but Zeus struck him with a thunderbolt. Orion descended into the realm of Hades, where his shade with a brazen club continued to hunt the wild beasts. But according to the more popular tradition Orion was transported to the sky where,

in golden armour and sword in hand, he shines on winter nights. His brilliance, however, fades when the constellation Scorpio appears.

Pleiades and Hyades. The Pleiades were daughters of Atlas and Pleione or Aethra. There were seven of them: Maia, Taygete, Electra, Alcyone, Celoeno, Sterope and Merope. The first three were loved by Zeus. Poseidon obtained the favours of Alcyone and Celoeno. Ares was Sterope's lover. Only Merope had to be content with the love of a mere mortal, Sisyphus – hence she shines less brightly in the sky than her sisters. They had all been changed into stars. They were being pursued across the mountains of Boeotia by the hunter Orion. They were about to fall into his clutches when they cried to Zeus for help. He turned them into doves, then placed them in the sky. It was also related that the Pleiades, inconsolable at the death of their sisters, the Hyades, killed themselves in despair and were then changed by Zeus into stars. They appeared in the sky in the middle of May and thus announced the return of the good weather.

The appearance of the Hyades on the contrary was the signal for the rainy season. Their very name meant the Rainy Ones. They were also daughters of Atlas and Aethra or Pleione. Their number varies among different authors from two to seven. Nor are their names fixed. The ones most frequently listed are: Ambrosia, Eudora and Coronis. It was related that they had brought up Zeus in Dodona, and later Dionysus in Nysa. In recognition of these services they were placed among the heavenly bodies, where they formed a group of stars in the constellation Taurus. Their metamorphosis was also explained as a recompense for the unhappiness they suffered at the death of their brother Hyas, who was killed while hunting by a serpent or a wild boar.

GODS OF THE WINDS

The empire of the winds was shared between the four sons of Eos, the dawn, and Astraeus, the starry sky. They were called: Boreas, the North Wind; Zephyrus, the West Wind; Eurus, the East Wind; and Notus, the South Wind.

Boreas dwelt in the mountains of Thrace. It was there that Iris came in search of him to fan the funeral pyre of Patroclus. It was said that Boreas carried off Oreithyia, daughter of Erechtheus, from the banks of the Ilissus, and by her had several children, notably Chione, who was loved by Poseidon; Cleopatra, who married Phineus; and the twins Zetes and Calais, also called the Boreades, who took part in the expedition of the Argonauts, fought victoriously against the Harpies, and were slain by the arrows of Hercules in the island of Zenos. They were changed into favourable winds which blew from the north-east and were given the name *Prodromes,* forerunners, because they came shortly before the rise of the Dog Star.

Boreas assumed the form of a stallion to mate with the mares of Erichthonius, and from this union were born twelve young mares so light of step that 'they ran across fields of standing corn without bruising an ear of grain and over the crests of the sea without wetting their feet'.

In memory of the abduction of Oreithyia the Athenians raised a temple to Boreas on the banks of the Ilissus. They especially venerated Boreas because he had dispersed the fleet of the invader Xerxes. Boreas was represented as a winged man of mature age with hair floating in the wind. On the chest of Cypselus, however, he is depicted as having serpents for legs.

The normal companion of Boreas was Zephyrus who was not, originally, the soft and beneficial wind at whose breath the spring flowers open. Like his brother he was a savage and baleful wind who took pleasure in brewing storms and tossing the waves of the sea. With Boreas he lived in the caves of mountainous Thrace. From his union with the Harpy Podarge were born the two horses Xanthus and Balius, who drew the chariot of Achilles.

Later Zephyrus' violent disposition softened. He became a sweet-scented wind which gently fanned the blessed regions of Elysium. For a wife he was given the gracious Chloris by whom he had a son, Carpus – or fruit.

The Athenians consecrated an altar to Zephyrus on the road to Eleusis.

Theseus receiving a jewelled crown from Amphitrite, the goddess of the sea. Challenged by Minos to prove his claim to be the son of Poseidon by retrieving a golden ring thrown into the sea, the Attic hero has plunged into its depths, escorted by a school of dolphin, and now stands before the goddess. Detail from the bottom of a Greek cup decorated with scenes showing the exploits of Theseus.

As for Notus and Eurus, their individualities were never clearly defined.

Aeolus. Another tradition, which has its source in the *Odyssey*, places the abode of the winds in the Aeolian Islands, where they were kept under the guardianship of Aeolus. Aeolus was the son of Poseidon and Arne, and a brother of Boeotus. After an adventurous youth he settled in the Lipari Islands and married Gyane, the daughter of King Liparus. Because of his piety and justice Aeolus became a friend of the gods. It was said that he invented ships' sails. Zeus appointed him guardian of the winds which he could, at will, excite or soothe. When Odysseus landed on his island Aeolus welcomed him hospitably and on his departure gave him a wine-skin in which were tied up those winds which would impede his voyage. Overcome by curiosity the companions of Odysseus untied the wine-skin and let the deadly contrary winds escape.

At first Aeolus was simply the guardian of the winds, but later he became their father and, in Roman mythology, the god of wind. He resided, they said, on the isle of Lipara, where he kept the winds chained up in deep caverns.

The Chimaera and the Harpies. In opposition to these regular winds there were various monsters who personified the storm winds who, 'pouncing suddenly on the darkened waves, unleashed the raging tempests to destroy men'. Their father was Typhon, son of Typhoeus, spirit of the hurricane, and their mother was Echidna, the upper part of whose body was that of a young nymph but whose lower part was that of a horrifying serpent covered with scales. Among these monsters it will be sufficient to mention the Chimaera and the Harpies.

The Chimaera had the head of a lion, the body of a goat and the tail of a dragon. She vomited forth horrible flames. It is agreed that she was a personification of the storm-cloud.

The Harpies – who were also said to be daughters of Thaumas and Electra – were tempest-goddesses, 'the ravagers'. Homer only names one of them, Podarge. Hesiod mentions two, Aello and Ocypete, winged creatures as swift as birds and the winds. Later the Harpy type became definite: they were monsters with the face of an old hag, the ears of a bear, and the body of a bird with long hooked claws. It was their habit to snatch and devour food from tables, or else to soil the table, spreading filth and stench and causing famine. Thus when the soothsayer Phineus was condemned by Zeus to eternal old age and everlasting hunger, the Harpies came to steal the food which was laid before him, soiling with their excrement what they did not carry away. They were attacked by the Argonauts and particularly by the Boreades Zetes and Calais, who pursued them through the air and vanquished them. They granted them their lives, however, at the request of Iris. According to other traditions one of the Harpies drowned herself in the Tigris, a river in the Peloponnese; the other fled to the Echinade Islands where she turned round and fell to the shore. Thus the islands took the name of the Strophades, from the Greek 'to turn'.

GODS OF THE WATERS

Pontus. The oldest divinity of the waters was Pontus, whom Gaea produced from herself at the beginning of time. Pontus is no more than the personified sea. He was without physiognomy or character, and all that remained of him was his name, which poets later used to designate the sea.

Oceanus. The primitive Greeks, like the Chaldeans, imagined an immense river which formed a liquid girdle around the universe. It lay beyond the sea and embraced the sea without, however, mingling with its waters. It was the River Ocean, or Oceanus, who, having himself neither source nor outlet, gave birth to 'all the rivers, the entire sea, to all waters which gushed from the earth, to all deep wells'. From him arose all the stars – with the exception of the Great Bear – only to plunge back again. On the shores of Oceanus were the fabulous lands of the virtuous Ethiopians, the fog-bound Cimmerians, the minute Pygmies.

Son of Uranus and Gaea, the Titan Oceanus was one of those elemental forces which had contributed to the formation of the world. In him Homer salutes the essence of all things, even of the gods, and regards him as a divinity whose power was inferior to none but Zeus'.

Oceanus married his sister Tethys and by her had the three thousand Oceanids and the three thousand rivers. According to one tradition Oceanus and Tethys cared for the infant Hera, whom they sheltered in their palace in the west of the world.

The Olympians, however, finally established their empire over the waters, as over the rest of the universe, and the watery element was inherited by Poseidon, who from then on became the uncontested lord of the sea and the rivers, while the aged Oceanus was confined to his distant place of retirement.

DIVINITIES OF THE SEA

The importance assumed by Poseidon in Greek religious belief caused the other and more ancient marine deities to play secondary roles, and their cult retained no more than a popular character.

Nereus. Nereus was the son of Pontus and Gaea. He was born in the first ages of the world, and the accumulation of centuries had made of him a venerable greybeard. He was, indeed, called 'The Old Man of the Sea'. He was kindly and helpful, 'having known only thoughts of justice and kindness'. He only left the dwelling he occupied with his wife Doris in the depths of the Aegaean Sea in order to come to the assistance of sailors and give them useful advice. Like other marine deities, however, he only spoke when he had to. Hercules resorted to force in order to learn from him how to reach the land of the Hesperides. Nereus also possessed the gift of prophecy; Paris one day beheld him emerging from the waves and heard from his mouth the announcement of the coming destruction of Troy.

Of the marriage of Nereus and Doris were born fifty daughters, the Nereids, fair virgins with golden hair who lived with their father in his submarine abode, but who might sometimes be seen when the sea was calm frolicking with the Tritons on the crest of the waves.

Of most of the Nereids we know only the names; some of them, however, played a part in the legends of Greece.

Arethusa was seen one day by the hunter Alpheius, who immediately fell in love with her. He pursued her, and to escape him Arethusa took refuge on the isle of Ortygia, where she was changed into a spring. Alpheius, who remained in the neighbourhood of Olympia, was himself changed into a river and his waters, crossing the sea without mingling with it, then joined the waters of the spring Arethusa on the isle of Ortygia.

Galatea, another Nereid, was courted by the Cyclops Polyphemus, but she preferred a young herdsman of Sicily, named Acis. Polyphemus surprised the two lovers one day while they were conversing in the hollow of a grotto and crushed Acis under an enormous boulder. Galatea, however, succeeded in having Acis changed into a river.

Psamathe had a son by Aeacus, Phocus, who reigned over the island of Aegina and who was assassinated by Peleus and Telamon. To avenge the murder of her son Psamathe sent a monstrous wolf who devastated Peleus' flocks.

The most celebrated of the Nereids was Thetis. For her beauty she was sought in marriage by both Zeus and Poseidon. But Themis declared that Thetis would give birth to a son more powerful than his father, and both gods prudently renounced their project. Zeus decided to marry Thetis to a mortal, and chose Peleus, King of Thessaly. Thetis did not accept this alliance which she, being immortal, considered beneath her dignity, without protest. She attempted to escape from Peleus by taking on various shapes: she changed herself into a fish and then into an animal, into a fluid wave, then into burning flame. Thanks to the advice of the centaur Chiron, Peleus finally succeeded in seizing her and their marriage was celebrated with great pomp in the presence of the gods, who showered handsome gifts on the couple. To Thetis and Peleus was born a son, Achilles. Some said that Achilles was their seventh child and that Thetis had thrown the first six into the fire to destroy such evidence of an unworthy union. This story agrees rather badly with the tenderness which Thetis always showed towards Achilles. When she learned the fatal destiny which awaited her son she tried to prevent it by rendering Achilles invulnerable. In order to do this, she exposed him every night to the flames and dressed his wounds with ambrosia. But Peleus caught her unawares one night and, terrified, snatched the child away. According to a more accredited version, as soon as Achilles was born Thetis plunged him into the Styx, thus making his body invulnerable, all except the heel by which she held him.

Thetis plays a part in many legends. It will be recalled that she came to the assistance of Zeus when he was nearly overcome by Hera, Apollo, Poseidon and Athene: she brought the giant Briareus to defend Zeus. Thetis and her sister Eurynome sheltered Hephaestus after his fall from Olympus. She also sheltered Dionysus when he fled before Lycurgus.

She was honoured in various parts of Greece, in Thessaly, in Messenia and at Sparta.

Proteus. Proteus was another 'Old Man of the Sea'. He was the son of Oceanus and Tethys, and his duty was to guard Poseidon's herd of seals. At noon each day he would emerge from the waves and come ashore to rest in the shelter of a rock. Around him slept the tight-packed herd of seals, sons of the fair Halosydne. It was the propitious moment to obtain from wise Proteus a revelation of what fate held in store; for he saw into the future and he spoke the truth. But, since he never spoke oracularly unless forced to do so, it was first necessary to catch hold of him – no simple matter, for Proteus could change shape at will and in order to escape from whoever held him would in succession turn himself into a lion, a dragon, a panther, into water, fire, a tree... The important thing was not to be intimidated by these metamorphoses, for then Proteus would admit himself vanquished and talk. In this manner Menelaus, following the advice of Idothea, Proteus' own daughter, learned from him how to return to his own country. Proteus was represented with the features of an old man, and he lived on the isle of Pharos on the Egyptian coast.

This localisation no doubt resulted from a confusion with a fabled King of Egypt who was also named Proteus. It was said that this king welcomed Paris and Helen when they fled from Sparta, but that he kept Helen with him in order to return her to her legitimate husband. It was also said that he went from Egypt to Thrace, where he married. Later, angered by the cruelty of his two sons, Tmolus and Telegonus, he decided to return to Egypt, and Poseidon hollowed out for him under the sea a road which led him back to Pharos.

Phorcys. The character of Phorcys is more vague. Homer calls him 'the old man who rules the waves'. He says that his daughter was the nymph Thoosa who by Poseidon had the monstrous Polyphemus. According to Hesiod, Phorcys was the son of Pontus and Gaea. He married his sister Ceto and fathered the Graeae, the Gorgons, the dragon Ladon and, perhaps, the Hesperides. It was also said that Scylla was born of his love for Hecate. To judge by his wild progeny Phorcys must in the eyes of the Greeks have personified the perfidious and evil sea. His very name seems to indicate the whitish foam which crowns the crest of the waves.

Glaucus. The name Glaucus evokes a picture of the dark greenish-blue which the sea assumes when the winds begin to rise. There were various legends about Glaucus. One related that he was a humble fisherman from Anthedon. One day when he returned from fishing he set down his fish among some herbs which grew beside the shore. He saw them immediately leap up and fling themselves back into the sea. He tasted the herbs himself and was changed into a Triton. He jumped into the sea and was admitted among the marine deities as one of their own number. Another legend recounts that while pursuing a hare Glaucus saw the creature swallow a blade of this herb and at once recover its agility. In curiosity Glaucus also tasted the mysterious herb and thus acquired immortality. He took to the sea either in obedience to a secret impulse sent by Zeus, or because he was vexed at being unable to make his fellow men acknowledge his immortality.

Glaucus normally dwelt in Delos. Apollo conferred on him the gift of prophecy which he transmitted to his daughter, the sibyl Deiphobe. Once a year Glaucus left his abode in Delos and made a tour of the islands of the Aegean Sea. He would appear to sailors, with his thin body covered with seaweed and seashells, and predict sinister occurrences.

He was a lugubrious divinity and even his love affairs were unhappy. Except for Syme, whose love he won and whom he carried to a small island near Rhodes, all to whom he paid court repulsed him. He discovered Ariadne on the isle of Naxos and attempted to console her, but Dionysus arrived, bound him up with vine-shoots, and consoled Ariadne himself. It was also said that Glaucus turned Scylla into a monster out of resentment though, it is true, Scylla's metamorphosis was also attributed to the jealousy of Amphitrite.

Sometimes confused with Glaucus was another personage of human origin who was raised to the rank of a marine divinity: Melicertes Palaemon.

Melicertes was the son of Athamas and Semele's sister Ino who had incurred the wrath of Hera for having fed and sheltered young Dionysus after his mother's death. Hera, in vengeance, unbalanced Athamas' mind and Athamas slew one of his own sons, Learchus. To save the other son, Melicertes, from his father's madness, Ino seized the child and jumped with it into the sea. She was welcomed by the Nereids and became, under the name Leucothea, a divinity who protected mariners. As for Melicertes, his body was carried by a dolphin to the coast of Corinth. Sisyphus found it and erected a tomb for Melicertes on the shore. Under the name Palaemon, Melicertes was from then on venerated as a god. On the instructions of the Nereids the Isthmian games were instituted in his honour. He is usually represented as a child carried by dolphins.

Triton. Around the chariot of Amphitrite, who was escorted by the gracious Nereids, frisked strange creatures, half-men, half-fish, whose bodies were covered with scales, whose teeth were sharp and whose fingers were armed with claws. Their breast and belly were supplied with fins, and instead of legs they had the forked tail of a marine monster. This lascivious troop played among the waves, noisily blowing on conch shells. They were the Tritons. Some of their number, who were furnished with a pair of horse's legs as well, were known as Centaur-Tritons.

Although they lived in the sea the Tritons sometimes ventured on to land. At Tanagra, people remembered a Triton who had desolated the country and ravished the women. To capture him they placed a vase filled with wine on the beach. The Triton drank it, and during his drunken slumber a fisherman cut off his head. They placed a statue of a headless Triton in the temple of Dionysus at Tanagra to commemorate the event.

These marine genii took their name from a primitive god, son of Poseidon and Amphitrite, whose name was Triton. He also was half-man, half-fish, and lived with his father in the depths of the sea, although his favourite place of abode was near the coast of Libya. It even seems that in origin Triton was a purely Libyan divinity, unless the Minyaen colonists had brought with them to Africa the former god of the river Triton which flowed into Lake Copais in Boeotia.

As Poseidon's son, Triton shared some of his father's powers: like him he could raise or quieten the waves. He could be seen riding the waves on his chariot drawn by steeds whose hooves were the claws of crayfish.

On two occasions he did Zeus a good turn. During the war with the Giants, Triton contributed to the victory of the Olympians by frightening the giants with the terrible sounds he made with his conch. Later, it was Triton whom Zeus made responsible for seeing that the waters withdrew after the deluge.

Benevolent and obliging, Triton saved the Argonauts when a tempest drove their ship on to the Libyan coast. He helped them, and his advice enabled them to continue their voyage.

Triton shared the gift of prophecy with the other marine gods, Nereus and Proteus, of whom he was originally, perhaps, only a local form. It seems, however, that he more especially personified the roar of the sea or its wild movement, as his attribute, the conch, tends to indicate.

Sea Monsters: The Sirens. The name Siren derives from a Greek root meaning 'to bind or attach' and clearly alludes to the role the Sirens played in mythology. One is inclined, however, to consider them as divinities who symbolised the souls of the dead. They would thus be funerary genii, avid for blood and hostile to the living. With their bird's body and woman's head, they recall the human-headed Egyptian hawk who also incarnated the souls of the dead. The Sirens were invoked at the moment of death, and their

Head of Demeter with her attributes: sheaves of corn, poppies and snakes. Terra-cotta. Terme Museum, Rome.

images are frequently found on tombs. Legend, however, has retained nothing of this conception of them, and depicts the Sirens only as malevolent monsters of the sea.

At first they were represented with the head and bust of a woman and the body of a bird, and only later depicted as women whose bodies terminated in fish tails. Their attribute was a musical instrument – a lyre or a double flute. They had a temple at Sorrento.

When Odysseus was about to leave Circe and take to his swift ships again, she warned him of the dangers of the voyage and in particular said:

'First thou shalt arrive where the enchanter Sirens dwell, they who seduce men. The imprudent man who draws near them never returns, for the Sirens, lying in the flower-strewn fields, will charm him with sweet song; but around them the bodies of their victims lie in heaps.'

And so it was that Odysseus came in sight of a rocky islet where he perceived the bizarre creatures, half-women, half-birds, who, seeing his ship, began to sing. They were the Sirens and what they sang was:

'Draw near, illustrious Odysseus, glory of the Achaeans, stop thy ship and come to us. None has yet passed by this isle without having listened to the enchantment of our voices and heard us sing of the mighty deeds done by the Greeks beneath the walls of Troy. For we know all that happens on the fruitful earth.'

The sweetness of their voices was such that Odysseus could not have resisted their invitation had he not followed Circe's advice and taken the precaution of having himself lashed to the mast of his ship. As for his companions, he had cautiously stopped up their ears with wax.

Thus they escaped the fearful danger. But the human bones scattered over the green fields of the Siren Island bore mute witness to the imprudence of former sailors and to the ferocity of these insidious-voiced creatures.

They had not always been like this. In primitive times the Sirens, who were daughters of the river Achelous, had been river deities.

In number they were – depending on different authors – two, three, four or even eight. They had names which emphasised the charm of their voices: Aglaophonos or Aglaophone (of the brilliant voice); Thelxepeia (of the words which enchant); Peisinoë (the persuasive); Molpe (song).

There were various explanations of their strange shape. According to some they were with Persephone when she was ravished by Hades, and it was at their request that Zeus gave them wings so that they could fly in pursuit of the ravisher. According to others they owed their birds' bodies to the wrath of Aphrodite who punished them in this way for having been rebellious to love.

The Sirens were excessively proud of their voices and their musical talent and had, it was said, dared one day to challenge the Muses. But the Muses vanquished them and pulled out their wing feathers. They then abandoned the springs and dales and went to hide their shame among the jagged rocks along the coasts of Southern Italy. Their abodes were Cape Pelorus, Capri, the isle of Anthemusa, and the Siren Isles. There from the shores they attracted sailors by their songs and devoured the unhappy wretches who had been unable to resist their seduction.

In the end, however, they found their master. When the ship of the Argonauts sailed past their island they tried as usual to exert their power. But only Butes, son of Zelion, jumped overboard to join the treacherous goddesses. The others were prevented by Orpheus who was with them. He tuned his lyre and began to sing; and his persuasive voice overcame the allure of the Sirens.

Vanquished, the Sirens from that moment lost all power to do harm and were changed into rocks. One of them, Parthenope, threw herself into the sea in vexation. Her body was tossed on to the shore by the waves, and a tomb was erected for her on the very spot where later the city of Naples rose.

Charybdis and Scylla. This same Sicilian sea where the Sirens dwelt also harboured two other redoubtable monsters, Charybdis and Scylla.

Of Charybdis we know little more than what Homer tells us. 'Divine Charybdis with a terrible roar swallows the waves of the bitter sea and three times each day she throws them up again.' She lived under a rock crowned by a green fig tree. She was called the daughter of Poseidon and the Earth and it was because she had stolen the oxen of Hercules that Zeus struck her with a thunderbolt and changed her into a whirlpool whose vortex swallowed up ships.

The legend of Scylla was more extensive. She was the daughter of Phorcys and Crataeis, or of Typhon and Echidna, or of Poseidon. According to others, her mother was Lamia, that queen of Libya who was loved by Zeus and saw her children perish as a result of Hera's jealousy. In her misery she went out of her mind and devoured babies whom she tore from their mothers' arms. Scylla was at first a nymph of rare beauty. Whether it was because she repelled the advances of Glaucus and Glaucus punished her for disdain, or whether, on the contrary, she had given herself to Poseidon and thus excited Amphitrite's jealousy, Scylla was changed by Circe into a monster. While she was bathing in a pool into which Circe had thrown certain magic herbs, six necks suddenly sprang from her shoulders, necks of monstrous length, surmounted by six frightful heads, each supplied with a triple row of teeth. She lurked in a dark cavern hollowed in the middle of a reef from which emerged only her heads, which snapped up passing dolphins, the dogs of the sea, and those of 'the enormous monsters nurtured by the noisy Amphitrite whom she was able to seize'. When a ship passed within her reach each of her heads would carry off a man from the bench of rowers, and no vessel could boast of escaping Scylla without loss.

When Hercules brought Geryon's herd through the straits of Sicily, Scylla seized and devoured one of the oxen. Hercules killed her, but she was resuscitated by her father Phorcys, and mariners passing the straits of Sicily continued to dread the twin perils of Charybdis and Scylla.

FRESH-WATER DIVINITIES

The Rivers. There were three thousand rivers according to Hesiod, sons of Oceanus and Tethys, who partook of the divine nature of their parents and were worshipped by mortals.

Young folk consecrated their hair to them; rams were immolated to them and into their waters were cast living horses and bulls.

The rivers were represented as vigorous men with long beards; their strength was symbolised by the pair of horns which adorned their brow.

The most celebrated and venerated of rivers was the Achelous, which was also the largest watercourse in Greece. Achelous fought against Hercules for the hand of Deianeira. Vanquished, he changed himself into a serpent, then into a wild bull, Hercules, however, overthrew him and tore off one of his horns, with which the nymphs made the Horn of Plenty. Achelous, ashamed of his defeat, threw himself into the river which thenceforth bore his name. Achelous was revered throughout Greece and even in Sicily – six rivers were named after him – and he was invoked when taking oaths. It was for having omitted to do him honour during a sacrifice that the daughters of the soothsayer Echinus were changed into islands and became the Echinades.

Almost as famous was the Asopus, a name also found in Thessaly and the Peloponnese. Asopus was a river-god of Boeotia. By his wife Merope he had two sons, Pelasgus and Ismenius, and twelve daughters, among them Sinope, who was carried off by Apollo; Corcyra and Salamis, who were loved by Poseidon; and Aegina, who was ravished by Zeus. Asopus went in search of Aegina and learned from Sisyphus – in exchange for a spring which he made gush forth on Acrocorinth – the name of his daughter's ravisher. He attempted to obtain justice, but Zeus struck him with a thunderbolt and forced him to return to his river bed.

Inachus, river-god of Argolis, also had one of his daughters, Io, seduced by Zeus. During the dispute between Hera and Poseidon for possession of Argolis, Inachus was chosen to arbitrate. He pronounced in favour of Hera, and Poseidon, in annoyance, dried up his waters.

Cephissus was a river-god of Phocis and Boeotia. He only appears in mythology as the father of Narcissus, whom he had by the Oceanid Liriope. There was a sanctuary consecrated to him at Argos.

Among the other river-gods may be mentioned: Peneius in Thessaly; in Arcadia, Ladon, who was the father of Syrinx and Daphne; in the Peloponnese, Alpheius, who, they said, fell in love with Artemis. To elude him Artemis took refuge in Elis and when she reached Letrini made herself unrecognisable by daubing herself with mud. It was also related that Alpheius was a hunter who fell in love with the nymph Arethusa and pursued her to the isle of Ortygia, where she changed into a spring. Alpheius, in his turn, was changed into a river, but he still obstinately pursued Arethusa. He crossed the sea without mingling with its waters and in Ortygia rejoined her whom he loved. When bulls were sacrificed in Olympia, past which the Alpheius flowed, it appeared that the waters of the fountain of Arethusa were also tinted with blood. The Eurotas in Laconia had, it was said, been a king of that country, and son of Taygete. Among his daughters was Sparta, who was married to Lacedaemon. He was responsible for draining the marshes which covered Laconia, and his name was given to the canal he dug to carry away the waters. Others said he threw himself into the river which bears his name in despair at having lost a battle.

In Phrygia the two principal river-gods were the Scamander (or Xanthus) and the Maeander. It was Hercules, seized by thirst, who had scooped out the earth and caused the Scamander to gush forth. Scamander took part in the Trojan war and Homer describes his battle with Achilles. He caught up the hero in his nets and it required the intervention of Hephaestus to appease the river-god. As for the Maeander, it owed its name to Maeander, King of Pessinonte, who in the course of a war made a vow that if he were victorious he would immolate the first person who came to congratulate him. The first person to do so was his son. Maeander fulfilled his vow, but threw himself in despair into the river which took his name.

Water Nymphs. Just as every river had its own divine personality, so every stream, brook, spring and pool harboured in its waters a divinity who was known as a nymph.

Water nymphs were classified according to their place of abode. Potamids were nymphs of rivers and streams; Naiads were nymphs of brooks; Crenae or Pegae were nymphs of springs; Limnads were nymphs of stagnant waters.

Although in the divine hierarchy they occupied an inferior rank, they were occasionally admitted to Olympus, and mortals honoured them with a religious cult.

Their functions were many. They had the gift of prophecy and could deliver oracles. They were benevolent deities and cured the sick; they watched over flowers, fields and flocks.

Sometimes they lived in the depths of the waters, sometimes in grottoes near the springs over which they presided. There they would busy themselves weaving and spinning. Sometimes they would mingle with the retinue of certain divinities.

In spite of their divine character they were not immortal. According to Plutarch the average life span of a nymph did not exceed nine thousand six hundred and twenty years. But it was their privilege always to remain young and beautiful, for their nourishment was ambrosia.

Although they were generally benevolent, they could become dangerous to those mortals whom they distinguished with their favours. Like the Rusalki of the Slavs, they sometimes dragged such mortals down into the depths of the waters. This, as we have seen, was the fate of Hermaphroditus, victim of the nymph Salmacis. A similar fate overtook young Hylas, the handsome companion of Hercules. When the ship of the Argonauts reached the coasts of the Troad, Hylas, who was a member of the expedition, was sent to shore by his companions in search of water. As it happened he discovered a fountain, but the nymphs of the place were so charmed by his beauty that they carried him to the depths of their watery abode, and in spite of the cries of Hercules which made the shores reverberate with the name Hylas, the young man was never seen again.

Among the nymphs whose name is known to legend may be mentioned Aganippe, nymph of the spring of that name which flowed at the approaches of Mount Helicon and whose waters inspired those who drank of them; Cassotis and Castalia, nymphs of prophetic springs on Parnassus; Hago, who presided over a fountain on Mount Lycaeus. During periods of drought the priest of Lycaean Zeus would touch the surface of the fountain with an oak branch. At once a mist would arise which would thicken into a cloud and soon pour forth the wished-for rain. There were also Pirene whose tears at the death of her son formed a fountain which could be seen near Corinth; Cyane, a Sicilian nymph who accompanied Persephone when she was carried off by Hades: heartbroken, she turned herself into a fountain. According to another tradition this fountain sprang from the hole Hades made when he plunged into the earth. Every year the people of Syracuse would come there and throw in a bull. Argyra, nymph of a fountain in Arcadia, loved the shepherd Selemnos. When she deserted him Selemnos was so broken-hearted that Aphrodite took pity on him and changed him into a river, granting him oblivion to cure the sickness of his heart. Thus whoever bathed in the river Selemnos found oblivion from the sorrows of love.

Calypso was the daughter of Atlas and Tethys and reigned, according to ancient tradition, over the isle of Ortygia in the Ionian Sea. When Odysseus was thrown by a tempest on her shores she welcomed him hospitably and kept him with her for seven years. To retain him forever she offered him immortality, but Zeus ordered her to release him. As her name – derived from a root which means 'to hide' – indicates, Calypso personified the depths of the waters.

DIVINITIES OF THE EARTH

GAEA, RHEA AND CYBELE

A personification of the earth, Gaea was, as we have already seen, the primitive goddess of the Greeks. Though her cult persisted throughout the ages her individuality became submerged in that of other similar divinities. The Pelasgian Gaea was early supplanted by Rhea whose origin was probably Cretan and who was herself only the earth deified. Her very name seems to derive from an archaic word meaning earth.

The legend of Rhea was formed by more or less repeating that of Gaea. The couple Rhea-Cronus correspond exactly to the couple Gaea-Uranus. Both goddesses have the same maternal anxieties and both husbands come to the same unhappy end. In the same way that the primitive Greeks made Gaea the Great Mother and and author of all beings, so the supremacy of Rhea was affirmed by the fact that she was made mother of the great ruling gods of Olympus.

In spite of her foreign origin Rhea soon took on a physiognomy which was plainly Greek. Several regions of Greece claimed the honour of having been the theatre of the divine episodes of her legend. For instance, it was near Chaeronea, on the cliff of Petrachus, that Rhea presented the stone to Cronus; the same scene was also localised at Methydium in Arcadia. Thebans pointed out the place where Rhea brought Zeus into the world, while the Arcadians said he was born on Mount Lycaeus. The god had grown up either in Olympia of Elis, or on Mount Ithome in Messenia. Finally Rhea was supposed to reside on Mount Thaumasium in Arcadia.

The Hellenic character of Rhea was, however, altered by the influence of the great Phrygian goddess Cybele whose cult was early introduced into Greece; but in the end the two goddesses were merged.

Etymologically Cybele was the goddess of caverns. She personified the earth in its primitive and savage state and was worshipped on the tops of mountains: on Ida in Phrygia, on Berecyntus, Sipyle, Dindymus. She exercised dominion over wild beasts who habitually formed part of her retinue.

Greek representations of Cybele retained an Asiatic character. The goddess with her turreted crown – the normal attribute of Asian mother-goddesses – is seated on a throne flanked by two lions, or else is placed in a chariot drawn by the same animals. Sometimes she holds a whip decorated with knuckle-bones. This attribute, emblem of power, was the instrument with which the *Galli*, priests of Cybele, flagellated themselves.

The Galli were an odd fraternity who celebrated the cult of their goddess with convulsive dances to the sound of flutes, drums and cymbals, while clashing their shields with their swords. In their orgiastic fury they would sometimes voluntarily mutilate themselves. They were known in Greece under the name of the Corybantes and were the issue, it was said, of a certain Corybas, son of Cybele.

Later they were identified with the Cretan Curetes.

With the great Phrygian goddess a god of lesser rank was associated: Attis, whose role in respect to Cybele was analogous to that of Tammuz to the Babylonian Ishtar, or Adonis to the Phoenician Astarte. Like them he was a vegetation god; the Phrygians honoured him under the name *Papas,* the father.

As the cult of Cybele spread through Greece the figure of Attis became modified. He was presented as a young and handsome shepherd from Celaenae with whom Cybele fell in love. She chose him as her priest and imposed upon him a vow of chastity. When Attis broke his vow and espoused the daughter of the river Sangarius, Cybele struck him with frenzied delirium in the course of which he mutilated himself. When he recovered from his madness he was on the point of killing himself when Cybele changed him into a fir-tree. According to another tradition – obviously inspired by the myth of Adonis – Attis perished a victim of the jealousy of Zeus who sent a wild boar against him. The tomb of Attis was at Pessinus, and each year at the beginning of spring his festival was celebrated for five days. The first was a day of mourning when in the midst of lamentation a sacred fir wound with woollen bands was carried through the streets. On the second day the Galli worked themselves into a fever to the sound of savage music. The third day was marked by bloody mutilations. On the fourth day joyful dancing commemorated the resurrection of Attis. Finally the fifth day was devoted to rest.

Cybele became united with the King of Phrygia, Gordius, who had devised the famous Gordian knot. By him she had a son, Midas, who succeeded to his father's throne. He was a wise and pious king who established the cult of the Great Zeus of Ida and instituted the mysteries of Cybele. His kindness to Silenus who, on the banks of the Sangarius one day was drunk and had been tied up by peasants, earned Midas the gratitude of Dionysus. The god asked him to make a wish and Midas asked that everything he touched should be turned into gold. He soon regretted this indiscretion, for even the food he ate immediately turned into gold. Dionysus took pity on him and sent him to purify himself in the river Pactolus, which thenceforth flowed with gold dust.

Midas was less fortunate with Apollo. Asked to arbitrate between Apollo and Marsyas as to which played the lyre or the flute better, Midas voted against Apollo who, as a reward, gave him a pair of ass's ears. Midas was able to hide these ears under his Phrygian cap and his disgrace was known only to his barber. The secret weighed heavily on the poor barber who dug a hole in the ground and confided it to the earth. Now reeds grew in this spot and whenever the wind stirred among them they could be heard to repeat: 'King Midas has ass's ears.' In despair Midas killed himself by drinking, they say, the blood of a bull.

DEMETER

Character and Functions. Gaea and her substitutes, Rhea and Cybele, personified the earth as such, while Demeter represented the fertile and cultivated soil. Of the two elements which compose her name – an alteration or a more ancient form of a word meaning 'earth mother' – the maternal part finally assumed the greater importance among the Greeks.

Without doubt the primitive character of Demeter was preserved in certain regions of Greece, notably in Arcadia where the goddess was represented with a horse's head, surrounded by serpents and ferocious beasts, bearing in one hand a dolphin and in the other a dove. But elsewhere, and particularly in Attica, Demeter appeared above all as a goddess of the fruits and riches of the fields. She was especially the corn-goddess. She presided over the harvest and all the agricultural labours which attend it.

Goddess of the earth, Demeter's sphere of influence also reached the underworld; though her character of underworld divinity soon devolved on a special goddess – Persephone – who was made the daughter of Demeter.

Demeter always remained in contact with mortals whom she heaped with the benefits of civilisation. Thus she was called *Thesmophoros* 'who gives laws', though this title may have been given to her in her capacity of goddess of marriage.

Cult and Representations. Demeter was worshipped in Attica, Arcadia and Argolis, at Delos, in Crete, in Asia Minor and in

Eleusinian divinities. Tripotolemus between Demeter and Kore. Bas-relief of the fifth century B.C. National Museum, Athens.

Sicily. Her cult remained mysterious and was accompanied by orgies. Her temples, called *Megara,* were often found in forests.

It is above all Demeter's maternal aspect that art has accentuated in the various portrayals of the goddess. She appears sometimes seated, sometimes walking, dressed in a long robe and often wearing a veil which covers the back of her head. Sometimes she is crowned with ears of corn or a ribbon, and holds in her hand either a sceptre, ears of corn, or a torch.

Demeter's Suitors. Demeter was a daughter of Cronus and Rhea and thus belonged to the group of the great Olympians. She was of a severe beauty, a beauty scarcely relieved by her hair, which was as fair as ripened grain.

Poseidon coveted her, but Demeter refused herself to him. To escape him she fled to Arcadia where, assuming the shape of a mare, she mingled with the herds of King Oncus. Poseidon, however, succeeded in finding her, changed himself into a stallion and made her the mother of the horse Arion who was endowed with the gift of speech and had the right feet of a man. By Poseidon Demeter also had a daughter whose name has remained concealed and who was known only as the mistress – Despoena. She was particularly honoured in Thessaly.

Demeter was infuriated at the outrage to which Poseidon had submitted her and left Olympus. She took on the aspect of a Fury – thus in Arcadia she was entitled Erinnys – and hid her shame in a cavern. In order to bring her back to Olympus Zeus himself had to intervene. She resumed her place among the Immortals after purifying herself in the waters of the Ladon.

Demeter was also coveted by Zeus whom she resisted in a similar fashion. Zeus, however, deceived her by turning himself into a bull and made her mother of Kore.

But the heart of Demeter was not always untouched by sentiment. It was said that she loved Iasion, 'lay with him in a thrice-ploughed field' and had by him a son, Plutus. According to some Zeus was jealous of Iasion and struck him with a thunderbolt; according to others, he lived for a long time with Demeter and introduced her cult into Sicily.

Demeter and Kore. Demeter, however, was chiefly celebrated for her maternal tribulations. She loved her daughter Kore tenderly. One day Kore was gathering flowers in the fields of Nysa with her companions when she suddenly noticed a narcissus of striking beauty. She ran to pick it, but as she bent down to do so the earth gaped open and Hades appeared. He seized her and dragged her with him down into the depths of the earth. According to another tradition, the abduction of Kore took place on the heights near the town of Enna in Sicily. And in the neighbourhood of Syracuse they showed the place where Hades plunged back into the earth, hollowing out a vast cavity in the process, since filled by waters from the spring of Cyane. Colonus in Attica, Hermione in Argolis, Pheneus in Arcadia and even Crete, likewise claimed for their territory the honour of this divine abduction.

Demeter meanwhile had heard her child's despairing cry for help. 'Then,' says the poet of the Homeric hymn, 'bitter sorrow seized her heart...Over her shoulders she threw a sombre veil and flew like a bird over land and sea, seeking here, seeking there...For nine days the venerable goddess ranged the world, bearing flaming torches in her hands. At last on Hecate's advice, she went to consult the divine Helios who revealed to her the name of her daughter's ravisher. 'No other god is guilty,' he said to her, 'but Zeus himself, who awarded thy daughter to his brother Hades so that he might call her his flowering bride.' This revelation overwhelmed Demeter. In rage and despair she withdrew from Olympus and in the guise of an old woman sought refuge among the cities of men. For long she wandered aimlessly. One day she arrived in Eleusis and sat down to rest near the palace of the wise Celeus, who reigned in that country. The king's daughters saw her and questioned her kindly. Demeter told them that she had been carried off by Cretan pirates who had brought her to these parts where she was a stranger. She was, she added, in search of refuge and would be glad to work as a servant or nurse.

Now it happened that Metaneira, the wife of Celeus, had just been delivered of a son, Demophoön. Metaneira, therefore, welcomed the goddess under her roof; but when Demeter crossed the threshold her head brushed the rafters and from her emanated a divine radiance. Metaneira was filled with respect and offered her her own seat. But Demeter remained standing and silent, her eyes fixed on the ground, refusing food and drink; for longing for her flower-girdled daughter consumed her. Finally young Iambe who, though she was the daughter of Pan and Echo, served as a slave in Celeus' palace – and to whom was attributed the invention of iambic verse – succeeded in cheering up Demeter with her buffoonery. She persuaded Demeter to drink a little *kykeon,* a beverage made of water, flour and mint.

Later legend substituted Baubo for Iambe. Baubo was upset when Demeter refused the drink she offered her and made an obscene gesture at which the goddess, in spite of herself, laughed.

Demeter was put in charge of bringing up the infant Demophoön. She gave him nothing to eat, but instead breathed softly on him, anointed him with ambrosia and at night hid him in the fire, like a burning coal, in order to destroy all that was mortal in him. Thus, to the amazement of his parents, the child grew like a god. Intrigued by this prodigy Metaneira spied on the nurse and caught her just as she was placing the little boy in the middle of the flames. Metaneira screamed with terror. Incensed, the goddess withdrew Demophoön from the fire and put him on the ground. 'Had it not been for your imprudence,' she said to his mother, 'I should have put this child forever beyond the reach of old age and death; but now it is no longer possible for me to shelter him from death.' Then she appeared before the wife of Celeus in her divine form. She revealed her name and ordered that a temple be erected for her in Eleusis where the initiated should celebrate her mysteries. Then she went forth from the palace.

Before departing, however, she wished to show her gratitude to her hosts; she gave Triptolemus, Celeus' oldest son, the first grain of corn, and taught him the art of harnessing oxen to the plough and how to sow the soil with grain from which would spring fair harvests. She gave him as well a winged chariot harnessed with dragons, and bade him travel the world spreading the benefits of agriculture among all men. Thus Triptolemus ranged all Greece, taught Arcas, King of Arcadia, how to make bread, and in Arcadia founded many towns. He also visited Thrace, Sicily and Scythia where King Lyncus tried to murder him while he was asleep and was changed by Demeter into a lynx. He visited Mysia where the King of the Getae, Carnabon, tried in vain to harm him, and finally returned to Eleusis. There Celeus plotted to have him slain, but was prevented by Demeter. Celeus was then forced to resign the throne to Triptolemus.

It should be pointed out that originally no bond of relationship united Celeus and Triptolemus who in the Homeric hymn is merely described as one of the kings who were guardians of justice. Very much later Triptolemus was identified with Demophoön and attributed with the marvellous adventure in infancy of which Demophoön was originally the hero.

Demeter's stay at Eleusis was the chief episode in the course of her wanderings on earth, but she also stayed with Pelasgus in Argos. She visited Phytalus to whom she gave the olive tree. She was received in Attica by Misme whose son Ascalabos made Demeter the butt of his jokes and was punished by being turned into a lizard.

Still inconsolable at the loss of her daughter, Demeter retired to her temple at Eleusis. There 'she prepared for mankind a cruel terrible year: the earth refused to give forth any crop. Then would the entire human race have perished of cruel, biting hunger if Zeus had not been concerned.' He hastened to send his messenger Iris to Demeter, but without success. Then all the gods came one by one to supplicate the implacable goddess. She stated flatly that she would not permit the earth to bear fruit unless she saw her daughter again. There was no solution except to give in. Zeus commanded Hermes to descend into the kingdom of Hades and obtain Hades' promise to return young Kore – who since her arrival in the underworld had taken the name Persephone – to her mother. Hades complied with the will of Zeus, but before sending his wife up to earth tempted her to eat a few pomegranate seeds. Now this fruit was a symbol of marriage and the effect of eating it was to render the union of man and wife indissoluble.

When Kore returned to the world of light her mother hastened to her and embraced her with transports of joy. 'My daughter,' she cried, 'surely thou hast eaten nothing during your imprisonment in the dark regions of Hades! For if thou hast not eaten thou shalt

718

Dionysus, holding in one hand the thyrsus and in the other a cantharus. The god is portrayed as an ephebe. Bas-relief from Herculaneum. National Museum, Naples.

The Nymph Leucothea (Ino) gives the infant Dionysus a drink from the Horn of Plenty. Antique bas-relief. Lateran Museum, Rome.

live with me on Olympus. But if thou hast, then must thou return to the depths of the earth!' Kore admitted that she had tasted of the fatal pomegranate. It seemed that Demeter was again to lose her daughter.

As a compromise Zeus decided that Persephone should live with her husband for one-third of the year and pass the other two-thirds with her mother. The august Rhea herself brought this proposal to Demeter who agreed to it. She set aside her anger and bade the soil again be fertile. The vast earth was soon covered with leaves and flowers. Before she returned to Olympus, Demeter taught the kings of the earth her divine science and initiated them into her sacred mysteries.

And thus they explained why each year when the cold season arrived the earth took on an aspect of sadness and mourning: no more verdure, nor flowers in the fields, nor leaves on the trees. Hidden in the bowels of the ground the seeds slept their winter sleep. It was the moment when Persephone went to join her husband among the deep shadows. But when sweet-scented spring came the earth put on its mantle of a thousand flowers to greet the return of Kore, who rose in radiance, 'a wondrous sight for gods and men'.

The Eleusinian Mysteries. This double event – the disappearance and return of Kore – was the occasion of great festivals in Greece. In the *Thesmophoria* which were celebrated in Attica in the month of October, the departure of Kore for the sombre dwelling was commemorated. According to Herodotus the origin of these festivals went back to the daughters of Danaus who imported them from Egypt. They were exclusively reserved for married women and lasted three days.

The return of Kore was celebrated in the *Lesser Eleusinia*, which took place in the month of February.

As for the *Greater Eleusinia*, which took place every five years in September, it seems that they had no direct connection with the story of Kore. It was a solemn festival – the greatest festival of Greece – in honour of Demeter, and its principal object was the celebration of the mysteries of the goddess. The scene of the Greater Eleusinia was Athens and Eleusis.

On the first day the *ephebi* (youths) of Athens would go to Eleusis to fetch the sacred objects (*hiera*) kept in the temple of Demeter, and bring them back with great pomp to Athens where they were placed in the Eleusinion, at the foot of the Acropolis. The following day the faithful (*mystae*) who were judged to be worthy of participating in the mysteries would assemble in Athens at the call of the hierophant. Afterwards they would go to purify themselves in the sea, taking with them pigs which were bathed and then sacrificed. Finally the solemn procession towards Eleusis took place and the *hiera* were returned with the same ceremonial as before. At the head of the procession was carried the statue of Iacchus, a mystic name for Dionysus who was early associated with the cult of Demeter.

In Eleusis the actual mysteries themselves were then celebrated. Only the initiated could participate and they were forbidden to divulge what occurred. Initiation comprised two stages; the second, the *epoptae*, could only be undertaken after a year's probation.

As far as one can conjecture, the *mystae*, after drinking the *kykeon* and eating the sacred cakes, entered the *Telesterion*, where they attended a liturgical drama concerning the abduction of Kore. The *epoptae* – or those belonging to the highest grade – attended another liturgical drama the subject of which was the union of Demeter and Zeus, and of which the priestess of Demeter and the hierophant were the protagonists.

It is not easy to understand the exact meaning of these mysteries. They were, however, probably more than a simple commemoration of the legend of Demeter and must also have had to do with the problem of future life, the revelation of which the initiated awaited from the goddess.

DIONYSUS

Character and Functions. Dionysus is etymologically the 'Zeus of Nysa' and seems, by several similarities of legend and function, to be the Greek form of the Vedic god *Soma*. The cradle of his cult was Thrace. It was brought to Boeotia by Thracian tribes, who established themselves in that country, and was afterwards introduced to the island of Naxos by Boeotian colonists. The cult

Votive relief from Eleusis showing Persephone pouring water on an initiate. It was from Eleusis, according to the priests of Demeter, that the goddess' daughter Persephone, or Kore, was abducted by Hades and carried off to the Underworld and it was here that Demeter had her great sanctuary where mother and daughter were worshipped conjointly and where their Mysteries were celebrated. Only the initiated were allowed to take part in these.

of Dionysus spread throughout the islands, whence it returned to continental Greece, first to Attica, then later to the Peloponnese.

The figure of the primitive Dionysus is complicated by traits borrowed from other and foreign gods, notably the Cretan god Zagreus, the Phrygian god Sabazius, and the Lydian god Bassareus. Thus his sphere of influence widened as his character became enriched with fresh contributions. In origin Dionysus was simply the god of wine; afterwards he became god of vegetation and warm moisture; then he appeared as the god of pleasures and the god of civilisation; and finally, according to Orphic conceptions, as a kind of supreme god.

Cult and Representations. Dionysus was honoured throughout Greece; but the character of the festivals which were dedicated to him varied with regions and epochs.

One of the most ancient festivals was that of the *Agrionia*, first celebrated in Boeotia, especially at Orchomenus: the Bacchantes immolated a young boy. Human sacrifice was also practised at Chios and at Lesbos; it was later replaced by flagellation. In Attica, they celebrated rural *Dionysia*: in December the *Lenaea*, festival of the wine press, when the god was offered the new wine; at the

Demeter and Persephone. This votive relief from Eleusis shows Persephone's return to her mother in the springtime after her winter's sojourn in the Underworld. The corn goddess is seated on the left grasping her staff in one hand and with her attribute – three ears of corn – in the other while her daughter stands before her holding two flaming torches. It seems probable that Persephone was originally merely another aspect of Demeter. Fifth century B.C.

end of February the *Anthesteria*, floral festivals which lasted three days, during which wine of the last vintage was tasted. In the sanctuary of Lenoeon there was a procession followed by a sacrifice offered by the wife of the archon-king, and finally boiled seed was offered to Dionysus and Hermes. The most brilliant festivals were the *Greater Dionysia*, or urban Dionysia, at the beginning of March. It was during these festivals that dramatic representations were given. In addition to those dignified ceremonies all Greece celebrated festivals of orgiastic character as well, such as those which took place on the slopes of Mount Cithaeron.

The appearance of Dionysus altered at the same time as his legend. He was first depicted as a bearded man, of mature age, with brow generally crowned with ivy. Later he appears as a beardless youth of rather effeminate aspect. Sometimes the delicate nudity of his adolescent body is half-covered by the *nebris,* a skin of a panther or fawn; sometimes he wears a long robe such as women wore. His head with its long curly hair is crowned with vine leaves and bunches of grapes. In one hand he holds the *thyrsus,* and in the other, grapes or a wine cup.

The Birth and Childhood of Dionysus. When the earth has been made fertile by life-giving rains it must, in order that its products may reach maturity, endure the bite of the sun which burns and dries it up. Only then do its fruits develop and the golden grapes appear on the knotty vine. This seems to be the meaning of the myth of Semele who was normally considered to be the mother of Dionysus.

Semele, daughter of Cadmus, King of Thebes, was seen by Zeus and yielded to him. Zeus would come to her father's palace to visit her. One day, at the suggestion of the treacherous Hera who had assumed the guise of her nurse, Semele begged Zeus to show himself to her in his Olympian majesty. She was unable to endure the dazzling brilliance of her divine lover and was consumed by the flames which emanated from Zeus' person. The child she carried in her womb would also have perished had not a thick shoot of ivy suddenly wound around the columns of the palace and made a green screen between the unborn babe and the celestial fire. Zeus gathered up the infant and, as it was not yet ready to be born, enclosed it in his own thigh. When the time was come he drew it forth again, with the aid of Ilithyia, and it is to this double birth that Dionysus owed the title *Dithyrambos.*

Zeus confided his son to Ino, sister of Semele, who lived at Orchomenus with her husband Athamas.

Such was the commonest version of the story. It was also related that Cadmus, learning of the guilty liaison of his daughter Semele, had her shut up in a chest and thrown into the sea. The chest was carried by the waves as far as the shores of Prasiae in the Peloponnese; when it was opened Semele was dead, but the child was still alive. He was cared for by Ino.

Hera's jealous vengeance was unappeased and she struck Ino and Athamas with madness. Zeus succeeded in saving his child for the second time by changing him into a kid whom he ordered Hermes to deliver into the hands of the nymphs of Nysa.

Where was Nysa? Was it a mountain in Thrace? One seeks its precise situation in vain; for every region where the cult of Dionysus was established boasted of having a Nysa.

Dionysus, then, passed his childhood on this fabled mountain, cared for by the nymphs whose zeal was later recompensed: for they were changed into a constellation under the name of the Hyades. The Muses also contributed to the education of Dionysus, as did the Satyrs, the Sileni and the Maenads. In Euboea, according to tradition, Dionysus was confided by Hermes to Macris, the

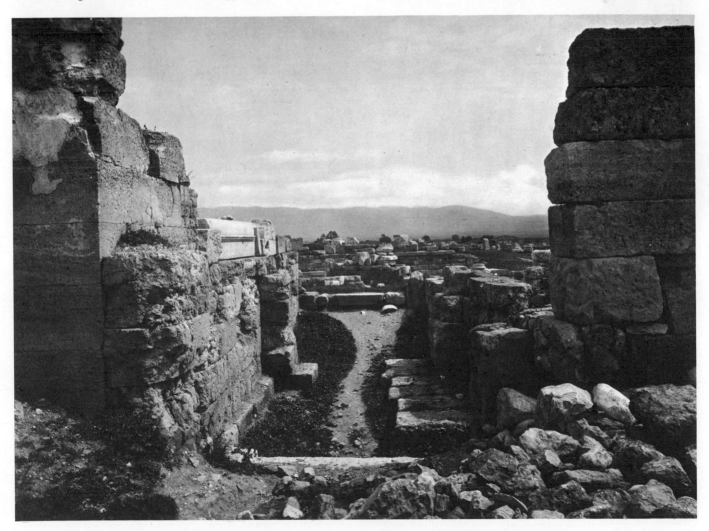

The wall surrounding the sacred precinct at Eleusis. Some fourteen miles west of Athens, Eleusis was the home of the most holy rites of the Greek religion until the end of the pagan period. Its sacred precinct was filled with altars and inscriptions while within it stood the great hypostyle hall called the Telesterion in which the mysteries of Demeter and Persephone were celebrated. The sacred buildings were destroyed by Alaric in A.D. 396.

Persephone and Hades. Condemned by Zeus to spend a third of each year in the Underworld with her husband Hades after eating the fatal pomegranate seeds, the symbol of marriage, Persephone is shown here seated at the foot of her husband's couch while he reclines upon it clasping a cornucopia or horn of plenty. Feared as the god of the Underworld, Hades was more widely venerated as Pluto, the god of riches.

daughter of Aristaeus, who then nourished him with honey.

With his head crowned by ivy and laurel the young god wandered the mountains and forests with the nymphs, making the glades echo with his joyful shouts. In the meanwhile old Silenus taught his young mind the meaning of virtue and inspired him with the love of glory. When he had grown up Dionysus discovered the fruit of the vine and the art of making wine from it. Doubtless he drank of the wine without moderation at first, for they said Hera had stricken him with madness. But the disease was short-lived. To cure himself Dionysus went to Dodona to consult the oracle. On the way he came to a marsh which he crossed by mounting an ass. To reward the animal he bestowed on it the gift of speech. When he was cured Dionysus undertook long journeys across the world in order to spread the inestimable gift of wine among mortals. Marvellous adventures marked his passage through the countries he visited.

The Travels of Dionysus. Coming from the mountains of Thrace he crossed Boeotia and entered Attica. In Attica he was welcomed by the king, Icarius, to whom he presented a vine-stock. Icarius had the imprudence to give his shepherds wine to drink; as they grew intoxicated they thought they were being poisoned and slew him. The daughter of Icarius, Erigone, set out to look for her father and, thanks to her dog Maera, at last discovered his tomb. In despair she hanged herself from a nearby tree. In punishment for this death Dionysus struck the women of Attica with raving madness. Icarius was carried to the heavens with his daughter and her faithful dog. They were changed into constellations and became the Waggoner, Virgo and the Lesser Dog Star.

In Aetolia Dionysus was received by Oeneus, King of Calydon, and fell in love with Althaea, his host's wife. Oeneus pretended not to notice and the god rewarded his discretion by giving him a vine-stock. From the fleeting union of Dionysus and Althaea was born Deianeira.

In Laconia Dionysus was the guest of King Dion who had three daughters. Dionysus fell in love with the youngest, Carya. Her two older sisters threatened to expose the affair by warning their father. Dionysus struck them with madness, then changed them into rocks. As for Carya, it was her fate to be turned into a walnut tree.

After continental Greece Dionysus visited the islands of the Archipelago. It was in the course of this voyage that the god, walking one day by the seashore, was abducted by Tyrrhenian pirates and carried aboard their ship. They took him for the son of a king and expected a rich ransom. They tried to tie him up with heavy cords, but in vain. The knots loosened of their own accord and the bonds fell to the deck. The pilot, terrified, had a presentiment that their captive was divine and attempted to make his companions release him. The pirates refused. Then occurred a series of prodigies. Around the dark ship flowed wine, fragrant and delicious. A vine attached its branches to the sail, while around the mast ivy wound its dark green leaves. The god himself became a lion of fearful aspect. In horror the sailors leapt into the sea and were immediately changed into dolphins. Only the pilot was spared by Dionysus.

On the isle of Naxos Dionysus one day perceived a young woman lying asleep on the shore. It was the daughter of Minos, Ariadne, whom Theseus had brought with him from Crete and just abandoned. When she awoke Ariadne realised that Theseus had left her and gave way to uncontrollable tears. The arrival of Dionysus consoled her and shortly afterwards they were solemnly married. The gods came to the wedding and showered gifts on the couple. Dionysus and Ariadne had three sons: Oenopion, Euanthes and Staphylus. The Homeric tradition has a different version of the Ariadne episode. Ariadne was supposed to have been killed by Artemis and it was only after her death that Dionysus married her. In Naxos they showed the tomb of Ariadne and in her honour two festivals were celebrated: one mournful, bewailing her death; the other joyful, commemorating her marriage to Dionysus.

The travels and adventures of Dionysus were not limited to the Greek world. Accompanied by his retinue of Satyrs and Maenads he went to Phrygia, where Cybele initiated him into her mysteries. At Ephesus in Cappadocia he repulsed the Amazons. In Syria he fought against Damascus who destroyed the vines which the god had planted and was punished by being skinned alive. Then he went into the Lebanon to pay a visit to Aphrodite and Adonis whose daughter, Beroë, he loved. After having reigned for some time over Caucasian Iberia, Dionysus continued his journey towards the East, crossing the Tigris on a tiger sent by Zeus, joined the two banks of the Euphrates by a cable made of vine-shoots and ivy-tendrils, and reached India where he spread civilisation. We also find him in Egypt where he was received by King Proteus; and in Libya where he helped Ammon to reconquer his throne from which he had been deposed by Cronus and the Titans.

After these glorious expeditions Dionysus returned to Greece. He was no longer the rather rustic god recently come down from the mountains of Boeotia. His contact with Asia had made him soft and effeminate: he now appeared in the guise of a graceful adolescent, dressed in a long robe in the Lydian fashion. His cult became complicated by orgiastic rites borrowed from Phrygia. Thus he was received in Greece with distrust, sometimes even with hostility.

When he returned to Thrace, notably, the king of that country, Lycurgus, declared against him. Dionysus was obliged to flee and seek refuge with Thetis, in the depths of the sea. Meanwhile, Lycurgus imprisoned the Bacchantes who followed the god, and Dionysus struck the country with sterility, depriving Lycurgus of his reason. In his madness Lycurgus killed his own son, Dryas, whom he mistook for a vine-stock. The desolation of Thrace did not cease until the oracle ordered that Lycurgus be conducted to Mount Pangaeum where he was trampled to death under the hooves of wild horses.

Dionysus was no better received by Pentheus, King of Thebes, who threw the god into prison. Dionysus escaped without trouble and struck Agave, the mother of Pentheus, as well as the other women of Thebes, with madness. They were transformed into Maenads and rushed to Mount Cithaeron where they held Dionysian orgies. Pentheus had the imprudence to follow them and was torn to pieces by his own mother. This terrible drama forms the subject of Euripides' *Bacchae*.

A similar tragedy overtook the inhabitants of Argos who had also refused to recognise the divinity of Dionysus: the women, driven out of their minds, tore up and devoured their own children.

Among the chastisements which Dionysus inflicted, one of the most famous concerned the daughters of Minyas, King of Orchomenus. They were three sisters: Alcithoë, Leucippe and Arsippe.

Pan Teaching Olympus to play the syrinx. National Museum, Naples.

Since they refused to take part in the festivals of Dionysus, he visited them in the guise of a young maiden and tried to persuade them by gentleness. Being unsuccessful, he turned himself successively into a bull, a lion and a panther. Terrified by these prodigies, the daughters of Minyas lost their reason and one of them, Leucippe, tore her son Hippasus to pieces with her own hands. Finally they underwent metamorphosis: the first became a mouse, the second a screech-owl, the third an owl.

Thenceforth no one any longer dreamed of denying the divinity of Dionysus or of rejecting his cult.

The god crowned his exploits by descending into the infernal regions in search of his mother, Semele. He renamed her Thyone and brought her with him to Olympus among the Immortals. At Troezen, in the temple of Artemis Soteira, they showed the exact place where Dionysus had returned from his subterranean expedition. According to the tradition of Argos the route to the underworld had been shown to the god by a citizen of Argos, one Polymnus, and Dionysus had come up again via the sea of Alcyon.

On Olympus Dionysus took part in the struggle against the Giants; the braying of the ass on which he rode terrified the Giants and Dionysus killed Eurytus or Rhatos with his *thyrsus*.

Foreign Divinities Assimilated by Dionysus. The exuberance of the legends of Dionysus is explained not only by his great popularity but also because the personality of Dionysus absorbed, as we have already said, that of several foreign gods, notably the Phrygian Sabazius, the Lydian Bassareus and the Cretan Zagreus.

Sabazius, who was venerated as the supreme god in the Thracian Hellespont, was a solar-divinity of Phrygian origin. Traditions concerning him were very diverse. Sometimes he was the son of Cronus, sometimes of Cybele whose companion he became. His wife was either the moon-goddess Bendis or Cotys (or Cottyto), an earth-goddess analogous to the Phrygian Cybele. Sabazius was represented with horns and his emblem was the serpent. The *Sabazia* were celebrated in his honour – nocturnal festivals of orgiastic character.

When Sabazius was later assimilated by Dionysus their legends became amalgamated. Some said that Sabazius had kept Dionysus enclosed in his thigh before confiding him to the nymph Hippa; others claimed on the contrary that Sabazius was the son of Dionysus. It was in consequence of such confusions that Dionysus was finally supposed to have come from the Thracian Hellespont.

Sometimes the Bacchantes were called *Bassarids* and Dionysus himself had the epithet *Bassareus,* in which case he was represented wearing a long robe in the Oriental fashion. The lexicographer Hesychius considered this to be a reference to the fox-skins which the Bacchantes wore; but it would rather seem to be an allusion to an Oriental divinity absorbed by Dionysus. Indeed, in Lydia a god similar to the Phrygian Sabazius was venerated. The place of his cult was Mount Tmolus where, according to Orphic-Thracian legend, Sabazius delivered the infant Dionysus to Hippa. Tmolus actually became one of the favourite haunts of Dionysus. What was the name of the Lydian god? It has been conjectured that his name was Bassareus. He was doubtless a conquering god and to him may be attributed the origin of Dionysus' distant conquests. Bassareus could also explain the visit of Dionysus to Aphrodite and Adonis, and perhaps also the legend of Ampelus, a youth of rare beauty whom Dionysus cherished with particular affection. One day when he was attempting to master a wild bull Ampelus was tossed and killed by the animal. Dionysus was heartbroken and obtained the gods' permission to change Ampelus into a vine.

The identification of Dionysus with the Cretan god, Zagreus, who was very probably in origin the equivalent of the Hellenic Zeus,

introduced – under the influence of Orphic mysticism – a new element into the legend of the god, that of the Passion of Dionysus.

This is what they said of Dionysus-Zagreus:

He was the son of Zeus and Demeter – or of Kore. The other gods were jealous of him and resolved to slay him. He was torn into pieces by the Titans who threw the remains of his body into a cauldron. Pallas Athene, however, was able to rescue the god's heart. She took it at once to Zeus who struck the Titans with thunderbolts and, with the still beating heart, created Dionysus. As for Zagreus, whose remains had been buried at the foot of Parnassus, he became an underworld divinity who in Hades welcomed the souls of the dead and helped with their purification.

On these sufferings and resurrection the adepts of Orphism conferred a mystic sense, and the character of Dionysus underwent profound modification. He was no longer the rustic god of wine and jollity, formerly come down the mountains of Thrace; he was no longer even the god of orgiastic delirium, come from the Orient. Henceforth Dionysus – in Plutarch's words – 'the god who is destroyed, who disappears, who relinquishes life and then is born again', became the symbol of everlasting life.

Thus it is not surprising to see Dionysus associated with Demeter and Kore in the Eleusinian mysteries. For he, too, represented one of the great life-bringing forces of the world.

THE RETINUE OF DIONYSUS: RURAL DIVINITIES

From early times in Greece the vintage festivals were occasions for joyful processions in which priests and the faithful, men and women, of the cult of Dionysus took part. These devotees were called Bacchants and Bacchantes or Maenads. It was the habit to provide the god with a cortège or *thiasus* composed of secondary divinities more or less closely bound up with his cult: Satyrs, Sileni, Pans, Priapi, Centaurs, Nymphs.

Satyrs and Sileni. The Satyrs represented the elementary spirits of the forests and the mountains. They were a kind of wood-genii whose sudden appearance would terrify shepherds and travellers. There was something about them of both monkey and he-goat with their low forehead, their snub nose, their pointed ears, their hairy body ending in a goat's tail, their cloven hooves. Such at least was their primitive aspect; later traces of the beast which at first do-

Dionysus, Pan and a Bacchante. Antique bas-relief. National Museum, Naples.

minated survived only in their pointed ears and the small horns on their brow, while their features took on an expression of youth and gentleness. Their character also altered. According to Hesiod the Satyrs were originally a lazy and useless race who loved only pleasure and good cheer. Sensual and lascivious, they delighted in chasing the nymphs through the forests. Later, although they preserved their malicious nature, they acquired more grace and specialised in the pleasures of music and the dance. They were thought to be brothers of the nymphs and the Curetes. Another tradition relates that they were originally men, sons of Hermes and Iphthima, but that Hera turned them into monkeys to punish them for neglecting to keep watch on Dionysus. They were, however, faithful companions of the god and played the principal role in his orgiastic festivals.

One of the most picturesque figures in the retinue of Dionysus was Silenus, a fat old man, bald, snub-nosed, always drunk, who followed the god sometimes supported by Satyrs, sometimes swaying precariously on an ass. Nevertheless this cheerful drunkard was full of wisdom. He had been the tutor of Dionysus and had helped to form his character. His knowledge was immense, he knew both the past and the future, and could reveal the destiny of anyone who succeeded in tying him up during the heavy slumber which followed his drinking-bouts. Plato felt no irreverence in comparing his master Socrates with Silenus. Silenus was, it appears, the son of Hermes and the Earth. Others say that he was born of the blood of Uranus after Cronus had mutilated him. Pindar says his wife was Nais.

In reality the name Silenus is a generic term which applies to a category of rural divinities, rather similar to the Satyrs and often confused with them. The Sileni were native not to Greece, but to Phrygia, and personified the genii of springs and rivers. Their name seems to mean 'water which bubbles as it flows' and their fluvial character is evident from certain peculiarities of their bodies: unlike the Satyrs who derive chiefly from the he-goat, the Sileni derive rather from the horse – a water symbol – whose tail, hooves, and even ears they possess. Marsyas, who is generally made a Satyr, was in reality a Silenus and, at the same time, a river-god of Phrygia. That was why the Phrygian Midas – whose legend is closely connected with that of the Sileni – voted for Marsyas in the famous music contest with Apollo.

Pan, Aristaeus, Priapus. Another divinity later incorporated in the retinue of Dionysus, and often confused with the Satyrs because of his physical resemblance to them, was the god Pan, whose cult was for long localised in Arcadia. Hence he was made the son of Hermes, the great Arcadian god. His mother was either the daughter of King Dryops, whose flocks Hermes had tended, or Penelope, whom he had approached in the form of a he-goat. Pan himself came into the world with the legs, horns and beard of a goat.

Various etymologies have been proposed for the name Pan. The Homeric hymn connects it with the adjective which means 'all' under the pretext that the sight of Pan on Olympus amused *all* the Immortals. The same etymology was invoked by the mythologists of the school of Alexandria who considered Pan to be the symbol of the Universe. Max Muller found a connection between Pan and the Sanskrit *pavana*, the wind, and believed that Pan was the personification of the light breeze. In our opinion, however, it seems more likely that the name comes from the root which means 'to eat' which gave the Latins the verb *pascere*, 'to graze or pasture'. Pan, indeed, was above all a shepherd-god, of woods and pastures, protector of shepherds and flocks. He lived on the slopes of Mount Maenalus or Mount Lycaeus, in grottoes where the Arcadian shepherds came to worship him. He made their goats and ewes prolific – whence his aspect of a phallic divinity – and caused wild beasts to be killed by hunters; when the hunt was unsuccessful they would whip his image by way of reprisal. Pan himself delighted in roving the forests, frisking with the nymphs whom he sometimes terrified with his appearance. One day he was chasing the nymph Syrinx and had nearly caught her when she cried aloud to her father, the river-god Ladon, to change her into a reed. Her prayer was granted. Pan consoled himself for his disappointment by cutting some reeds with which he made a flute of a new sort, giving it the name Syrinx, or Pan-pipes. He was more successful with the nymph Pitys who preferred him to Boreas. Boreas, the bitter North Wind, was enraged and flung himself on

Pitys, throwing her against a rock where her limbs were crushed. In pity Gaea transformed her into a pine. It was told that Pan succeeded in seducing the moon-goddess Selene; he disguised himself in the fleece of a dazzling white ewe and drew her into the forest with him, or he himself assumed the shape of a white ram.

For long he was confined to the mountains of Arcadia where he amused himself by giving the lonely traveller sudden frights, called for this reason panics. He penetrated into Attica only at the time of the Persian wars. Shortly before the battle of Marathon he appeared to the ambassadors whom the Athenians had sent to Sparta and promised to put the Persians to flight if the Athenians consented to worship him in Athens. In gratitude they erected a sanctuary for him on the Acropolis and from there the cult of Pan spread throughout Greece.

We have said that Pan finally symbolised the universal god, the Great All. In this connection Plutarch recounts how in the reign of Tiberius a mariner sailing near the Echinades Islands heard a mysterious voice call out to him three times, saying: 'when you reach Palodes proclaim that the great god Pan is dead.' This was at the exact time that Christianity was born in Judea. The coincidence has always seemed strange; but Reinach has demonstrated that the sailor simply heard the ritual lamentations in honour of Adonis.

Every region in Greece had its own Pan. That of Thessaly was called Aristaeus. Without doubt this Aristaeus was a great primitive deity of this land, for his name means 'the very good', which was also the epithet of Zeus in Arcadia. Moreover Pindar says that 'Aristaeus was carried after his birth by Hermes to Gaea and the Horae who fed him on nectar and ambrosia, and transformed him into Zeus, the immortal god, and into Apollo, the pure, the guardian of flocks and the chase and pasturage.' According to legend Aristaeus was the son of Uranus and Gaea or of Apollo and Cyrene. He was brought up by the Centaur Chiron and instructed in the arts of medicine and soothsaying. He was considered as the protector of flocks and agriculture, particularly of the vine and olive. It was he who taught men bee-keeping.

His civilising influence was felt throughout Greece. In Boeotia he married the daughter of Cadmus, Autonoë, by whom he had a son, Actaeon. During his stay in Thrace he fell in love with Eurydice, the wife of Orpheus. It was in fleeing from Aristaeus that she was mortally bitten by a serpent. The end of Aristaeus was mysterious; he vanished from the earth on Mount Haemus.

The Pan of Mysia, in Asia Minor, was Priapus. He was particularly venerated at Lampsacus. His orgin is rather vague. His mother was said to be Aphrodite or Chione and his father Dionysus, Adonis, Hermes or Pan.

It was told that Hera, jealous of Aphrodite, caused him to be born with the extraordinary deformity to which he owes his name. His mother abandoned him and he was taken in by shepherds. Priapus presided over the fecundity of fields and flocks, over the raising of bees, the culture of the vine and over fishing. He protected orchards and gardens where his phallic image was placed. He was evidently introduced into the retinue of Dionysus by way of Asia.

The Centaurs. In addition to the Satyrs and the Sileni another kind of monstrous creature formed part of the cortège of Dionysus: the Centaurs. Their torso and head were those of a man; the rest of their body belonged to a horse. They had not always been like this: the first representations of Centaurs show them as giants with hairy bodies; then they were depicted as men with the hindquarters of a horse. Their definitive appearance goes no farther back than the period of Phidias.

Natives of Thessaly, the Centaurs were descendants of Ixion, son of Ares. Ixion was engaged to marry Dia, daughter of Eioneus. There was a dispute between Ixion and his future father-in-law and Ixion threw him into a burning ditch. This crime earned universal reprobation and Ixion was forced to seek refuge with Zeus who offered him hospitality. But Ixion had the audacity to covet Zeus' own wife, Hera. In order to test how far his impudence would go, Zeus formed a cloud into the likeness of Hera and gave it to Ixion. From this strange union was born a monster, Centaurus, who, himself uniting with the mares of Pelion, fathered the race of the Centaurs.

Some have interpreted all this as a Hellenic equivalent of the Vedic Gandharvas. But it is more likely that the Centaurs – whose name etymologically signifies 'those who round up bulls' – were a primitive population of cowmen, living in Thessaly, who, like American cowboys, rounded up their cattle on horseback. Their behaviour was rude and barbarous, whence the savagery which was always attributed to the Centaurs – gross creatures, cruel, and given to lechery and drunkenness.

Some of their number were, however, famed for their wisdom. Such was Pholus who entertained Hercules. Such, especially, was Chiron who was educated by Artemis and Apollo themselves, and who in his turn was the teacher of many heroes. He perished in consequence of a wound made by Hercules with a poisoned arrow. The wound was incurable and Chiron exchanged his immortality for the mortality of Prometheus. Zeus placed him among the stars where he became part of the constellation Sagittarius.

The chief episode in the legend of the Centaurs was their battle with the Lapiths on the occasion of the nuptials of Peirithous. The Lapiths were also a fabulous people from Thessaly. Their king, Peirithous, was marrying Hippodameia and had invited the Centaur Eurytion to the festivities. Excited by the wine Eurytion attempted to abduct the bride, but was prevented from doing so by Theseus. Eurytion returned to the attack with a troop of Centaurs armed with slabs of stone and the trunks of pine trees. A general battle took place from which the Lapiths at last emerged victorious, thanks to the courage of Theseus and Peirithous. The Centaurs were driven to the frontiers of Epirus and took refuge on the slopes of Mount Pindus.

The Nymphs. Among these graceless and brutal divinities the nymphs were conspicuous for the charm of their youth and beauty. The nymphs of Dionysus' retinue were in all points similar to their sisters who peopled the rivers and springs. Like the nymphs also found in the retinue of Artemis and Apollo they were tutelary deities of the forests and mountains. Their names varied according to their place of abode. The Oreads were nymphs of the mountains and the grottoes. The Napaeae, the Auloniads, the Hylaeorae and the Alsaeids haunted the woods and valleys. Only the Dryads, forest nymphs responsible for trees, never mingled with divine processions. Crowned with oak-leaves, sometimes armed with an axe to punish outrages against the trees which they guarded, they would dance around the oaks which were sacred to them. Certain of their number, the Hamadryads, were still more closely united with trees of which, it was said, they formed an integral part.

Among the nymphs who followed Hera there was an Oread named Echo who, every time that Zeus paid court to some nymph, would distract Hera's attention with her chattering and singing. When Hera discovered this she deprived Echo of the gift of speech, condemning her to repeat only the last syllable of words spoken in her presence. Now shortly afterwards Echo fell in love with a young Thespian named Narcissus. Unable to declare her love she was spurned by him and went to hide her grief in solitary caverns. She died of a broken heart, her bones turned into stone, and all that was left of her was the echo of her vioce. Her unhappy end was also attributed to the wrath of Pan who was unable to win her love and had her torn to pieces by shepherds. Gaea received her mortal remains but even in death she retained her voice.

As for Narcissus, the gods punished him for having spurned Echo by making him fall in love with his own image. The soothsayer Teiresias had predicted that Narcissus would live only until the moment he saw himself. One day when he was leaning over the limpid waters of a fountain Narcissus caught sight of his own reflection in the water. He conceived so lively a passion for this phantom that nothing could tear him away from it, and he died there

Votive relief to Asclepius. The faithful come to beseech the god's aid. With him are his wife Epione, his sons Machaon and Podaleirius, and his daughters Hygieia, Aegle and Panacea. National Museum, Athens.

of languor. He was changed into the flower which bears his name and which grows at the edge of springs.

Another victim of the nymphs was the handsome Sicilian herdsman Daphnis. Daphnis was the son of Hermes and a nymph. He was abandoned by his mother and taken in by shepherds whose daily life he shared at the foot of Etna. He was loved by a nymph, Echenais, Xenaea or Lyce, who made him swear eternal fidelity to her under pain of going blind. Intoxicated by the princess Chimaera, Daphnis broke his vow and at once lost his sight. He tried to console himself with poetry and music; he was called the inventor of pastoral poetry. He killed himself one day by falling from the top of a cliff.

THE LIFE OF MAN

Zeus, sovereign lord of mortals, did not rule directly over their fate. He delegated this task to secondary divinities who accompanied men throughout their physical and moral life.

DIVINITIES OF BIRTH AND HEALTH

Ilithyia. In primitive times there were two Ilithyias, daughters of Hera, who presided over birth and brought to women in labour both pain – the keen arrows of the Ilithyias – and deliverance. No child could be born unless they were present, no mother could find relief without them. Thus, when Apollo was born, the jealous Hera detained Ilithyia on Olympus for nine days and nine nights when she had been on the point of going to the aid of Leto. Hera repeated this manoeuvre when Alcmene was about to give birth to Hercules.

The two Ilithyias finally merged into a single person, the goddess of childbirth. She was, in fact, a very ancient divinity believed to have originated in Crete. She is most often depicted kneeling, a position which was believed to aid delivery, and carrying a torch, symbol of light, while with her other hand she makes a gesture of encouragement.

Certain goddesses known to be particularly concerned with women were sometimes given the epithet Ilithyia: Hera at Argos, for instance, and Artemis at Delos. It may even be asked if Ilithyia is not simply a double of Hera's.

Asclepius. We have seen, in discussing Apollo, the tragic circumstances of the birth of Asclepius, son of Apollo and Coronis. Apollo snatched him from the burning pyre on which his mother's body had just been consumed and carried him to Mount Pelion where he was confided to the care of the Centaur Chiron. Chiron taught him to hunt and instructed him in the science of medicine. The medical career of Asclepius then began. With his miraculous cures he soon earned immense renown. He even succeeded in restoring the dead to life, thanks either to the Gorgon's blood which Athene had given him or to the properties of a plant which a serpent had told him about. Hades felt that he was being wronged. He went to Zeus to complain, and Zeus agreed that mortals must follow their destiny. Thus Asclepius was guilty of thwarting the order of nature and Zeus struck him dead with a thunderbolt.

Apollo avenged the death of his son by exterminating the Cyclopes who had forged the thunderbolt. Apollo was banished from Olympus for a considerable time as a result of this massacre.

At Epidaurus another tradition of the birth of Asclepius was current. They said that Coronis gave birth to her son Asclepius while her father, Phlegyas, was on an expedition to the Peloponnese. She exposed the new-born child on Mount Titthion where a goat fed it and a dog guarded it. One day Aresthanas, a shepherd, discovered it and was struck by the supernatural light which played over the child.

Be that as it may, the god of health was always considered to be the offspring of light or fire. To the sick he restored the warmth they had lost. Hence he was the object of great veneration in Greece. He was surrounded by auxiliary divinities: to begin with, Epione, his wife, who bore the two Asclepiads, Podaleirius and Machaon. Both took part, at the head of the Thessalians of Tricca, in the Trojan war. They were as skilled in medicine as their father. Machaon, especially, cured Menelaus of an arrow wound. He also cured Philoctetes. He himself was killed before Troy and Nestor brought his body back to Greece. Podaleirius survived the expedition and on his return was cast by a tempest on to the shores of Caria where he settled.

Asclepius also had daughters: Iaso, Panacea, Aegle and, above all, Hygieia, who was closely associated with the cult of her father as goddess of health. Finally we must mention the guardian spirit of convalescence, Telesphorus, who was represented wearing a hooded cape, the costume of those who had just recovered from illness.

Asclepius was sometimes represented as a serpent, but more frequently as a man of middle age with an expression of benevolence, and his cult was at the same time a religion and a system of therapeutics. His sanctuaries, such as those at Tricca, Epidaurus, Cos and Pergamus, were built outside the towns on particularly healthy sites. The priests in charge of them at first held a monopoly of medical knowledge which was handed down from father to son. It was only later that they admitted outsiders as neophytes.

In the *Asclepeia* special rites were observed. After much purificatory preparation, baths, fasting, sacrifices, the patient was permitted to spend the night in the temple of Asclepius where he slept either on the skin of the sacrificed animal or on a couch placed near the statue of the god. This was the period of incubation. During the night Asclepius would appear to the patient in a dream and give him advice. In the morning the priests would interpret the dream and explain the god's precepts. Patients would thank Asclepius by tossing gold into the sacred fountain and by hanging ex-votos on the walls of the temple.

DIVINITIES CONCERNED WITH MORALITY

The Moerae or Fates. The Moerae, whom the Romans called the Parcae, were for Homer the individual and inescapable destiny which followed every mortal being. Only in Hesiod's *Theogony* are they treated as goddesses. They were three in number, daughters of Night, and they were called: Clotho, Lachesis and Atropos. Clotho, the spinner, personified the thread of life. Lachesis was chance, the element of luck that a man had the right to expect. Atropos was inescapable fate, against which there was no appeal. The whole of man's life was shadowed by the Moerae. They arrived at his birth with Ilithyia. When he was married the three Moerae had to be invoked so that the union should be happy. And when the end approached the Moerae hastened to cut the thread of his life. Hesiod placed them with the Keres, thus giving them the role of divinities of violent death.

The Moerae were submitted to the authority of Zeus who commanded them to see that the natural order of things was respected They sat in the assemblies of the gods and possessed the gift of prophecy.

Nemesis. Like the Fates, Nemesis had at first been a moral idea, that of the inexorable equilibrium of the human condition. Man could displease the gods in two manners, either by offending the moral law – in which case he incurred their wrath – or by attaining too much happiness or riches – in which case he excited their jealousy. In either of these cases the imprudent mortal was pursued by Nemesis, or the divine anger. If he had offended only by an excess of good fortune he might hope to propitiate the goddess by sacrificing a part of his happiness.

Polycrates, tyrant of Samos, was terrified of the unheard-of luck which followed him, and wished to forestall the jealousy of the gods by throwing into the sea a priceless ring of which he was especially fond. But when the ring was returned to him by a fisherman who had found it in the belly of a fish, Polycrates realised that Nemesis had refused to accept his sacrifice and that unhappiness was in store for him. And, indeed, it overtook him shortly afterwards.

Nemesis later became a goddess with more definitely defined personality, and various genealogies were ascribed to her. According to some she was the daughter of Oceanus. According to others she was born of Night and Erebus, in which case she was a deadly power. But when Dike was made her mother she became an equitable divinity. She was, however, always responsible for seeing that order was maintained. One of her titles was Adrasteia – the Inevitable. She is sometimes depicted with a finger to her lips – suggesting that silence is advisable in order not to attract the divine anger. The principal sanctuary of Nemesis was at Rhamnus, a small town in Attica. There was a statue of the goddess there

The Eumenides. Greek crater. The Eumenides sleep while Apollo purifies Orestes with a young pig. Louvre.

which Phidias carved from the marble which the Persians, rashly counting on victory in advance, had brought with them before the battle of Marathon, expecting to erect a trophy with it.

Tyche, Ate, Litae. To complete the list of divinities whose functions were moral, there is Tyche, goddess of fortune. Hesiod calls her the daughter of Oceanus and Tethys. She was represented variously by various cities, each having its own Tyche. Adorned with the mural crown, she wears the attributes of abundance.

Ate, daughter of Eris or of Zeus, was on the other hand a malevolent divinity who prompted men to irresponsible acts. She led both men and gods into error and aberration. It was she who, when Hercules was born, suggested to Zeus the imprudent vow which caused the hero such subsequent misery. Hence the master of the gods punished the wicked goddess by banishing her permanently from Olympus and 'from the heights of heaven flung her into the midst of man's affairs'.

In order to repair the damage done by the treacherous Ate, Zeus sent the Litae after her. The Litae were Prayers and also daughters of Zeus. Wrinkled and lame, they limped after their sister Ate, trying to mitigate the evils she caused. Whoever welcomed the Litae with respect was showered with blessings.

THE UNDERWORLD

In Greek mythology the Infernal Regions were the mournful abode where, separated from their bodies, the souls of those who had finished their earthly existence took refuge. There were two successive conceptions of where the afterworld was situated. 'The Afterworld,' says Circe to Odysseus, 'lies at the extremity of the earth, beyond the vast Ocean.' The earth was thought of as a flat surface limited by an immense encircling river Ocean. One must cross this river in order to reach the desolate and uncultivated shore of the infernal regions. There few things grew, the soil was barren and no living being could survive, for the sun's rays could not penetrate so far. Black poplars were found there, and willows which never bore fruit. The ground supported asphodel, a funerary plant of ruins and cemeteries.

This was the tradition of the epic poems. It was altered with the progress of geography when navigators discovered that very far to the west – where the infernal regions were supposed to be – there existed lands which were in fact inhabited. Popular belief then placed the kingdom of Shadows elsewhere: from then on it was situated in the centre of the earth. It continued to remain a place of shadows and mystery, of Erebus. Its approaches were no longer the Ocean. The Underworld communicated with the earth by direct channels. These were caverns whose depths were unplumbed, like that of Acherusia in Epirus, or Heraclea Pontica. Near Cape Taenarum there was one of these entrance gates and also at Colonus in a place dedicated to the Eumenides.

In the same way certain rivers whose course was partly underground were thought to lead to the infernal regions. Such was the Acheron in Thesprotia into which flowed the Cocytus. It must be remarked, moreover, that the names of these rivers were given to them because they were believed to flow into the underworld. Acheron derives from the word which means 'affliction'. It was the river of sadness and Cocytus was the river of lamentation.

Though the ancients carefully described the exterior appearance and approaches of the underworld, they were vaguer about its interior. On this aspect of the Infernal Regions we have little information. According to what we have, the actual Underworld was preceded by a vestibule called the Grove of Persephone. Here the black poplars and sterile willows were again found. It had to be crossed before reaching the gate of the Kingdom of Hades. At the gate was posted Cerberus, the monstrous watch-dog with fifty heads and a voice of bronze. He was born of the love of the giant Typhoeus for Echidna. Cerberus was variously represented. Sometimes he had only three heads, sometimes he bristled with serpents and his mouth dribbled black venom. He was always to be feared. When entering the underworld, to be sure, the terrible beast would appear prepossessing, wagging its tail and ears. But never again could one come out. Cerberus, however, could be appeased by tossing to him cakes of flour and honey. Hermes could calm him down with his caduceus and Orpheus charmed him with his lyre. Only Hercules dared measure his strength with Cerberus and, vanquishing him, carried him for a moment up to earth. Cerberus infected certain herbs with his venom which were afterwards gathered by magicians and used in the preparation of baleful philtres.

Within the Underworld flowed subterranean rivers: Acheron with its affluent the Cocytus swelled by the Phlegethon, Lethe and, finally, the Styx. Acheron was the son of Gaea. He had quenched the thirst of the Titans during their war with Zeus and been thrown into the Underworld where he was changed into a river. To cross Acheron it was necessary to apply to old Charon, the official ferryman of the Underworld. He was a hard old man, difficult to deal with. Unless before embarking the shade of the deceased newcomer presented Charon with his obolus, he would mercilessly drive away an intruder so ignorant of local usage. The shade was then condemned to wander the deserted shore and never find refuge. The Greeks therefore carefully put an obolus into the mouths of the dead.

The Styx surrounded the Underworld with its nine loops. The Styx was personified as a nymph, daughter of Oceanus and Tethys. She was loved, it was said, by the Titan Pallas and by him had Zelos (Jealousy); Nike (Victory); Kratos (Force); and Bia (Violence). As a reward for the help she rendered the Olympians during the revolt of the Titans it was decided that the Immortals should swear by her name, and such vows were irrevocable.

Those who drank of the waters of Lethe forgot the past. Lethe flowed, according to some, at the extremity of the Elysian fields; according to others at the edge of Tartarus. The Elysian fields and Tartarus were the two great regions of the Underworld.

THE SOVEREIGN OF THE UNDERWORLD

It seems that the name of the ruler of the Underworld derives from the privative prefix 'a' and the verb 'to see', evoking an idea of mystery. He was the Invisible. He was also called Pluto, from the word for 'riches'. It was he who received buried treasure: he was then considered the god of agricultural wealth. From the centre of earth he exerted his influence on cultivation and crops.

Hades – he was also called Aidoneus – was the son of Rhea and the ferocious Cronus who devoured him as he devoured his brothers and sisters. Fortunately he was delivered by his brother Zeus, from whom he received as his share of the inheritance the Kingdom of the Underworld.

Over this domain Hades ruled as absolute master. He seemed happy there and was only seen to leave his Kingdom on two occasions: once to abduct Persephone and the other time to go in search of Paean in order to be cured of a wound inflicted by Hercules who struck his shoulder with a sharp-pointed arrow. On the other hand, if an impulse to emerge from the Underworld seized him, no one could see him; for his helmet made him invisible.

Hades was not a particularly inconstant husband. Persephone had only twice to complain of his infidelity. First he became interested in Minthe, a nymph of the Cocytus. Persephone – or perhaps it was Demeter – pursued the unfortunate nymph and trod her ferociously underfoot. Hades transformed her into a plant which first grew in Triphylia; it was mint which was afterwards sacred to Hades.

Hades also brought a daughter of Oceanus to his kingdom, one Leuce, who died a natural death and became a white poplar, the tree of the Elysian Fields. When Hercules came up from the Underworld he was crowned with its foliage.

Hades was very little venerated, though as Pluto he received much more homage. This was because Hades was essentially a god of terror, mystery and the inexorable. Pluto, on the contrary, was regarded as a benevolent deity and his cult was sometimes associated with that of Demeter.

To pray to him – Homer says – one struck the ground with bare hands or with rods. One sacrificed to him a black ewe or a black ram. Plants sacred to the god of the Underworld were the cypress and the narcissus.

Persephone. The name of the wife of Hades occurs in several forms: Persephone, Persephoneia, Phersephone, Persephassa, Phersephatta. It is difficult to discover the etymology of all these variations. It is believed that the last half of the word Persephone comes from a word meaning 'to show' and evokes an idea of light. Whether the first half derives from a word meaning 'to destroy' – in which case Persephone would be 'she who destroys the light' – or from an adverbial root signifying 'dazzling brilliance' as in the name Perseus, it is difficult to decide.

The problem is complicated by the fact that Persephone is not a purely infernal divinity. Before marrying Hades she lived on earth with her mother Demeter who had conceived her by Zeus. Her name had then been Kore.

It is probable that originally mother and daughter were merged in one and the same divinity. Demeter, as we have seen, had in her province not only the surface of the earth, but also its interior. Subsequently the personality of Demeter split and her subterranean function devolved on a distinct goddess who was, however, an offspring of the primitive goddess. This is the meaning of the Kore-Persephone myth.

The dramatic circumstances of Kore's abduction will be recalled: how Hades surprised her while she was gathering flowers in a field, carried her away in his chariot and plunged with her into the depths of the earth; how Demeter, unable to regain full possession of her daughter, accepted the gods' proposal that Persephone should pass at least part of the year with her.

Persephone's legend is limited to this single episode, though the initiates of Orphism tried to enrich it by making the goddess the mother of Dionysus-Zagreus. Confined, like Hades, to her shadowy empire, Persephone was exempt from the passions which swayed other divinities. At most she was said to have felt a certain tenderness for the beautiful Adonis.

As goddess of the Underworld Persephone's attributes were the bat, the narcissus and the pomegranate. She was honoured in Arcadia under the names Persephone Soteira and Despoena. She was also venerated at Sardes and in Sicily. But usually her cult was joined to Demeter's and the rites of both were almost always similar.

Hecate. Hecate is best treated as a divinity of the Underworld, though she was in origin a moon-goddess. She was a native of ancient Thrace and in some ways she resembled Artemis with whom she was sometimes merged. Her name seems to be the feminine form of a title of Apollo's – the far-darter. Thus Hesiod makes her the daughter of the Titan Perses and the Titaness Asteria, both symbols of shining light. Hecate's lunar character always remained: she and Helios together witnessed the abduction of Kore by Hades.

Hecate was powerful both in the sky and on earth: she gave men riches, victory and wisdom; she watched over the prosperity of flocks and presided over navigation. During the war with the Giants she was the ally of Zeus; thus she continued to be honoured on Olympus.

A later tradition says that Hecate was the daughter of Zeus and Hera. It was said that she incurred her mother's wrath by stealing her rouge to give to Europa. She fled to the earth and hid in the house of a woman who had just been brought to bed with a child, contact with whom rendered Hecate impure. To remove the stain the Cabeiri plunged her into the Acheron, and that was how Hecate became a divinity of the Underworld. In the infernal regions Hecate's authority was considerable: she was called Prytania of the dead or the Invincible Queen. She presided over purifications and expiations. She was the goddess of enchantments and magic

Hercules wrestling with Achelous. The river-god has turned himself into a speckled serpent in an attempt to overcome his rival for the hand of the lovely Deianeira but he was finally overcome by the hero who snapped off one of his horns. Rivers were worshipped by the Greeks who believed them to be the divine offspring of Oceanus and Tethys. The Achelous was the largest watercourse in Greece. Detail from a Greek red-figured vase.

charms as well. She sent demons to the earth who tormented men. She herself would appear at night accompanied by her retinue of infernal dogs. The places that she haunted most frequently were crossroads, or near tombs or the scenes of crimes. Thus at crossroads her image could be found, either columns or statues of the goddess with three faces – they were called triple Hecates – and, on the eve of the full moon, offerings would be left before these images to propitiate the redoubtable goddess.

THE AUXILIARIES OF HADES

Thanatos and Hypnos. Thanatos – Death – naturally supplied Hades with his subjects. He was the son of Night. Euripides shows him dressed in a black robe holding in his hand the fatal sword, as he walks among men. But normally Death did not appear in this sinister aspect; Thanatos was more usually represented as a winged spirit. He then completely resembled his brother Hypnos – Sleep – who lived with him in the Underworld. Hypnos put men to sleep by touching them with his magic wand or by fanning them with his dark wings. He had power also over the gods and Homer tells us how at Hera's request he took the form of a night bird and sent Zeus to sleep on Mount Ida. The son of Hypnos was Morpheus, god of dreams.

The Keres. The Keres executed the will of the Moerae or Fates and were no doubt originally confused with them. When the implacable deities had fixed the fatal hour, it was the Keres who appeared. They would then seize the unhappy mortal, deliver the decisive blow, and carry him down to the land of shadows. In the midst of battle especially they could be seen to hover, with a sparkling eye, grimacing mouth, and sharp teeth whose whiteness contrasted with the sombre hue of their visage. They wore red robes and cried out dismally as they finished off the wounded. They would dig in their sharp claws, then greedily drink the streaming blood. Not without reason were they called the dogs of Hades.

The Erinnyes. The Erinnyes were also sometimes called the 'dogs of Hades'. They, too, were infernal deities whose special mission was to punish parricides and those who had violated their oaths. Their genealogy was rather vague: according to Hesiod they were born to Gaea fertilised by the blood of Uranus. Aeschylus calls them 'the children of Eternal Night' and Sophocles 'Daughters of the Earth and the Shadow'. It seems that they were first venerated in Arcadia where a Demeter Erinnyes, from whom they were perhaps derived, was worshipped. Their number for long remained undetermined, but was later fixed at three when they were given the individual names of Tisiphone, Megara and Alecto.

When a crime was committed in a family – above all when a son's hands were stained with the blood of his parents – the black goddesses would immediately appear, their hair bristling with serpents, armed with torches and whips. They would sit at the threshold of the guilty one's house and it was in vain to attempt escape. Even in the Underworld they pursued their vengeance and tormented the guilty in Tartarus.

The cult of the Erinnyes was spread throughout all Greece, above all in Athens where they had a temple near the Areopagus. Here they were honoured under the name of the Eumenides – the Benevolent Ones – in memory of the mildness they had shown towards Orestes, who, after the murder of his mother, had come to seek refuge in Athens.

Life in the Underworld. Souls of the dead, when they had left the earth, only retained a pale reflection of their former personality. Physically they were diaphanous and insubstantial. Morally they were also shadows: their courage and intelligence had disappeared. Only a few privileged persons lived in the Underworld as they had lived on earth, following the same occupations. Orion continued to hunt, Minos judged souls, Hercules was always ready to overthrow some monster or other.

In brief the Underworld, in this primitive conception of it, was a sort of dismal house of retirement. Only the outstandingly guilty suffered eternal torture.

Little by little, however, the Underworld came to be thought of, not as a limbo, but as a place of justice where each received exactly what he deserved.

Souls on their arrival appeared before a tribunal composed of Hades and his three assessors: Aeacus, Minos and Rhadamanthys.

The latter two were sons of Zeus and Europa and had reigned, Minos over Crete and Rhadamanthys over the Cyclades. Aeacus was the son of Zeus and Aegina and during his life had been distinguished for his piety and love of justice. The gods themselves had chosen him as an arbiter. After his death he was appointed in the Underworld especially to judge Europeans, while Rhadamanthys tried Asiatics. It was Aeacus who held the keys of the Underworld.

After they had been examined and judgment pronounced, the souls of the dead were either cast into Tartarus or conducted to the Elysian Fields or to the Islands of the Blessed.

Tartarus with its gates of bronze was the sombre gaol of those who had committed crimes against the gods. It was surrounded by a triple wall and bathed by the waters of the Phlegethon. The avenue which led to Tartarus was closed by a diamond gate. Here the most notorious prisoners were the Titans and the giant Tityus on whom two vultures fed because he had attempted to violate Leto. Tantalus could also be seen, eternally tortured by hunger and thirst; Sisyphus, who without respite rolled his rock up a steep cliff; Ixion, bound to his flaming wheel spinning in the air; and the Danaids, condemned eternally to fill a bottomless barrel.

In Elysium, on the contrary, snow and rain and tempests were unknown. Soft breezes forever refreshed this abode of happiness which was at first reserved for the children of the gods, but later opened to the favourites of the Olympians and the souls of the just.

THE HEROES

The Greeks' Idea of the Hero. The Greek Hero was not always a supernatural being related to the gods. Homer made him a man of strength and courage or one who was especially venerated for his wisdom, like Laertes, Aegyptus and Demodocus. The hero could also be simply a prince of an illustrious family like Odysseus and Menelaus, for example. It is only incidentally that the heroes of Homer's poems are related to gods.

Hesiod on the other hand generalised the idea of the superman and recounted his origin. According to him, heroes were the offspring of the fourth generation of mythical men, that is to say the generation which took part in the battles of Troy and Thebes. At that epoch, indeed, gods and mortals often mingled.

Cult of the Heroes. The cult which the Greeks rendered to their heroes closely resembled the devotion with which they honoured their own ancestors. The hero, they believed, was in fact their most illustrious ancestor. Heroes and ancestors alike were offered sacrifice at the end of the day: the sacrificial victim was turned towards the West and at the foot of the altar a trench was dug to receive the victim's head. But the chief role of the hero was to act as intermediary between men and the gods. While men after death became insubstantial shadows, heroes retained their original

Dancing Maenad. With her head thrown back in ecstasy, one of Dionysus' female retinue follows in the wake of the god. Modelled in an idealised fashion upon the god's frenzied Thracian worshippers, the Maenads accompanied Dionysus on his travels crowned with wreaths of ivy, oak or fir and draped in the skins of animals. Under a more peaceful aspect they gathered grapes and prepared wine. Statue ascribed to the fourth century B.C. sculptor, Scopas.

Silenus supported by a young satyr. One of the most picturesque figures in the retinue of Dionysus, Silenus was always depicted as a drunken, fat old man. In spite of his unprepossessing appearance he was nevertheless possessed of great wisdom and had formerly been the god's tutor. He is assisted by a young satyr wearing a panther skin, or *nebris*, and carrying the *thyrsus*. Detail from the Borghese vase.

qualities and could intercede for mortals. In brief, the heroes, who were originally idealised men, became demi-gods and in the hierarchy occupied a position midway between men and the Olympians.

HERCULES

We are not very certain about the etymology of the word Heracles (the Latinised form being Hercules, which is used here throughout). Various hypotheses have been suggested to explain the name. The ancients claimed that Heracles was thus named because he owed his glory to Hera. The name has also been translated as 'glory of the air'. But no one of the theories advanced is more convincing than the others.

The Functions of Hercules. Hercules was thought of as the personification of physical strength. In his aspect of athlete-hero the foundation of the Olympic Games was ascribed to him. Pindar says that he arranged all the rules and details. But the chief function of Hercules was to play the part of a protector. When men were in danger Heracles *Alexikakos* was their chief resort. In consequence he even had medical powers: he was invoked in case of epidemics, while certain medicinal springs at Himera and Thermopylae were sacred to him. Finally, sometimes as Heracles Musagetes he played the cithara. To sum up, he presided over all aspects of Hellenic education and, after being the god of physical prowess, he was the god who sang of victory and accompanied himself on the lyre. More than any other he was the friend and counsellor of men.

Representation and Cult. The glorious hero, the invincible athlete, is depicted as a man of mature strength, endowed with muscular power, whose head is rather small in relation to his body. Generally Hercules stands, leaning on his heavy club. In his statues and busts we observe a rather sad and severe expression, as though Hercules, the eternal conqueror, never knew repose. His appearance suggests that he is waiting for yet another superhuman task to fulfil.

Hercules was venerated like other heros and with the same rites, but his cult was much more general. All Greece honoured him. His exploits, indeed, took place all over the Hellenic world. Thebes and Argos were the centres from which his legend spread.

The Birth of Hercules. His Childhood and First Exploits. Hercules descended from Perseus, whose son Alcaeus (the Strong) was the father of Amphitryon, the supposed father of Hercules. On the other hand, Electryon (the Brilliant), another son of Perseus, was the father of Alcmene (woman of might). Hercules, then, was born under the sign of strength and light; and, into the bargain, his paternity was divine. Zeus, wishing to have a son who should be a powerful protector of both mortals and Immortals, descended one night to the city of Thebes where he assumed the appearance of Amphitryon and lay with Amphitryon's wife, Alcmene. Shortly afterwards Amphitryon himself returned from a victorious expedition and took his wife in his arms. From the two successive unions Alcmene conceived twins: Hercules and Iphicles.

Their birth was not without difficulties. On the day Hercules should have been born Zeus swore a solemn and irrevocable oath before the Olympians that the descendant of Perseus who was about to be born should one day rule Greece. At these words Hera, doubly jealous, hurried to Argos where she caused the wife of one Sthenelus – himself a son of Perseus – to be brought prematurely to bed. She gave birth to Eurystheus. Hastening to Thebes, Hera simultaneously retarded the birth of Hercules. Thus Eurystheus came into the title of ruler of Greece and Zeus, bound by his solemn oath, was obliged to recognise him. And that was why Hercules all his life found the hardest tasks imposed on him by the rival whom Hera had set up against him. Nor was her vengeance yet satisfied. One night while all in the palace of Amphitryon were asleep, two serpents attacked the infant Hercules. While Iphicles screamed pitifully, Hercules firmly grasped the two monsters, one in each hand, and wrung their necks. To encourage such promise Hercules was then handed over to illustrious tutors. Rhadamanthys taught him wisdom and virtue while Linus taught him music. Linus was killed by the young hero in a fit of temper. Amphitryon then confided his divine offspring to some shepherds who lived in the mountains. There Hercules gave himself over to physical exercise and developed his strength. At the age of eighteen he killed

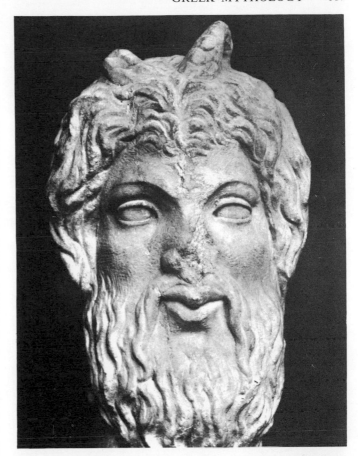

Head of Pan. An Arcadian shepherd-god who protected flocks and herds and made them prolific, Pan loved to roam the woods and mountains of Arcadia joining in the revels of the nymphs and playing on the pipes. He was later incorporated into the retinue of Dionysus. Half man and half goat, he was portrayed with a man's body but with the legs, ears, horns and beard of a goat.
Athenian sculpture in Pentelic marble, *c.* 400 B.C.

Centaur fighting a Lapith. The Centaurs, half man and half horse, also formed part of the retinue of Dionysus and were probably originally inspired by the horse-breeders of Thessaly. Though barbarous and sensual for the most part, some of them were famed for their wisdom. Here a Centaur struggles with a Lapith at the wedding feast of King Peirithous. It was this series of reliefs by Phidias and his assistants that fixed their appearance definitively. Metope from the Parthenon. Pentelic marble. *c.* 445 B.C.

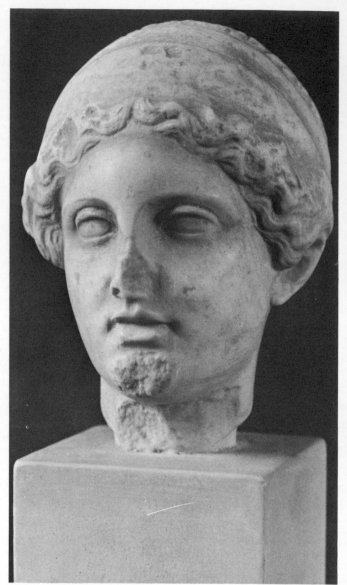

Asclepius. The god of health and healing leans on a tree-trunk
lost in meditation grasping a scroll representing medical learning.
The son of Apollo, he had learned the science of medicine from
the Centaur Chiron but was later killed by Zeus for raising the dead.
His image was set among the stars. Greatly venerated throughout Greece,
he had numerous shrines, his priests holding a monopoly of
medical knowledge.

Head of Hygeia. The daughter of Asclepius, Hygeia was closely
associated with her father's cult as the goddess of health and was frequently
portrayed with him. The most important of his attendants, her mother,
brothers and sisters also being auxiliary divinities of the god,
she had a cult at Titane which was almost as honoured as his.
Her name follows immediately after his and before that of her sister
Panacea in the Hippocratic oath.

a ferocious lion which came to devour Amphitryon's herds. The
hero, while waiting for the beast, hid in the house of King Thespius
and, legend recounts, he made use of the occasion to lie in a single
night with his host's fifty daughters.

Hercules shortly afterwards defended his native city against
Orchomenus. He met the herald of Orchomenus, who had come to
Thebes to collect the tribute, and cut off his nose and ears, thus
starting the war. Amphitryon, fighting beside his two sons, was
killed. But Hercules, aided by Athene, defeated Erginus, King of
Orchomenus. Creon became king of that country and gave his
daughter Megara to Hercules as a wife. Their marriage was unhappy.
Hera sent Lyssa, the Fury of madness, to Hercules. The hero was
seized with the deadly malady, mistook his own children for those
of Eurystheus, and massacred them and their mother. After this
grim crime Hercules had to flee the country. He went to Argolis
where he spent twelve years under the orders of Eurystheus who
imposed upon him the most arduous labours. For thus the oracle
of Delphi had commanded when Hercules, wishing to remove the
stain of his crime, consulted her.

THE TWELVE LABOURS

The Nemean Lion. The first monster that Hercules had to exterminate was the Nemean Lion, the skin of which Eurystheus ordered

him to bring back. Hercules attempted in vain to pierce the beast
with his arrows, then he engaged it hand to hand and finally strangled
it in his powerful grip. But he kept the skin and from it made a
garment which rendered him invulnerable. He then returned to
Tiryns with his trophy.

The Lernaean Hydra. This hydra, born of Typhon and Echidna,
was an enormous serpent with nine heads. Its den was a marsh
near Lerna in the Peloponnese. It would issue forth to ravage the
herds and crops; its breath moreover was so poisonous that whoever
felt it fell dead.

Accompanied by Iolaus, son of Iphicles, Hercules arrived at
Lerna, found the monster near the spring of Amymone and forced
it to emerge from the marshes by means of flaming arrows. Then
he tried to overwhelm it by means of his mighty club. But in vain:
for every time he struck off one of the hydra's nine heads two
grew in its place. Then Iolaus set the neighbouring forest on fire
and with the help of red-hot brands burnt the serpent's heads.
Hercules cut off the final head and buried it. Then he soaked his
arrows in the hydra's blood which made them poisonous and
deadly.

The Wild Boar of Erymanthus. This savage beast came down from
Mount Erymanthus, on the borders of Arcadia and Achaia, and

Head of Hypnos. An auxiliary of Hades, Hypnos (or Sleep) lived in the Underworld with his brother Thanatos (or Death), the son of Night. Unlike his brother he was beneficial to men and was represented as a winged youth who touched the foreheads of the weary with his magic wand or fanned them with his wings to bring them sleep. His son was Morpheus, the god of dreams. Bronze. Greek late fourth-century original or a copy of the Roman period.

devastated the territory of Psophis. Hercules succeeded in capturing it and carried it to Tiryns. Eurystheus was so terrified at the sight of the monster that he ran away and hid himself in a bronze jar.

On his way to Mount Erymanthus Hercules had received the hospitality of the Centaur Pholus, who in his honour broached a barrel of delicious wine which had been a present from Dionysus. The other Centaurs were attracted by the bouquet of the wine and came running to the house of Pholus, armed with stones and uprooted fir trees, to demand their share of the wine. Hercules drove them off with his arrows. The Centaurs were decimated, and took refuge near Cape Malea.

The Stymphalian Birds. The marshes of Stymphalus in Arcadia were peopled by monstrous birds whose wings, beaks and claws were of iron. They fed on human flesh and were so numerous that when they took wing the light of the sun was blotted out. Hercules frightened them with brazen cymbals and slew them with arrows.

The Ceryneian Hind. Eurystheus then ordered Hercules to bring him back the hind of Mount Ceryneia alive. Her hooves were of bronze and her horns of gold. Hercules chased her for an entire year before he at last caught her on the banks of the Ladon.

The Stables of Augeias. Augeias, King of Elis, owned innumerable herds of cattle among which were twelve white bulls sacred to Helios. One of them whose name was Phaethon was privileged to shine like a star. Unhappily these magnificent animals lived in foul stables, heaped high with manure of many years' accumulation. Hercules undertook to clean them out in one day on condition that the king gave him a tenth part of the herd. In order to do this he breached the walls of the building and, altering the course of the rivers Alpheus and Peneius, made them rush though the cow-sheds. When the job was done Augeias, under the pretext that Hercules was merely executing the orders of Eurystheus, refused to fulfil his part of the bargain. Later the hero was to punish this dishonesty.

The Cretan Bull. Poseidon had given Minos a bull, believing that Minos would offer it in sacrifice to him. As the king did nothing

of the sort, Poseidon drove the animal mad. The country was terrorised and Minos appealed to Hercules who at the time happened to be in Crete. The hero managed to capture the animal which he carried on his back across the sea to Argolis.

The Mares of Diomedes. Diomedes, son of Ares and king of the Bistones, owned mares which he fed on human flesh. Hercules, accompanied by a few volunteers, approached Thrace and captured these terrible mares, having first killed their guardians. The alert was given, the Bistones rushed upon him and the battle began. Hercules at last vanquished his assailants and Diomedes was given to his own mares to eat.

The rescue of Alcestis is usually said to have taken place at this same time. Admetus, King of Pherae, had obtained from the Fates, through the intermediary of Apollo, an assurance that he would not die if someone consented to die in his stead. When the fatal moment arrived his wife, Alcestis, took his place. They were about to bury the unhappy woman when Hercules passed by and engaged in dreadful struggle with Thanatos – Death himself. Hercules succeeded in wrenching Alcestis from death's grasp and returned her to her husband.

The Girdle of Hippolyte. Hippolyte, whom some call Melanippe, was the Queen of the Amazons in Cappadocia. As a mark of her sovereignty she possessed a magnificent girdle given to her by Ares. Admete, daughter of Eurystheus, greatly coveted this marvellous adornment, and Hercules was therefore given orders to go and fetch it. Accompanied by several celebrated heroes – Theseus, Telamon, Peleus – he embarked. His first port of call was Paros where he fought with the sons of Minos. Next he reached Mariandyne in Mysia where he helped King Lycus to conquer the Bebryces. In gratitude Lycus built the town of Heracles Pontica.

When at last he reached the country of the Amazons Hercules at first encountered no obstacle: Hippolyte agreed to give him the girdle. But Hera was enraged and, disguising herself as an Amazon, spread abroad the story that Hercules planned to abduct the queen. The Amazons seized their weapons. Hercules, believing they had betrayed him, slaughtered the Amazons, together with their queen. He took the girdle and then proceeded towards Troy.

The Hind with the Brazen Hooves. The Cretan bull. Greek cup. Louvre.

The Cattle of Geryon. Geryon was a triple-bodied monster who reigned over the western coast of Iberia or, according to others, over the Epirus. He owned a herd of red oxen which were guarded by the herdsman Eurytion and the dog Orthrus. Hercules, on the orders of Eurystheus, took possession of the oxen after killing Eurytion, Orthrus and finally Geryon. On his return journey he had various adventures. He slew the sons of Poseidon who attempted to steal the oxen, and he had to go to Eryx, king of the Elymans, in Sicily, to recapture an ox which had escaped and been put in the stables of Eryx. Eryx refused to return the beast unless Hercules beat him in a series of boxing and wrestling bouts. Hercules finally overthrew and killed him. In the hills of Thrace Hera sent a gadfly which drove the animals mad; they dispersed through the mountains and Hercules had great trouble in herding them together again. When he had done so he brought the cattle to Eurystheus who sacrificed them to Hera.

It was in the course of this expedition that Hercules penetrated Gaul where he abolished human sacrifice. He fought the Ligurians with the aid of stones which Zeus caused to rain down from the sky and which covered the plain of the Crau. The river Strymon refused to let him cross and he filled up its bed with stones.

The Golden Apples of the Hesperides. Eurystheus next commanded Hercules to bring to him the golden apples which the Hesperides, daughters of Atlas and Hesperus, guarded in their fabulous garden at the western extremities of the world. Hercules first travelled towards the north where, on the banks of the Eridanus, the nymphs of the river advised him to consult Nereus about the route. Hercules succeeded in capturing the prophetic god who told him how to reach the garden of the Hesperides. Crossing Libya Hercules measured his strength with Antaeus, a monstrous bandit who forced all travellers to wrestle with him. Antaeus was the son of Gaea, Mother Earth, and had the power of regaining his strength by touching the earth with his feet. Hercules in the end choked him to death by holding him high in the air in his arms. Hercules was next attacked while asleep by the Pygmies. He sewed them up in his lion skin. Then he arrived in Egypt where Busiris, the king, sacrificed a foreigner every year in order to put an end to a terrible famine. Hercules was chosen as victim, put in chains and conducted

to the temple. But he threw off his chains suddenly and slew Busiris and his son Amphidamas (Iphidamas). He then resumed his journey. He crossed Ethiopia where he killed Emathion, son of Tithonus, and replaced him by Memnon. He crossed the sea in a golden barque which the Sun had given him. In the Caucasus he slew with his arrows the eagle which gnawed the liver of Prometheus and finally reached the garden of the Hesperides. He killed the dragon Ladon which guarded the entrance, seized the apples and delivered them to Eurystheus. Eurystheus made him a gift of them and Hercules in his turn presented them to Athene who returned them to the Hesperides.

It was also related that Hercules was aided by Atlas on this enterprise. He persuaded Atlas to pick the apples while he, Hercules, meanwhile supported the world on his shoulders. When Atlas returned with the apples he was reluctant to reassume his traditional burden and would have refused to do so had not Hercules outwitted him.

Hercules' Journey to the Underworld. In despair of ever getting the better of Hercules, Eurystheus, as a final labour, commanded him to fetch Cerberus, guardian of the infernal gates. Hercules first had himself initiated into the infernal mysteries at Eleusis and then, guided by Hermes, he took the subterranean passage which descended at Cape Taenarum. Everything fled before him except Meleager and the Gorgon. Farther on Theseus and Peirithous, who had imprudently ventured into the Underworld, implored his assistance. Hercules saved Theseus, but was prevented from rescuing Peirithous by a sudden earthquake. He relieved Ascalaphus of the boulder which was crushing him, overthrew Menoetes, or Menoetius, the herdsman of Hades, wounded Hades himself and finally obtained the permission of Hades to carry off Cerberus, provided that he could conquer the monster without other weapons than his bare hands. Hercules leapt on Cerberus and at last mastered him by strangulation. Then he dragged the brute by the scruff of its neck back to earth, showed him to Eurystheus, and sent him back to Hades again.

Other Exploits of Hercules. When he was at last freed from servitude Hercules, far from resting on his laurels, set forth on new adventures.

When King Eurytus promised the hand of his daughter Iole to him who vanquished him in an archery contest, Hercules arrived and triumphed. The king refused to keep his word. Shortly afterwards the king's son, Iphitus, asked Hercules to help him search for some stolen horses, and Hercules, distraught with fury, killed him. For this crime Hercules went to Delphi to be purified. The Pythia refused to answer him and Hercules made off with her tripod. A bitter quarrel with Apollo ensued in which Zeus himself had to intervene. At last the oracle condemned Hercules to a year's slavery, and obliged him to hand over his year's wages to Eurytus. It was Omphale, Queen of Lydia, who bought the hero when he was offered for sale as a nameless slave, for three talents. In spite of the tradition which showed Hercules during this period softened by pleasures and dressed in a long oriental robe while he spun wool at the feet of his mistress, he did not remain inactive. He captured the Cercopes, evil and malicious demons who were, perhaps, only a horde of brigands camped near Ephesus. He killed the king of Aulis, Syleus, who forced strangers to work in his vineyards and then cut their throats. He rid the banks of the Sagaris of a gigantic serpent which was ravaging the countryside, and finally threw the cruel Lityerses into the Maeander. Lityerses had been in the habit of forcing strangers to help with his harvest and then of cutting off their heads with a scythe. Omphale was overcome with admiration and restored the hero's freedom.

Hercules then offered to rescue Hesione, daughter of Laomedon, King of Ilium. This unfortunate princess had been chained to a rock, as an expiatory victim against an epidemic. A dragon had come to devour her. Hercules prevented the tragedy, but Laomedon refused to give him the reward which had been agreed upon. The hero returned to Ilium with six ships, besieged the town, took it by assault, killed Laomedon and his sons, and gave Hesione in marriage to his friend Telamon. On his return journey he was thrown onto the shores of the island of Cos by a storm raised by Hera. The inhabitants received him badly and he avenged himself by sacking the island and slaying its king, Eurypylus. Next, he took part at Phlegra in the battle between the gods and the giants.

Hercules had not forgotten the dishonesty of Augeias in the matter of the Augean Stables. He marched against him and devastated his domain. He had on this occasion to fight the Molionids,

sons of Poseidon. It was said that they had been hatched from a silver egg and had but one body with two heads, four arms and four legs.

While he was laying siege to Pylus Hercules did battle with Periclymenus who had the power of metamorphosis. When Periclymenus turned himself into an eagle Hercules destroyed him with a blow of his club.

Hercules also restored Tyndareus to his throne after he had been deprived of it by Hippocoon and his sons. Passing through Tegea in Arcadia Hercules seduced Auge, daughter of Aleus and a priestess of Athene. She bore him a son Telephus, whom she hid in the temple of the goddess. Athene, angered by this profanation, sent a plague to the country. Aleus discovered his daughter's shame and drove her away. She took refuge with King Teuthras in Mysia and exposed her child on Mount Parthenius. When Telephus grew to manhood he went in search of his mother. He found her in Mysia and, not recognising her, was on the point of marrying her when Hercules intervened and prevented the incest.

The last adventure of Hercules took place in Aetolia and in the land of Trachis. He obtained the hand of Deianeira, daughter of Oeneus, king of the Aetolians, after having triumphed over another suitor, the river-god Achelous. But shortly afterwards the accidental murder of young Eunomus, who served at his father-in-law's table, obliged Hercules to fly from the country, together with his wife. When he arrived at the river Evenus Hercules gave Deianeira to the Centaur Nessus to carry across to the opposite bank. But halfway across Nessus attempted to violate Deianeira. Hercules saw this and at once struck him with an arrow. As Nessus died he gave his blood to Deianeira, telling her that it would preserve the love and fidelity of her husband.

Unfortunately Hercules then conceived the fateful idea of going back to punish Eurytus. He slew Eurytus, together with his sons, and brought away Iole whom he had never ceased to love. On his return he stopped at Cenaeum in Euboea to offer a sacrifice to Zeus. Before doing so he sent his companion Lichas to Deianeira in Trachis to fetch a white tunic. Deianeira was worried at the thought that Iole was with her husband and, remembering the words of Nessus, soaked the tunic in the Centaur's blood before sending it to Hercules, hoping thus to regain his love. Scarcely had Hercules put

Hercules strangling the Nemean Lion. Silver platter. Bibliothèque Nationale, Paris.

on the tunic when he felt himself devoured by inner fire. Maddened with pain, he seized Lichas by the feet and flung him into the sea; then, tearing up pine-trees by their roots he made himself a funeral pyre, mounted it and ordered his companions to set it alight. All refused. Finally Poeas, father of Philoctetes, lighted the pines and Hercules rewarded him by giving him his bow and arrows.

The flames crackled and rose around the hero. At the moment they reached his body a cloud descended from the skies and in an apotheosis of thunder and lightning the son of Zeus disappeared from the eyes of men. He was admitted to Olympus where he was reconciled with Hera. He was married to her daughter Hebe and from then on lived the blissful and magnificent life of the Immortals.

The Progeny of Hercules. Legend ascribes nearly eighty sons to Hercules; their fortunes varied. Certain of them, more especially designated the Heraclids, distinguished themselves by conquering the Peloponnese.

After their father's death the sons of Hercules, fearing Eurystheus' persecution, left Mycenae and for a long time searched for refuge in vain. Finally Demophon, son of Theseus, received them in Athens. This was sufficient pretext for war between Eurystheus and the inhabitants of Attica. Iolaus, a former companion of Hercules, killed Eurystheus. The Heraclids then thought they could return to the Peloponnese. Their return was premature and caused an outbreak of the plague, and again they had to exile themselves.

Afterwards they attempted five consecutive invasions. Only the last one was successful. Its leaders were Temenus, Cresphontes and Aristodemus, great-grandsons of the hero. Allied with them were Dymas and Pamphylus, sons of the king of the Dorians. They chose the sea route and embarked at Naupactus to sail through the straits of Corinth. Before they left they had the misfortune to kill a prophet of Apollo. In anger the god destroyed their fleet and struck the expedition with famine. When the oracle of Delphi was consulted, it told the allies that they required a guide with three eyes. In the end they discovered a one-eyed man, Oxylus, who rode towards them on a horse and thus, with his mount, fulfilled the conditions of the oracle. Oxylus became leader of the expedition.

Tisamenus, son of Orestes, who reigned in Argos, perished in battle against the Heraclids and their Dorian allies, who then divided his country among themselves. Oxylus received Elis, Temenus was given Argos, the sons of Aristodemus obtained Sparta and Cresphontes took Messenia.

Hercules seizing Cerberus.
Amphora of Andocides. Louvre.

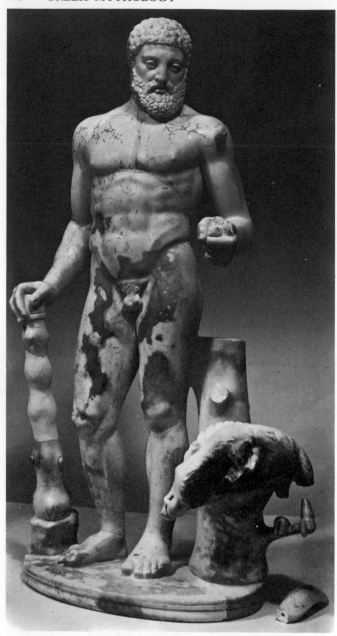

Hercules. The most popular of the Greek heroes, Hercules was worshipped throughout the whole of Greece. The personification of physical strength and the protector and counsellor of men, he was the son of Zeus and Alcmene who was herself descended from another hero – Perseus.

This statuette depicts him leaning on his club with a boar – possibly that of Erymanthus – caught in the branches of a tree beside him. Marble. Roman copy of a fifth-century Greek original.

THESEUS AND THE HEROES OF ATTICA

The Birth and Youth of Theseus. Theseus, like Hercules, was a great destroyer of monsters; and like Hercules he perished tragically. His birth was also analogous to the Theban hero's. His mother was Aethra, daughter of Pittheus, King of Troezen. She was loved at the same time by Aegeus, King of Athens, and by Poseidon. Theseus, who was conceived by this double union, thus had two fathers, a mortal and a god. Aegeus was obliged to return to Athens before the child was born and he hid his sword and his sandals under a heavy rock. When Theseus had grown strong enough to lift the rock and find these, he was to come to Athens and rejoin his father. So Theseus spent his childhood with his mother. When he was sixteen years old Aethra revealed the secret of his birth and showed him the famous rock of his father. Theseus had already shown bravery. As a child he had attacked, thinking it was alive, the body of the Nemean Lion which Hercules, visiting Pittheus, had placed on a table. Theseus now lifted the mighty rock, took possession of his father's sword and sandals and set forth for Athens.

His First Exploits. His first adventures occurred on his journey to Athens. Near Epidaurus, he killed a dangerous bandit, Periphetes, son of Hephaestus, and took from him his terrible club. In the forests of the Isthmus he inflicted on Sinis, son of Poseidon, the same torture which Sinis imposed on others; namely, tearing them asunder by tying them to sprung pine-trees. He killed the wild sow of Crommyon, called Phaea. On the slopes of Megaris he dashed Sciron against a boulder. Sciron had forced travellers to wash his feet and when they stooped to do so he would kick them over the cliff into the sea where they were devoured by a monstrous turtle. At Eleusis he vanquished Cercyon the Arcadian and, a little farther on, put an end to the criminal career of the giant Polypemon, known as Procrustes, who forced his victims to lie on a bed too short for them and then cut off whatever overlapped. Alternatively he would stretch them if the bed proved too long. Theseus made him undergo the same treatment. When he had purified himself after all these killings on the banks of the Cephissus, Theseus at last reached Athens.

He had donned a white robe and carefully arranged his beautiful fair hair. Hence, the workmen building the temple of Apollo Delphinios mocked at his innocent air and foppish appearance. Without deigning to reply Theseus picked up a heavy ox-cart and tossed it clean over the temple. Then he arrived at his father's palace. Aegeus had meanwhile married Medea who was instinctively jealous of the unknown newcomer and during the ensuing feast attempted to poison him. When Theseus drew his sword, his father recognised it and him. Aegeus then drove Medea and her children away and shared his throne with his son. From then on Theseus fought to strengthen his father's authority. First he exterminated the Pallantids who were nephews of Aegeus and had schemed to overthrow their uncle. Then he went in search of a wild bull which was devastating Attica. He succeeded in capturing the beast near Marathon, brought it back to Athens and sacrificed it to Apollo Delphinios.

Theseus and the Minotaur. In the midst of all this arrived ambassadors from Crete who for the third time had come to collect the annual tribute – seven virgins and seven young men – which had been imposed on Athens since the murder of Androgeus. These unfortunate young people were, when they arrived in Crete, thrown as food to a monster called the Minotaur. Theseus embarked with the victims with the intention of destroying the monster. He told his father that if he were victorious the ship when it returned would carry a white sail; if he were vanquished the black sail would be retained. When he arrived in Crete Theseus said that he was the son of Poseidon. Minos, to test this boast, tossed a golden ring into the sea and requested the hero to bring it back to him. Theseus dived in and returned not only with the ring but with a crown which Amphitrite had given him. Ariadne, the daughter of Minos, fell in love with Theseus and furnished him with a ball of string by means of which he could guide himself through the Labyrinth in which the Minotaur was kept and, after killing him, return. When Theseus had slain the beast he left Crete and took Ariadne and her sister Phaedra with him; but he abandoned Ariadne on the isle of Naxos. We have already seen how she was consoled by Dionysus.

In the joy of victory Theseus forgot to change the black sail which his ship was carrying. Aegeus saw it from the shore and, believing that his son was dead, threw himself into the sea. The ship which had been used on this expedition was piously preserved by the Athenians and carefully kept in a state of repair. It was named the Paralia and every year took gifts from Attica to Delos.

The Last Exploits of Theseus. At the death of his father Theseus became King of Attica and endowed his people with wise institutions. He united them in a single group, built a communal prytaneum in Athens, divided the citizens into three classes, erected temples and instituted the Panathenaea. At the same time he continued his wandering life of adventure.

He accompanied Hercules on his expedition against the Amazons, took part in hunting the wild boar of Calydon and sailed with the Argonauts. He was usually accompanied by his faithful friend Peirithous who at first had been his enemy. With Peirithous he also attacked the Amazons and abducted one of them, Antiope – which was the motive for an Amazonian invasion of Attica. Antiope bore him a son, Hippolytus, but he repudiated her and instead married Phaedra. Again with Peirithous he went to Sparta and carried off

Hercules carrying the Cercopes. While spending a year as the slave of Omphale, queen of Lydia, as his punishment for carrying off the Pythia's tripod from Delphi, Hercules did not entirely relinquish his heroic character and succeeded in capturing the two Ephesian Cercopes who travelled the world working mischief and who had constantly plagued him. Here he carries off the two brothers dressed in the invulnerable pelt of the Nemean lion.

Atlas bringing Hercules the apples of the Hesperides. As the eleventh of his twelve labours Hercules had been ordered to bring back the golden apples guarded by Atlas' daughters, the Hesperides. In the second version of the story Atlas himself fetched the apples while the hero supported the world on his shoulders in his place. In this relief he is assisted in this task by Athene. Metope from the temple of Zeus at Olympia. Parian marble, c. 450 B.C.

Hercules and Nessus at the river Evenus. Obliged to flee from Aetolia with his wife and son, Hercules had been held up by the river Evenus which was in flood. Here, with his son on his back, he asks the Centaur Nessus to carry Deianeira across to the other bank. The Centaur attempted to carry her off and Hercules killed him with a poisoned arrow. Wall-painting from Pompeii.

Peleus wrestling with Thetis. Humiliated at being ordered to marry a mortal, the Nereid Thetis attempted to escape from her future husband by turning herself successively into fire, water, a lion and a serpent. With Chiron's advice the Thessalian hero succeeded in overcoming her resistance and they were finally married. Their son was Achilles. Bottom of a Greek cup by the painter Peithinos. Late sixth century B.C.

young Helen. The two friends drew lots for her and she fell to Theseus. To console himself Peirithous decided to abduct Persephone, and the two heroes set forth for the Underworld. They succeeded in getting in, but they could not get out again and it required Hercules to rescue Theseus. When he returned to Athens the king found his house in an uproar. The Dioscuri, as Helen's brothers were called, had come to take their sister back; and Phaedra had conceived an incestuous passion for her son-in-law Hippolytus, who, being consecrated to Artemis, had made a vow of chastity and refused her. In chagrin Phaedra told Theseus that his son had made an attempt on her honour, and Theseus, too credulous, banished Hippolytus and called down Poseidon's wrath on the youth. The god summoned up a marine monster who terrified Hippolytus' chariot horses, and Hippolytus was crushed to death. At Troezen his tomb could be seen near the tomb of Phaedra. In the temple which was consecrated to him maidens, on the vigil of their wedding, would hang up a lock of their hair.

Sorely stricken by these tragedies, Theseus left Athens and retired to Scyros, to the palace of King Lycomedes. But Lycomedes was jealous of his guest's great fame and treacherously threw him into the sea. The remains of Theseus were interred at Scyros and later found by Cimon who brought them back to Athens and placed them in the sacred enclosure of the Theseum.

OTHER HEROES OF ATTICA

Cecrops. Cecrops, who was called Autochthonus or 'born of the earth', was regarded as the founder of Athens. It was during his reign that the dispute between Athene and Poseidon for the possession of Attica took place.

Erichthonius. Erichthonius was the son of Hephaestus who had engendered him by Gaea, the Earth, after being repulsed by Athene. In spite of this, Athene took charge of the infant, enclosed him in a chest which she confided to Pandrosos, the eldest daughter of Cecrops, forbidding her to open it. But the sisters of Pandrosos could not control their curiosity. When they saw that the newly born child was entwined by a serpent they were seized with terror.

The battle between the gods and giants. The gods are advancing from left to right against the attacking giants in this archaic relief from Delphi. On the left one of the lions drawing Cybele's chariot seizes a giant while Apollo and Artemis advance before him shooting arrows behind a fleeing giant. On the right three more giants advance over the body of a fallen comrade. Detail from the north frieze of the Siphnian treasury at Delphi. Parian marble, *c.* 525 B.C.

Theseus is recognised by his father. Bas-relief. Villa Albani, Rome.

Theseus killing the Minotaur. When Minos sent to Athens for the third time for his annual tribute of seven youths and seven maidens to be fed to the Minotaur, Theseus offered himself as one of the victims and sailed with them to Crete. With the assistance of Ariadne, the daughter of Minos, he succeeded in finding the monster within the labyrinth and slew him with his club.

Persus fleeing after slaying the Gorgon, Medusa.
The hero of Argolis makes off towards the left, his head turned to look at the decapitated body of the Gorgon which sinks to the ground behind him. In his left hand he carries the *harpe* with which he has just killed her while in a wallet round his neck he bears her severed head. The goddess Athene follows behind him. Greek red-figured vase.

Perseus rescuing Andromeda.
Mural painting from Pompeii in the National Museum, Naples.

In their wild flight they fell from the top of the Acropolis and were killed.

Erichthonius was King of Athens; he introduced the worship of Athene and the use of silver. He made war on Eumolpus and the Eleusinians. This Eumolpus, son of Poseidon, had come from Thrace to Eleusis and there instituted the mysteries of Demeter. It was told how Eumolpus was slain by Erichthonius and how, in expiation of the murder, Poseidon demanded the death of one of the King of Athens' daughters. There were four of them and they decided to die together. As for Erichthonius, Zeus struck him dead with a thunderbolt.

Descendants of Erichthonius. One of his daughters, Oreithyia, was seen one day by Boreas while she was playing on the shore; he carried her off and married her. Another daughter, Creusa, was loved by Apollo and by him had a son, Ion, whose adventure has been related in the chapter on Apollo.

Pandion, son of Erichthonius, succeeded him to the throne of Athens. He had three daughters: Procris, Philomela and Procne. All three had tragic fates. Procris was married to Cephalus and we have already seen how the jealousy of Eos brought unhappiness to the couple.

Philomela and Procne. When Pandion made war on Labdacus, King of Thebes, he was assisted by Tereus, King of Thrace, to whom he had given his daughter, Procne, in marriage. Procne bore Tereus a son, Itys. But when Tereus laid eyes on Philomela, his sister-in-law, he fell in love with her, violated her and, for fear that she would reveal the crime, cut out her tongue. Nevertheless the wretched Philomela was able to tell her sister what had occurred by embroidering the shocking story on a peplos. Procne, out of her mind with rage, killed Itys and served him to Tereus for dinner. Then she and Philomela fled while the tyrant Tereus pursued them with drawn sword. A benevolent deity intervened and turned Tereus into a hoopoe, Procne into a swallow and Philomela into a nightingale. As for Itys, he was resuscitated and changed into a goldfinch.

BELLEROPHON AND THE HEROES OF CORINTH

Sisyphus. If Bellerophon was Corinth's most valiant hero, his grandfather, Sisyphus, was its most cunning. Sisyphus was the son of Aeolus and founded Ephyra, the ancient name of Corinth. As far back as Homeric times he was reputed to be the craftiest of men. Sometimes he was even alleged to be the father of Odysseus, so great was their resemblance in this respect. It was Sisyphus who told the river-god Asopus that his daughter Aegina had been abducted by Zeus. Zeus in fury sent Thanatos for him, but the cunning Sisyphus succeeded in trapping the god of death and it required Ares to set him free. This time Sisyphus had to submit to his destiny. But before dying he advised his wife not to pay him funeral honours. He had scarcely arrived in the Underworld when he went to Hades to complain of his wife's negligence and to ask for permission to go back to earth for a moment in order to punish her. Permission was granted and Sisyphus, back on earth again, refused to return to the Underworld. Hermes had to deal personally with this recalcitrant shade. Sisyphus was punished for his bad faith by being condemned eternally to roll up the slope of a mountain an enormous boulder which, each time it nearly reached the summit, rolled down again.

Bellerophon. Sisyphus had a son, Glaucus, who offended Aphrodite and, in the course of funeral games, was trampled and killed by his horses, whom the goddess had driven mad. Afterwards the ghost of Glaucus continued to frighten horses. The son of Glaucus, Hipponous, was more celebrated under the name of Bellerophon, which was given to him after he had murdered a Corinthian named Bellerus. In expiation of the murder Bellerophon went to the palace of Proetus, King of Tiryns. The King's wife, Stheneboea, at once fell in love with the young hero. Bellerophon scorned her and she told her husband that he had attempted to seduce her. Proetus did not dare to kill a man who was his guest and, instead, sent him to his father-in-law, Iobates, with a sealed message containing his death sentence. Iobates imposed various tasks on Bellerophon, trusting that in the attempt to accomplish them he would perish. First, he ordered Bellerophon to fight the Chimaera. Now Bellerophon had a marvellous winged horse called Pegasus, born of the Gorgon's

Chariot race between Pelops and Oenomaus. Bas-relief on a sarcophagus in the Vatican Museum, Rome.

blood, which he had succeeded in taming thanks to a golden bridle that Athene gave him. Mounted on Pegasus, Bellerophon flew over the Chimaera and stuffed the monster's jaws with lead. The lead melted in the flames which the Chimaera vomited forth and killed it.

Bellerophon next triumphed over the savage tribes of the Solymia and the Amazons. On his return he successfully overcame an ambuscade which Iobates had laid for him. Iobates was so filled with admiration that he gave the hero his daughter in marriage. The end of Bellerophon's life, however, was tragic. His two children, Laodameia and Isandrus, were slain, the first by Artemis, the second by Ares. According to Pindar Bellerophon himself attempted to reach Olympus on his flying steed, but was flung to earth by Zeus and lamed by his fall. Odious to all the Immortals, Homer says, Bellerophon wandered the earth, his heart consumed with misery, alone, fleeing the haunts of men.

PERSEUS AND THE HEROES OF ARGOLIS

When Io, daughter of the river-god Inachus, arrived in Egypt after all her tribulations she brought a son into the world, Epaphus. The great-grandsons of Epaphus were Aegyptus and Danaus. Both married, and Aegyptus had fifty sons while Danaus had fifty daughters. A quarrel broke out between the two brothers and on Athene's advice Danaus embarked with his fifty daughters and sailed towards Greece. He landed on the Peloponnesian coast and was received at Argos by Gelanor, the King, whose crown he shortly afterwards seized.

Some time later the sons of Aegyptus came to find their uncle, Danaus, and as a token of reconciliation asked him for the hand of his daughters. Danaus consented, but his rancour still seethed. On their wedding day he gave each of his daughters a dagger and ordered her to kill her husband during the night. All obeyed with the exception of Hypermnestra, who fled with her husband Lynceus. We have seen how the Danaids were condemned to everlasting torture in the infernal regions.

The grandsons of Hypermnestra, Proetus and Acrisius, were also brother enemies. Proetus was finally driven from Argos by his brother and retired to Lycia where he married the daughter of Iobates, Stheneboea. Then he laid claim to his share of Argolis and seized Tiryns where he settled, after having made peace with his brother Acrisius.

Acrisius, who grieved at having no heir, learned from the oracle at Delphi that his daughter Danaë would have a son who would kill his grandfather, namely himself. In vain he shut Danaë up in a subterranean chamber. We have already seen how Zeus, in the guise of a shower of gold, reached Danaë and made her the mother of a son, Perseus. Again, in vain, Acrisius put mother and son into a chest which he cast into the sea: they were washed ashore at Seriphos and taken in by Polydectes, king of that country. Some years later Polydectes fell in love with Danaë, but was embarrassed by the presence of Perseus who had become a robust young warrior. He therefore pretended that he wished to marry Hippodameia and asked his vassals to bring wedding gifts. Each did his best and Perseus, anxious to distinguish himself, promised to bring back the Gorgon's head. Polydectes was relieved to think he had seen the last of him.

Perseus then left Seriphos and reached the abode of the Graeae, frightening old shrews who among them had but one tooth and one eye which all three used in turn. Perseus stole their single tooth and only eye, and in this way persuaded them to tell him where the Gorgons lived. From them he also stole a magic wallet and a dark

helmet which rendered its wearer invisible.

Thus equipped Perseus reached the westernmost extremities of the earth where, says Aeschylus, 'dwell monsters abhorred by mortals, with locks of serpents, whom none look upon without perishing'. They were the three sisters Stheno, Euryale and Medusa, daughters of Phorcys and Ceto. Instead of teeth they had the tusks of wild boars, their hands were of bronze, golden wings were fixed to their shoulders, and whoever dared to look them in the face was instantly turned to stone. Only one of them was mortal, Medusa. It was therefore she whom Perseus attacked. Armed with a bronze

Meleager. This statuette by the Italian sculptor Antico probably depicted the Aetolian hero dispatching the Calydonian boar. Unfortunately, in an ensuing quarrel over its pelt, Meleager killed his two uncles and some say that to revenge their deaths his mother then destroyed the brand which preserved his life. Others say that she merely cursed him and that he was finally killed in battle by Apollo. Bronze, parcel gilt. Late fifteenth or early sixteenth century.

Perseus killing the Gorgon. Metope from Selinus. Palermo Museum.

Facing: Pegasus followed by a Centaur. Born of the Gorgon's blood, the winged horse Pegasus was later tamed by Bellerophon with the help of Athene and finally ascended to Olympus where he carried Zeus' thunderbolts. A favourite of poets and painters, it was he who had stamped out the spring Hippocrene on Mount Helicon for the Muses. The Centaur is shown as a man with only the hindquarters of a horse in this early portrayal.

The Dioscuri carry off the daughters of Leucippus. Bas-relief on a sarcophagus in the Uffizi Gallery, Florence.

harpe which Hermes had given him, he averted his eyes and, letting Athene guide his arm, he struck. Or, some say, he fixed his eyes on her reflection in the polished surface of his shield. Then he cut off Medusa's head with one stroke of the sickle, and from her bleeding neck sprang Pegasus and Chrysaor, father of the infamous Geryon. Perseus put the terrible head into his wallet and fled on Pegasus' back while the other two Gorgons pursued him in vain.

Perseus reached Ethiopia to find the country in a state of desolation. Cassiopeia, wife of the king, Cepheus, had offended the Nereids by proclaiming that she was more beautiful than they. In this quarrel Poseidon had taken the part of the Ocean nymphs and sent a marine monster to devour men and beasts. When the oracle of Ammon was consulted he answered that only Andromeda, daughter of King Cepheus, could save the country by offering herself as a victim to the monster. When Perseus arrived on the scene he found the unhappy Andromeda chained to a rock, awaiting death. He fell in love with her at first sight. The sequel may be guessed: he killed the monster, freed Andromeda and married her. He took her back with him to Seriphos, where he found that his mother was being persecuted by Polydectes. He put an end to this and to Polydectes by holding up the head of Medusa. Polydectes saw it and was turned to stone then and there.

Perseus returned the magic wallet and dark helmet to Hermes and presented Athene with the head of the Gorgon which she placed on her shield. Then, with his mother and his wife, he set forth for Argos. Acrisius, remembering what the oracle had said long ago, fled at the approach of his daughter's son. But fate ordained that one day while Perseus was throwing the discus during funeral games Acrisius was present and the discus struck and killed him. Perseus did not wish to succeed to his grandfather's throne and instead reigned only over Tiryns and Mycenae. He founded the family of the Perseids of which one day Hercules was to be such a glorious representative.

OTHER HEROES OF ARGOLIS.

The Pelopids. Although the race of Pelopids took their name from Pelops, they owed their origin to Pelops' father, Tantalus.

Tantalus was king of Phrygia or of Lydia. He was invited to dine with the gods on Olympus and he stole their nectar and ambrosia. He returned their invitation, and when they sat at his table he served to them, in order to test their divinity, the body of his own son, Pelops. The guests immediately realised this; Demeter alone, more absent-minded or else more hungry than the others, ate flesh from the shoulder. Zeus ordered that the child's remains should be thrown into a magic cauldron and Clotho restored Pelops to life. Only one of his shoulders was missing and had to be replaced in ivory.

For these crimes Tantalus was cast into the infernal regions. He stood waist-deep in the middle of a lake in Tartarus surrounded by trees laden with delicious fruit. Thirst and hunger which he could never satisfy tortured him: for when he reached out his hand the fruit evaded him, when he leaned down to drink the water receded.

When he was grown up Pelops left Phrygia and went to Pisa in Elis where he competed for the hand of Hippodameia. Her father, Oenomaus, had promised to give his daughter to the first suitor who vanquished him in a chariot race. Fifteen suitors had already been defeated and killed. Pelops bribed Myrtilus, Oenomaus' charioteer, to loosen one of his master's chariot wheels, and thus he won the race and the hand of Hippodameia. Afterwards he killed Myrtilus in order to get rid of an embarrassing accomplice. But the father of Myrtilus was Hermes, and Hermes avenged the death of his son by laying a curse on Pelops and all his house.

By Hippodameia Pelops had several children, among them Atreus and Thyestes. By another wife he had a son Chrysippus, whom he particularly loved. At Hippodameia's instigation Atreus and Thyestes murdered Chrysippus and for this crime were forced to go into exile. They reached Mycenae. At the death of Eurystheus, King of Mycenae, Atreus succeeded to the throne. His brother Thyestes was jealous and seduced the wife of Atreus, Aerope, and in addition stole from him a ram with a golden fleece which had been a present from Hermes. He was driven from Mycenae but left Pleisthenes to avenge him. Now Pleisthenes was Atreus' son, who had been brought up by Thyestes as his own son. Pleisthenes was on the point of striking down Atreus, but Atreus killed him instead, realising too late that it was his son. To avenge himself Atreus pretended to be reconciled with Thyestes and invited him and his children to return to Mycenae. In the course of a feast he served to

Pollux killing Lynceus. Antique bas-relief. School of Phidias. Villa Albani, Rome.

Thyestes the bodies of two of his sons. The sun, it was said, hid in order not to cast light on such a crime. Later Atreus was killed by Aegisthus, another son of Thyestes, whom Atreus had brought up with his own children, Agamemnon and Menelaus.

The series of these revolting crimes did not stop at this point. Thyestes who had succeeded his brother to the throne of Argos was driven from it by his nephews Agamemnon and Menelaus. On his return from the Trojan War, Agamemnon, in his turn, was murdered by Aegisthus who was living in adultery with Agamemnon's wife, Clytemnestra. Eight years later Aegisthus and Clytemnestra perished by the hand of Clytemnestra's son, Orestes, who expiated this matricide by a long period of suffering. Then only were the Furies satisfied and an end put to the atrocities which had stained the family of Atreus with blood.

THE DIOSCURI AND THE HEROES OF LACONIA

The Dioscuri. The founder of the Laconian dynasties was Lelex who, by his union with a Naiad, had a son Eurotas, whose daughter Sparta married Lacedaemon. Lacedaemon reigned over Sparta and gave his name to that city. The most famous of his descendants were Hippocoön, who was killed by Hercules: Icarius, to whom Dionysus taught the secret of wine-making and who was killed by drunken shepherds; and finally Tyndareus, husband of Leda and father of Helen, of Clytemnestra, and of the Dioscuri: Castor and Pollux.

It was said that Zeus had played a certain part in this paternity since, in the guise of a swan, he had visited Leda. Leda had been brought to bed with two eggs from one of which issued Pollux and Helen, regarded as the children of Zeus, and from the other Castor

The Abduction of Helen. Greek bas-relief in the Lateran Museum, Rome.

and Clytemnestra, who were reputed to be the children of Tyndareus.

In spite of their different paternity Castor and Pollux were both qualified as Dioscuri, which meant young sons of Zeus. They always lived on terms of close friendship.

The semi-divine character of the Dioscuri has been explained by A. H. Krappe as the superstition which surrounds the birth of twins among most primitive peoples. The phenomenon, being not common, was interpreted either as ill-omened – hence the persecutions often inflicted on twins and their mother – or as fortunate. In either event the anomaly was justified by assuming that one at least of the children was of divine origin; this was the case with Hercules and Iphicles, and also with Castor and Pollux.

Among the exploits of the Dioscuri may be mentioned their expedition against Athens to rescue their sister Helen from Theseus who had abducted her. They also joined Jason on the Argonauts' expedition, and Zeus showed his benevolence towards them during a storm which assailed the ship *Argo* in the sea of Colchis. While Orpheus called upon the gods, two flames descended from the sky and hovered over the heads of the Dioscuri. It was the origin of Saint Elmo's Fire which still today announces to sailors the end of a storm.

Afterwards Castor and Pollux carried off the two daughters of Leucippus and married them. This was the occasion of their quarrel with the Aphareids, Idas and Lynceus, who were also paying court to the young women. This rivalry must have been unfortunate for the Dioscuri although no one knows exactly how it turned out. According to Pindar the Dioscuri went on an expedition with the Aphareids and cheated them out of their share of the booty. Ac-

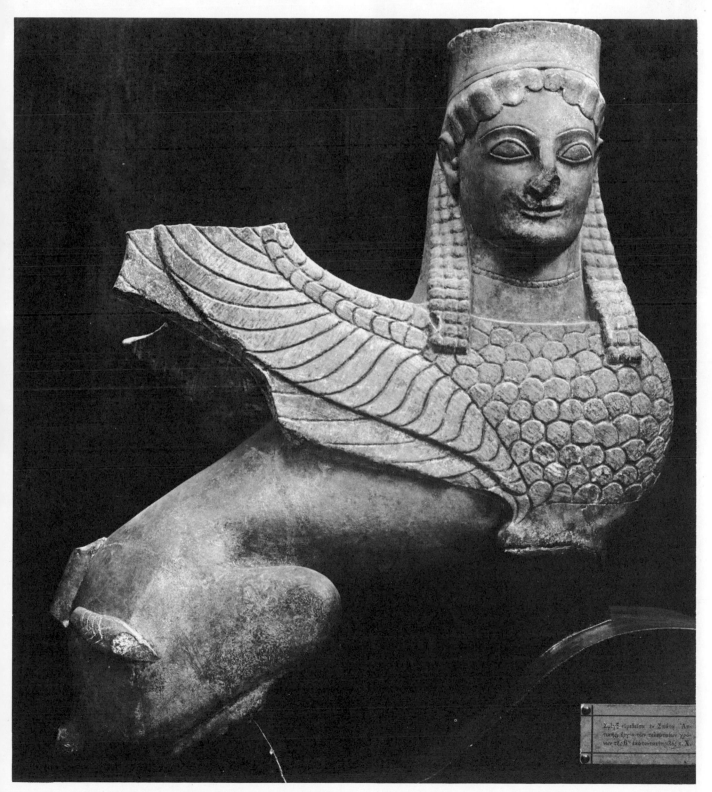

The Sphinx. Archaic statue found at Sparta. National Museum, Athens.

Oedipus and the Sphinx. 'What is the animal that has four feet in
the morning, two at midday and three in the evening?'
Perched on Mount Phicium near Thebes the Sphinx has just
put her riddle to Oedipus who is in the process of answering her.
A monster, part woman, part lion and part bird, she was accustomed to
devour all those who could not solve it. Oedipus succeeded,
however, and she threw herself to her death. Etruscan seal.

cording to other authors the four young men had a dispute over the
division of a herd of oxen. Idas quartered an ox and ruled that half
the spoil should go to the man who ate his share first, the other half
going to the man who finished second. So saying he swallowed his
own quarter and his brother's quarter and drove off the whole herd.

The Dioscuri then led an expedition against the Aphareids and
in the course of the battle Pollux killed Lynceus while Castor was
mortally wounded by Idas. Pollux wept over the body of his brother;
for being himself immortal he could not follow him to the kingdom
of Hades. Zeus was touched by this fraternal devotion and authorised Pollux to share with his brother the privilege of immortality: thus the Dioscuri continued to live each on alternate days.
Another tradition says that Zeus placed them among the stars, in
the constellation Gemini, The Twins.

Venerated at first in Achaia, the Dioscuri were afterwards
honoured throughout Greece as the tutelary divinities of sailors
and as protectors of hospitality. Sometimes they can be seen,
dressed in white robes and purple mantles, starred bonnets on their
heads, arriving in cities to test what sort of welcome the inhabitants
will give to strangers.

Helen. Their sister Helen was celebrated for her beauty. When she
had scarcely reached the age of ten Theseus carried her off, but the
Dioscuri brought her home again. She was besieged by suitors.
Her father Tyndareus made each of them swear that he would in
case of need come to the aid of the lucky man who became Helen's
husband. He then chose Menelaus. For three years the couple lived
happily together. Then Paris, son of the Trojan King Priam, visited
the court of Menelaus, fell in love with Helen and carried her off.
This was the cause of the Trojan War. All the princes of Greece,
faithful to their oaths, took arms under the command of Agamemnon to avenge the outrage done to Menelaus. For ten years the
struggle raged before the walls of Troy. Neither the craft of Odysseus,
the bravery of Diomedes, nor the dash of Achilles could conquer
the resistance of the Trojans, led by the valiant Hector. Finally the
Greek warriors were able to enter the city by hiding in the hollow

The death of Pelias. One of his daughters leads the old man from
his seat while another waits by a cauldron with a sword in her hand.
On the left Medea looks on. In order to effect her revenge Medea
had told Pelias' daughters that she could rejuvinate their father if they
first cut him up and boiled him in a cauldron. Two of them obeyed
her and thus killed their father. Detail from a Greek red-figured vase,
c. 420 B.C.

flanks of a huge wooden horse which the Trojans themselves dragged
into the city. Troy was taken and set on fire. Old Priam was slain and
the rest of his family immolated or carried away as slaves. Menelaus
regained his wife and was reconciled with her. To be sure it was said
that the real Helen had always remained in Egypt where her husband
later found her, and that Paris had brought only the phantom of
Helen back with him to Troy. However, it seems obvious that this
account was invented simply to save the self-esteem of the unfortunate Menelaus.

The end of Helen was variously reported. After her husband's
death she was admitted among the stars with the Dioscuri. Or else
she was united to Achilles in the Islands of the Blessed. Or, again,
she was driven from Sparta and sought refuge in Rhodes where
she was hanged from a tree on the orders of the queen, Polyxo.

She was venerated on this island of Rhodes under the epithet Dendritis.

Clytemnestra. The second daughter of Tyndareus, Clytemnestra, was first married to Tantalus, and subsequently to Agamemnon. She could never forgive Agamemnon for having sacrificed their daughter Iphigenia to the gods, and on his return from Troy she slew him in his bath, with the complicity of her lover Aegisthus. The two murderers were put to death by Orestes, the son of Clytemnestra.

OEDIPUS AND THE HEROES OF BOEOTIA

Cadmus. The principal heroes of Thebes belonged to the family of the Labdacids whose founder was Cadmus. He was the son of Agenor and Telephassa. Phoenix and Cilix were his brothers and Europa his sister. When Europa was carried off by Zeus, the three brothers set out to find her. Cilix and Phoenix soon tired of the search and settled down in the countries which were to be known as Cilicia and Phoenicia. Cadmus was more persistent and consulted the oracle of Delphi who advised him to abandon his search and when he came across a cow to let her guide him, and where she stopped, there to build a city. In Phocis Cadmus found the fateful animal and

followed her into Boeotia where she stopped. There he founded the city of Thebes and constructed the Cadmean Acropolis. He then decided to sacrifice the cow to Athene. In preparation for this ceremony he sent servants to fetch water from the Spring of Ares; but at the spring they encountered a dragon which devoured them. When Cadmus heard this he attacked the monster and killed it. Athene had helped him and she now advised him to draw the teeth of the dragon and sow them in a nearby furrow. The teeth at once began to sprout and from them sprang forth warriors, the Sparti (from the Greek 'to sow'), who immediately began to fight among themselves and kill each other. Only five survived and they became the ancestors of the Thebans.

Meanwhile in order to expiate the murder of the dragon who was a son of Ares, Cadmus had to spend a few years serving as a slave. After this Athene recompensed him by awarding him the crown of Thebes, while Zeus granted him the hand of the shining Virgin Harmonia, daughter of Ares and Aphrodite, or perhaps, of Zeus and Electra.

The couple lived happily together. Their children were Semele, mother of Dionysus; Ino, mother of Melicertes; Autonoë, mother of Actaeon; Agave, mother of Pentheus; and Polydorus, father of Labdacus who was the ancestor of the Labdacids. Towards the end of their lives Cadmus and Harmonia went to reign over Illyria, then were changed into dragons and transported to the Islands of the Blessed.

In Greece Cadmus was considered to be a divine legislator and the promoter of Boeotian civilisation: to him were ascribed the discovery of casting metal and the invention or importation of the alphabet.

Amphion and Zethus. Amphion and Zethus were twins, and the legends concerning them belong to the earliest days of Theban royalty. They were sons of Zeus and Antiope. Persecuted by her father, Antiope sought refuge with Epopeus at Sicyon. Epopeus married her, but her brother, Lycus, marched on Sicyon, killed Epopeus and brought Antiope back a captive. On the return journey, in a wayside thicket, Antiope brought her twins into the world. They were exposed on Mount Cithaeron and taken in by shepherds. Antiope was long held prisoner, but one day her chains fell from her of their own accord. She fled and rejoined her sons, Amphion and Zethus, who then attacked Thebes where Lycus now reigned. They killed Lycus and also his wife, Dirce, who was tied to the horns of a wild bull. The two brothers then fortified the city. Zethus carried

stones while Amphion, with the magic sounds of his lyre, caused the stones to move of their own will and gently slide into the desired position in the walls.

Afterwards Zethus married Thebe and Amphion married Niobe who bore him twelve children. Niobe was proud of her twelve children and unfortunately dared to scoff at Leto, who had only had two. Apollo and Artemis punished this insult to their mother by shooting down all of Niobe's children. The unhappy mother, prostrate with grief, was changed by Zeus into a rock on the deserted summits of Mount Sipylus.

Oedipus. Laius, son of Labdacus, king of Thebes, had married Jocasta. Having been warned by an oracle that his son would one day kill him Laius carried the child to which Jocasta had just given birth to Mount Cithaeron. He pierced the infant's feet with a nail and tied them together solidly, hoping thus to be rid of him. But a shepherd found the child and took him to Polybus, King of Corinth, who adopted him and named him Oedipus because of his wounded foot. When Oedipus had grown up he learned his destiny from an oracle who told him that he would kill his father and marry his mother. Oedipus believed that he could escape this fate by exiling

The building of the ship Argo. Antique bas-relief in the Villa Albani, Rome.

himself for ever from Corinth, never again seeing Polybus and his wife whom he assumed to be his true parents. This scruple was his own undoing. He went to Boeotia and on the road quarrelled with an unknown man whom he struck with his staff and killed. The victim was, indeed, Laius, his own father. Oedipus continued on his journey without suspecting that the first half of the oracle's prediction had been fulfilled. He arrived in Thebes where he learned that the region was being devastated by a fabulous monster with the face and bust of a woman, the body of a lion and the wings of a bird. Guarding the road to Thebes the Sphinx – as the monster was called – would stop all travellers and propose enigmas to them; those who were unable to solve her riddles she would devour. Creon, who had governed Thebes since the recent death of Laius, promised the crown and the hand of Jocasta to the man who delivered the city from this scourge. Oedipus resolved to attempt the feat. He was successful. The Sphinx asked him: 'Which is the animal that has four feet in the morning, two at midday and three in the evening?' He answered: 'Man, who in infancy crawls on all fours, who walks upright on two feet in maturity, and in his old age supports himself with a stick.' The Sphinx was vanquished and threw herself into the sea.

And thus, still without realising it, Oedipus became the husband of his mother, Jocasta. From their union two sons were born, Eteocles and Polyneices, and two daughters, Antigone and Ismene. Oedipus, in spite of the double crime he had innocently committed, was honoured as a sovereign devoted to his people's welfare, and appeared to prosper. But the Erinnyes were waiting. A terrible epidemic ravaged the land, decimating the population, and at the same time an incredible drought brought with it famine. When consulted, the oracle of Delphi replied that these scourges would not cease until the Thebans had driven the still unknown murderer of Laius out of the country. Oedipus, after having offered ritual maledictions against the assassin, undertook to find out who he was. His inquiries finally led to the discovery that the guilty man was none other than himself, and that Jocasta whom he had married was his mother. Jocasta in shame and grief hanged herself and Oedipus put out his own eyes. Then he went into exile, accompanied by his faithful daughter Antigone. He took refuge in the town of Colonus in Attica and, at last purified of his abominable crimes, disappeared mysteriously from the earth.

As for his sons, victims of the paternal curse, they perished by each other's hand. They had agreed to reign for alternate years. But when the time came Eteocles refused to hand over the crown. Polyneices gathered together an army of Argives and laid siege to Thebes. It was during this siege that the two brothers slew each other in the course of single combat. The senate of Thebes decreed that the body of Polyneices should be left unburied, but Antigone nevertheless rendered her dead brother funeral honours. For this she was condemned to be buried alive. Her sister Ismene shared her fate. And thus the unhappy family came to an end.

MELEAGER AND THE HEROES OF AETOLIA

The ancestor of the Aetolians was Aetolus, son of Endymion. Because of an accidental murder Aetolus was forced to leave the land of his father and he established himself in the region of Greece which afterwards took his name. Among his descendants was Oeneus, to whom Dionysus made a gift of the first vinestock. Oeneus had by two different wives two sons, Meleager and Tydeus.

Meleager. Meleager's mother was Althaea, the first wife of Oeneus. When he was seven days old the Fates appeared to his mother. Clotho predicted for the child great generosity; Lachesis, extraordinary strength; Atropos declared that he would live only so long as a certain brand which was burning on the hearth continued to exist. Althaea hastened to rescue the brand, extinguished it and put it in a place of safety. Meanwhile Meleager became, as the Fates had foretold, a hero full of valour. His father Oeneus once forgot to offer to Artemis the first fruits of his harvest and the angry goddess sent a monstrous wild boar to ravage Aetolia. To hunt the monster Meleager invited all the most celebrated heroes of Greece, among them a young Arcadian woman named Atalanta. The hunt was cruel and hard. Many were killed by the wild boar. Atalanta was the first to wound it with an arrow in the back and Meleager finished it off with his spear. A dispute arose among the huntsmen over the monster's remains which Meleager had presented to Atalanta.

Meleager's uncles attempted to take it away from her and Meleager killed them. When she learned how her brothers had been slain by her too quick-tempered son, Althaea, it was said, threw the fatal brand into the fire and Meleager immediately died. Another tradition says that Althaea merely dedicated her son to the Furies.

According to this latter version, war meanwhile broke out between the Aetolians and the Curetes over whom Meleager's uncles had reigned. The hero fought valiantly at first, but when he learned that his mother had cursed him he shut himself up in his house. The Curetes thus gained the advantage and broke into the town, setting fire to the houses. Stubbornly Meleager ignored the entreaties of relations and friends and refused to fight. He gave in at last to the prayers of his wife, Cleopatra, and resuming his place at the head of his troops put the enemy to flight. During the battle he was killed, they said, by Apollo.

Atalanta. Atalanta, the unconscious cause of Meleager's troubles, was the daughter of the Arcadian Iasus. Iasus had wanted a son and he exposed his infant daughter on Mount Parthenius where she was suckled by a bear and taken in by hunters whose rough life she shared. When she had grown up Atalanta continued to live in rural solitude, taking pleasure only in the chase and despising the thought of marriage. She slew the Centaurs, Rhaecus and Hylaeus, who had tried to ravish her. She took an illustrious part in Meleager's boar hunt, and vanquished Peleus in wrestling at the funeral games held in honour of Pelias. Her father Iasus finally recognised her and decided to have her married. She declared that she would only marry the man who could beat her in a foot race. More than one suitor had competed and been killed by Atalanta when a certain Melanion thought of a trick. While he ran he dropped one by one three golden apples which Aphrodite had given him. Atalanta paused to pick them up. She was thus beaten and married Melanion. The couple were later turned into lions for having profaned a temple of Zeus.

Tydeus and Diomedes. Meleager's half-brother, Tydeus, killed his cousins who had plotted against his father. He had to leave Aetolia and went to Argos where he married the daughter of King Adrastus. He took part in the expedition of the seven chieftains against Thebes and distinguished himself by various exploits, notably by killing fifty Thebans who had laid an ambush for him. He fell, however, under the blows of the Theban Melanippus. Though grievously wounded Athene brought him an elixir which would have cured and made him immortal. She was about to offer it to him when the soothsayer Amphiaraus who was a personal enemy of Tydeus, presented him with the head of Melanippus. In a transport of rage Tydeus split open his recent enemy's skull and devoured his brain. Outraged by such savagery, Athene left him to his fate and Tydeus died shortly afterwards.

His son Diomedes avenged him by sacking Thebes with the Epigoni. The same Diomedes was renowned for his exploits before Troy: he wounded Aphrodite and even Ares. With Odysseus he seized the Palladium on which the safety of Troy depended. After the war his return to Greece was marked with adventures. He was tossed by a storm on to the coast of Lycia and very nearly immolated to Ares by King Lycus, but was saved by the king's daughter, Callirrhoë, who loved him and when he departed killed herself in despair. When he returned to Argos he learned that his wife was unfaithful to him. He left Argos, which he later reconquered. He finished his valorous career in Italy with King Daunus whose daughter he married.

PELEUS, THE ARGONAUTS AND THE HEROES OF THESSALY

Peleus. Although Peleus was one of the most famous heroes of Thessaly he was not a native of that country. He was the son of Aeacus who reigned over the island of Aegina. Peleus with his brother Telamon fled from Aegina after they killed their half-brother Phocus. Telemon established himself in Salamis where he inherited the crown of Cychreus, the king. Peleus first went to Phthia where he visited Eurytion. Unwilling to present himself without an escort, he prayed to Zeus who changed certain ants into men who were henceforth called *Myrmidons*. Eurytion welcomed him warmly and gave him a third of his estates, together with the

The Argonauts gather under the protection of Athene. Detail of a crater from Orvieto. Louvre.

hand of his daughter Antigone. Unfortunately Peleus and Eurytion took part in Meleager's boar hunt during which Peleus accidentally killed his father-in-law. He then took refuge in Iolcus with Acastus who purified him. The wife of Acastus conceived an amorous passion for Peleus, but was repulsed by him. She avenged herself by falsely telling Antigone that Peleus had been unfaithful to her. Antigone hanged herself in grief. She also told her husband the same story. The laws of hospitality forbade Acastus to kill Peleus; instead he took his guest hunting on Mount Pelion, hoping to see him killed. But Peleus vanquished the wildest and most dangerous beasts, thanks to a fabulous dagger which had been made by Hephaestus. While Peleus was asleep Acastus stole this dagger and hid it, thinking in this way to leave him without defence against the

ferocious Centaurs who peopled the mountain. The project nearly succeeded, but by luck Peleus was saved by the Centaur Chiron who returned his dagger. Peleus used it to punish Acastus and his treacherous wife, and himself became king of the land.

Shortly afterwards Peleus married the Nereid Thetis, not without resistance on the part of the bride who, once courted by Poseidon and Zeus himself, considered marriage to a mortal to be an insult to her dignity. Thanks to the advice of Chiron Peleus overcame the efforts of Thetis to elude him and the marriage was sumptuously celebrated in the crests of Mount Pelion. From their union Achilles was born. We have already seen how Thetis attempted to bestow immortality on her son. The achievement of this work was interrupted by Peleus, and Thetis in vexation rejoined her sisters, the Nereids.

Young Achilles was confided to the Centaur Chiron who fed him on the marrowbones of bears and the entrails of lions.

Achilles. Thus Achilles grew in years and strength. He was nine when the seer Calchas predicted that he alone would conquer Troy. Thetis, who knew that in Troy he would meet his death, tried to avoid the peril by hiding him, disguised as a girl, in the palace of Lycomedes, King of Skyros. But the Greeks, helped by Odysseus, discovered the so-called 'maiden' by an ingenious trick. Odysseus one day came to Lycomedes' palace with gifts for the king's daugh-

ters. Among them he slipped a shield and a spear. Then he and his companions gave battle cries and sounded the trumpets. Achilles thinking they were being attacked, rushed for the weapons. The Greeks then took him with them; for he could not escape his destiny. We know what valour he displayed beneath the walls of Ilium; in single combat he killed the valiant Hector. But he himself perished before Troy was taken, pierced in his vulnerable heel by an arrow, shot either by Apollo or by Paris.

But to return to Peleus: while his son grew up his own adventurous life continued. He took part in the voyage of the Argonauts. He

The Centaur Chiron instructing the young Achilles. When Thetis deserted her husband Peleus, their son, Achilles, was entrusted to the care of the wise old Centaur Chiron on Mount Pelion who fed him on the entrails of lions and the marrowbones of bears to give him courage and instructed him in the arts of riding, hunting, pipe-playing and healing. Here he teaches him to play on the lyre. Wall-painting from the basilica of Herculaneum.

Priam pleading with Achilles for the body of his son Hector. Achilles reclines on his couch with his head averted while the aged Priam addresses him. Above him hangs the armour forged for him by Hephaestus while beneath his couch lies the mangled body of the Trojan hero. Though Achilles had refused Hector's dying plea that his body might be ransomed for burial he finally yielded to Priam's entreaties and accepted Hector's weight in gold. Greek vase painting.

fought with the Lapiths against the Centaurs. He seconded Hercules during his own expedition against Ilium. He outlived his son and had a listless old age. The circumstances of his death are unknown.

Jason and the Argonauts. The expedition of the Argonauts was celebrated in the annals not only of Thessaly but of all Greece. Its object was the conquest of the Golden Fleece, the origin of which was this: Phrixus and Helle, the two children of the Boeotian King Athamas, were hated by their step-mother Ino. Their very lives were threatened and they fled, mounted on a fabulous ram which was a gift of Hermes. This ram was endowed with reason and speech; had a fleece of gold and could move through the air as well as it could over the earth. In the course of their flight Helle fell into the sea and gave her name to the Hellespont. Phrixus was luckier and reached Colchis on the Black Sea. There he sacrificed the ram to Zeus, and offered its fleece to the king of the country, Aeëtes, who hung it from a tree and set a dragon who never slept to guard it.

Meanwhile at Iolcus in Thessaly reigned Pelias who had wrenched the throne from his brother, Aeson. Aeson's son, Jason, had been confided to the care of the Centaur Chiron. When he reached man's estate Jason went to his uncle and demanded his share of the kingdom. Pelias was sorely disturbed, for an oracle had once told him to 'beware of the man who wears but one sandal', and Jason had appeared before him with only one foot shod. He therefore told his nephew that he would willingly comply with his demand on condition that Jason first brought him back the Golden Fleece.

With the help of Hera or Athene Jason immediately built a ship with fifty oars, the *Argo*, in which he had set a bough of the prophetic oak of Zeus at Dodona. He gathered together the most famous heroes, among whom were Amphion, the Dioscuri, Hercules, Orpheus, Peleus, Theseus and Meleager. Then the hardy adventurers set forth in search of the fabled Golden Fleece. Their voyage was full of incident: they were forced to struggle against the elements as well as against men. Finally they reached the mouth

The young Apollo. Bronze statue of the fifth century B.C.

Two figures from the palace of Knossos, now in the Heraklion Museum. They probably represent priestesses of the great earth-mother and fertility goddess of the eastern Mediterranean. The serpents which they carry are age-old symbols of fertility *c.* 1600 B.C.

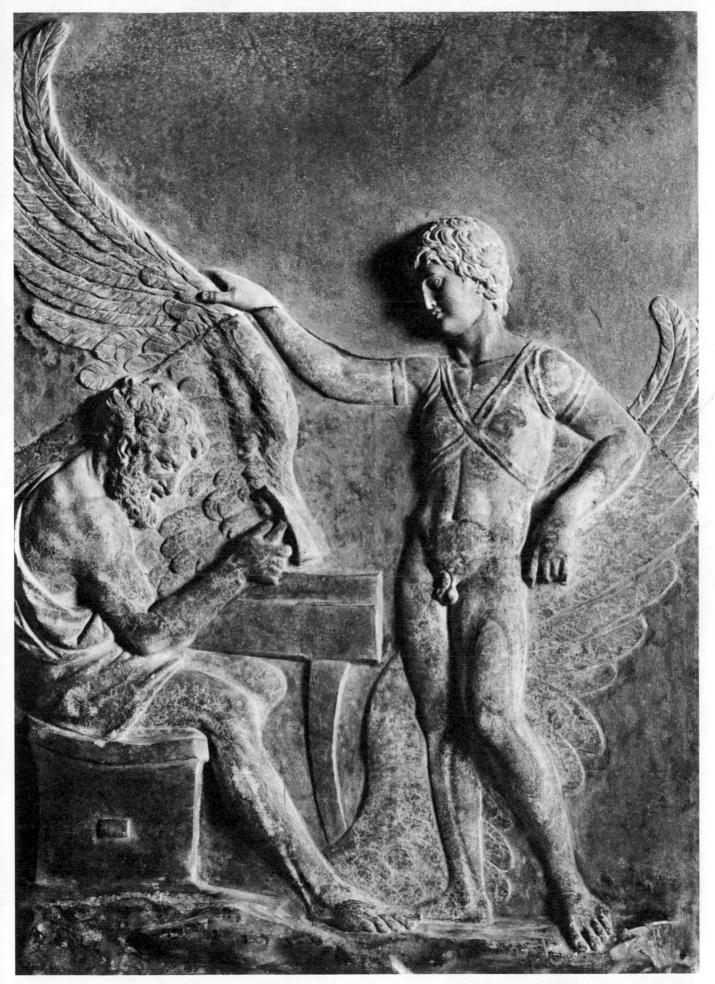

Daedalus and Icarus. Antique bas-relief. Villa Albani, Rome.

of the Phasis and rowing up the river came to the kingdom of Aeetes. Aeetes consented to give up the Golden Fleece, but imposed his own conditions. Jason had first to harness a plough with two wild bulls whose hooves were of bronze and whose breath was of flame. With them he must plough a field and plant it with dragons' teeth. Luckily for Jason the daughter of Aeetes, Medea, fell in love with him and, as she was a skilled magician, showed him how to overcome these fearful conditions. Then Aeetes refused to keep his word; Medea again helped Jason to vanquish the dragon who guarded the Golden Fleece and to seize the precious trophy. Both left the country in haste, pursued by Aeëtes. In order to delay her father's pursuit Medea did not hesitate to scatter the route with the dismembered body of her own brother whose throat she had cut. After a long and perilous voyage which took them across the Danube, the Ocean, the Libyan deserts, the Red Sea and the Mediterranean, the Argonauts finally returned to Iolcus. During Jason's absence Pelias had put Aeson to death. Others say that Aeson was still alive and was even rejuvenated by one of Medea's magic philtres. In any case, Jason avenged himself on his uncle. Medea persuaded the daughters of Pelias that she could with her charms rejuvenate their father, but that first they must cut him up into pieces and cook him. They carried out these instructions and Medea left matters as they were. After this atrocious murder Medea and Jason withdrew to Corinth. There they lived happily for ten years, whereupon Jason fell in love with Creusa (or Glauce), daughter of King Creon, and abandoned Medea. Medea avenged herself by sending a wedding present to the new bride: a magnificent robe which consumed her with inextinguishable fire. Medea then cut the throats of the children she had had by Jason and fled to Athens where she married Aegeus. She had to leave Athens when she tried to poison Theseus and went to her father at Colchis.

As for Jason, some say that he grew weary of life and killed himself. Others say that while resting in the shade of the ship *Argo,* the poop fell on him and accidentally crushed him to death.

ORPHEUS AND THE HEROES OF THRACE

Orpheus, the great hero of Thrace, was very different in character from the other Greek heroes. He was not distinguished for his warlike exploits. He was in origin perhaps a Thracian king, and he owed his fame above all to his amazing musical talent. Son of Apollo, he sang and played the lyre with such art that the savage beasts came running to listen and even trees would follow him. His talent performed miracles during the voyage of the Argonauts. The ship *Argo,* high on the beach, descended to the sea of its own accord at the sound of his singing. His songs arrested the Symplegades, those terrible moving rocks which threatened to crush the ship, and sent them down to the bottom of the sea. He lulled the dragon, guardian of the Golden Fleece, to sleep by singing, and thus facilitated the Argonauts' escape.

Such was the power of his voice and the harmony of his lyre that even the infernal deities submitted to them. He had married the nymph Eurydice whom he passionately loved. One day when Eurydice was fleeing from Aristaeus she was mortally bitten by a snake hidden in the grass. Orpheus was heartbroken at the death of his wife and resolved to descend into the Underworld to reclaim her. He was able to charm Hades and Persephone who gave him permission to take Eurydice back to earth on the sole condition that he should not turn to look at her during the journey. The couple had almost reached the gates of Hades when Orpheus impatiently and imprudently turned to look at his wife. At once she was whisked back into the sombre abode of the dead and vanished, this time for ever.

Orpheus was inconsolable and, some said, killed himself. But the more widely held opinion was that he was torn in pieces by Thracian women who were infuriated at this single-minded love for his wife. His head and his lyre were flung into the River Hebrus and carried as far as Lesbos. The head of the divine singer was caught in a fissure of rock where for long it delivered oracles. In the days of Lucian his lyre could still be seen in a temple at Lesbos and it was sacrilege to lay hands on it. One day Neanthus, son of the Tyrant of Lesbos, tried to play the wondrous lyre and was devoured by dogs who had been attracted by the sound. They also said that the head of Orpheus was found by a shepherd on the banks of the Melas, and in the town of Libethra in Macedonia they pointed out his tomb.

Other Thracian Poets. Thrace took pride in other famous poets and musicians, such as Philammon, also said to be a son of Apollo, and to whom was attributed the institution of choral dance in the temple of Delphi.

Philammon's son, Thamyris, an equally celebrated musician, once dared to challenge the Muses. For his presumption they deprived him of his voice and, into the bargain, blinded him.

To Thrace also belonged Eumolpus, son of Poseidon and Chione who was a daughter of Boreas. Eumolpus was thrown into the sea by his mother who wished to conceal her shame. He was found by Boreas who carried him to Ethiopia. From there Eumolpus went to the court of Tegyrius, King of Thrace. He was killed by Erechtheus when he was fighting with the Eleusinians against Athens. Some say that Eumolpus instituted the Eleusinian mysteries in honour of Demeter who had taught him how to cultivate the vine and trees. He also taught Hercules to sing and play the lyre.

MINOS AND THE HEROES OF CRETE

The ancient legends of Crete were early imported into Greece and were, as we have seen, a basis of Hellenic mythology, taking on new aspects as they became adapted to continental traditions. They centred for the most part around the figure of the fabulous King Minos. It seems, however, that more personages than Minos were concerned, and we should distinguish at least two Minoses of which one was the grandson of the other. But makers of myths are never worried about chronology or verisimilitude and wove all their legends around the single figure of Minos.

Minos then – with Rhadamanthys and Sarpedon – was a son of Zeus and Europa. Europa after her arrival in Crete married the king of the island, Asterius, who adopted her children. Minos succeeded Asterius to the throne of Crete. He distinguished himself by the wisdom of his laws and his sense of justice which, after his death, earned him promotion to the dignity of judge of the Underworld.

Minos had married Pasiphae. She had already given him several children when Poseidon, angered by Minos, inspired her with a monstrous passion for a bull. From this union was born the Minotaur, a monster half-human, half-bull.

The Athenians had killed the son of Minos, Androgeus, and in consequence Minos laid siege to Athens. Previously he had besieged Megara and vanquished the king Nisus, thanks to the treason of Scylla, Nisus' daughter. Scylla was in love with Minos and had therefore cut a golden lock of hair – on which the safety of the city depended – from her father's head. Minos took advantage of this treacherous act, but punished its author. He had the infatuated Scylla drowned in the Saronic Sea, where she was changed into a lark. Before Athens, however, Minos was less successful. The siege dragged on. Minos implored the aid of Zeus who visited Athens with a plague. To rid themselves of this plague the Athenians consented to send Minos an annual tribute of seven youths and seven maidens who were to be fed to the Minotaur. We have already seen how Theseus freed his city from this wretched servitude.

The Minotaur, who fed exclusively on human flesh, had been enclosed by Minos in an amazing palace from which no one could find an exit: the Labyrinth. The Labyrinth had been constructed by Daedalus, an Athenian distinguished for his ingenuity and cunning. To Daedalus was ascribed the invention of the axe and the saw. It was he, they said, who first fixed arms and legs to the *xoana,* the shapeless primitive statues of the gods. He killed his nephew who was a rival craftsman and sought asylum with Minos. Daedalus helped Ariadne when she gave Theseus the precious ball of thread which enabled the hero to find his way out of the Labyrinth. For this act of treachery Minos had Daedalus and his son Icarus locked up in the Labyrinth for a while. They flew to freedom by means of an ingenious pair of wings which Daedalus devised. In the course of their flight Icarus was imprudent enough to approach too near the sun. The wax by which his wings were attached melted and he plummeted into the sea which henceforth took his name, the Icarian Sea. Daedalus landed in Cumae, and from there went to Sicily where he gained the favour of King Cocalus. Thus when Minos pursuing Daedalus landed on the island, Cocalus refused to hand over his guest. Indeed, he smothered Minos in a bath. Such was the end of this famous monarch whose tomb was, nevertheless, shown in Crete.

ROMAN MYTHOLOGY

INTRODUCTION

The term Roman Mythology requires some explanation, even justification. The religious system whose centre is placed for convenience in Rome was not in fact purely Roman; the elements which composed it were numerous and varied. It was not monolithic, but a mosaic in which can be recognised contributions which were Etruscan, Alban, Sabine, Greek, Syrian, Persian, Egyptian. Obviously there were Roman elements too; but not to such a degree that they dominated the system and gave it a specifically national character.

Roman mythology seems poor when compared with the poetic and spiritual richness of Greek and Oriental mythologies. The Romans were a practical people with little imagination and they sought to form a religion which corresponded to their needs. It was important to them to feel sheltered from the perils which threatened the group or the individual; but they experienced no mystic necessity to love and worship the superhuman powers to whom they had recourse. Their gods were protectors for whose services they paid; and in case of failure their wages were withheld. *Do ut des:* I give to thee so that thou givest to me; such was the cynical profession of faith that one might inscribe above the entrance of the Roman Pantheon.

We use the term Roman pantheon inaccurately, for there was no genuinely Roman pantheon. The term was a Greek importation of the third century B.C. Was there not, then, a hierarchy of divinities worshipped in Rome? There was. But it was not at all like that great assembly of splendid personages, all possessing their individual traits and each easily recognised, which composed the Greek pantheon. It was something more abstract and utilitarian: a register, an actual catalogue (*Indigitamenta*) in which those who were interested could find the names of protective powers with special functions attributed to them and the rites which must be performed in order to purchase their favours.

In the course of time, when the fortunes of war had given the Romans empire over the ancient world, this utilitarian spirit which they had shown in constructing their own religious system led them without effort to build on their own soil the temples of the peoples they had defeated. These foreign gods whom they installed in the family circle, as it were, were new protectors who joined those who already stood guard over the Roman family and city. Rome, capital of the Empire, accepted within its walls gods who were formerly enemies but henceforth formed part of Roman political organisation.

ITALIC GODS

There were a certain number of purely Italic gods. It must not, however, be forgotten that foreign influences, and above all Greek influence, were felt from very early times. To give a few dates: the traditional foundation of Rome was 753 B.C. Now during the course of that century Greek colonies were established in Sicily and in southern Italy which was, indeed, called Magna Graecia. The Dorians founded Syracuse in 734 and Tarentum in 707. The Achaeans founded Sybaris in 721, Metapontum and Croton. The Euboeans installed themselves on both sides of the Straits of Messina, at Rhegium (Reggio) in Italy and at Messina in Sicily.

Mars, the most Roman of the gods, second in importance only to Jupiter himself. Originally an agricultural deity his character changed with that of the Roman people and he became instead the god of war of a conquering and warring nation, his agricultural functions devolving on to lesser gods. Mars had numerous temples both in Italy and throughout the empire, his chief festivals being in the spring. Roman marble.

Romulus and Remus discovered by the shepherds.
Deposited at the foot of the Palatine by the flooded river Tiber,
the twin baby sons of Mars and Rhea Silvia are shown being suckled by the
she-wolf on this bas-relief from Ostia. On the right is the Tiber.
Romulus and Remus later returned to the Palatine to found the city of
Rome – according to tradition in 753 B.C. Roman altar discovered at Ostia.

Relations obviously sprang up between these Greeks and the
Italic tribes. In particular, Etruscan towns like Tarquinii, Vulci
and Caere were in regular touch with the Hellenic colonies. Now the
Etruscans were closely involved in the history of primitive Rome,
which they perhaps conquered. In any case, during the sixth century
tradition speaks of the Etruscan kings of Rome: Tarquinius the
Elder – who was of Greek origin – Servius Tullius and Tarquinius
Superbus. Hence it is evident that the Romans, through the intermediary of the Etruscans, were very early exposed to Hellenic
influence, which explains why in these notes devoted to the Italic
gods we shall encounter certain details already observed in Greek
mythology. This early hellenisation of the Roman pantheon fore-
shadows the more complete assimilation which took place in the
course of the third and second centuries B.C.

We have seen that the Romans considered their gods as protectors.
There were thus two chief classes of Italic gods: those whose function
it was to guard the State, and those who watched over the family –
the family being considered as an integral cell of the State.

We shall study first the gods of the State; but this does not imply
that in the eyes of the Romans these were in any way more important
than the gods of the family. Indeed the cult rendered by the *Pater-
familias* – who acted as an actual priest – to his lares, his penates
and his manes was just as important as the cult of Janus or Jupiter.

GODS OF THE STATE: PRINCIPAL DIVINITIES

Janus. Janus is unique in that he was an essentially Italic god or,
more precisely, Roman. He appears in no other mythology.

The origin of his name is uncertain. Cicero tried to find it in the
verb *ire*. Others preferred the root *div* (*dividere*), and assumed
that the first form of the name was *Divanus*. A third hypothesis
suggests a form *Jana*, sometimes employed for Diana, of which
the root *dius* or *dium* evokes the idea of the luminous sky.

This last etymology agrees with the established fact that Janus
was in origin a solar deity. But his functions were wide and important
and derived one from another.

Bearded Janus. Roman Coin. Bibliothèque Nationale, Paris.

Beardless Janus. On the reverse, Jupiter mounted on a quadriga.
Roman Coin. Bibliothèque Nationale, Paris.

Mars bearded and helmeted. Roman Coin. Bibliothèque, Nationale, Paris.

Janus was first the god of all doorways: of public gates (*jani*)
through which roads passed, and of private doors. His insignia
were thus the key which opens and closes the door, and the stick
(*virga*) which porters employed to drive away those who had no
right to cross the threshold. His two faces (*Janus bifrons*) allowed
him to observe both the exterior and interior of the house, and the
entrance and exit of public buildings.

Being god of the gates he was naturally the god of departure and
return and, by extension, the god of all means of communication.
Under the name Portunus he was the god of harbours; and since
travel can be either by land or sea, he was supposed to have invented
navigation.

Janus was also the god of 'beginnings'. As a solar god he presided
over daybreak (*Matutinus Pater*). He was soon considered as the
promoter of all initiative and, in a general way, he was placed at
the head of all human enterprises. For this reason the Romans
ascribed to him an essential role in the creation of the world. He
was the god of gods, *Janus Pater*. Ovid relates that Janus was called
Chaos at the time when air, fire, water and earth were all a formless

Jupiter Tinia and Juno Supra.
Etruscan statuettes in
bronze. Louvre.

A Roman sacrifice. This relief probably depicts the *suovetaurilia*, a sacrifice consisting of a bull, a ram and a pig (the most valuable items of Roman livestock) which was offered to Mars in his original capacity as an agricultural deity during the spring festival of the *Ambarvilia*. Prior to becoming a war-god Mars had been responsible for protecting crops and fields and for increasing the fertility of animals. A horse was sacrificed to him each October.

mass. When the elements separated, Chaos took on the form of Janus: his two faces represented the confusion of his original state. Other legends made Janus a king of the golden age of Latium. He was said to have welcomed Saturn driven from the sky by Jupiter.

The cult of Janus was established either by Romulus or by Numa and always remained popular among the Romans. Janus appeared at the head of religious ceremonies and, in his quality of father of the gods, was the first on the Romans' list, coming even before Jupiter. He was honoured on the first day of every month and the first month of the year (*Januarius*) bore his name.

In the Forum he had a temple whose gates were open in times of war and closed in times of peace. The reason for this custom is not certain. The gates of the temple of Janus were, however, rarely closed: once under Numa, three times under Augustus, then under Nero, Marcus Aurelius, Commodus, Gordius III, and in the fourth century.

It was told of this temple how, during an attack on Rome by the Sabine Tatius, a Roman woman was bribed by jewels to show the enemy the path to the citadel. But Janus — whose function it was to open a channel for fountains — caused a jet of boiling water to gush forth which stopped Tatius short. On the spot where the water spurted the temple of Janus was erected.

We possess no statue or bust of Janus, but on coins his effigies are numerous. He is normally represented with a double face, or as an older man with a beard. The crown of laurel does not appear on all his images.

Mars. Mars is without doubt the most Roman of the gods. His cult was more important than that of Jupiter. This was due to the fact that Mars was very intimately concerned with Roman history, first because tradition made him the father of Romulus, then because of his functions as an agricultural god, and finally because he was the god of war. He thus corresponded to the two successive conditions of the Roman citizen, who was himself first a farmer and then a conqueror.

The origin of his name is disputed. Some connect it with a root *mar* or *mas* which signified the generative force. Others give to the root *mar* the sense of 'to shine', which would imply that Mars was at first a solar divinity.

The most ancient forms of his name are *Maurs* and *Mavors* which were contracted into the usual form Mars. Other forms — *Marspiter* and *Maspiter* — were created by the addition of the word *pater*.

The Latins believed that Mars was the son of Juno. Juno gave birth to him, not with the assistance of Jupiter, but by means of

a mystic union with a fabulous flower. Mars was the husband of the vestal Rhea Silvia. He took her by surprise while she was sound asleep, and he became the father of Romulus and Remus.

His functions were at first rustic. In ancient times he was the god of vegetation and fertility. Under the name of *Silvanus* — who afterwards became a distinct divinity — he presided over the prosperity of cattle. He lived in forests and in the mountains. In a general way he protected agriculture; in this aspect he is found associated with *Robigus* who preserved corn from the blight (*robigo*). Several animals were sacred to him: the woodpecker, the horse and the wolf whose image frequently appears in the sanctuaries of the god; it was a she-wolf who had suckled Romulus and Remus. Among the plants and trees which were dedicated to him were the fig-tree, the oak, the dog-wood, the laurel and the bean.

These details, together with the fact that Mars was the god of Spring, when his most important festivals were celebrated, demonstrate that Mars was essentially an agricultural god. He was called Mars *Gradivus*, from *grandiri*, 'to become big, to grow'.

His warrior functions only came afterwards, but in the end they supplanted his former duties which were then transferred to Ceres and Liber. Mars became the god of battle. Honour was paid to him in his temple at Rome before setting out on military expeditions. Before combat sacrifices were offered to him, and after victory he received his share of the booty. Moreover he sometimes appeared on the field of battle, escorted by Bellona and Vacuna, warrior-goddesses, by Pavor and Pallor, who inspired terror in the enemy ranks, and by Honos and Virtus, who instilled in the Romans honour and courage. Mars still preserved his former title of *Gradivus*, but it had changed in meaning and by corruption was now connected with the verb *gradi* 'to march'. Mars was now a foot-soldier. After victory he was accompanied by Vitula and Victoria.

Mars was venerated in Etruria, in Umbria, among the Sabines who associated him with the goddess Nerio, in Samnium and among the Oscans and in Latium. His temples were very numerous and the Romans erected more of them in the conquered territories.

At Rome where he was worshipped as Mars and as Quirinus he had a *sacrarium* on the Palatine Hill in the *Roma Quadrata* of Romulus. It was there that the god's sacred spears were kept and the twelve shields, *Ancilia*, which were objects of his cult. Wishing to bestow upon King Numa a token of his benevolence Mars — or according to Ovid, Jupiter — caused a shield to fall from the sky, to which the fate of Rome was thenceforth attached. In order to avoid all risk of theft or destruction, Numa had eleven identical shields constructed and placed them under the guardianship of a special college of priests, called the Salii. Primitively the rites of the Salii were intended to protect the growth of plants.

Mars appeared as a purely agricultural god in the festivals of the *Ambarvalia* which were celebrated in Rome on the twenty-ninth of May. They were purification festivals. During them Mars was offered the *suovetaurilia,* in the course of which a pig, a ram and a bull were led around before being immolated to the god.

Mars also figures in the chanting of the *Arvales,* a college of priests who were responsible for the cult of Dea Dia, a rural goddess, closely related to Ceres.

Representations of Mars almost all derive from Greek art. The most Roman image of him is probably a bearded Mars, with cuirass and helmet, reproduced from a statue of Mars Ultor in the temple constructed by Augustus. As for the numerous figures of Mars engraved on medals, they are in the Greek style and copy the Ares type.

Bellona, his companion – sister, wife or daughter – had a celebrated temple in Rome near the gate of Carmenta. There the senate gave audience to ambassadors. In front of the temple rose the 'war column' which the fetialis struck with his lance when war was declared. The priests of Bellona were chosen from among the gladiators.

Jupiter. In the name Jupiter can be found the root *di, div,* which corresponds to the idea of brilliance, the celestial light.

The function of the Etruscan Jupiter, who was called *Tinia,* was to warn men and, on occasion, to punish them. For this purpose he possessed three thunderbolts. He could hurl the first whenever he felt like it, as a warning; but to hurl the second, which was also premonitory, he had to obtain the permission of twelve gods, *consentes* or *complices.* The third thunderbolt was the one which punished. It could only be released with the consent of superior or hidden gods – *dii superiores, involuti.* This primitive Jupiter can be compared with Summanus, another Etruscan thunder-god who presided over the night sky.

The Latin Jupiter was first of all the god of light – sun and moon – and of celestial phenomena: wind, rain, thunder, tempest and lightning. His role was thus important to the agricultural population. Several epithets correspond to his diverse duties: Jupiter Lucetius was the god of light; Jupiter Elicius (*elicere,* to elicit, to draw forth) caused the rain to fall; Jupiter Liber was the god of creative force; Jupiter Dapalis presided over sowing; Jupiter Terminus watched over the boundary stones of fields.

Jupiter rapidly lost his rural functions and became the great protector of the city and the State. He was a warrior-god (Jupiter Stator, Feretrius, Victor). He symbolised the great virtues of justice, good faith and honour; he protected youth. In short he was the great tutelary power of the Empire: Jupiter Optimus Maximus. Solemn titles were reserved for him: Conservator orbis, Conservator Augustorum, Propugnator, etc. A more prosaic title, Pistor – 'baker' – recalled that Jupiter once advised the Romans, who were besieged in the Capitol by the Gauls, to throw bread over the walls in order to show the enemy that they were in no fear of starvation.

Jupiter was worshipped throughout Italy. On the Quirinal he had a very ancient temple, the Capitolium vetus, where he formed a triad with Juno and Minerva. This temple was built on the Capitoline Hill under the Tarquins and the three gods there formed the Capitoline Triad. There Jupiter bore the name Optimus Maximus.

It was under the aegis of the Capitoline Jupiter that the senators assembled to declare war. Generals appeared before him prior to setting out to war and after victory returned to offer him a crown of gold and part of the booty.

The *ludi romani,* annual games, were celebrated in the circus in his honour. Their foundation was attributed to the Elder Tarquin. They consisted of athletic contests, especially chariot races.

As well as the ludi romani there were the *ludi plebeii* which consisted of foot races and theatrical entertainments.

Images of Jupiter are practically all derived from Greek art. The Volscian Jupiter is, however, curious in that it is beardless and the god is depicted as a young man.

Juno. Sister and consort of Jupiter, Juno was a very great Italic goddess. In the remotest epochs she was found among the Sabines, the Oscans, the Latins, the Umbrians and the Etruscans.

Her oldest titles, Lucetia and Lucina, correspond to her chief functions.

Juno Lucetia was the feminine principle of the celestial light, of which Jupiter was the masculine principle. Like Jupiter she was also a moon-goddess; in this latter aspect she was coupled with Diana.

Goddess of light, she was by derivation the goddess of childbirth, for the new-born baby is brought into the light. The goddess was then Juno Lucina.

In this aspect she occupied an important part in the ceremonies of marriage and afterwards. She had many titles: Juno Pronuba watched over the arrangement of marriages; Juno Domiduca conducted the bride to the house of her husband and saw that she crossed the threshold; Juno Nuxia coated the doorposts with perfume; Cinxia unknotted the bride's girdle. Later Juno Lucina protected the pregnant wife, strengthened the bones of the infant (Juno Ossipago) and assured the mother's supply of milk (Juno Rumina). Juno Sospita received fervent invocations at the time of labour and delivered the baby.

As a goddess of childbirth she was naturally invoked by wives who were barren. It was Juno Lucina who rescued the Sabine women from the scourge of sterility with which they had been stricken after their abduction.

The Venus of Arles. The Roman goddess of love is shown holding an apple and admiring herself in a mirror in this antique sculpture restored by Pradier in the nineteenth century. Originally an Italian goddess of horticulture who brought beauty and fruitfulness to gardens, Venus later became identified with the Greek goddess Aphrodite and extended her influence to human beings as well.
Probably a copy of a Praxitelean work of *c.* 360 to 350 B.C.

To sum up, Juno Lucina was the goddess and symbol of the Roman matron – a logical consequence of her own title of spouse of Jupiter, the supreme god.

Her role of goddess of childbirth was not confined to the protection of the Roman wife. Under the name Populonia, Juno also watched over the multiplication of the race. Under the name Martialis, mother of Mars, she was the goddess of birth and finally of fertility – Caprotina. This is what they said of the origin of this epithet: taking advantage of Rome's weakness after the invasion of the Gauls, the neighbouring tribes marched against the city under the leadership of Posthumius Livius. They threatened to destroy Rome unless all the women and girls were turned over to them. Some female slaves offered to go to the camp of Posthumius, disguised as free women. The stratagem was successful. But that night, when the enemy was asleep, they unfurled from the top of a wild fig-tree (*caprificus*) a signal to the Romans who hastened to come and slaughter the aggressors. The slaves were set free and rewarded by the State; and their act of heroism was commemorated every year on the seventh of July, known as the Nonae Caprotinae.

Juno Moneta, after having been the adviser of those about to be married, became the adviser of the Roman people. When the Gauls attempted to scale the walls of the citadel of the Capitol it was Juno's sacred animals, the geese, who warned (Latin *monere,* to warn) the defenders of the peril. Later this epithet Moneta changed its meaning, due to the installation near the temple of Juno of the mint where *money* was coined.

Juno Sospita, protectress of confinements, became in a broader sense she who was always willing to help, the liberator. She had two temples at Rome. At Lanuvium, Juno Sospita had a temple which was guarded by a serpent. Every year a maiden would offer cakes to the serpent. If it accepted, this was a sign that the girl was a virgin. Its refusal was an evil omen and a year of sterility was to be feared.

A temple to Juno Lucina was built on the Esquiline in 735 B.C. only a few years after the foundation of Rome. In the temple of the Capitoline Triad, built by the Tarquins, Juno's title was Regina. There she held the golden sceptre, the Patera and the thunderbolt. She then played the role of august consort of Jupiter and protectress of the Roman people. Her cult was spread throughout the Empire.

The festivals of Juno Lucina, the *Matronalia*, were celebrated by Roman matrons at the Kalends of March. After a ceremony in the sacred grove of the Palatine it became a family festival. The mistress of the house was its central figure; she received a present from her husband and served her slaves at the table.

Juno Regina is almost always represented standing; her attributes are the sceptre, the patera, the veil and the peacock.

Juno Sospita is armed with spear and shield.

Juno Lucina carries a child in her arms; there are two more at her feet. She is also represented with a child in her arms and in her hand a flower which recalls the circumstances in which she conceived the god Mars.

Vesta. Vesta is the most beautiful of Roman divinities, bright and pure like the flame which is her symbol. Her name derives – like the name Hestia – from a Sanskrit root, *vas,* which expresses the idea of 'shining'.

The Latins had made Vesta a goddess who personified the earth and fire. The Romans kept only the second of these personifications. Nor was Vesta the goddess of fire in its broadest sense, but only of fire required for domestic use or in religious ceremonial.

In the beginning Vesta was associated with Janus Pater and Tellus Mater, and was the protectress of sown fields. She was also a symbol of idealised maternity – although she was a virgin – because fire nourishes.

As a goddess of fire she received both a private and a public cult.

Every hearth had its Vesta. With Jupiter Dapalis she presided over the preparation of meals; she was offered the first food and drink. With the Lares and the Penates she held a pre-eminent position in the house.

At Rome the centre of her cult, which was said to have been originated by Romulus, was in the Regia. It lasted almost all the year, being interrupted only during the months of January and November. The chief festivals of Vesta were the Vestalia which were celebrated on the seventh of June. On that day her sanctuary (which normally no one except her priestesses, the Vestal Virgins, entered) was accessible to mothers of families who brought plates of food. The Vestals officiated. The ceremonies were simple and unsanguinary. The objects of the cult were essentially the hearth fire and pure water drawn into a clay vase, handmade, and narrow at the base so that it could not stand on the ground.

The Vestals, who played a role of first importance in Roman liturgy, enjoyed exceptional prestige. When Numa first instituted them they were two in number; Servius increased them to six. They were chosen by lot from patrician families and entered the college between the ages of six to ten. They remained there for thirty years. During the first ten years they received instruction in their duties which they exercised for the following ten years. Then, in their turn, they taught the younger Vestals.

They took vows of absolute chastity. Those who broke their vows were punished by death. Originally they were whipped to death, but the Elder Tarquin modified this torture: they were then whipped and walled-up alive in a tomb which was sealed after a few provisions had been deposited in it. Vestals accused of impurity sometimes managed to clear their reputation. It was told how Tuccia proved her virginity by bringing back water from the Tiber in the sacred sieve. The accomplice of the guilty Vestal was whipped to death in the Forum Boarium. During the course of eleven centuries only twenty Vestals broke their vow and suffered punishment.

If a Vestal let the sacred fire go out she was whipped by order of Pontifex Maximus.

When the Vestals had finished the thirty years of their engagement they could marry. They rarely took advantage of this right, however, preferring to maintain the privileges of their position. Whenever they appeared in public they were preceded by a lictor, and if a man condemned to death chanced to meet a Vestal he was immediately reprieved.

Statues of Vesta are not numerous. Her image is found on coins, mostly imitations of Greek art. She is always veiled.

Vulcan. Vulcan was one of the oldest of Latin gods, ante-dating even Jupiter. Under the name Volcanus, he was the first Jupiter of Rome whose foundation he protected. In his aspect of Jupiter he formed a couple with Juno. He was also associated with Maia, an incarnation of the Earth Mother, and with Vesta, considered as goddess of the earth. He was not allied with Venus who in those remote times still played a small part in Roman mythology. Volcanus was the father of Cacus, whose legend will be recounted later. To him was also attributed the paternity of Servius Tullius, king of Rome.

A maiden in the neighbourhood of Praeneste was seated one day near the fire when a spark fell on her; some months afterwards she gave birth to a son. She exposed him in the forest where some girls found him beside a lighted fire. For this reason he was regarded as a son of Vulcan and because of the smallness of his eyes they named him Coeculus. When he grew up he founded the town of Praeneste, celebrating the occasion with public games. As some of those present cast doubts on his paternity he invoked his father Vulcan and the crowd was immediately surrounded by flames.

Vulcan was the god of the thunderbolt and of the sun, then the god of fires whose ravages he could arrest, and finally became the god who was associated with the attribute of life-giving warmth.

He was invoked as the divinity of the hearth and, as he was united with Maia, mother of springs, he was considered the first god of the Tiber. He even possessed warlike functions and may have preceded Mars as god of battles. In the early history of Rome, then, Volcanus was a more important personage than the later Vulcan.

The *Volcanalia* were celebrated on the twenty-third of August. On the twenty-seventh of August Vulcan was fêted in the *Volturnalia* in his role of god of the Tiber, Volturnus being one of this river's religious names. The seventeenth of August was the festival of the *Portunalia,* also consecrated to the Tiber. It is probable that in ancient times human sacrifices were offered to Vulcan. His altar in the Forum was the Volcanal.

The Romans always represented him as bearded, sometimes with a slight facial deformity which doubtless recalled his infirmity. Near him stand the hammer, tongs and anvil, attributes which came from Greece. He wears a bonnet (*pileus*) and a short tunic which leaves his right arm and shoulder free.

Saturn. Saturn was a very ancient agricultural divinity of Latin and Roman origin; he was of the same rank as Janus and Jupiter. His name may be connected with *satur* (stuffed, gorged) or with *sator* (a sower); in either case he is synonymous with abundance.

Saturn was a working god and a vine-grower (*vitisator*). Under the name Stercutius he saw to the manuring of fields. He was associated with Ops, who was a personification of the earth's riches. Saturn was supposed to have been king of Italy during the golden age. Driven from the sky by Jupiter he hid himself (*latuit*) in the country since called Latium, and indeed beneath the Capitol at Rome itself. His reign brought prosperity and abundance.

The *Saturnalia,* celebrated on the seventeenth of December, originally consisted of a series of rural festivals, *sementivae feriae, consualia larentalia, paganalia.* The Saturnalia assumed their real importance in 217 B.C., a time when the defeat at Lake Trasimene, a prelude to the disaster of Cannae, caused a religious revival among the Romans.

The Saturnalia lasted seven days, from the seventeenth to the

Tellus Mater with Air and Water. An earth-goddess and goddess of fecundity, Tellus Mater protected the fruitfulness of the soil and watched over marriage and the procreation of children. Here she is portrayed holding two children while fruit, flowers, plants and corn fill her lap and grow beside her. On her right is Air seated on the back of a swan while on her left Water is shown with a marine monster. Bas-relief from the Ara Pacis, or Altar of Peace, erected on the Campus Martius between 13 B.C. and 9 B.C.

Jupiter. The supreme god of the Roman pantheon, he was the great protector of the city and the state and the guardian of public morality being concerned with oaths, treaties and leagues. Originally an Italian sky-god he was later closely identified with the Greek Zeus, his cult being introduced to Rome by the Etruscan kings shortly before their fall.
With Juno and Minerva he formed the Capitoline triad.

Minerva. This Etruscan figure of the goddess shows her wearing a helmet and breastplate like the Greek goddess Athene, with her right arm raised to hurl her spear. One of the twelve great figures of the Roman pantheon, Minerva first appeared in Etruria and was possibly a goddess of the thunderbolt. She was merged with Athene very early however and was consequently the least Roman of the divinities of the Capitoline triad. Bronze of the sixth century B.C.

twenty-third of December. It was a period of unrestrained festivity. After the religious ceremony there was an immense feast: people even took the precaution of bathing in the morning in order to remain all day at table. Encumbering togas were removed and they ate at ease in tunics. In memory of the golden age the masters served the slaves who, during the festivals, could say and do what they liked. There was a general suspension of public activity. Law courts did not sit, schools were closed, commercial and military operations were suspended.

In the temple of Saturn near the Capitol the State treasury was kept, as well as the standards of the legions which were not on campaign. The god's effigy was bound with woollen strips which prevented him from leaving Roman territory. His bands were untied during the Saturnalia.

In a painting from Pompeii Saturn is standing, his chest half bare, a sickle in his hand. On coins he carries a sickle or ears of corn.

Minerva. The name Minerva is connected with the root *manas* or *mens*. She first appeared in Etruria under the names of *Menrva, Menrfa, Meneruva, Menarva,* and was perhaps a goddess of the thunderbolt. It seems that this Etruscan Minerva very early merged with the Greek Athene. Minerva is hence the least Italic of the divinities with whom she formed the triad Jupiter-Juno-Minerva.

The Roman Minerva was especially the protectress of commerce and industry and of schools. It was only later that she assumed the character of a warrior-goddess.

According to Roman tradition the cult of Minerva originated in Falerii. When in 241 B.C. the Romans took this town they carried Minerva off, built her a temple at the foot of Mount Coelius and gave her the name Minerva *Capta.* There was, however, a temple already consecrated to Minerva in Rome on the Aventine. In any case her cult was not ancient in Latium or among the Sabines.

Minerva was honoured, in association with Mars, in the *Quinquatrus* which lasted five days during the Spring equinoxes.

Minerva was venerated throughout the Empire. Particularly homage was paid to her by corporations of artisans, flute-players, doctors and so forth.

There was no purely Roman figure of Minerva. The Etruscans had represented her with wings, holding a screech-owl in her hand. It will be remembered that this bird was sacred to Athene.

Mercury. The name Mercury is connected with the root *merx* (merchandise) and *mercari* (to deal, trade). He is not very ancient for he does not appear in the *Indigitamenta.* The early Romans, being above all countrymen, had no need for a god of commerce.

The Roman Mercury appeared only about the fifth century B.C. and was exclusively the god of merchants. For long he was known only in this capacity, so that Plautus, in his prologue to *Amphitryon,* reminds his audience that Mercury presided over messages and commerce. Like certain other minor divinities – Pecunia, Aesculanus, Argentinus – he watched over tradesmen's profits.

Mercury had a temple on the Aventine. Among animals the cock was especially sacred to him.

To portray him Roman artists generally drew upon representations of Hermes. They gave Mercury a beardless face and, for attributes, the caduceus and the winged petasus, with a purse in his hand.

AGRICULTURAL DIVINITIES

Faunus. Legend made Faunus the son of Picus and the grandson of Saturn. He was thought to have been one of the first kings of Latium. He gave laws to the still barbarous tribes and invented the shawm or rustic pipe. He deified his father Picus and his mother Canente who on the death of her husband wasted away with grief until there was nothing left of her. Faunus was one of the first Roman rustic divinities and, above all, a fertility god. He also possessed the gift of prophecy and caused voices to be heard in the countryside. But to obtain oracular information from him he had first to be bound, as King Numa succeeded in doing. Under the name Lupercus he had a temple on the Palatine, the Lupercal – the name of the grotto where the she-wolf suckled the twins, Romulus and Remus. The *Lupercalia* were celebrated on the fifteenth of February and were among the most important festivals on the Roman calendar. Their function was purificatory. Goats

Minerva, portrayed as the goddess Roma. Roman Coin.
Bibliothèque Nationale, Paris.

Mercury. Effigy on a Roman Coin. Bibliothèque Nationale, Paris.

Head of Minerva. To the Romans Minerva was above all the goddess of
handicrafts, learning and the arts and as such was particularly venerated by
the guilds of artisans, artists and professional men.
She later assumed Athene's other role as a warrior-goddess and
was worshipped in association with Mars in the *Quinquatrus* – a festival
which finally came to be considered her own.
Statue after the Athene Parthenos of Phidias.

and he-goats were sacrificed, and perhaps dogs. After the animals
were immolated two youths were led to the altar. The priests touched
their brows with the bloody knife and wiped them with a wad of
wool soaked in milk, after which the youths would burst out
laughing. The priests of the college of the Luperci, half naked,
draped only in the skins of the sacrificed goats, would then perform
a ceremony during which women who wanted to become pregnant
would hold out their hands and turn their backs to be struck with
a whip of goat's hide. Ovid gives a rather amusing explanation of
the nudity of the Luperci. One day Faunus surprised Hercules and
Omphale asleep in a grotto. Faunus wished to take advantage of
the sleeping young woman, but the lovers had playfully exchanged
garments. In the darkness Faunus did not notice this and, deceived
by the softness of the robe Hercules was wearing, approached him
instead of Omphale. He was, as can be imagined, rudely repulsed.
To avoid such misadventures in the future, Faunus insisted that
his priests should be naked when they celebrated his festivals. The
Lupercalia were only suppressed in 494 A.D. by Pope Gelasius who

replaced them by a festival in honour of the ritual Purification
of the Virgin.

With Faunus, god of fertility, was associated Fauna, who was
his wife or daughter. Fauna was invoked under the name of *Bona
Dea:* women celebrated her cult at the beginning of December
with a mysterious festival which was forbidden to men and degenerated into an orgy. Also associated with Faunus was Ops, a
very ancient Sabine goddess whom Rome adopted. Ops was a
personification of creative force and agricultural fertility. She was
venerated in the *Opalia* on the nineteenth of December and invoked
by sitting down and touching the earth with the hand. Fauna, or
Bona Dea, was also closely related to Maia who symbolised the
earth's Spring fertility and was honoured in May. Another goddess
of Latium, Marica, was loved by Faunus who, according to

The Apollo of Veii. Apollo was introduced into Italy at a very early date and his cult was first established in Rome in the fifth century B.C. following an outbreak of plague. During the Republican period he was chiefly worshipped as a god of healing and prophecy but under Augustus he became one of the chief gods of Rome and as Apollo Palatinus was in some ways the equal of Jupiter Optimus Maximus. Etruscan terracotta, late sixth century B.C.

The Diana of Gabii. An Italian goddess of mountains and woods and of women and childbirth, Diana was anciently identified with the Greek goddess Artemis who possessed a similar character and functions. Her cult was widespread, her most famous shrine being at Nemi while at Rome she was worshipped in a temple on the Aventine traditionally founded in the sixth century B.C. This life-size Roman marble statue possibly reproduces Praxiteles' Artemis Brauronia of 346 B.C.

Virgil's interpretation, made her the mother of the king, Latinus.

Consus. Consus was one of the most ancient gods of Rome. He presided over sowing. His festivals, the *Consualia*, consisted of two distinct ceremonies. In the first, which took place on the twenty-first of August after the harvest, Consus was associated with Ops. There were chariot races and horse races, entertainments, dancing and a curious race on oxhides rubbed with oil. The second ceremony of the Consualia took place on the fifteenth of December after the sowing. Chariot races with mules were held in the circus. Consus had an altar near the Circus Maximus. During the year this altar was covered with earth to evoke the idea of sowing. It was only swept for the Consualia. It was during the festivals of Consus that the Romans abducted the Sabine women.

Pales. Pales was at first a masculine divinity attached to the person of Jupiter. Afterwards Pales took on feminine form and became the protectress of flocks, giving vigour to the males and fecundity to the females. Her festivals, the *Palilia,* were celebrated on the twenty-first of April, the date of the foundation of Rome. On the eve of the festival a purification ceremony took place in houses and stables in which a sacred mixture made by the Vestals was employed. Then the livestock and stables were sprinkled with lustral water. Pales gave her name to the hill where Roma Quadrata rose, the Palatine.

Liber Pater. This Italic god's first function was to preside over the fertility of the fields. He was also a god of fecundity. He was honoured on the seventeenth of March in the *Liberalia.* This was

The Antium Girl. This life-size statue from Antium depicts a young temple servant or priestess performing a religious rite.
On her arm she balances a circular salver on which were originally arranged a rolled-up strip of woollen cloth, a laurel twig and a vessel, of which only one foot remains. She wears a linen chiton and a woollen cloak. Probably a Roman copy of a Hellenistic bronze of the mid third century B.C. Parian marble.

the day on which adolescents left off wearing the *praetexta* and assumed the apparel of a man (the *toga virilis*). Liber Pater did not become the god of vine-growers until after he had been confused with Iacchus Dionysus. His consort was Libera, an ancient Italic goddess about whom there is little information.

Silvanus. This Latin divinity was popular in Rome from very early days. As his name indicates Silvanus was a forest god. He was, they said, the son of a shepherd of Sybaris and a she-goat or else a maiden named Valeria Tusculanaria. He watched chiefly over the work of clearing land and making pastures in wooded country. His province extended to all arboriculture, as well as to guarding herds and to the tilling of the soil. Domestic cattle were sacrificed to him. He was often confused with Faunus or with Pan whose physical aspect he had. Silvanus was particularly feared by children and by women in labour.

Tellus Mater. In the remotest times Tellus Mater was a goddess of fecundity in company with a male divinity, Telluno. Afterwards she was associated with Jupiter. In her role of mother she watched over marriage and the procreation of children. The bride would offer her a sacrifice when she entered her husband's house. She had her part in the *porca praecidanea*, the sow immolated to Ceres 'before the harvest'. As an agricultural deity she protected the fruitfulness of the soil and all the states which the seed passes through when it is sown in the soil.

Flora. In primitive central Italy Flora was the goddess of budding springtime, of cereals, fruit trees, the vine and flowers. With Robigus (or Robigo) she prevented wheat-rust. With Pomona she watched over fruit trees. She had a temple on the Quirinal and another near the Circus Maximus. Her festivals, the *Floralia*, lasted from the twenty-eighth of April to the third of May and were rather licentious. On the twenty-third of May there was another festival in her honour, a rose festival. The Sabines and the Latins venerated another goddess, Feronia, who shared some of Flora's functions and watched over spring flowers and vegetation. It is possible that Feronia was originally an underworld divinity. She was associated with Soranus, a Sabine divinity who became a solar god after first having been a god of the underworld. In the course of a sacrifice which mountaineers were offering on Mount Soracte wolves appeared and seized the offerings; they then took refuge in a cave from which escaped pestilential vapours. The oracle declared that these wolves were under the protection of the god Soranus and instructed the mountaineers to live by rapine, like the wolves. Whence arose the name *Hirpi Sorani* which was given to them. The name was perpetuated in a Roman family, especially devoted to the cult of Soranus and Feronia. During the festivals of Feronia members of this family, the Hirpini, would walk bare-footed over glowing coals without burning themselves.

Divinities of the Waters. All stretches of water, all springs and all rivers were deified. The nymph Juturna – or rather Diuturna – a native of Latium, was the goddess of still waters and of rivers over which Jupiter gave her empire in reward for her love. She was venerated in the *Juturnalia* on the eleventh of January by the college of the *Fontani* who were artisans assigned to aqueducts and fountains.

Neptunus was perhaps originally a water-god or a protector against drought. During the *Neptunalia* on the twenty-third of July they would build huts of branches for shelter against the sun.

As for the Nymphs, they were in a general way water divinities. Usually they were associated with some superior deity like Jupiter, Diana or Ceres. Their cult originated in Latium. Their springs were found near the Capena gate. The most famous was the fountain of the nymph Egeria whom Numa, the king, would come to consult during the night. According to Ovid she married Numa and after his death retired to the woods in the valley of Aricia where Diana changed her into a fountain. She is reputed to have foretold the fate of new-born babies.

Among the other nymphs may be mentioned the Camenae who were prophetic nymphs. One of them, Antevorta, knew the past; another, Postvorta, the future. The most important of the Camenae was Carmenta who first dwelt in Arcadia where she had a son by Mercury, Evander. When Evander left his native land and came to Italy, where he founded the town of Pallantium, Carmenta came with him. She changed the fifteen Greek letters brought by Evander into Roman letters; she had the gift of prophecy and lived until she was a hundred and ten. After her death she received divine honours.

Ceres and Diana. In their aspect of Italic divinities Ceres and Diana offer no particular interest. Ceres, who came from Campania, had a temple in Rome; but her rites, like the temple itself, were Greek. Diana retained only briefly her primitive character as a goddess of light, mountains and woods. She was rapidly hellenised. Among other sanctuaries Diana had a temple on the shores of Lake Nemi whose priest was traditionally an escaped slave. In order to obtain this office he had first to kill his predecessor in single combat. From then on he, too, was a target for any assassin who might wish to supplant him.

Venus. Venus, too, in early days occupied a very modest position in the Roman pantheon. With Feronia and Flora she symbolised spring and fruitfulness. She had her place in the *Floralia* (twenty-eighth of April to the third of May) and in the *Vinalia rustica* on the ninth of August.

Vertumnus. It is not known whether Vertumnus was Etruscan or Latin. In any case the origin of his name is clearly Latin: *vertere*, 'to change'. He was a god of fruit trees like Ceres and Pomona. Pomona was courted by all the rural gods, but she yielded only to Vertumnus. In order to seduce her he was forced to assume several different guises, appearing before her as a labourer, a vinegrower and a harvester. In the end he overcame her suspicions by assuming the aspect of an old woman. Vertumnus was also associated with Silvanus, and he was venerated with the god of the Tiber, the course of which he was supposed to have altered. Tradition shows him revolving in the assembly of gods, where he was constantly changing shape.

GODS OF THE UNDERWORLD.

It was above all from primitive Etruria that the Romans borrowed their conception of the infernal regions and its inhabitants. In the Etruscan underworld the naive and terrifying visions common to all primitive religions mingle with the abstract conceptions of more developed systems. Both were submitted to Greek influence while they retained their national characteristics. In the infernal regions Eita or Ade (Hades) with his consort Persipnei (Persephone) reigned. The chief infernal figures were Charun (Charon) and Tuchulcha, a female demon with ferocious eyes, the ears of an ass, a beak in place of a mouth, two serpents twined around her head and a third around her arm. At the moment of death the soul was seized by two groups of genii. The first were malevolent and were led by Charun who carried a mallet or a torch. The second group were benevolent and were led by Vanth. Their dispute symbolised the struggle between good and evil. The deceased travelled to the afterworld either in a chariot, on horseback, or on foot. He is sometimes depicted with two genii, one leading him by the hand and the other following him; sometimes accompanied by a winged divinity who carries in his right hand a scroll on which is inscribed the dead man's record. Another subterranean divinity, Tages, taught the Etruscans haruspicy – that is to say the rules for foretelling the future by the examination of entrails and by the observation of lightning. Tages in the guise of a child suddenly rose from a furrow before a certain labourer, Tarchon, and revealed to him certain magic formulas which were afterwards gathered together in books.

The Romans had no great Underworld divinities. Those of whom we shall speak have a confused personality which only developed under Hellenic influence. In the primitive epoch the real infernal gods were the Manes.

Dis Pater. His name signified that he was the richest of all the gods – *dis* is a contraction of *ditis*, 'rich' – and indeed the number of his subjects continued ceaselessly to increase. In much the same way the Greeks called the god of the dead Pluto, *ploutos* being 'riches'. Dis Pater was never popular; his altars were rare. The Romans being superstitious did not care to worship a personification of death; or perhaps they reserved their homage for the Manes.

Maenad. The worship of Dionysus was introduced into Rome from lower Italy, its popularity being attested by numerous artistic representations. Here one of the god's female followers brandishes the knife with which she has just cut off the head of a wild animal which she will devour raw in the *omophagia*. Women, as successors of the Maenads, had a special place in the worship of Dionysus. Antique bas-relief.

A soul escorted to the underworld between two funerary genii. Fresco from Cervetri. Louvre.

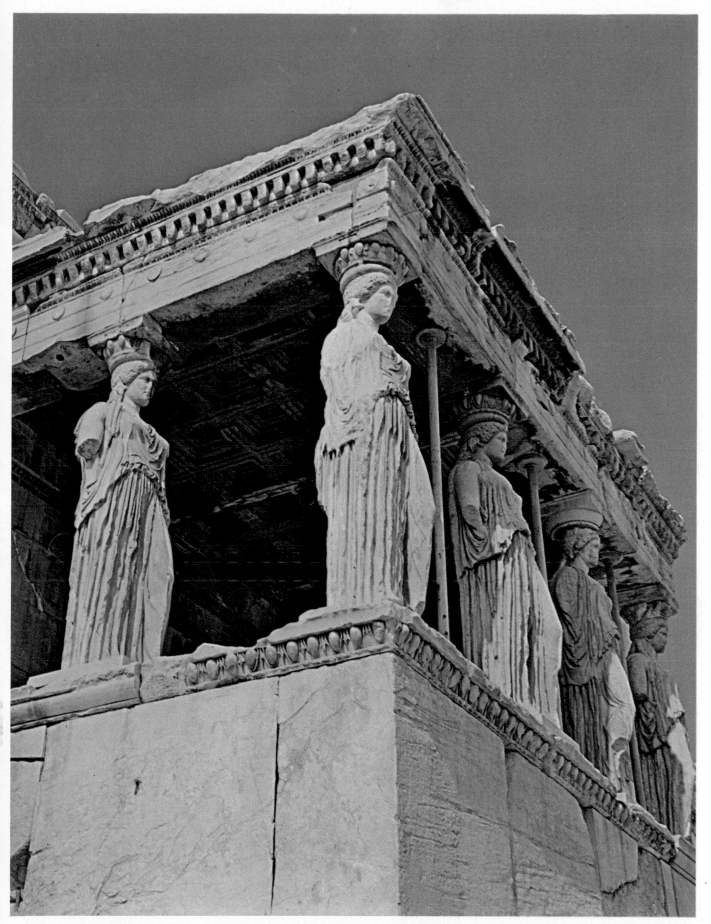

The Acropolis of Athens from the south west. Occupied from the earliest times, the sacred hill with its temples towers some five hundred feet above the modern city which stretches away to the north. Set on fire and laid waste by the Persians in 480 B.C., its present buildings date from the restoration of Pericles. On the left, where the ground rises less precipitously, is the entrance with the little temple of Athene Nike while in the centre of the hill stand the Erechtheum and the great temple of the Parthenon dedicated to the worship of Athene Parthenos, or 'Athene the Virgin', the protectress of the city.

One of the Dioscuri, seen in the Roman theatre at Leptis Magna. Castor and Pollux were hatched from eggs like Helen and Clytemnestra –
a sequel to the coupling of Leda with a swan, who proved to be Jupiter (Zeus) in one of his many guises. The Romans embraced the cult
of the Dioscuri at an early date; it was probably adapted from an Etruscan source but this did not prevent the Romans from claiming
that the twins in fact fought on their side at the Battle of Lake Regillus. Statues of Castor and Pollux stood at either side of the orchestra
in the Leptis Magna theatre and were recently restored to the position they occupied in the first century A.D.